European Expansion and Migration

In this collective volume one of the most dramatic consequences of the expansion of Europe is analysed. Why is it that now many millions of ex-Europeans live in the Americas, while so few are present in Asia and Africa? Why were Africans almost absent in the flow of migrants after the slave trade had been abolished? How many Asians participated in intercontinental migration and were they able to benefit from it as much as the Europeans did or did Asian migration resemble that of the Africans? While addressing these wide-ranging questions, the authors focus on the same set of main issues: i) push-pull factors, ii) the demography of the sending regions, iii) female migration, iv) transportation, v) integration or isolation in the receiving areas, vi) return migration, vii) capital movements related to migration.

Pieter C. Emmer is a Professor of the History of European Expansion in the University of Leiden, The Netherlands. His publications in English include *Reappraisals in Overseas History*, with H.L. Wesseling and *Colonialism and Migration*. He is presently researching nineteenth-century colonial labor migration.

Magnus Mörner was a Professor at the University of Gothenborg, Sweden, from 1982 to 1990. Prior to that he taught at several universities in the United States. He has published dozens of books and about three hundred articles on Latin American social history in Spanish, English, and other languages.

European Expansion and Migration

Essays on the Intercontinental Migration from Africa, Asia, and Europe

Edited by
P.C. EMMER *and* M. MÖRNER

BERG

New York / Oxford

Distributed exclusively in the U.S. and Canada
by St. Martin's Press, New York

Published in 1992 by

Berg Publishers, Inc.
Editorial offices:
165 Taber Avenue, Providence, RI 02906, U.S.A.
150 Cowley Road, Oxford OX4 1JJ, UK

British Library Cataloguing in Publication Data
European expansion and migration: Essays on the
intercontinental migration from Africa, Asia and
Europe.
I. Emmer, P.C. II. Mörner, M.
304.809

ISBN 0–85496–300–6

Library of Congress Cataloging-in-Publication Data
European expansion and migration: essays on the intercontinental migration from Africa, Asia, and Europe / edited by P.C. Emmer and M. Mörner.
p. cm.
Includes bibliographical references and index.
ISBN 0–85496–300–6
1. Emigration and immigration–History. I. Emmer, P. C.
II. Mörner, Magnus.
JV6021.E87 1991 91–18969
325″. 09–dc20 CIP

Printed in Great Britain by
Billing and Sons Ltd, Worcester

Published with the financial assistance of the European Science Foundation, Strasbourg.

A special thank you is given to Remco Raben, a Ph.D. student at the Institute for the History of European Expansion, University of Leiden, for providing valuable editorial assistance.

Tables

Figures

I

European Expansion and Migration: The European Colonial Past and Intercontinental Migration; An Overview

P.C. EMMER

The ethnic composition of the contemporary world has become very confusing. Recently, the thirty year anniversary of the Cuban revolution was commemorated, and some journalists remembered that in 1959 it was not yet clear as to whether Castro headed a nationalist or a communist insurrection against Batista, the then ruling dictator of Cuba. At the time, in fact, a commentator of the *New York Times* made much of a photograph showing a triumphant Castro with a Chinese face among his entourage. Was that not a sure sign of the influence of Communist China on the future direction of Cuba's revolutionary movement? Fortunately, a reader's letter pointed out that more than 100,000 Chinese had moved to Cuba when the island was a Spanish colony and when many governments with sugar colonies had concluded treaties obtaining the right to recruit migrant Chinese laborers. Thus, the Chinese face on the picture did not necessarily belong to a newly arrived Chinese; it might have belonged to someone from the Cuban Chinese community established more than a hundred years ago.

Confusion about a similar point occurred when V.S. Naipaul received the Nobel prize for literature. He looked Indian. Was he an Indian from India or an Indian who had moved to Britain? It took some time to explain that Naipaul actually belonged to those Indians who had migrated to the Caribbean during the nineteenth century and from there had migrated to Britain after World War II, taking advantage of the fact that all these areas belonged to one empire.

* I would like to thank my co-editor, Magnus Mörner, for his comments on an earlier draft of this contribution.

These two examples clearly show that there existed a link between European expansion and international migration. In surveying these long distance migrations we will first attempt to establish the relative quantitative volume of the various movements. Secondly, attention will be paid to the demographic, socioeconomic, and cultural differences that existed, and still exist, between the international migrants from Europe, Africa, and Asia. Finally, a balance sheet of the various migration movements will be drawn up in an attempt at predicting the future of intercontinental migrations now that Europe has virtually dissolved its empires.[1]

The Volume of European, African, and Asian Intercontinental Migration Since 1500

One of the most important and visible remnants of the expansion of Europe is the change in the ethnic composition of the world. Until 1800 intercontinental migrations were still relatively modest due to

1. There exists an extensive body of literature on international migration, but no general survey comparing the European, African, and Asian migrations since 1500. The usual piecemeal approach is best illustrated by two collective volumes on international migration, which have appeared recently: William McNeill and Ruth S. Adams, eds., *Human Migration; Patterns and Policies* (Bloomington and London 1978) and Ira Glazier and Luigi de Rosa, eds., *Migration across Time and Nations* (New York and London 1986). As far as the European participation in intercontinental migration is concerned, I consulted chapter 2 of William Woodruff, *Impact of Western Man; A Study of Europe's Role in the World Economy, 1759–1960* (New York 1967). The various factors that have influenced the demographic development of both the colonies of European settlement as well as that of the plantation colonies in North America and the Caribbean: John J. McCusker and Russell M. Menard, *The Economy of British America, 1607–1789* (Chapel Hill and London 1985), 211–35. For Latin America: Magnus Mörner, *Adventurers and Proletarians; The Story of Migrants in Latin America* (Pittsburgh 1985). The volume and direction of the African slave trade are summarized in Philip D. Curtin, *The Atlantic Slave Trade; A Census* (Madison 1969) and David Eltis, *Economic Growth and the Ending of the Transatlantic Slave Trade* (New York and Oxford 1987). The effects of the Atlantic slave trade on West Africa are discussed in the contributions collected by J.E. Inikori, ed., *Forced Migration; The Impact of the Export Slave Trade on African Societies* (London, 1982). The consequences of the slave trade and of slavery on the New World are surveyed by Herbert S. Klein, *African Slavery in Latin America and the Caribbean* (New York and Oxford 1986). The only survey of the migration of Indian indentured labor: Hugh Tinker, *A New System of Slavery; The Export of Indian Labour Overseas, 1830–1920* (London 1974). The Chinese indentured laborers, who migrated to Latin America, have been studied by Arnold Joseph Meagher, *The Introduction of Chinese Laborers to Latin America: the 'Coolie Trade', 1847–1874* (Ann Arbor University Microfilms 1985). On the immigration of Chinese labor into South Africa see Peter Richardson, "Coolies, Peasants and Proletarians: The Origins of Chinese Indentured Labour in South Africa, 1904–1907," in *International Labour Migration; Historical Perspectives*, Shula Marks and Peter Richardson, eds. (London 1984), 167–85.

the limited technical and financial possibilities, at the time, of transporting massive numbers of migrants across the seas. After 1800 these various limitations had been considerably reduced and it had become possible to transport more migrants in a decade than in any of the three centuries before 1800.

During the period of the ancien régime between 1500 and 1800 the expansion of Europe caused two big migration streams to come into existence, both directed toward the New World: (1) the forced emigration of about six million Africans, and (2) the migration of about two to three million Europeans. These two migratory movements enabled the foundation and consolidation of colonies of settlement in the New World, as well as the foundation and expansion of a number of plantation colonies in the Caribbean, in north-eastern Brazil and in the southern part of North America.

During the first half of the nineteenth century the situation remained unchanged both with respect to the ethnic composition as well as to the destination of the intercontinental migratory movements. After 1850, however, the volume of international migrations increased in an explosive way because of the dominance of European migrants. Between 1800 and 1960 at least 61 million Europeans participated in intercontinental migration. North America remained the main recipient of these migrants: 41 million or 70 percent of the Europeans went to the United States and Canada. The other European migrants went to South America (12 percent), to South Africa, Australia, and New Zealand (9 percent), and to the Asian part of Russia (9 percent).

After 1800 the share of non-European migrants in the international migratory flows was much smaller than before, both in absolute as well as in relative terms. In total, about five to six million Asians and Africans participated in these migrations. About half of this number – approximately three million – were made up by African slaves, who were forcibly removed to the New World. This migratory movement of Africans constituted a direct, as well as an indirect, continuation of the slave trade, which had been the most voluminous migration stream before 1800. Most of the Africans who migrated during the nineteenth century were slaves; only about 100,000 to 200,000 went as "voluntary" labor migrants. Also connected with the African slave trade were the migrations of Asian indentured laborers, totaling about one million. Half of these indentured laborers went to plantations in the Americas just as slaves had been forced to do before the end of the slave trade. The other half of the indentured laborers went to South Africa, La Réunion, Mauritius,

Australia, Fiji, and Uganda. In concluding this survey, we now come to the most recent group of international migrants from the Third World: those who moved to Europe after World War II, coming from Asia, Africa, and the Caribbean. If we limit ourselves to those migratory flows after World War II which were directly connected with the contraction of Europe, and if we exclude the returning expatriate Europeans, it seems unlikely that the number of migrating ex-colonial Africans, Asians, and West-Indians was larger than one to two million.[2]

In adding all these figures on the volume of intercontinental migration, both before and after 1800, we arrive at a grand total of about 60 to 65 million European participants and to a total of about 15 million African and Asian (mainly forced) migrants taking part in international migrations. The figures allow us to conclude that the relatively small population of Europe has used the "emigration escape hatch" many more times than the inhabitants of other continents. Even if we limit ourselves to the period after World War II, the dominance of Europeans in international migration remains impressive. During the period 1945 to 1960, the total number of European emigrants came to about seven million, while the number of non-European migrants amounted to less than half of that.

In discussing these figures, three caveats should be kept in mind. First, it should be stressed that all these figures are extremely imprecise; they are only used in order to quantify the relative volume of the participation in international migrations by Europeans, Africans, and Asians.

Second, it should be kept in mind that the expansion of Europe not only caused migratory movements to occur between the three continents but that it also triggered considerable population movements within these three continents. Let us start with Europe, where the expansion overseas stimulated and increased the size of the various merchants marine, navies, and armies. Consequently, the demand for young, unmarried males on the European labor market also increased considerably, surpassing the usual supply of local labor. Subsequently, young men came from increasing distances to the harbors of western Europe causing a considerable inter-European migration.

For other reasons, a similar phenomenon occurred in North and South America, where growing numbers of Amerindians moved

2. Unfortunately, no surveys of the post-Second World War migration have been composed to date. My impression of its volume is based on James Walvin, *Passage to Britain; Immigration in British History and Politics* (Harmondsworth 1984).

away from the frontier created by the penetrating Europeans. In West Africa the "production" of slaves for the increasing Atlantic slave trade caused internal migration within Africa to occur, as did the settlement of European colonists in South Africa, Kenya, and North Africa. European penetration into Asia has also caused internal migrations. Both Indians and Chinese, with or without contracts, have moved to those regions in Asia where the Europeans had established trading posts and agricultural enterprises. Labor migration also took place to those areas within Asia where local agriculture and indigenous manufacturing industries produced for the European markets. The Chinese minority in Indonesia and the Tamils on Ceylon are only two groups whose present locations are a direct result of inter-Asian migration induced by the process of European expansion.

The third caveat points to the fact that the numbers mentioned here only refer to actual migrants. Counting the descendants of these intercontinental migrants would provide us with a completely different picture. The most telling example is that of the number of ex-Europeans and ex-African inhabitants of the New World around 1800. At that time, the New World counted about 13.5 million inhabitants of European origin, while between 1500 and 1800 only about 2 million Europeans had migrated to the New World. In the same year, the number of New World inhabitants of ex-African origin amounted to about 6.5 million, and that number only equals the number of imported slaves between 1500 and 1800. Obviously, the demographic growth that occurred among some groups of African slaves in the Americas had been completely annihilated by the demographic decline among other groups of African immigrants. Research has indicated that both European and African immigrants in North America showed considerable demographic growth. Instead, the African slave populations in the Caribbean experienced a steep demographic decline, probably matched by that of the European immigrants into this region. The first group of immigrants who seemed to have quickly overcome the demographic drawbacks of the Caribbean were the Indians. All this proves our point that the volume of intercontinental migration, and the size of the subsequent immigrant communities, were not necessarily related because of differences in demographic performance between the various groups of intercontinental migrants.

The Price of Moving: The Demographic, Socioeconomic, and Cultural Developments of Migrant Communities

Demography usually provides us with the most realistic answer to the question as to whether particular migrations were successful or not. In using this yardstick, the European intercontinental migrants have been very successful: due to their participation in intercontinental migration, Europeans have been able to increase considerably their share in the world population. First, the mortality among the Europeans overseas was different from the one in Europe. The mortality among Europeans who had migrated to the tropical areas was much higher than in Europe, but only relatively few European migrants went there. The European immigrant communities established in regions with a temperate climate experienced a lower mortality than the prevalent rate in Europe, due to the absence of major epidemic diseases in the new settlement colonies. In addition to providing an environment with a relatively low mortality, the European settlements overseas also allowed its settlers to produce more food per head of population than would have been possible at home. These two conditions allowed the European population overseas to increase dramatically. In the European colonies overseas virtually all women married and did so earlier than in Europe, thus allowing for a considerable increase in the number of births per woman. As an extreme example, eighteenth century French Canada should be mentioned; there the average number of children per woman was slightly higher than eight and 42 percent of the settlers were under fifteen.[3]

The favorable demographic development among the Europeans overseas can be sharply contrasted to that of the overseas Africans. They were forced to leave their continent and migrate as slaves to the dangerous disease environment of the New World where the bacteriological setting was probably as hostile to humans as it was in tropical Africa at the time. In addition, the slave trade was heavily dominated by male slaves, causing a sexual imbalance in most of the slave communities of the New World similar to that in the early overseas settlements of Europeans. The sexual imbalance among African slave communities, however, was continually reinforced by the constant importation of new groups of forced migrants from

3. K.G. Davies, *The North Atlantic World in the Seventeenth Century* (Minneapolis and London 1974), 79.

Africa, equally dominated by male slaves. The strong demographic growth of the European settler communities overseas, on the other hand, almost compensated for this imbalance after some time. In concluding these remarks on the differences in demographic performance between ex-Europeans and ex-Africans in the New World, it should be pointed out that African plantation slaves had more difficulty in finding a partner and creating a family than other groups of migrants. The "production" of slaves in Africa, as well as the way in which Europeans purchased slaves on the coast of Africa, made it practically impossible for African families to arrive intact at their destination. In contrast, the lists of European passengers to the New World always show a nucleus of migrating families. Also, slaves were usually prohibited from leaving the plantation and, thus, had a more limited choice in selecting a partner of the opposite sex than other groups of immigrants. In addition, it should be remembered that the heavy labor on plantations in the tropical parts of the New World was exclusively performed by African slaves and that these labor conditions also must have had a negative effect on their demographic performance. Research of plantation records has shown that on average slave women employed on sugar plantations had their first child at a later age than other slave women.[4]

The Asian migrants of the nineteenth century were able to escape the predicament of the migrating Africans because in migrating they were usually able to retain part of their Indian family structure. In recruiting laborers in India for overseas destinations, a legally set sexual ratio of one hundred males to forty females had been instituted by the colonial authorities. This set percentage stimulated the recruiters to convince as many couples as possible to indenture themselves for service overseas. Such practice was utterly impossible in the operation of the African slave trade. In addition to this advantage, the Asian migrants also profited from the improvement in medical care, which had simply not existed during the slave trade. These two factors are important in explaining why the demographic performance of the ex-Asians in the New World was usually so different from that of the Africans, in spite of the similar sexual imbalance existing among these two groups at their arrival overseas. Obviously, more research is needed in order to explain why the ex-Asian communities in the New World have been able to reach

4. The demographic performance of the slave populations in the United States' South and in the Caribbean/Brazil was totally different. See Herbert G. Gutman, *The Black Family in Slavery and Freedom, 1750–1925* (Oxford 1976) and B.W. Higman, *Slave Populations of the British Caribbean, 1807–1834* (Baltimore and London 1984).

quickly the relatively high demographic growth of India, while most communities of ex-Africans in the New World took centuries to reach even the relatively modest demographic growth of Africa.[5]

The demographic differences between the three migrant groups more or less coincided with the differences in their socioeconomic developments. In this field, the European migrants have been most fortunate. They managed to obtain a better, or at least a similar, socioeconomic development than they had at home. The high, impenetrable social barriers of Europe could hardly be transplanted to the colonies. Differences in income did exist, but the average income per head of population overseas usually was considerably higher than that in Europe. The many economic crises that occurred in the Old World could not affect the economies of the colonies of settlement in the same way, as these colonies obtained a high degree of self-sufficiency.

The disparity between the positive socioeconomic consequences of intercontinental European migration and those of the African and Asian migrants could not have been larger. The Africans and Asians usually arrived in colonies where the socioeconomic development was unifocally directed toward the development of a tropical export agriculture. Alternatively, African and Asian migrants arrived in areas where extra labor was temporarily needed in order to construct railways or to exploit mines. In the host colonies of Africans and Asians it was impossible to amass considerable amounts of capital and also difficult to diversify the economy as in the case of the colonies of European settlement. Not only were the economic prospects relatively bleak for the immigrants, the social barriers were also many times larger in their new host countries than they had been at home. The word "racism" will be a sufficient indication for this. These two developments show why the chances for socioeconomic improvement for ex-Africans and ex-Asians overseas were so much smaller and much more difficult to come by than for European migrants.[6]

5. P.C. Emmer, "The Great Escape: the Migration of Female Indentured Servants from British India to Surinam, 1873–1916," in *Abolition and its Aftermath; the Historical Context, 1790–1916* David Richardson, ed. (London 1985), 245–63. The demography of the British Indians in Guiana was different from that in Surinam: Basdeo Mangru, *Benevolent Neutrality; Indian Government Policy and Labour Migration to British Guiana, 1854–1884* (London 1987).

6. Much new research has been done into the pattern of European investment overseas during the era of "Modern Imperialism." See chapter 4 of Woodruff and also Lance E. Davis and Robert A. Huttenback, *Mammon and the Pursuit of Empire; The Political Economy of British Imperialism, 1860–1912* (Cambridge 1986).

It should be added that the Asian migrants again experienced a different development overseas from that of the Africans. The African migrants and their descendants were first and foremost confronted by the many social and economic limitations of the slavery system. Even after abolition, however, many of these obstacles remained in place as well as the continued racism of the colonial ex-European and non-European elites. By the time the Asian immigrants arrived, some of these barriers had disappeared and this allowed the Asians to use migration as a way to personal material improvement, like the Europeans and not like the Africans.[7]

Lastly, the differences between the cultural developments of the three groups of migrants coincided with the demographic and socioeconomic differences between the ex-Europeans, ex-Africans, and ex-Asians overseas. The Europeans used their political and military dominance in retaining almost all of their cultural habits when moving overseas. In most of the New World, as well as in large parts of Africa and Asia, the various languages of the European colonizers were made into the official languages of administration, of Christian churches, and of the judiciary. In addition, the Europeans were able to transfer their political ideologies, as well as to develop their own imitations of the European political institutions overseas. Some of this even applied to the few non-colonized countries such as China, Japan, Turkey, and Egypt.

The Africans, on the other hand, had the greatest difficulty in preserving their culture overseas. European racism considered African culture and African culture in the New World (language, religion) as inferior. Thus, the Africans on the small plantations in North America and in Brazil – embedded in societies with an abundant white presence – experienced considerable pressure pushing them to divorce themselves from their African past. On the large plantations in the Caribbean, however, the Africans and their descendants could feel less intimidated. The relatively small group of Europeans in these plantation colonies were usually not interested in conversion and assimilation. This laissez-faire attitude also helped the Asian immigrants in the West Indies to preserve their culture. The Asians were usually not subjected to a forced assimilation, since the European and Creole inhabitants of the area viewed the Asian immigrants as temporary workers and not as permanent settlers.

7. A general discussion of this issue in Robert Ross, ed., *Racism and Colonialism; Essays on Ideology and Social Structure* (The Hague 1982).

Progress and Intercontinental Migration

Many of the contributions to this volume show that there existed considerable differences not only between the three ethnic groups of intercontinental migrants but also within each of these groups. Some of these issues should be studied further. As one example within the group of European immigrants in Australia there appears to have developed a striking difference between the participation in higher education of second generation Greek and Dutch immigrants. Within the group of Asian migrants to the Caribbean there developed important demographic differences between British Indian and Javanese women, in spite of the fact that both groups migrated to Surinam under very similar conditions and during the same period. Within the African group of migrants, important differences in social mobility have appeared between the descendants of those Africans who came to the Caribbean and moved to the big cities in North America and the descendants of those Africans who arrived in the southern United States and whose offspring also moved to these cities. More research into these matters is needed in order to find out whether the historical background of international migration can help us to explain some of the differences that surface in present day multi-ethnic Europe.

Historical migration research will provide results that can be of immediate use, for instance, to the housing authorities of big cities in France, the United Kingdom, and the Netherlands in their plans to provide subsidized housing to the various ethnic groups arriving in these cities from the Caribbean. Only historical research can explain why the percentage of female-headed households among the ex-African group of immigrants is so much higher than that among ex-Indian migrants from the Caribbean.[8]

Many of these topics within the history of intercontinental migration need additional research. Nevertheless, the contributions to this volume on intercontinental migrations already allow us to draw some general conclusions relating the past and the future of intercontinental migration insofar as it is connected to the process of European expansion.

1. The study of migration as part of the process of European expansion and contraction clearly shows that Europeans have

8. *Surinamers en Antillianen in Amsterdam; verslag van een in 1977 gehouden enquête*, I (Amsterdam 1979), 39.

participated much more extensively in intercontinental migrations than Africans and Asians. In absolute terms, Europeans are now ahead by 80 percent.

2. Europeans have profited more than Africans and Asians from international migration. By changing continents, Europeans managed to live longer and better than their fellow Europeans who did not migrate.
3. Europeans who stayed behind, however, also profited from intercontinental migration. Before 1800 the loss of about two to three million European emigrants to the New World, and an outflow of a similar number of Europeans going overseas in the service of an army, navy, or merchant marine, helped to decrease population pressure, particularly in some of the fastest growing economies of Europe. In addition, the new plantation and settlement colonies overseas provided an extra economic stimulus for those who remained at home in, again, some of the fastest growing economies. Modern research has resurrected a link, although indirect, between colonial trade and the creation of Europe's Industrial Revolution.[9]
4. After 1800 the increase in the velocity of economic growth in Europe could only be maintained by using international migration as an "escape hatch." The exodus of sixty-one million Europeans after 1800 allowed European economies to create an unknown prosperity and escape a situation in which economic growth was absorbed by an increase in population. After World War II, Europeans also benefited from the intercontinental migration since the dissolving colonial empires forced many colonial subjects to migrate to the metropolis. During this period there was no danger of overpopulation, but rather of a labor shortage. Many colonial migrants coming to Europe had been well trained, and they arrived exactly at a time when skilled labor was at a premium in rebuilding Europe's economy. Thus, large groups of ex-colonial civil servants from French, British, Portuguese, Dutch, and Belgian Africa and Asia could easily be assimilated into the labor force of their respective mother countries.
5. Study of the history of European expansion shows that, thus far, Africans and Asians not only have participated less in intercontinental migrations than Europeans, but they have been unable to

9. A recent survey regarding a possible connection between the rise of plantation slavery and the Atlantic economy at large (including the Industrial Revolution in the United Kingdom): Barbara L. Solow and Stanley L. Engerman, eds., *British Capitalism and Caribbean Slavery; The Legacy of Eric Williams* (Cambridge 1987).

gain as much from it. In fact, Africans, Amerindians, and Aborigines in the New World and Austral-Asia paid most of the demographic, socioeconomic, and cultural costs of international migration.

6. In view of the future volume and ethnic composition of international migration it should be kept in mind that even today the mix between the migrating Europeans, Asians, and Africans is still very unbalanced. Even after World War II, many more Europeans have migrated overseas than have Asians and Africans. Some of the African and Asian immigrants now living in the former colonial metropolis timidly explain that "we are here because you were there." In view of the increasing limitations put in the way of intercontinental migration, however, it is doubtful whether the Africans and Asians will ever be able to draw similar advantages from moving around the world in search of a better life as the Europeans have done and still do.

2

Portuguese Emigration from the Fifteenth to the Twentieth Century: Constants and Changes*

VITORINO MAGALHÃES GODINHO

The Volume of Portuguese Emigration

During the 1960s a young Galician poet, Manuel Maria, succeeded better than anyone else in putting into words the search for employment and for a better life that in fact set in motion the migrations in the world, as shaped by World War II:

A emigración	*The Emigration*
Pra ver marchar aos emigrantes	To see the emigrants march
(ibanse case todos polo mar)	(they were all going by sea)
nos tempos de denantes	in past times
somentes se había que achegar	it was necessary only to go
a un porto calisqueira :	at any port :
había alf tantisimo xentío	there was such a crowd
que semellaba unha feira	that resembled a fair
de dór e de arrepío.	of pain and of shudder.
Cando saía un vapor	When a steamer left
pra calquer lado	in any direction
iba carregado	it used to go loaded
de mágoas e de dór.	with grief and pain.
Os labregos galegos	The poor Galician farmers
iban como cegos	went like blindmen

* This article appeared as a paper presented to the European Science Foundation May, 1977 and is the only survey, to our knowledge, of Portuguese emigration. Readers will note that many factors, including Portugal's entry into the European Economic Community, might change some of the author's prognostications on the current scene were he writing today.

a ser gomitados
en Bós Aires, A Habana, Nova York
ou a ser desembarcados
noutros portos menos nomeados.
Agora non é como denantes:
os emigrantes
non van en vapores
pra América sonhada:
venden os seus suores
i as suas dóres
a Europa cultivada,
industrializada
e supercivilizada.
Ou vanse pra Bilbaó,
que queda mais a mao,
o tambén pra Madrid e Barcelona,
cidades de primeira, de boa sona,
nas que hai barrios turbios,
suburbios,
arrabales
e mínimos xornales
pra emigrantes normales.

to be thrown out
in Buenos Aires, Havana, New York
or to be disembarked
in other less known ports.
Now it is not like before:
the emigrants
do not go in steamers
to the America of their dreams:
they sell their sweat
and their pains
to developed Europe,
industrialized
and supercivilized.
Or they go to Bilbao,
that is close by,
or also to Madrid and Barcelona,
first class cities, of good fame,
where there are dubious quarters,
suburbs,
slums
and minimal salaries
for ordinary emigrants.

Before World War II, the European emigration of poor farmers boarded ship in the direction of the New World. Today, it is the labor market in Europe itself, fostered by the development of industry and the tertiary sector, that attracts Spaniards, Portuguese, Italians, Turks, Algerians, and Tunisians. They come, of course, by land routes: by train, automobile, and coach. Some of the countries, or at least some of their districts that formerly exported workers, are participating in this industrialization and, in their turn, attract domestic migrants. The industrialization in Portugal, unlike in Spain, started off only very belatedly and remained timid; forming cysts, not centers of development.

Today, some 800,000 Portuguese are in France. On the remote shores of the Pacific, half a million Portuguese or Luso-Americans live in California; not to mention Brazil, Venezuela, Canada, Germany, Morocco, and Spain. During the five-year period from 1966 to 1970, some 700,000 left peninsular Portugal, or its adjoining islands, without returning. It is not surprising, therefore, that the census of 1970 has recorded, for the first time since the demographic fluctuations of the Napoleonic period and the struggles surrounding the installation of the institutional monarchy, a noticeable drop in the population. Yet, this first negative result in almost one and a half centuries has thwarted all predictions and ruined the annual calculations of the demographers. For the middle of 1970, a total population of 9.7 million residents was estimated; in reality only 8,668,267 people were effectively registered by the end of the year. The divergence of more than one million exceeds the difference between official domicile and actual presence; rather, it expresses an underestimation of the phenomenon of emigration, having counted only on official figures. Considering the actual emigration, already by 1966 the surplus birth rate did not make up for the departures, even when taking into account the 22,454 returnees.

The departure movement started off slowly in 1947, but two years were sufficient for it to accelerate like a whirlwind, reaching its height from 1966 onward. The economists thought of this as a passing phenomenon which would soon level off. They could not be excused for such a grave mistake because a period of calm had settled in between 1930 and 1945 due to the policy of closed doors as practiced by Brazil and the United States and later reinforced by World War II. It seems to have been forgotten that from at least the last third of the nineteenth century the Portuguese had always left their homeland in great numbers. Indeed, within one century plus fifteen years, from 1855 to 1970, more than 3.1 million have left, never to return to their native land; this accounts only for the legal departures. Including the clandestine departures, the total amount certainly exceeds four million; that is to say, as many as the population of the home country and the archipelagos at the beginning of the envisaged period.

We are thus struck by the cry of anguish of the poet Guerra Junqueiro:

Look, look at them, the emigrants who leave in herds . . .
Howlings of loneliness swept the roads and the quays,
Surge from the side of vessels that move away.
Old men, fiancées, children,
Ah, my God, my God,
While their last hopes fly away,

Clutching their hands, biting their lips;
Seething with anger.
They are carried along, they are going away carried on the
  high seas . . .
Will they return? And when, oh deep sea?

The great thinkers of the last third of the nineteenth century – the historians, economists, sociologists, and politicians like Herculano, Rodrigues de Freitas, Oliveira Martins, and, in this century, Alfonso Costa – were all the more touched. They have studied profoundly the conditions of this exodus, discovered the effects, and proposed its remedies. They were aware of the fact that the evil came from the root of national life itself; they knew that the exodus had actually begun five centuries before.

Already around 1534 the impassioned secretary to King John II, in a rhyming chronicle of "fresh novelties" of the second half of the quattrocento and the first decades of the cinquecento, did not conceal his astonishment:

We have seen the Portuguese, dispersing in great numbers,
seeking to live everywhere,
populating Brazil and the Islands,
going to settle down in the Indies
and even forgetting their natural roots.

In the era in which Garcia de Rèsende worried about the scale of the departures of the Portuguese – and the arrival of slaves – his countrymen had already populated the previously uninhabited Atlantic archipelagos of Madeira, the Azores, Cape Verde, and São Tomé. In Morocco they occupied the seaports of Ceuta, Tangiers, Arzila, Elksar-es-Kebir, Azemmour, Mazagan, and Cape Guir. They were busy settling themselves, with their sugar kettles, their way of life, and their institutions, in vast Brazil, which was created by the extraordinary expeditions of the *bandeiras*. They had trading posts on the Saharan coast, the rivers of Guinea, in Sierra Leone, and all around the Gulf of Guinea – let us not forget the gold of Elmina – just as on the Congo-Angolan shores. They even had permanent residence in inland areas, in between the black villages. On the other side of the Cape of Good Hope, we encounter them in the seaports of East Africa where they entered the hinterland and established agglomerations on riverbanks, disappearing into the wilderness. They settled in Ormuz in the Persian Gulf, Goa and Diu in

India, in Cochin and Quilon in Cannanore, and put their hands on Bassein and Chaul; they trafficked and settled on the coast of Coromandel and in Bengal. Further east, the powerful emporium of Malacca and the Moluccas, the islands of rich spices, were touched on. The Portuguese also frequented the Banda archipelago and the Chinese coast and, little later, Japan, Solor, and Timor. As a matter of fact, we find them on all the islands in Asian waters. In the western hemisphere, Portuguese cod fishermen were fishing in the waters of the New World while their compatriots were coming into the Rio de la Plata, passing on to Peru. At that time Portugal had 1.4 million inhabitants. In Europe, without speaking of the colonies of Jews who were expelled or who fled from the intolerance, there were Portuguese nations in Antwerp, Seville, Venice, and on the island of Chios.

This dispersion, which has gone around the world in a few decades, had started in 1415 with the capture of Ceuta, on the Straits of Gibraltar, and the populating of Porto Santo and Madeira in 1420 to 1425, soon followed by the colonization of the Azores since their discovery in 1427. Still moderate and geographically restricted during the fifteenth century, the dispersion spread like an electric current from the last years of the quattrocento and the dawn of the cinquecento. Let us try to calculate its volume – the estimate will not be too far from the mark.

By the Cape route, allowing for returnees, there were not less than 2,000 Portuguese who left the Kingdom every year; this figure was diminishing throughout the seventeenth century, as soon as commerce gave way to Dutch and English imperialism. Also, the Portuguese more and more sought their fortune in the empires and principalities of the Orient. The population of the Atlantic archipelagos was increasing, and the Moroccan presidios constantly absorbed soldiers, sailors, fishermen, merchants, and indeed peasants. From the middle of the sixteenth century, Brazil attracted most settlers; the Canaries saw Portuguese of all social levels settle in great numbers. They infiltrated everywhere in the Spanish empire. This all means that the departures, on the whole, must be set around 3,500 annually, never coming down below 2,000 nor passing probably an upper limit of 5,000. In relation to the total population, the emigration counted for about 2.5 per thousand inhabitants, without dropping below 1.5 per thousand and not rising above 3.5. When all is said and done, these are sensible enough proportions, which explains why the number of Portuguese in the home country never diminished, except cyclically, from the end of the fifteenth century until the Restoration of 1640.

Emigration increased toward the last decades of the sixteenth century and during the first of the seventeenth century. Involuntary converts continued to flee from the Inquisition, settling in the Netherlands – Amsterdam received them in large numbers – and, during a short period, the French southwest. Still, it was above all Brazil and the Spanish empire that attracted these emigrants; they often crossed the border in the direction of nearby Castile. In 1620 Frei Nicolau de Oliveira estimated the departures at about 8,000 each year. Even if we have to reduce this estimate, it still should not come to less than 5,000, even 6,000. The population having increased – it would approach two million in 1640 – it was a yearly drain of about 3 or 3.5 per thousand. After the Restoration, this loss seems to have narrowed, probably even considerably. When the century ended, on the eve of the irresistible gold rush or at the time of its launching, we can assess at some 2,000 the embarkations in Viana, Porto, and Lisbon bound for Pernambuco, Bahia, and Rio de Janeiro. If we take into account other harbors of departure and other destinations, this yearly average could be brought to 2,500 to 3,000 at the most; that is to say, 1.5 per thousand. The rush for Brazilian gold and diamonds again accelerated the drain, which we can estimate at 8,000 or 10,000 emigrants annually without fear of a grave error, during the first two-thirds of the eighteenth century. In 1732 the population of Portugal and the adjoining islands was some 2.3 million, approaching 2.6 million in 1766 to 1767. The emigration therefore represents 4.5 per thousand at the most, 3.5 at the very least, fluctuating on average around 4.

Let us take the risk of giving estimates of emigration totals, of which the very rough degree of accuracy may rightly give offense. From 1500 to 1580 Portugal was "drained" of some 280,000 individuals. During the sixty years that follow, the global figure leaped, passing 300,000 and reaching perhaps 360,000; afterward, from the Restoration in 1640 to 1700 it dwindled to around 150,000. But again, between 1700 and 1760, the drain increased to more than half a million, even to 600,000, to be reduced during the slack period in the exploitation of gold and diamonds in Brazil. In the fifteenth century the departures did not exceed about 50,000. In total, from the start of the overseas expansion until 1760, there were surely more than a million, probably one and a half million Portuguese emigrants, whereas the annual departures beginning at less than 1 per thousand, never go through the ceiling of 4.5 and are situated most of the time between 3 and 2.5 per thousand.

The population of metropolitan Portugal did not even double

between 1527 to 1531, the first census of homesteads, and 1766; far from it. If, however, there were slack periods, even momentary decline, it does not appear that long-lasting ebbs have occurred, contrasting what happened in Spain from 1590 until the mid seventeenth century. The relatively moderate rate of emigration probably explains the absence of extended periods of low population growth, but only partly. Moreover, one has to account for the immigration of slaves throughout the ancien régime. Around 1534, Rèsende feared that these slaves would come to surpass in number the Portuguese themselves; his fears were not justified. Nevertheless, it is possible that this work-force reached 10 percent of the population, at least in the coastal areas. Recent studies have proved its importance in the provinces, attached to all kinds of work. This was the case in the Algarve, as analyzed by Joaquim Magalhães.

A rough calculation can be made of the annual import of slaves. The 1541 figures of the humanist Góis seem exaggerated: 10,000 to 12,000 slaves per year. Another writer in 1578 provides a more acceptable estimate of 3,000. Let us accept 2,000 to 3,000 annually, that is to say 200,000 to 300,000 for the entire sixteenth century, the higher figure being more likely. Around 1523, the Italian Giulio Landi already noticed the twofold effect of the emigration of free Portuguese and the entry of slaves: in Portugal free manpower was so expensive that only the rich had means at their disposal to use it, while others had to take on slave labor (often farmed out by their masters). The economist Severim de Faria, writing in 1655, remarks that lack of Portuguese workers forced the ploughmen to use blacks from Guinea, mulattoes, and even Indians for agricultural jobs. In the seventeenth century, because of the growing demand for slaves in Brazil (due to the expansion of the sugar economy) and the difficulties raised by the fierce competition in purchasing slaves on the African coast, the influx into the home country slowed down. During the first sixty years of the eighteenth century, they were even re-exported from Brazil, partly to the metropolis. Between one and two thousand slaves disembarked yearly in the ports of the metropolis during this one and a half century, although somewhat less toward the end than at the beginning of this period.

The arrival of slaves in the metropolis has no doubt made up for more than one third, perhaps occasionally for half of the Portuguese emigration during the entire ancien régime. The influx of slaves had almost compensated emigration during the sixteenth century. Here we have an extremely important constant from the fifteenth century until 1760 in contrast with the period that follows. There was always this influx of very cheap labor that was placed at the lowest level of society, although these immigrants were often specialized in the service sector and in the primary sector. Most certainly, the effect of compensation with regard to the emigration is less significant than the figures seem to indicate as a result of a much higher mortality rate and the lower reproduction rate of the slaves, despite the accommodating attitude of the masters to help them produce offspring.

The end of the tidal wave of the Brazilian gold and diamonds, from the 1780s onward, and the industrialization movement that started in Portugal brought the exodus back to much lower levels – by half, at least. The economist and demographer Soares de Barros at the end of the eighteenth century estimated that the number of those who left their country in the hope of finding easier conditions every year exceeded 3,000, but not by much. Later, the transfer of the royal court across the Atlantic during the Napoleonic invasions, followed by the strong English domination, caused the emigration to rise again. The political crisis due to Brazil's rise to independence was too short to stop it; in fact, the absolutist persecutions drove a good number of Portuguese into exile. Until the second half of the nineteenth century, the departures scarcely exceeded 4,000 or 4,500 on annual average or about 1.5 per thousand of the overall population. It was the effective abolition of the slave trade to Brazil that once again triggered off the sensational increase in emigration, whereas the worsening internal conditions of Portuguese society also made their contribution. Between 1840 and 1850 the Brazilian empire had still taken in about 33,500 slaves per year. This figure was reduced to 3,287 in 1851, and in 1864 the last disembarkations took place. On the other hand, the War of Secession ended in 1865, and slavery was abolished in Brazil on May 13, 1888. Thereafter, the Brazilian economy entered the era of the expansion of coffee and also, at least in São Paulo, of cotton. The New World attracted numerous emigrants. Let us follow the curve of Portuguese emigration.

After a false start in 1855 to 1859, with 10,000 annual departures, there was a temporary return to the previous rhythm. In 1870, however, emigration soared, this time for good. In reality, the average in the period 1855 to 1880 was already 9,664, jumping to 37,289 from 1881 to 1930. The years 1911 through 1913 represented something of an attack of fever in Portuguese emigrations, which is usually explained by political reasons, specifically the institution of the republic. It is, however, the economic and social climate that has

TABLE 2.1 Portuguese Emigration from Metropolitan Portugal and Adjoining Islands to All Destinations

Period	Total		Annual average	
1855–1859	30,178		10,035	
1860–1865	31,241		5,206	
1866–1870	41,121		8,224	
1871–1875	70,906		14,181	
1876–1880	57,826		11,565	
1881–1885	84,682		16,936	
1886–1890	104,952		20,990	
1891–1895	158,380		31,676	
1896–1900	111,637		22,327	
1901–1905	128,341		25,668	
1906–1910	197,926		39,585	
1911–1915	271,279		54,255	
1916–1920	154,496		30,899	
1921–1925	157,157		31,431	
1926–1930	167,595		33,519	
1931–1935	37,459		7,492	
1936–1940	44,246		8,849	
1941–1945	19,199		3,839	
1946–1950	71,072		14,214	
1951–1955	244,811		48,962	
1956–1960	215,099	*	43,019	*
1961–1965	288,455	367,401	57,691	73,480
1966–1970	458,343	696,691	91,668	139,338
1971–1974	227,521	446,858	56,880	111,714
Total 1855–1974	3,393,682 (clandestine emigrants included)			

Note: * Clandestine emigration included. The figures of clandestine emigrants only concern entries into France.
1974: provisional results.

to be questioned. World War I had obviously reduced emigration but it recovered from 1919 onwards. It was not for internal reasons that emigration dropped between 1930 and 1945 to less than one-fifth of the preceding average, with only 6,726 departures annually; it was because of the immigration policy followed by the countries traditionally receiving Portuguese migrants – Brazil and the United States – and World War II.

Immediately after peace was restored, the exodus started again: the years 1947 and 1948 already saw 10,422 emigrants leave on average, and the yearly average for the five-year period 1946 to 1950 reached 14,214; in the period 1951 to 1955 this number was multiplied by almost 3.5, after which it receded slightly during the following five years. The decade of 1960, however, brought a new, spectacular leap forward to more than double this figure. The quarter of a century between 1946 to 1970 saw a yearly average of 51,111 legal emigrants leave Portugal, after deduction of the returns. This constitutes an increase larger than 35 percent in comparison with the half century from 1881 to 1930. During fifteen years, from 1960 to 1974, at least 1,479,888 Portuguese left their home country without returning.

Alas, all these neat calculations (except in part the last one) reveal one great defect: that of taking into account only the legal emigration figures. During a long time, however, the clandestine emigration, or at least the non-registered one, has been extremely numerous. In 1883, in his report and plan for regulation Luciano Cordeiro cast doubt on the accuracy of the statistics of legal emigration. Concerning the clandestine emigration, Cordeiro did not regard it as reckless to estimate it at one-third of the volume of legal migration. A very well-informed economist and historian, Oliveira Martins, estimated the illegal migration to be more than half the legal one. We can be sure of not making a great error when we put it between one-fourth and one-third, as the ratio varied according to the circumstances. After World War II the unlegalized departures resumed in 1962 and later increased disproportionately: in 1969, 1970, and 1971 they came to exceed the official departures; the clandestine then made up 61 percent of the total. We only have figures for France; Spain and other countries have no data on illegal Portuguese immigration.

While taking these estimates of non-official emigration figures into account, we can correct some calculations of the demographic effects. From 1886 to 1959 the balance of the actual emigration has destroyed almost half of the demographic balance; from 1960 to 1969 the "drain" has reached 83.6 percent whereas from 1951 to 1962 it had only been 40.1 percent. More serious is the fact that for the years 1966 to 1972 the emigration reached 136.4 percent of the demographic balance. In comparison with the total population, there have been 8.3 emigrants per thousand inhabitants during the years 1961 to 1965 and 14.6 during 1966 to 1969; in the last year the rate even came to 18.4. In 1970 the rate reached to 20.77 per thousand. In our opinion the 1970 census results stand out as excessive.

The Areas of Reception and Settlement

In Morocco where the expansion began, there were only a few hundred Portuguese settlers until around 1470. Later, because of the strengthening of the Portuguese occupation, there came to be 5,000 soldiers in the Luso-Moroccan towns, and the Portuguese population came to 25,000 inhabitants (of which there were 4,000 to 5,000 in Safi alone). This number dwindled with the royal ascendancy that provoked the crisis of the 1540s. Madeira is the first archipelago to have been colonized. In the middle of the fifteenth century there were already 3,000 inhabitants on the main island, whereas Porto Santo was left with only 160 or 200 at the beginning of the sixteenth century. Around 1550, the island of sugar and wine reached 20,000 inhabitants, among whom were 3,000 slaves; the density was 23 inhabitants per square kilometer, against 15 to 16 in Portugal. On the Azores, Fayal and Pico already numbered 1,500 inhabitants at the end of the reign of King João II. The rapid development of the archipelago was considerable in the sixteenth century thanks to the production of wheat, crayon, and cattle. Of the islands of Cape Verde, in 1480 only Santiago was inhabited, and a quarter of a century later a second one, Fogo, also was populated. On the other islands there was nothing but cattle left to roam. While their start had been slow, the role of the Cape Verde islands was increasing during the following centuries: ports of call on the long distance routes to the Cape, to Brazil, to the Castilian Indies, to the slave market of Guinea, and to the markets of cotton, orchil, leather, and salt. Beneath the Equator, São Tomé began to be colonized during the reign of João II, who dispatched hundreds of young Jews there; of that forced emigration, there were still some 600 of both sexes in 1506. Povoação, with 200 to 250 homes, already had one thousand inhabitants; on the whole island, including the town Povoação, there were about 4,000 of whom half were slaves employed in farming. Moreover, there were 5,000 to 6,000 slaves destined for re-exportation. Toward the middle of the sixteenth century the town grew: 3,000 to 3,500 inhabitants at that time, around 4,000 fifteen years later, and toward 1590 some 8,000 to 9,000, including the Atlantic blacks and the prisoners. The whites were small in number since the climate barely suited them. Apart from the colonization of their own possessions, the Portuguese were about to settle permanently in foreign possessions. For example, in the Canaries they formed 70 percent of the immigration after the Inquisition trials.

In the Orient, the Portuguese emigration also provided settlers for colonization. In 1513 there were slightly more than 2,500 Portuguese capable of soldiering in Asia; three years later there were 4,000. Toward 1540 there were between 6,000 and 7,000. Under Sebastião, the number of Portuguese scattered throughout the Indies approached 16,000 according to an estimate of the chronicler Diogo do Couto, who lived on the spot. In reality, an incredible dispersion went together with controlled settlement. Toward the middle of the century, we count at least 200 "very rich" Portuguese in Abyssinia. In Muscat, at the Gulf of Oman, there were about thirty Portuguese residents. In the great emporium of Ormuz, the married Portuguese numbered between 150 and 200 during the second half of the sixteenth century. In Diu, besides 350 garrison soldiers, there were some sixty families. On the island of Mozambique there were forty to fifty settlers; in the interior at Sena a dozen. It was, of course, Goa that gained the upper hand, particularly after the middle of the century. The inhabitants who came from the Metropolis numbered 5,000 to 6,000. In Cochin, even though it was the great loading port for spices, there were only a thousand Portuguese residents (in 1546 they did not even number 350, except for the season when the "royal ships" were present). On the east coast of India, 1,000 were counted at São Tomé de Meliapor. In Malacca, the key to all the fabulously rich traffic between the Far East and the Indian Ocean, the number of Portuguese families did not exceed 1,000 toward the end of the sixteenth century. The Portuguese were also present at Lar (in Persia) and Baghdad. In the service of the Mughal squadron in Bengal, there were more than 900 Portuguese in 1582. One thousand Portuguese inhabited Macao at the beginning of the seventeenth century.

Let us return to the shores of the Atlantic. At the beginning of the sixteenth century in Brazil, there were only 2,000 Portuguese, having more than double that amount of slaves at their service. Toward the middle of the sixteenth century the white colonists exceeded this figure ten times. There were at least 30,000 around 1600 and rising to 50,000 in 1612, when the number of slaves came to more than 120,000, half of them Indians and half blacks.

In constructing a synthesis, however dangerous this may be, we can say that in the course of the sixteenth century some 100,000 to 150,000 Portuguese resided outside the metropolis, scattered in an astonishing diaspora, across the entire globe.

Let us now survey, alas very sketchily, the evolution during the whole seventeenth century. The Spanish empire had become the main market of silver, the white metal. Since the *reales* began to control the international trade, the Portuguese had never ceased infiltrating Spain and the Castilian Indies. They had a major trump card in that they were in control of the slave trade. From 1577 Frei João de São José noticed the demographic decline of a town like Tavira: numerous merchants and other rich Algarvians had transferred their residence to Seville and to other ports of Andalusia, tempted as they were by the profits to be earned in the trade of the Castilian Indies. In order to take part in it, it was necessary to settle in Castile so as to evade the edicts directed against foreign participation. The decrease in population which afflicted Spain at the end of the sixteenth and during the first half of the seventeenth century attracted foreign labor. In addition to the Portuguese, the Auvergnats went there in large numbers. The Portuguese craftsmen crossed the border willingly, attracted by higher salaries and better job opportunities. By the same token, the higher level of prices also attracted Portuguese merchandise. Until the Restoration of 1640 the Portuguese merchants were also in possession of the *asiento*, of the supply of slaves to the New World, having ousted the Genoese. At that time one-fourth of the inhabitants of Seville had been born in Portugal, and the majority of the skilled workers in Old Castile and Estremadura also were of Portuguese origin. Even assuming that these statements were somewhat exaggerated, the Portuguese were counted by the thousands in Spain in that period. On the other side of the Atlantic, it was said that one-third of the population of Buenos Aires was Portuguese. In Peru there were a few thousand, including wealthy capitalists, craftsmen, navigators, and fishermen, according to research of Gonçalo de Reparaz. These groups of *peruleiros* developed close relations with Brazil. The Portuguese were still persecuted by the Holy Office in Mexico, which provides proof of the fact that they were numerous and that their competition was feared. The Restoration of 1640 reduced these Portuguese groups in the Spanish empire, but it could not annihilate them completely.

Toward the end of the seventeenth century, when metropolitan Portugal barely counted 2 million inhabitants, the rich archipelago of Madeira was very heavily populated; 50,000 inhabitants, with the density exceeding 58 persons per square km. On the Azores, São Miguel, the granary of the kingdom, had already more inhabitants than Madeira. On the islands of the western and central groups taken together the number did not come to 15,000; on Santa Maria there were 3,200, on Terceira more than 19,000. In total the archipelago of the Azores was inhabited by some 90,000 people, the average density being 37.5 per square km. The adjoining islands had a density which was by far superior to that of the metropole, and they never gave up this supremacy until our days. The main town, Angra, had more than 14,000 inhabitants in those days, and if Ponta Delgada had only 9,500, they were both on the scale of metropolitan cities. In the archipelago of Cape Verde, in Guinea, and on the island of São Tomé there lived 25,000 to 30,000 Portuguese.

We do not have the sources allowing us to reconstruct the number of those who went to Angola and Mozambique. They numbered perhaps 80,000, perhaps even a hundred thousand. In India, Goa was in full decline; its population was probably not more than 50,000, of whom only a small number are *reinóis*, that is to say, of metropolitan origin. All over the East Indies the number of Portuguese emigrants could not have been much more than about ten thousand. Macao was unquestionably their most lively center, in spite of the loss of trade with Japan; about 6,000 non-Christian Chinese and, moreover, a few hundred converted Chinese, lived there together with a thousand Portuguese families. Brazil was developed during the seventeenth century by the *bandeiras* looking for gold and hunting slaves. The population grew progressively during the first third of the century. This growth suffered heavily from the Dutch wars and the sugar crisis later in the century, to show a slow rise only toward the end of the century. The colonization covered particularly the northeast, the plateau of São Paulo, the area of Rio, the Amazon basin, and the Maranhão. With the addition of whites, Indians, and blacks, the population was likely to exceed half a million. On the whole, the Portuguese overseas empire must have had a total "weight" of almost one million people, of whom one-fourth to one-third were of peninsular origin.

From the end of the seventeenth century two characteristic features enter into the history of Portuguese emigration. In turn, the colonization zones became centers of emigration. That was the case with the adjoining islands, which were to send off entire groups of families to Brazil, Mozambique, and later to North America. At the same time, the dispersion of the Portuguese to all corners of the world dwindled considerably; from then on Brazil was to absorb the overwhelming majority.

As for the Cape Verde islands, it does appear that the Portuguese settlement process did progress, as well as on the coast of Guinea and in Africa south of the Equator. These areas under Portuguese domination continued to count around 80,000 to 100,000 settlers. In Asia we can suppose 120,000 colonists of Portuguese origin. The growth of Portuguese colonization in Brazil had become impressive:

its population tripled, or even more, in one century – the century of the gold rush; the number of settlers counted 1,850,000, against 390,000 inhabitants on the adjoining islands and the other regions of the empire. And Brazil would continue to grow at a rhythm much more intense than that in Portugal. Numerical equality of the populations was reached at the beginning of the nineteenth century. At the time of independence, the population of Brazil exceeded that of Portugal by 50 percent.

It is noteworthy that the independence of Brazil neither stopped nor diverted the emigration drain of which the ancient home country was suffering. From 1820 to 1909 it averaged 7,808 annually, reaching a total of 702,790 Portuguese emigrants for the above mentioned period. Certainly, these overall figures covering such a long period conceal the broad lines of the evolution of emigration. Actually, from 1855 to 1865 the average was only 4,055, but it leaped to 11,689 in 1871 to 1874 and to 14,000 in 1880 to 1881. We have already seen the causes of this increase: the end of the era of slavery and the expansion of coffee and cotton cultivation. There were not only Portuguese in this tidal wave that inundated Brazil. The strongest contingent consisted of Italians, with 45.2 percent against 25.6 percent Portuguese, with the Spaniards bringing in 11.6 percent, three times the German contribution: in total, 2,742,622 immigrants. Brazil's population had risen from three million (of which a third were slaves) in 1800 to eight million in 1850, to ten million in 1872, and to seventeen million in 1900, reaching thirty million in 1920. At Santos and Rio alone, 131,268 immigrants disembarked in 1888, almost three times the number of the previous year and five times the average of 1878 to 1886.

Let us return to the Portuguese emigration. Of the emigrants of the years 1880 to 1888, more than 85 percent landed in Brazilian ports. Other regions of the New World received 7.2 percent, of which the majority – that is to say 4 percent – went to the United States, 2 percent to Argentina, and the rest to English Guyana. Oceania received 2.6 percent of the Portuguese emigrants, Europe and Asia 2 percent, while Portuguese Africa received only 3 percent. The overwhelming preponderance of the Brazilian outlet during the 1880s had only established itself recently: from 1855 to 1865 the new empire of Portuguese language and culture had only welcomed 55.5 percent of the Portuguese emigrants, because the archipelagos had poured out their surplus above all to the United States. This calls for two observations. An extremely voluminous emigration flowed toward a single destination, Brazil. On the other hand, there occurred an astounding dispersion to all corners of the world. Notice for example that the emigration flow to remote Hawaii was of the same size as the flow to Africa. In the Hawaiian archipelago at that time there were, among the 17,000 whites, 9,377 Portuguese against 60,000 natives. Until the end of the nineteenth century, however, Brazil would continue to absorb more than 80 percent of the Portuguese emigration.

In the twentieth century the attraction of the Brazilian bottomless pit subsided only slightly. It still received 75 percent of all Portuguese emigrants during the first decade. From 1900 to 1930, this percentage fell to 70 percent. Afterward, despite Brazil's closed-door policy, it climbed to 76.1 percent from 1931 to 1946 and even to 78.6 percent from 1947 to 1954. Until 1923, the second most receiving area was the United States, with 18.6 percent on average from the beginning of our century. From that year onward, Argentina took over from the United States.

After World War II, it was initially still Brazil that attracted most Portuguese emigrants, but after a few years, its role faded. Venezuela and Canada were gaining importance as lands of destination, and the United States recovered a good portion of its attraction. Above all, in an almost vertical take-off, France soon came to take over the role reserved in the past for Brazil.

Table 22 shows the developments in legal emigration figures, according to destinations, from the decade of 1950 to 1959 to that of 1960 to 1969.

During the first decade, 82.3 percent still went to South America, 8 percent to North America, and almost none toward Europe. During the second decade, the percentage of South America fell to 17.4 percent, that of North America rose to 18 percent, and Europe took a great spurt. The share of France swelled even more disproportionally if we take the clandestine emigration into account. It was, therefore, the industrial nations that attracted Portuguese labor since about 1950.

We have not included in these calculations the flow of Portuguese of the metropolis and the adjoining islands toward the overseas territories. Only some fifty emigrants per year embarked to Portuguese Africa during the last quarter of the nineteenth century. From 1901 to 1906 this average went up to 2,033, a modest number compared with the total average of 25,000 departures. In Brazil alone, there were between 150,000 and 200,000 Portuguese who were not naturalized in 1890, and in 1917 they had reached the 800,000 mark, ten times their numbers in the provinces overseas. In

TABLE 2.2 Legal Emigration According to Destination, 1950–1959, 1960–1969

Destinations	1950–1959		1960–1969	
	Total	%	Total	%
Argentina	8,549	2.5	2,828	0.4
Brazil	237,327	69.5	73,267	11.3
Canada	11,350	3.3	50,405	7.7
France	14,924	4.3	329,050	50.8
Germany	0	0	45,474	7.0
Netherlands	0		2,085	
Republic of South Africa	6,193	1.8	15,793	2.4
United States	16,193	4.7	66,674	10.5
Venezuela	35,236	10.3	37,318	5.7
Others (Netherlands included in %)	11,356	3.3	24,068	4.0

1940 the population of the African territories numbered 10,880,000 inhabitants, and ten years later 12,113,000. On the first date, the number of whites was 81,911 and on the second 185,609; the number of half-castes being 168,473 and 171,693, respectively. From these figures the small migration to Africa immediately stands out. In Africa and also on Timor and São Tomé there was substantial interbreeding, which was the major contributor to demographic growth on the islands of Cape Verde. The Portuguese of metropolitan origin in the overseas territories were clearly outnumbered by the colony of Rio de Janeiro alone: some 600,000 and in São Paulo more than 300,000. From 1937 to 1945 the number of metropolitans which on annual average settled in Portuguese Africa did not even come to 1,800. From 1946 to 1950 the average rose to 6,857, and during the following decade, leaped to more than 12,000. Toward the end of World War II and during the first years of peace, as long as the emigration to foreign countries had not yet started, these modest figures represented high percentages: 51.9 percent from 1944 to 1949. The percentage went down again, however, to 15 percent for the period 1950 to 1959. In the years 1965 to 1970 the departures toward overseas territories were no more than 6.5 percent of the total emigration (clandestine emigration included).

From these trends and figures regarding emigrants and destinations, an overall conclusion is to be drawn. The Portuguese emigrants have never succeeded in contenting themselves with the territories governed by Portugal, but they have always broken away to foreign lands. It is true they have built up the Atlantic archipelagos and Brazil, but they have too often shown their preference to go and fit into the framework of societies that already existed and were of a superior level of development – India in the sixteenth century, the industrialized nations, and even those of the tertiary revolution during our times. In Brazil, where the Portuguese have laid the foundations and built the framework of society, they have profited, especially during the nineteenth century, from the supply of foreign capital and infrastructure. And yet, the Great Discoveries and the rapid development of expansion in the fifteenth and sixteenth centuries do not owe much to foreign contributions. The great mass of emigrants was made up by people of little importance, without means to invest; rather, searching to improve their fate, to earn money based on hard labor, and to rise socially. It was, and is, always easier to try one's luck in those social contexts where the infrastructure is already in place. The emigrants found their way, particularly toward the tertiary activities, the service sector. In 1779 the viceroy of Brazil, the Marquis de Lavradio, observed in a report to his successor that the colonist who came to settle in Brazil, even if he or she was a farmer at home, only wanted to devote himself to shopkeeping.

Return Migration

It remains impossible – especially for the more distant epochs – to determine if the emigrants left while cherishing the hope to return to their native country. Still, we possess some information about actual returns. In 1610 Pyrard de Laval writes that at the end of a stay of nine or ten years in Brazil, many Portuguese "come back from it all rich; and there are among others, many of these New Christians who are baptized Jews, who are rich with sixty, eighty and a hundred thousand crowns, and more; but they [the Old Christians] do not take much notice of these people." As a matter of fact, there have always been people from the upper or middle strata, who left either to do business or to hold public office in the hope of accumulating riches. They returned when they had reached their objectives or at the expiration of their duties: viceroys, governors, captains of fortresses and of ships, magistrates, finance and trading post personnel, privates, and specialized craftsmen working on behalf of the State. Only the highly placed and the powerful had the possibility of transporting back home the treasures they had gained such as gold, diamonds, supplies of precious fabrics, and loads of spices; for the little man, the transfer of his modest savings met with strong obstacles.

Thus, the majority of the emigrants stayed overseas, often shifting to other places in order to hunt for fortune, and settling down in the end. The great majority did not really succeed in making a fortune, and the accumulated money allowed them to live better in their new environment than in their home country. For the sixteenth century, the historian Costa Lobo estimated that the returns amounted only to 10 percent of the total number of emigrants. We can assume that this percentage had always been rather low, except in the case of the dominant strata. We have already seen that Garcia de Resende, around 1534, complained that the Portuguese who went to settle in Brazil, on the islands or in the East Indies too often forgot their "nature" that is to say, their native roots. They were building up other roots overseas. The Dutch Governor-General Van Diemen explained in 1638 to the directors of the East India Company: "The vast majority of Portuguese colonists consider the Indies to be their native land, and they do not think about Portugal. They do very little business with their land of origin, preferring to live and to get rich thanks to the treasures of the Indies, as if they were natives and do not know any other fatherland." Van Diemen was not wrong, because half a century before, a Portuguese navigator had observed: "These Indies are so large and so fertile that no Portuguese has a desire any more to return to Portugal, at least when he is not made to return by force; because the soil is so abundant with goods and people enjoy so much their pleasures, that they abandon their wives and their children, and they live there without ever intending to see them back."

In the nineteenth century, the Portuguese who was driven into emigration went to till the land with the spade and the hoe or to serve as apprentice or desk employee in the retail business. Those who were successful in agriculture often purchased plots of land and stayed in Brazil; sometimes they preferred to set up a business with their accumulated savings. Those apprentices and employees who had been successful, established themselves at their own expense, and later, if they succeeded in gathering sufficient savings, returned to Portugal. Alternatively, they bought land and houses or they devoted themselves to speculate in public loans. According to the estimates of the economist Oliveira Martins, around 1888, almost half of the emigrants returned sooner or later. This constituted an exceptional percentage, being no doubt due to the circumstances of the time. Very soon this percentage dropped sharply and, except for the years after 1930 when emigration fell back, it must not have gone beyond 10 percent. During the low tide of emigration, from 1936 to 1949, the return migration reached a record of 52.8 percent. But during the years 1951 to 1962 it had already dropped again to 4.9 percent. During the twenty years 1950 to 1970, the rate further fell to 3.4 percent. It was only 1.4 percent in 1970, almost all emigrants coming from South America. In these calculations we have only taken the legal emigration into account, which was solely destined for foreign countries; overseas territories, therefore, are not included.

The Sending Regions

We do not have sources at our disposal for the period before the nineteenth century that provide us with numerical data about the regions of origin of the emigrants. Nevertheless, a systematic summary of qualitative indications allows us to determine at least the relative importance of the different places of origin. A very suggestive approach has been tried by Jorge Dias and Orlando Ribeiro, using the ethnographic method: they have compared the cultural characteristics of metropolitan regions with those of the Atlantic islands. The hand mill, which could only be met with in the Algarve, is found back in the archipelagos of Madeira, the Azores, and Cape Verde. This leads to the assumption that there was a first wave of colonization that took off from this southern region. We know, furthermore, that the voyages of discovery and the colonization started and continued, until the last third of the fifteenth century, from Algarvian ports; this makes such an ethnographic conclusion very likely. Nevertheless, some other characteristics of the cultural complex of Madeira point to the northwest of the home country; whereas those of Santa Maria remain Algarvian, those of São Miguel are linked to the Estremadura and to the Alentejo. As far as the other islands of the Azores are concerned, some resemblance occurs with the Minho and Beira. As to the archipelago of Cape Verde, it was culturally linked to the south of Portugal with, of course, black contributions such as the African pestle.

The Algarvian period of expansion encompassed precisely the discovery of the adjoining islands, of the Saharan and Guinean coasts, and of the archipelago of Cape Verde. After this first wave of discoveries, Lisbon and other ports on the western coast became prominent as points of departure when new waves of emigration started setting off from the Alentejo – having easy communications with Lisbon – from the Estremadura, and subsequently from other regions united with Lisbon. Later contributions to the emigration stream came from the Minho, served by the ports of Viana, Porto, and Beira. The atmosphere of emigration expanded very fast. From my sample surveys regarding the origins of the Portuguese who went to the East Indies during the first half of the sixteenth century, it stands out that the emigrants came from everywhere in Portugal but mainly from the regions south of the Tagus. Alentejanos could be found even on the sugar-producing island of São Tomé. The north-east and the inland center of Portugal did not seem to have escaped from this flood of departures, but departures there were fairly widespread geographically and moderate in scope. The geography of the Portuguese sending regions is not surprising, bearing a strong resemblance to the other Iberian kingdoms in the same period. It was especially the central band of the Meseta, from the Cantabrians to Andalusia, that sent emigrants, whereas the East, and indeed Galicia, hardly took part in it. The reason for this was that before the seventeenth century the center of the Peninsula, including the interior regions of Portugal, was relatively more populated in those days in comparison to the periphery.

By the last third of the sixteenth century the Portuguese northwest took first place among the sending regions. In 1583 to 1584 Fernão Cardim noted in Pernambuco that the majority of people came from Viana do Minho. At that time, Algarvians settled especially in Andalusia. It seems beyond doubt, however, that as the years went by, the sending regions in the metropolis became less important. From the last quarter of the seventeenth century, if not earlier, the adjoining archipelagos at their turn started to send out emigrants along the Atlantic routes. This situation would persist until after Wold War II, only to be modified by small movements to the north. From 1866 to 1871, among the 51,509 Portuguese emigrants 14,065 had embarked on Madeira and on the Azores; 16,450 came from the department of Porto. Together these two places of origin represented 59 percent of the total. The regions that followed them were Aveiro, Braga, Viana, Viseu, Vila Real, and Coimbra; thus, the metropolitan northwest and adjoining archipelagos. If we take a longer period, from the same starting date of 1866 until 1888, with 309,547 departures, the Entre Douro e Minho and the two Beiras – the Alta and the Littoral – provided more than 58 percent; the Azores and Madeira, 27 percent of these emigrants. Therefore, the northwest and the islands contributed a total of 85 percent while the contribution of the Estremadura was still 7.2 percent. The same percentage was split between the provinces of the Algarve, Alentejo, the Lower Beira, and Trás-os-Montes; that is to say, all the south and the northeast. Among these four last provinces, Trás-os-Montes is the one which supplied the highest contingent, due to the ruin of the vineyards and the opening of a rail connection.

During the twentieth century a new widening of the sending regions followed. During the years 1900 to 1957, the Azores participated with 16.7 percent; next came, in descending order, the departments of Viseu, Porto (gone down to third place), and Aveiro, each of these three contributed more than 10 percent and, together with the islands, they represented 51.22 percent of the emigration. A second group was formed by the departments of Coimbra, Guarda, Vila Real, Braga, and Bragança, each contributing between 7.55 percent and 5.9 percent, together approximately 32.9 percent. The two first groups, that is the northwest and the northeast, comprised a total of 84 percent. A third group consisted of Leiria, Viana, Lisbon, and Faro, whose percentages ranged between 4 percent and 2 percent. The regions contributing less than 1.5 percent each were Santarém, Castelo Branco, Beja, Portalegre, and Evora. In comparison with the nineteenth century, the widening of the sending regions stands out. They now include the northeast because the railway enabled the emigration from the interior on a large scale. The department of Viana do Minho, which played an important part for three centuries, was reduced to fit into the third group after Leiria.

This recent evolution spreads the emigration phenomenon over the entire metropolitan and island territory, with frequent changes in the order of the various departments.

Let us advance to 1969. The Azores, whose role had faded during the years 1960 to 1965, recaptured first place with 17.1 percent. On the peninsular territory, the northwest and the coastal center represented 51.8 percent; the two together reached a total of 69 percent. The exodus from the extreme north was losing momentum, while the emigration from Estremadura increased. In 1970 it was the department of Lisbon that raised itself to first rank, and the Algarve returned to an honorable place. Unfortunately, these deductions only take the legal emigration into account. There is nothing to indicate that the clandestine departures are proportional to the legal emigration. Since we know the real entries into France, we have to see whether or not these two are similar. We looked more closely at the same year 1969:

TABLE 2.3 Emigration by Department

1961		1965		1969		1970	
Funchal	4,797	Porto	10,743	P. Delgada	8,250	Lisbon	7,060
Aveiro	2,798	Lisbon	10,593	Porto	7,274	P. Delgada	6,393
Porto	2,582	Braga	9,404	Braga	6,529	Braga	5,770
P. Delgada	2,371	Leiria	8,162	Lisbon	5,973	Porto	5,707
Viseu	2,282	Guarda	7,980	Leiria	5,171	Viseu	5,089
Bragança	2,074	Viana	6,470	Viseu	4,855	Leiria	4,665
Braga	2,058	Aveiro	6,412	Aveiro	4,598	Aveiro	4,231
		Castelo Br.	6,077	Faro	3,771	Faro	2,889
		Viseu	4,914	Vila Real	3,598	Vila Real	2,608
		Santarém	4,371	A. Heroìsmo	3,036	Coimbra	2,581

TABLE 2.4 Emigration to France, 1969

1. Braga	12,369	6. Bragança	4,873
2. Porto	10,259	7. Viana	4,829
3. Vila Real	6,294	8. Castelo Branco	4,818
4. Leiria	5,483	9. Aveiro	4,702
5. Viseu	5,256	10. Guarda	4,522

The two departments of Braga and Porto taken together supplied almost 28 percent of the total of 80,829 entries into France. The regions north of the central mountain range Estrela-Montejunto contributed 77.2 percent. There are differences between the geographical origins of this emigration from Portugal to France and that of the legal emigration; this stands to reason. It was not the population of the islands that turned to France; the clandestine emigration to France is, self-evidently, easier from the northern and central border zones of Portugal itself. What stands out, without doubt, is the growing impact of the emigration fever on the whole of the metropolis.

This tidal wave can even be more easily judged from the figures indicating the number of emigrants per thousand inhabitants. Indeed, we must not confuse the share of each department in the total emigration with the "drain" that the exodus inflicted on each department. Unfortunately, these figures are badly distorted. Clandestine emigration would actually double the percentages of emigrants. Let us pick the year 1965, when these distortions were less serious than in other years.

The departments that supplied the biggest contingent to the flow of emigrants were not, as the table shows, those that suffered the

TABLE 2.5 Clandestine Emigration, Number of Emigrants per Thousand Inhabitants, 1965

1. Guarda	29.4 per thousand	7. Braga	15 per thousand
2. Viana	23.5	8. Faro	13.7
3. Leiria	20.4	9. Vila Real	12.5
4. Castelo Branco	19.7	10. Aveiro	11.8
5. Bragança	16	11. Viseu	10
6. Ponta Delgada	15.8	12. Funchal	9.6

worst consequences. The northeast and the extreme south, of which the contribution was not very significant, are listed among the most severely "drained" regions.

Two nineteenth-century historians, Alexandre Herculano and J.P. Oliveira Martins, have analyzed the same regional imbalances, which were equally visible in their own day. Unfortunately, their conclusions are as well applicable to the present situation and recent studies have revived them.

We have to see the problem in a wider perspective: throughout five centuries of Portuguese history, minorities have had to expatriate themselves in order to avoid persecution or at least discrimination. Tens of thousands of Jews were forced to leave Portugal by the end of the fifteenth century due to the Inquisition, which tried to defend an established oligarchy, noble, ecclesiastic, and deeply in debt, against the rise of a bourgeoisie with a modern mentality. Moreover, the State has always made its weight felt in national life. At the time of the Cortes of 1472, the popular estates already complained that the laws, regulations, and constant interventions of the central power destroyed the liberty of the citizens and took away all possibilities to earn a decent living, to attend to their affairs, and "oppressing them to such an extent that they cannot lift up their heads and they live in financial difficulty and they are poor". Around 1534, the old secretary of the king, Resende, confessed that Portugal did not lack resources but only a good government and good legislation. The same tune was played through all the following centuries. In fact, the society has remained prisoner of a structure of the ancien régime that was held in place by the ruling classes wanting to prevent the participation of other strata in public life.

Herculano and Oliveira Martins have underlined a phenomenon whose collective character is so pronounced (as it developed over several centuries) that it could not be explained in terms of individual psychology. The structural reasons for this general movement of emigration need to be discovered before anything else. These two historians, and all the earlier and later economists, have put it into one phrase: it is poverty, a factor strongly rooted in the social economy, that has always forced the Portuguese to emigrate. First, there was a persistent lack of employment. Second, there was the very low level of salaries and other gains. We have seen that the "drain" of each department is often not proportional, either in comparison with the respective population or with the density. The causes are therefore not local or regional, but they can be related to the structure of the whole Portuguese political economy.

During the sixteenth century there was a Portuguese migration to the Canaries. The majority of these migrants consisted of humble peasants and laborers. In addition, we also encounter artisans, sailors, and, for different reasons, merchants. It is most astonishing that there are even men of letters, in fact three of them, one of whom was a teacher of grammar. When in the seventeenth century the priest and author Severim de Faria wanted to give an explanation for the large number of Portuguese settling in Spain, mostly to work in the industrial sector, he wrote that these mechanical artisans left for the neighboring kingdom because in Portugal they did not find out "how to work"; that is to say, they did not find employment. In 1580 two Venetian envoys went to Lisbon to congratulate Philip II upon his conquest of Portugal. They appeared to be struck by the low level of living standard of the working classes. "The humble folk live poorly, their daily food consists of sardines" and of unrefined bread; only fruits were plentiful. A minister of King João V, the Cardinal da Mota, recommended in 1734 the setting-up of a silk factory, because "in no other kingdom there are as many unemployed and poor people as a result of a lack of jobs. They will find employment in these factories." In the previous century, Faria e Sousa made a descriptive sketch of Portugal at the time of Philip IV. In the Alentejo, he said, the laborers were mostly rich in goods; their families were nurseries of the magistrature and of the higher government. The Estremadura enjoyed a moderate welfare, even the less favored managed to get by. In the Beira, however, (which is the region of Aveiro, Coimbra, Viseu, Guarda, Idanha (Castelo Branco)) the great majority lived in poverty and were forced to beg. Between the Douro and the Minho the agriculture was well-kept and the production was plentiful, but the multitude of people was so great as to force the *Minhotos* to emigrate and the nobility to live in discomfort – even castles were falling into ruins. In those days Manuel Severim de Faria emphasized the contrast between the great, but badly cultivated, properties beyond the Tagus and the small domains of the Minho. At the beginning of the nineteenth century, a lawyer, Almeida e Sousa de Lobão, who was supportive of the absolute monarchy, pointed on the one hand to the great *fazendas* (farms) of the Alentejo, where the rich owner had cattle in abundance and a great number of day laborers and on the other to the poverty of the farmers of the Beira, the Minho, of Trás-os-Montes, and even of the Estremadura, who had to work with their hands, assisted by a small number of *criados* (servants). In 1875, the economist and historian Rebelo da Silva studied the Portuguese rural economy and noticed the lack of strength of the population of the countryside as well as their apathy. He called the generally miserable diet of the poor classes into question. "The people live and work, but it would be more accurate to say that in many areas they only vegetate."

The Financial Consequences of Migration

The very low standard of living of the laboring classes was related to a lack of employment and insufficient salaries. The unemployment forced people into begging; veiled unemployment reduced the returns, not only in agriculture but also in industry. Increases in salaries, however, have never brought an end to the dramatic unemployment. Around 1870, the landowners and farmers complained that the salaries had gone up as a result of the lack of labor due to emigration; the consequence was an agricultural crisis. A century later, Portuguese industrialists agreed to pay higher wages in order to deal with the contraction of the labor market and to reduce the emigration debit. These measures, emphasized in a report of the Portuguese Industrial Association at the beginning of 1967, have not reached their goal at all since, as we have seen, the emigration has increased to sensationally high levels during the years 1967 to 1970. Such mass exodus quite often does not lead to an improvement of the standard of living as workers prefer to reduce the number of working days, only maintaining the level that they already had.

Salaries and employment are nevertheless only manifestations of an entire social structure. In 1632 the *juiz do povo* of Lisbon, Francisco Velho, stated in a report to the king: "In this kingdom there is no farmer who ploughs his land independently, because almost all the land belongs either to the church, or to the crown or he pays fees to several nobles, and such fees and charges and taxes and tributes are excessive." A century later, a politician with a very cultivated mind who carefully studied the Portuguese problems, D. Luís da Cunha, characterized Portugal as follows:

> a strip of land which can be divided in three pieces. The first is not well cultivated, though it could have been; the second belongs to the clergy, including the monastic orders. The third section produces a bit of corn, which is nevertheless not enough for the subsistence of its inhabitants, which therefore has to come from outside. It also produces a lot of wine, olive oil, salt. . . .

Let it come to mind that by the end of the eighteenth century 68 percent of the land in Spain belonged to the nobility and to the clergy. In Portugal the landholdings of the nobility and the clergy were considerable as well, and the weight of the charges providing the "income" of the upper strata was certainly also very high; in 1715 the abbot Mornay estimated it at two-thirds of the national income. One should not be deceived by the preponderance of small exploitation in the north and especially in the northwest. Agriculture in Portugal has always lacked capital. The Venetian Cà Masser took note of that at the beginning of the sixteenth century. A century later, judge Velho elaborated further on this absence of *cabedal* that, in combination with the lack of manpower, left the fields fallow. Herculano, in 1873 to 1875, also came back to this lack of *cabedais de grangeio*, the lack of investment capital. It is true that throughout Portuguese history, and even in our own days, those who had money were not inclined to invest it but preferred to make extravagant expenditures. As the propertied classes squeezed the peasant and did not renounce their income from land, they by preference turned to trade; to an economy of circulation and speculation rather than to one of production. The Portuguese trade balance has continuously remained in deficit ever since the country was launched into the Great Discoveries. The deficit was made up by re-exportation and the invisible exports, in which the exportation of labor takes a good share.

The mercantile economy has grown from the sixteenth century down to our times. This increase has prevented the development of the rural population. As a result, in Portugal and in Spain alike, the population involved in agriculture was unable to feed the national population until the nineteenth century. The preponderance of this ancient tertiary sector has smothered, and still suffocates, the chances for an agricultural and agrarian reorganization, which is the prerequisite for a really revolutionary and sustained industrial start. There has never been, however, a national prospect of a powerful industry as Portugal has always been very weakly urbanized. Over many centuries only Lisbon has been a city of some proportions; apart from her, there are only half-urbanized towns, contrary to the situation in Spain. Lisbon represents only 5 or 6 percent of the population of the metropolis. Only for a very short moment in the seventeenth century did it come near the 10 percent mark, and it never reached that level again until our days. Even today it is a city of less than 900,000 inhabitants; the entire department of Lisbon barely exceeds 1.6 million residents. Herculano perfectly realized this already: the Portuguese towns, for a lack of industry, are not in a position to absorb the rural exodus. Let us add also that there is a lack of size.

Another reason for the lack of industrialization in Portugal was its oligarchy, which was deeply involved in trade and did not open the doors for industrialization unless there was a crisis, as from 1670 to 1790 and during the Pombal era. As soon as the depression gave way and business was resumed, a new commercial expansion put the train back on the rails and dropped the industry that supported it. Certainly, new industrial nuclei remained from these often discontinued attempts. Nevertheless, these innovations only seemed to be reflected in some minor modifications in the traditional sectors. Banks were created, factories were built, and limited companies were founded. Yet, the overwhelming majority of the population hardly saw their conditions of existence improve. Interior demand did not increase, except on some restricted levels. The various nuclei of the modern economy were lost in a sea of apathy. Faced with the world of industrial capitalism and of middle-class civilization, the oligarchy always remained in charge of the reins of an economic and social structure rooted in the ancien régime, often utilizing machinery of the state in order to resist integration into the modern world.

Conversely, Portugal has always remained the center of handmade products. The commercial balance has constantly been negative since the Napoleonic invasions. This deficit became only worse toward the middle of the nineteenth century. Therefore, the remittances of emigrants always had the purpose of filling the chronic deficits of Portugal's balance of payments. Because of these remittances, there was no lack of capital in the Portuguese economy. Unfortunately, capital was unevenly distributed and it was not invested in the sectors that needed it most. Such shortages were noticeable for instance in agriculture. The majority of economists have cited this as a prime bottleneck in the development and modernization of Portugal. Capital that was available in Portugal was usually diverted to speculative investments.

Around 1873, Alexandre Herculano valued the remittances of the Portuguese emigrants living in Brazil at about 3,000 contos per year. The average surplus of imports over exports, from 1868 to 1872, came to about 3,500 contos. Thus, the monetary transfer resulting from emigration covered more than six-seventh of the trade deficit. The financial bureau of Portugal in Rio de Janeiro valued the bank transfers around 1900 at 10,000 contos at least, if not more. Silva Cordeiro calculated a total equal to or higher than 15,000 in 1896.

Oliveira Martins, in 1891, distinguished three types of transfers: (1) the savings of workers and the earnings accumulated by merchants and small shopkeepers, (2) the yearly income of investors overseas (estimated to have been 3,000 to 4,000 contos), and (3) the monthly payments, pensions, alms, and gifts sent by emigrants to their families and friends in Portugal (estimated at 2,000 to 3,000 contos). In total these transfers amounted to 12,000 to 15,000 contos yearly. To this should be added the proceeds from commerce between Portugal and Brazil of about 6,500 contos in value, bringing a profit of 600 to 700 contos. The essential role of the bills of exchange in these transfers is well explained in an elementary handbook on political economy by Luiz d'Almeida e Albuquerque, published in 1897. In Brazil bills of change were drawn on London since it was more difficult to draw directly on Lisbon as trading activities there were less extensive and the exchanges were generally more modest. In London the bill was sold to a Portuguese merchant who needed money on the English market, or the bill was sent to Lisbon in order to settle a debt. The debtor then paid the Portuguese beneficiary of the remittance that was sent by an emigrant in Brazil. This transfer mechanism provides us with an account of the predominance of the English pound sterling.

Miriam Halpern has uncovered the connection between the metropolitan regions of emigration to Brazil and the localization of banks, established in Portugal during the period 1873 to 1875. In less than twenty years the remittances by emigrants from Brazil increased fourfold. In the last decade of the nineteenth century the Brazilian remittances covered more or less the entire deficit of the commercial balance.

As the number of emigrants increased, so did the value of the remittances; the new arrivals more than made up for those who had ceased to remit. For the period between 1910 and 1917 the remittances are estimated at about 18,000 gold contos. The figure occasionally rose to 24,000 or 4.5 million pounds sterling. The end of the Great War would again bring a sharp increase. Veiga Simões, economist and diplomat, calculated the transfer to have been some 30,000 contos in 1917, while the Portuguese consul at São Paulo valued the transfer in 1920 at 32,000 contos. From April 1925 to March 1928, remittances exclusively coming from Rio de Janeiro were placed at 26,000 contos per year on average according to trustworthy banking sources. It is true that an English report of 1924 allocated two million pounds sterling to the Portuguese against 2.5 million to the Italians, but this figure was certainly too low. Carvalho Neves evaluated the contribution of the emigration to the Portuguese economy in 1928 to be 4.5 million pounds sterling. In short, in the course of the decade after World War I that contribution wavered between 4.5 and 6.5 million pounds sterling. During the years 1924 to 1925 the average imports were higher than 25.7 million and the exports stood at around 15.3 million contos, a coverage of hardly 60 percent. The deficit in foreign trade – 10.4 million pounds sterling – was only partly covered by the private remittances of emigrants.

After the intermezzo of 1930 to 1947, emigration picked up once more and soon the transfers flowed again. The development in present currency is presented in Table 2.6.

The remittances of emigrants should not be confused with the entries of the different private transfers. The table above only seeks to outline the contribution from emigration. In order to measure its impact on the Portuguese economy, let us compare it to the deficit on the balance of trade. This deficit amounted to between 10 and 12.8 million contos during the period 1965 to 1969. It was made up for by the remittances of the emigrants for about one-third and rising to more than 92 percent. For the years 1970 to 1973 it amounted to 87.8 percent. Not less enlightening is the comparison with Spain. The *remessas* of the emigrants there amounted to 38.62 million dollars in 1959, rising to 550.25 million in 1971. In this last year, the total value of entries of private transfers benefitting Portugal rose to 656 million dollars (636 million if we only count the transactions outside the escudo area). Note that Spain has a population nearly four times that of Portugal.

If we follow the table of the *remessas* of the emigrants, we are obliged to deflate these amounts accounted. The rate of price increases amounted to 5 percent in 1965 and to 11.9 percent in 1971.

TABLE 2.6 Remittances of Emigrants

Year	Thousands of Contos	Year	Thousands of Contos
1950	504	1963	2,371
1951	358	1964	2,679
1952	211	1965	3,378
1953	300	1966	4,618
1954	320	1967	6,267
1955	412	1968	7,902
1956	1,037	1969	11,612
1957	1,542	1970	14,343
1958	1,552	1971	18,848
1959	1,913	1972	22,388
1960	1,868	1973	26,452
1961	1,489	1974	26,500
1962	1,704		

Sources: Reports of the Banco de Portugal; Financial Statistics of the Instituto Nacional de Estatistica; Marinho Antunes, *A Emigração Portuguesa desde 1950* (Lisbon, 1973); Reports of different banks.

Thus, an index of 100 in 1970 rose to 177.7 in 1974. In this way the real value of the remittances in 1974 did not really exceed those of 1970 in constant currency. The great expansion took place between 1938 and 1966, a multiplication by three, and between 1966 and 1970, 2.3.

It is essential to study the absorption of these *remessas* by the Portuguese economy and society; their role in the investments appears to have remained modest. The remittances allowed for housebuilding, improving domestic equipment, supporting the elderly and the disabled, and buying more foodstuffs for consumption. In this way emigration supports the archaic structures that created and sustained this movement through the centuries. The small number of returning migrants did not allow them to play a stimulative role after their return, contrary to the everyday clichés in the literature. Let us look at the distribution of the working population.

Urbanization only occurred after 1960. But while the Portuguese towns are new, the urban mentality is still not properly rooted. Furthermore, emigration has changed the pyramid shaped diagram of population by age groups: between 1951 and 1967 the class of 15 to 29 year olds lost 10 percent of its number, if not more.

The traditional disparities in Portugal are emphasized dramatically by the process of emigration in view of the fact that the less

TABLE 2.7 Working Population

Sector	1960 Thousands	1960 %	1970 Thousands	1970 %	Variation %	% of Gross National Product
Agriculture	1,445	43.6	1,002.9	31.7	−30.6	13.7
Industry	958.7	28.9	1,021.4	32.3	+ 6.5	44.9
Services	911.9	27.5	1,139.6	36	+25	41.4
Total	3,315.6		3,163.9		− 4.6	

populated departments are proportionally the most affected. From the river Minho to the river Sado and in the departments of Viana, Braga, Porto, Aveiro, Viseu, Coimbra, Leiria, Santarém, Lisbon, and Setubal, which occupy 41.7 percent of the national territory of the peninsula, there live:

68.7% of the metropolitan population in 1801
67.7% of the metropolitan population in 1864
65.2% of the metropolitan population in 1911
73.9% of the metropolitan population in 1960
79.1% of the metropolitan population in 1970

The building of motorways makes this imbalance still worse. By strengthening the trunk road between Porto, Lisbon, and Setubal, and some branch roads, the transport system remains like that of the railway, which only sought to reinforce the traditional pattern of the domestic traffic. Outside the dominating north-to-south trunk road and the two tourist branches that lead from the eastern frontier to the coast, the Portuguese inner regions remain traffic deserts, yesterday and today.

Now, for the first time in five centuries, Portugal finds itself confronted by a reversal of the traditional situation. The decolonization, conducted in haste and disturbing the presence of Portuguese in the old territories overseas, has suddenly poured some 400,000 to 600,000 immigrants into the Portuguese homeland and the isles nearby. The unemployed workers exceed half a million, of an active working population that counts not even 3.5 million. In addition, the "oil and raw material crisis" and the inflation and recession in the highly industrialized or post-industrial countries, create new tensions in the fragile Portuguese community by sending back many

Portuguese migrant workers to Portugal. If all the Portuguese emigrants returned, it would be a disaster; not only because that would mean the end of the *remessas*, but above all because some 800,000 to one million new or returned hands will disrupt the labor market and food supply. Portugal is not in the position (and will not be for quite some time) to play host to more emigrants who should want to return. Nevertheless, the reorganization of the Portuguese economy cannot wait any longer: the problem remains above all rather more political than economical.

SOURCES AND BIBLIOGRAPHY

Period Before 1755

The earthquake of 1755 has swallowed up the most important bodies of documents from the great public institutions and seigniorial houses – such as from the Casa da India and the Vèdorias da Fazenda. The registers of departures and arrivals are missing. We still have numerous sources at our disposal, however, and occasionally a wealth of information, although very diverse and scattered, with enormous chronological gaps. It is not possible to list them all. Nevertheless, let us indicate some categories: (1) the censuses, sometimes of the entire population (major – minor), at least of "souls" for the years 1527 to 1532, 1638, 1724 to 1732, 1756, 1778, 1801; these are reported in various works; (2) the "chorographies", descriptions of the kingdom or of provinces, as well as of the viceroyalties or of the portcaptains of territories overseas; (3) the testimonies of foreigners, reporting information gathered by highly placed Portuguese in official registers; (4) the files of the Council of State, books of the Chancery, Council of Finance, Council of Overseas matters, minutes of the Cortes, registers of Town Halls, and of regional and of local bodies; (5) doctrinal works of economists and politicians (Severim de Faria, Duarte Ribeiro de Macedo, D. Luís da Cunha, etc.), who discussed at great length the problem of the "population" and "depopulation" of Portugal and the effects of the Conquests and the commercial and religious expansion.

From 1755 to the Middle of the Nineteenth Century

Some of the old institutions have not functioned as regularly as in the past, while others have come into being slowly and do not fill in the lacunae. The documentation, however, is rich, more or less systematic, and the collections are double in size as compared to the previous period of the Ministério do Reino, Junta do Comércio and, after the Revolution, the National

Assembly. The censuses are more frequent and more complete, the registers of Police henceforth form consistent and condensed series (also see the registers of Police in Rio de Janeiro, 1808 to 1842, Arquivo Nacional).

From the Middle of the Nineteenth Century

Sources

Marreca, António de Oliveira. "Da emigraçao e immigraçao." In *Parecer e Memória sobre proposta para um projecto de Estadística.* 77–91 Lisbon, 1854. (particularly the presentation of ideas and the comparison with the British Movement).

Castro, José Luciano de. *A Questão das Subsistências* 2d part, chap. I, "Emigração e colonização" Lisbon, 1856.

Primeiro Inquérito Parlamentar sobre a Emigração Portugueza. Lisbon, 1973. See the polemic between the agricultural engineer Paulo de Moraes and Alexandre Herculano.

Documentos sobre a Emigração Portugueza colligidos e publicados por ordem do Ministério dos Negócios Estrangeiros. Lisbon, 1873.

Freitas, J.J. Rodrigues de. *Notice sur le Portugal.* 9–10. Paris, 1867.

Percheiro, D.A. Gomes. *Portugal e Brazil – Emigração e Colonização.* Lisbon, 1880.

Cordeiro, Luciano. *Emigração – Relatório e Projecto de Regulamento.* Lisbon, 1883.

Queiroz, Eça de. *Relatórios sobre emigração.* Arquivo de Ministério dos Negócios Estrangeiros. Lisbon, 1874.

Anuário Estatístico de Portugal. Lisbon, annual. The Annual of 1884, published in 1886, contains the retrospective statistics of the emigration since 1866.

Estatísticas Demográficas: Continente e Ilhas Adjacentes. Lisbon, annual.

Censos da População (after 1864). The penultimate *Recenseamento da População: Continente e Ilhas Adjacentes* (1970) calls for strong restraint (approximation at 20 percent).

Boletim da Junta de Emigração – Lisboa, 1952–1969, since replaced by: *Secretariado Nacional da Emigração – Boletim Anual.* Lisbon 1970. ss. *Statistiques de l'Immigration.* National Office of Immigration, France.

Studies – sources

Queiroz, Eça de. *A Emigração como Força civilizadora.* Raul Rego ed. Lisbon 1979. Report to the Minister of Foreign Affairs. Lisbon 9/11/1974.

Rery, Gerardo. *Geographia e Estatística Geral de Portugal e Colónias.* Especially 92–94. Lisbon, 1875.

Herculano, Alexandre. "A Emigração" (1873–1875). Debate with Paulo de Moraes. Reproduced in *Opusculos* IV. 4th ed.; Lisbon, 103–282.

Martins, J.P. de Oliveira. "Emigração" (1881). Reproduced in *Obras Com-*

pletas I, having as a title: *Fomento Rural e Emigração* (Lisbon 1956). These two studies are the most profound and important.

Freitas, J.J. Rodrigues de. "A emigração portugueza para o Brazil" (1893). Reproduced as the posthumous compendium: *Páginas Avulsas*. 167–177. Porto 1906.

Carqueja, Bento, *O Povo Portuguez* (Porto, 1916) chap. 15, 377–441.

Studies

Apart from our synthesis, a few general studies:

Serrão, Joel, *A Emigração Portuguesa* 2d ed.; Lisbon 1974.

Costa, Afonso, *Estudios de Economia Nacional* I. *O Problema da Emigração*. Lisbon 1911.

Simões, Nuno. *O Brasil e a Emigração Portuguesa*. Coimbra 1934.

Almeida, Carlos de, Barreto, António, Krieger, L. and Petitat, A. *L'Emigration Portugaise: essai d'explication des récents développements du phénomène migratoire portugais en rapport avec les structures économiques, sociales et politiques du pays*. Geneva 1968.

Bettencourt, J. de Sousa. *O Fenómeno da Emigração portuguesa*. Luanda 1961.

Antunes, M.L. Marinho. *A Emigração Portuguesa desde 1950. Dados e Comentários*. Lisbon 1973.

Almeida, Carlos de and (António) Barreto. *Capitalismo e Emigração em Portugal*. 2d ed.: Lisbon 1974.

Trindade, Maria Beatriz R. *Immigrés Portugais. Observation psychosociologique dans la banlieue parisienne (Orsay)*. Lisbon 1973.

Silva, J. Gentil da. "A emigração para a América nos séculos 19 e 20 e a história nacional." *Jahrbuch für Geschichte Lateinamerikas* (1976) 107–131.

Silva, J. Gentil da. "L'histoire de l'expansion portugaise dans la perspective de la force de travail." *Wirtschaftskräfte und Wirtschaftswege* 4 (1978).

Estudos sobre a Emigração Portuguesa. Maria B.R. Trindade ed., Cadernos da Revista de História Económica e Social 1–2 (Lisbon 1981).

Carreira, António. *The People of the Cape Verde Islands – Exploitation and Emigration*. London and Connecticut 1982.

Anderson, Grace and David Higgs. *L'Héritage du Futur – Les communautés portugaises au Canada*. (s.l. 1976).

Higgs, David. *Les Portugais au Canada*. Ottawa 1982.

Brettell, Caroline B. *Já Chorei muitas Lágrimas*. Lisbon 1978.

Brettell, Caroline B., *Men who migrate, Women who wait. Population and History in a Portuguese Parish* (Princeton 1986).

Serpa, Caetano Valadão. *A Gente dos Açores*. Lisbon 1978.

Benis, Maria Johannis. "Rational Choice or Networking? Portuguese Emigration to the United States." Unpublished paper; History Department, University of Pennsylvania, May 1987.

Trindade, Maria Beatriz R. *Portuguese Migration Movements inside Europe*. Lisbon s.a.

Trindade, Maria Beatriz R. *The Politics of Migration Policies*. Chap. 13, "The Iberian Peninsula." New York 1979.

Nazareth, J. Manuel. "A Emigração Portuguesa no século XX – uma perspectiva demográfica." Unpublished paper; International Conference on Modern Portugal, University of New Hampshire, June 1979.

Nazareth, J. Manuel. "População, Emigração e Retorno." In Manuela Silva ed., *Portugal Contemporâneo Problemas e Perspectivas*. Chapter 1. Oeiras 1986.

3

Irish Emigration, 1700–1920

WILLIAM J. SMYTH

Located on the Atlantic fringe of western Europe, Ireland has long occupied a position of considerable geopolitical importance in the history of European demographic expansion. From the arrival of the Anglo-Normans in the twelfth century through to the English and Scottish colonizations of the seventeenth century, the island's society was transformed by successive immigrations, the last of which coincided with the emergence of a significant emigration movement. Seventeenth-century Ireland reflected a comparative demographic balance between immigration and emigration, but thereafter, and continuing until the present day, there has been a net outflow of population. No other European country has experienced such a sustained demographic hemorrhage. Among the transatlantic mass emigrations of the nineteenth century the Irish were early pioneers, and overall they constituted at least ten percent of the total movement; a proportion which was unjustified by the relative importance of the population of Ireland in contemporary Europe. From the early seventeenth century to the eve of World War I, seven million Irish have emigrated to North America, a further one-third of a million have gone to Australia and probably more than a million have settled in Britain. So prevalent has been the phenomenon of emigration in Irish society that one sociologist has dubbed it a rite de passage.

The exodus in the seventeenth century was episodic, associated primarily with wars, colonization ventures, land confiscations, military defeat, and enacted against a background of a British outreach to the Americas. British colonies stretching from the Caribbean to New England contained Irish-born populations – some of them willing settlers, others indentured and transported detainees. These

* The assistance of Nicholas Canny, Patrick Duffy, Cecil Houston, and Dympna McLoughlin is gratefully acknowledged.

early transatlantic migrations had their parallel within the European sphere and by 1700 most major ports in an area extending from Brittany to Cadiz housed an Irish presence. These seventeenth-century emigrations must also be viewed in the context of a century of overall net immigration in an Ireland undergoing colonization by English, Scottish, and a few European Protestant settlers.

By virtue of its scale, Irish emigration has proved of great interest to scholars working on the demographic history of Ireland and also to those researching the settlement histories of the United States and other former British colonies. Two distinct phases have produced the bulk of the literature on the topic. The first serious studies were developed in the 1930s, 1940s, and 1950s, and, in part, this interest was stimulated by the approaching centenary of the Great Famine. A pioneering work by William Forbes Adams, *Ireland and Irish Emigration to the New World from 1815 to the Famine*, published in 1932, contained a numerical assessment, that has yet to be superseded, of the dimensions of the emigration and also provided a detailed analysis of the major Irish source regions of emigrants.[1] Adams's study was augmented by a seminal essay published in 1956 by Oliver MacDonagh, *Irish Emigration to the United States and British Colonies during the Famine*[2] and this in turn was supplemented in 1958 by Arnold Schrier's *Ireland and the American Emigration, 1850–1900*.[3] These studies were complemented by the American-based researches of Oscar Handlin, whose Boston studies were the first serious investigation of the role of the Irish in the new land.[4] During the past twenty years there has been a virtual explosion of studies on Irish emigration, and among this group the influence of a rising international interest in ethnic studies and the methodological advances of the New Urban History movement are clearly discernable. The cumulative advances of much of this research have recently been synthesized in separate studies of the Irish in the United States, Canada, and Australia.[5] In terms of the periodicity of

1. Adams, *Ireland and Irish Emigration.*
2. Oliver MacDonagh, "Irish Emigration."
3. Arnold Schrier, *Ireland and the American Emigration, 1850–1900.*
4. Oscar Handlin, *Boston's Immigrants* (Harvard 1941); Idem., *The Uprooted* (Harvard 1951).
5. The last work on Irish emigration to the United States is to be found in Miller, *Emigrants and Exile.* A more critical and controversial review of recent writings on this topic is Donald H. Akenson, *Being Had: Historians, Evidence, and the Irish in North America* (Toronto, 1985). A bibliographical guide to the Irish in America as provided by Seamus P. Metress, *The Irish-American Experience. A Guide to the Literature* (Washington 1981). The Canadian Irish are best dealt with by John J. Mannion, *Irish*

research focus, most attention has been devoted to the nineteenth century, where statistical data, governmental, and private reports provide rich source material. Eighteenth-century migrations have, however, generated some interest, and in recent years the earlier writings of Gwynn and Quinn on seventeenth-century Irish emigration have been revised and extended by the work of Nicholas Canny.[6] As a result of these researches the volume, direction, and timing of Irish emigration during the past two hundred and fifty years is quite well documented. Large gaps in our knowledge remain, however, and in particular much more needs to be known about the familial, occupational, and religious composition of the emigrants. Furthermore, there is scope for further developing the analyses of the varying regional response of Irish society to the lure of emigration. In all of these areas, growing links within the international body of researchers and comparative analyses of other European migrants promise much for the future.

Numbers

Emigration to the American colonies in the seventeenth century may have totaled more than 100,000, but it was numerically dwarfed by the exodus of 250,000 to 400,000 in the years 1700 to 1776. During this latter period, the movement to colonial America averaged 5,000 per annum; this from an Irish population of approximately 2.4 million in 1750. In addition, by the late 1770s upward of 5,000 youths were annually traveling from southeast Ireland to the seasonal work of the Newfoundland fisheries, and a strong reciprocal link between emigration and commerce on the north Atlantic was firmly established. In particular, the provisions trade, the fisheries, and the eastward trade in flaxseed bound the Atlantic fringe of western Europe with the emerging colonial settlements of America, and in

Settlements; Akenson, *Irish in Ontario*. A bibliographic guide is provided by Seamus P. Metress and William M. Baker, "A Bibliography of the History of the Irish in Canada" in *The Untold Story: The Irish in Canada*, Robert O'Driscoll and Lorna Reynolds eds., (Toronto 1988), 977–1002. The history of Irish settlement in Australia is best summarized in O'Farrell, *Irish in Australia*. Eighteenth-century America is treated in a revisionist manner by Doyle, *Ireland, Irishmen and Revolutionary America*, while seventeenth-century transatlantic migration is the subject of Canny, *Kingdom and Colony*. From the perspective of the utility of Irish emigration data the most useful essay in Cormac O'Grada, "Note on Nineteenth-Century Irish Emigration Statistics," 143–149.

6. Canny, *Kingdom and Colony*.

that process a primary role was played by Ireland and her emigrants. This trade in cargo and people was interrupted by the American Revolution but by 1784 the flow had recommenced with 100,000 to 150,000 emigrating over the next thirty years. During this phase a perceptible northward shift in destination toward the remaining colonies of British America was apparent; furthermore, a rise in the cost of shipping during the Napoleonic War restricted the transatlantic option to a more select and self-reliant set of emigrants. This increased cost of passage, coupled with wartime agricultural prosperity in Ireland, served to minimize the outflow, with the result that after 1815 there was a rapid release of a pent-up emigration fueled by a looming agricultural recession. In the next thirty years, approximately one million crossed the Atlantic, going initially in almost equal numbers to the United States and Canada, although many of those landing in the latter territory rapidly made their way southward. During these years a further half million emigrated the short distance across the Irish sea to Britain. By virtue of its size and composition, this exodus differed greatly from the emigrations of the previous centuries.

In 1845, on the eve of the Famine, emigration was a mania within the country and a course of action, once confined to Ulster and the hinterland of major ports, was now universally regarded as a social option for all but the most destitute. Despite this sustained heavy out-emigration the national population continued to rise, and in 1841 there were 8.2 million inhabitants in Ireland as compared with 16 million in England and Wales and 2.6 million in Scotland. The disaster of the Famine years 1845 to 52 thrust a Malthusian-like solution onto this increasingly impoverished population, and in the decade 1845 to 55 one million died of disease and starvation and a further 1.8 million fled the country. By 1861 only 5.8 million remained in Ireland and for the next century continuous emigration served to lower even that figure. The Famine exodus consisted largely of panic-stricken flight but its long-term effects were of major significance. Henceforth, a new directional influence guided Irish emigrants in a chain-migration process to the urban industrial centers of northeast America, and in a very real sense the urbanization of the Irish occurred abroad.

In the seventy years following the Famine, the exodus continued unabated. During those years 3.8 million went to the United States, one-third of a million went to Canada, and a similar number settled in Australia and New Zealand. Despite the death and diaspora of the Famine years, the post-Famine period contributed more emi-

TABLE 3.1 Estimated Emigration Figures, 1700–1921

1700–1776	1784–1814	1815–1845	1845–1855	1855–1921
250–400,000	100–150,000	1.5M	1.8M	3.6M

TABLE 3.2 Irish National Population, 1700–1921

1712	1754	1800	1841	1851	1881	1901
2.0M*	2.4M*	3.8M*	8.2M	6.5M	5.1M	4.4M

* Estimated

grants than had the two centuries before 1845. Emigration was not the inevitable course of action for generation after generation, and even after two-thirds of Ireland attained political independence in 1920, the exodus continued, although, paradoxically, Britain replaced the United States as the preferred destination for the bulk of the emigrants from the newly independent state.

Push and Pull Factors

The dynamics of Irish emigration in the two hundred years following 1700 were representative of push- and pull-factors enjoined in a complex interrelationship and, for the most part, incapable of operating in isolation, one from the other. The emigration process, except on rare occasions, was not dominated by unidirectional forces; rather, it was a response to a varying set of push-factors operating against, and in conjunction with, pull-factors emanating from a number of potential destinations. Consequently, the geographical, social, economic, and religious backgrounds of those leaving Ireland during these two centuries varied enormously, and at no time were the emigrants confined in their choice to a single destination. The push of an immediate famine such as that of the late 1840s, or the more longsighted fear of diminished future prospects for the next generation, could equally propel an exodus, which in turn might be directed to Britain, British North America, the United States, Australia, or some other colony, depending upon a variety of personal, family, financial, and logistical factors that filtered the pull of the destinations.

The emergence of mass emigration from Ireland in the eighteenth century was prompted in large measure by economic factors. The creation of a Georgian Ireland characterized by fine city terraces and squares, elegant streetscapes, and distinguished public monuments had its counterpart in rural Ireland amid improved agriculture and farmhouses that departed markedly from the vernacular style. A growing commercial economy and enduring peace fostered the image of improvement and prosperity, yet the image it fostered was a façade. Behind the evident prosperity, not all regions and social groupings were equally content. In west Ulster, specifically the Foyle valley, a limitation on agricultural growth was imposed by the nature of the topography in a region where a century before immigrant Scottish colonists had carved out a comfortable niche. By the early eighteenth century there had occurred a transfer of economic and political power from Derry and the Foyle valley eastward to Belfast, the Lagan valley, and the lowlands to the east and south of Lough Neagh. This internal transfer generated a recognizable restlessness among a west Ulster Presbyterian society that was but three generations old and now, faced by a future loss of status rather than suffering from abject poverty, they turned once again to emigration as a potential solution.

The push of altered economic prospects was further reinforced by the politico-religious disadvantages under which Presbyterians labored. In a society dominated by an Established Anglican Church, Presbyterians were secondary in rank, excluded from the center of Ascendancy power, and consoled only by the fact that there lay below them on the social ladder the native Irish Catholics. It was this propellant that extended the appeal of emigration beyond west Ulster to embrace the Presbyterian communities of Antrim and Down in the east.

It is, however, questionable whether this voluntary out-migration of Ulster Presbyterians would have reached its eventual height had it not been reinforced by the pull of colonial America to which it was linked by trade in flaxseed. Ulster was the core region in Ireland for the cultivation of flax and the production of linen cloth, but because of the nature of the manufacturing process, the flax crop tended to be harvested before the seed was fully ripened. Imported flaxseed supported the Ulster flax economy and the bulk of the seed was obtained from the American middle colonies, Pennsylvania in particular. Derry, Belfast, and Newry were the most important ports involved in this trade and merchants within those ports acted as agents, procuring passengers for human ballast on the westward leg of the voyage. The logistics of transportation, focused by a specialized regional Irish economy, therefore served to reinforce the attractiveness of emigration as an option. It was an option that was taken up in the main by Ulster Presbyterians, although Anglicans and Catholics were not entirely absent.

Elsewhere in eighteenth-century Ireland, emigration was more limited in its appeal and was confined for the most part to the ports of Dublin, Wexford, Waterford, Cork, Limerick, and their immediate hinterlands. Recent studies have argued that these urban centers generated an emigration that was largely male, servant, or artisanal in background and Catholic in religion. Economic constraints, especially applicable to young males who newly finished their apprenticeship, were the primary push-factors involved in this movement, but again it was a propellant greatly augmented by the pull of the relatively easy access to passage on board transatlantic cargo ships.

In both the above cases, the pull exerted on the emigrants emanated largely from colonial America wherein the lure of land, employment as temporary indentured labor, and an expectation of personal freedom and social mobility, all provided powerful images. In the words of the time it was represented as "the best poor man's country," and for those sufficiently motivated and endowed with either personal funds or personally mortgaged as an indentured servant, it was a pull too strong to resist. Yet, the appeal of colonial America was selective and it was further mediated by the cost of transport, which was beyond the means of those lacking personal funds or skills. For the most impoverished layers of Irish society, colonial America was not attainable: for them the pull of emigration, if felt at all, was a force that directed them the short distance across the Irish sea. Already by the mid-eighteenth century the presence of Irish beggars was evident in Bristol and Liverpool and seasonal Irish harvesters were answering the call of improving British agriculturalists.

In the nineteenth century, after a temporary and partial lull during the Napoleonic wars, Irish mass emigration resumed. Its new phase was distinguished from that of the previous century by its greatly enlarged scale, its range of destinations, and its eventual appeal to almost the total range of groups in Irish society. The push-factor that operated throughout the century was that identified with a transformation in the Irish rural economy. Following the cessation of the Napoleonic wars, the agricultural economy after 1815 was characterized by a swing from tillage toward pasture, an overall trend toward greater regional specialization and a heightened awareness of commercial factors. Consequent upon this restructuring was a diminution of employment prospects for the swelling numbers of landless laborers. In addition, the emphasis upon commercially viable farming units had direct implications for the ability of the farming classes to maintain their offspring through subdivision of the family farm. As in the previous century, a prospect of limited future economic opportunity pushed many toward the emigrant boat as lack of development within the Irish urban system denied to rural out-migrants the facility of absorption in urban areas.

The out-migration was further prompted by the pent-up desire to emigrate that existed among those whose opportunities for earlier flight had been frustrated by the restriction of passenger movements during the years of international hostilities. It was that group that first seized the new opportunities for transatlantic movement. The potential for emigration was further extended by the rapid demographic growth, which had characterized Ireland since the mid-eighteenth century and had now generated a degree of population pressure that could not be contained within a restructured agrarian economy bereft of substantial urban-industrial outlets. By 1841 the population was recorded as being 8.2 million, and at that latter date, population density figures of over 300 per square mile characterized half the country; in some areas densities of twice that magnitude were recorded.

The push of demographic pressure was articulated most clearly in the years 1845 to 52 when a Malthusian-like catastrophe struck Ireland in the form of the Famine. A generation earlier the potato had become the staple of the laboring poor and small farming classes. When a fungoid disease struck the potato crop in 1845, the basic food supply for the lower orders was threatened. In 1846 and 1848 failure of the potato harvest was complete and in 1847 and 1849 to 50 partial failures of the crop occurred. As a result, one million people died of starvation and related diseases, while in the decade 1845 to 55, upward of 1.8 million emigrated. That complement of emigrants contained an element of relatively well-off groups who would have emigrated irrespective of the food supply, but the vast majority were pushed by the specter of the last great mass starvation in recent European history.

In the post-Famine era the noninheriting offspring of the farming class continued emigrating in large numbers, pushed by a family wish to preserve intact and, if possible, extend the boundaries of the family farm. Such a reluctance to subdivide farms was not unique within Europe, but whereas elsewhere this conservation of family resources generated internal migration, the scale and lack of dynamism within the Irish urban system ensured that the Irish would continue to urbanize abroad.

The forces emanating from a rural environment made emigration inevitable for millions of Irish in the nineteenth century. Within the resultant emigration process, strong directive influences were exerted by the logistics of transportation and the varying lures of a set of distinctive destinations. For the very poorest participants in the emigration process, the industrializing centers of England and southwest Scotland represented the easiest form of egress. A few hours by boat at a cost of one shilling per capita attracted both seasonal and permanent emigrants. The census of 1841 recorded 420,000 persons of Irish birth living permanently in Britain and a further 57,000 were enumerated as seasonal migrants in that year. The pull of British cities was duplicated somewhat by the lure of the industrializing cities of the northeastern United States, where New York, Boston, Pittsburgh, Philadelphia, and Chicago could all boast significantly large concentrations of Irish by the mid-nineteenth century.

Urban America was but one transatlantic destination that beckoned to the emigrant Irish. Further north, the forested valleys and lakeshore plains of British North America offered an alternative rural lifestyle that was taken up by tens of thousands. The pull of the British colonies was multi-dimensional. A life under the British Crown was in itself attractive to Irish Protestant colonists; that attraction was supplemented by free grants of land until 1825 and the opportunity of seasonal earnings in the timber industry. Perhaps one of the greatest attractions of British North America was its ease of access, for as a result of a developing transatlantic timber trade, the shipping and the offer of passage increased enormously on the North Atlantic. Between 1815 and 1845 the cost of transatlantic fares on converted cargo boats fell by 75 percent, and in terms of relative cost, Quebec City and Saint John, New Brunswick, had an advantage over Boston, Philadelphia, and New York. The logistics of the timber trade in the first half of the nineteenth century therefore sustained a role reminiscent of the flaxseed trade of the previous century and in the process linked Ireland with the settlement frontier of British North America. So great was the pull of these British Colonies and so directive were the logistics of the timber trade that for many of the years 1815 to 1845 more Irish disembarked in the British Colonies than in the neighboring United

States, although admittedly a large percentage of the Canadian arrivals rapidly moved southward.

Other specific examples of push- and pull-factors at work augmented the macro-emigration process described above. Government assisted emigration schemes in 1823 and 1825, and a series of landlord clearances, also pushed emigrants toward the colonies and expedited their removal by means of prepaid transportation costs. Dramatic as such movements were, they nonetheless applied to probably no more than five percent of the pre-Famine emigrants. Similarly, workhouse clearances in the latter half of the nineteenth century accounted for only a fraction of those emigrating. In the case of Australia, forcible transportation of convicts and, later, subsidized passages for free settlers, generated the basis of Irish Australia, but the numbers involved at no time rivaled those seeking a new home in Britain or in North America.

Once Irish communities were established abroad, they became for a generation or more a self-perpetuating force in the emigration process. Indeed, much of the pattern of Irish emigration can be explained by reference to prior routes and settlements. Irish emigration was highly selective in its range of destinations and the exodus, although high, was rarely a directionless and lemming-like abandonment of the homeland. Kin-related or chain migration was of major importance in refining the emigration process and educating the potential emigrants in the details of the macro-geographies of Irish settlement abroad. Upward of thirty percent of transatlantic emigration in the 1830s had been estimated to have been facilitated by prepaid passages and funds supplied directly by family members who had emigrated previously. Such a pull was highly selective and specifically targeted and, once the emigration route had been established, this was probably the single most important influence working on potential emigrants. Its impact was early recognized by contemporaries.

Migration and the Demography of Sending Regions

The rise of mass emigration from Ireland was in large measure a function of rising population pressure and a corresponding limitation of economic prospects. Yet, although such a causal relationship may be established, it is quite clear that the operation of that relationship was complicated by such factors as societal class, religious background, accessibility to ports, and the specific implication of restructuring within distinctive regional economies. There did not exist a simple correlation between population pressure and extent of emigration.

The eighteenth-century emigration of Ulster Presbyterians was clearly linked with a process of internal colonization within Ireland itself. Inmigration of Scottish and English settlers had been part of Ulster life for a century after the Ulster Plantation of 1609. For the most part, these immigrants were accommodated in agricultural and market-town settlements below the 500 feet contour line. By the early eighteenth century, this immigration, coupled with natural increase, had exhausted much of the settlement potential of west Ulster. In a process reminiscent of later Canadian and American settlement, the sons and grandsons of the immigrants turned toward further westward migration. The Atlantic merely replaced the North Sea; the back country of Pennsylvania replacing the Foyle valley of Derry.

In the remainder of Ireland outside of Ulster the eighteenth century had also witnessed an internal colonization process wherein Protestant landlords sought to establish upon their landed estates core groupings of their co-religionists in an effort to encourage better agricultural practices and industrial habits. Estate villages and surrounding large farmsteads in areas as far apart as Wicklow, Offaly, Limerick, and Cork witnessed these eighteenth-century in-migrations of Ulster, Scottish, English, and, occasionally, European Protestants, but in many instances, their roots were shallow and the opportunities limited for containing a second and third generation. These socioeconomic factors, combined with growing sectarianism in the late eighteenth century, were sufficient to ensure that these disparate Protestant cores were among the earliest and best organized of the communities which adopted emigration after 1815.

This ethnoreligious dimension, however, operated within the wider context of an Irish demographic experience, which in itself generated a demand for emigration. The rapid growth of the Irish population from 1750 onward was accommodated by a greater reliance upon a potato diet, subdivision of farms, and the emergence of a numerous landless laboring class. The rate of natural increase may in fact have been comparable to that of contemporary Britain but it was contained within a predominantly rural milieu. In 1841 86 percent of the national population were living in rural areas or in towns and villages of less than 2,000. They were mostly dependent upon agriculture and cottage production of textiles and other craft activities. The urban system contained only eighteen centers with population in excess of 10,000, and although Dublin had a population

TABLE 3.3 Urban Centers with a Population of more than 20,000, 1841

	Dublin	Cork	Belfast	Limerick	Waterford
	232,000	81,000	75,000	48,000	23,000
% National population	2.8%	1%	0.9%	0.6%	0.3%

of 232,000, the next largest center, Cork, had only one-third the population of the primate city.

With the exception of Belfast the industrial sectors of the other major urban centers tended to be dependent upon the processing of agricultural goods (e.g., tanning, brewing and distilling), and many of the enterprises were limited in scale. Irish cities and towns were overly dependent upon commerce and trade (all five largest centers were ports), and there was limited capacity for absorbing displaced rural migrants.

In the half century after the Famine, the proportion of the national population living in towns of more than two thousand people more than doubled, but this masks an overall decline in population size. In reality the total numbers living in towns increased only slightly, and outside of the textile area of Ulster, most urban centers either stagnated or lost population.

The inertia displayed by the Irish urban system, at a time when the urban systems of Britain and the United States were displaying unparalleled dynamism, created an imbalance in a world that had been closely integrated by the emigration process for several generations. Inevitably, the Irish continued to urbanize abroad.

The lack of a localized urban-industrial base had convinced contemporary observers that disaster was the inevitable outcome of the high rate of national increase. By the 1820s and 1830s it was clear that the farming classes were attempting to limit natural increase by raising the age of marriage. In some regions, at least the laboring classes were following suit by the 1840s. In the short term, however, these measures were insufficient to reverse the biological momentum of growth generated by a large and youthful population. The population proceeded toward its Malthusian climax, and in the disaster of the Famine, it was the landless laboring class that suffered most, being almost eliminated. Post-Famine Irish society adjusted its demographic behavior with a vengeance. The average age of males at marriage rose to thirty five by 1925 but fertility

TABLE 3.4 Proportion of Irish Living in Towns of more than 2,000 Inhabitants, 1841–1901

	1841	1851	1861	1871	1881	1891	1901
	13.9%	17.0%	19.4%	22.2%	24.1%	26.4%	31.1%
Total urban population	1.13M	1.12M	1.13M	1.2M	1.3M	1.2M	1.4M
Total population	8.2M	6.6M	5.8M	5.4M	5.2M	4.7M	4.5M

TABLE 3.5 Urban Centers with a Population of more than 20,000, 1901

	Dublin	Cork	Belfast	Derry	Limerick	Waterford
	350,000	349,000	76,000	40,000	38,000	27,000
% National population	8%	8%	1.7%	0.9%	0.9%	0.6%

within marriage remained at an unaltered high level. Celibacy was increasingly favored as a population check, and by the end of the nineteenth century, 20 percent of women and 24 percent of men over 45 years of age were unmarried. For many, the alternative to remaining on the family farm as the ill-paid unmarried brother or sister was to seek a life in the priesthood or the convent, or to emigrate. The economic rationalism of the post-Famine farming class, with its primary goal the maintenance of the family farm, offered to the noninheriting children a set of stark demographic alternatives. For many, emigration was the only means to marriage and family life.

Female Emigration

The sex balance among Irish emigrants differed greatly between the eighteenth and nineteenth centuries. Among the farming and largely Presbyterian emigrants from Ulster prior to the American Revolution, a striking characteristic was the presence of family groups. This was not a migration of the restless but rather the outcome of a careful evaluation of a set of options and, as might be expected, there was a relative balance between the sexes. Among the non-farming groups, however, the emigration process was one which emphasized the movement of indentured servants, a form of service that has been likened to a cross between apprenticeship and slavery. Few of these were female; rather, young males were reputed to account for 95 percent of the native Irish migrants, and similar sex proportions may have been applicable to the Anglican and Presbyterian artisanal and servant outflow. Similarly, the eighteenth century seasonal migrations from southeast Ireland to the Newfoundland fisheries were almost entirely composed of males. Not until permanent emigration gained in popular appeal in the decades following 1770 were the Newfoundland Irish to include women among their numbers. In the case of Colonial America the emphasis upon family elements in the Presbyterian group facilitated the intra-group marriage and the retention of some elements of an immigrant culture; the opposite was the case for the artisanal and largely Catholic Irish component. For this latter group, marriage to Irish Catholic women would have been rare owing to the imbalanced sex ratios and, in the words of one recent historian, "the very possibility of an Irish (Catholic) America was undermined" for a century.

From the beginning, nineteenth-century emigration emphasized a considerable balance between the sexes. From the perspective of those remaining in Ireland, one can identify from the 1841 census a residual population that was 51 percent female and 49 percent male; a ratio that revealed little distortion arising from the emigration of more than a half million from the country in the previous decade. If, however, the total emigrant outflow in the pre-Famine era is desegregated into components by destination, it is probable that the transatlantic flow was dominated by males and there may have been a corresponding imbalance in favor of females among these settling in Britain. Certainly port arrivals and passenger lists for Boston, New York, and Saint John display a preponderance of males, although the actual ratio varied from decade to decade and from port to port. Such a variance was in large measure a reflection of the selective pull of the different hinterlands: St. John, with an emphasis upon timber and farming, was less likely to appeal to women than New York, with its growing garment industry and demand for domestic servants. But in both cases males formed an overall majority.

The nature of the source material – disparate series of passenger lists and ship manifests – provides us with an accurate impression of sex ratios, but, by their very nature, these sources tend to give a rather erroneous impression of the marital characteristics of the emigrants. The process of Irish emigration was one wherein the initial step was frequently taken by one member of a family who subsequently provided passage money for brothers, sisters, wives,

TABLE 3.6 Sex Characteristics of Irish Emigration, 1851–1920 (in thousands)

	1851–1860	1861–1870	1871–1880	1881–1890	1891–1900	1901–1910	1911–1920
Males	578	427	339	395	202	172	76
Females	558	344	279	375	232	174	75

and children to follow. Family groups were therefore temporarily fractured by the process but were eventually reconstituted. Enumerations derived from passenger lists of single ships were, in the absence of cross linkages, bound to produce exaggerated impressions of the unmarried status of the emigrants. Closer analysis of the large numbers of children on board and genealogical investigations have revealed a very important family element in the transatlantic movement.

In the post-Famine era the strength of the push from Ireland, coupled with an increased range of jobs for both sexes in the industrial cities of America and Britain, produced an emigration flow that was well-balanced in terms of its sex composition. Of the total of 4.3 million who emigrated in that seventy-year period, 52 percent were males and 48 percent were females. As the dates indicate, however, a majority of males in the pre-1890 period had been transformed into a female majority during the next thirty years. This approximate balance among the emigrants is reminiscent of Jewish emigration to North America in the latter part of the nineteenth century. As with that group, the sex-ratio contained important implications for cultural cohesion within the immigrant population. Marriage within the ethnic boundaries was common among the Catholic Irish in North America, and there emerged a distinctive cultural grouping that, in terms of religion at least, had proved to be long-lasting. Nineteenth-century Irish Catholic America was not to contain a replication of the disappearance of their co-religionists as had occurred in the previous century.

Among the emigrant communities, the female Irish attained a reputation for domestic service. For the middle-class American family the Irish maid offered several advantages. Her color was acceptable, her level of homemaking skills adequate, and above all she spoke English. As nannies and servants, the Irish women therefore had an advantage over their non-English speaking competitors, and there was much truth in the stereotypical image of the Irish domestic servant versus the Italian female garment worker. Irish women, however were not confined solely to housework; in the textile towns of New England and of Lancashire their presence was evident in the mills, especially prior to their marriage. After marriage, as mother and landlady, many Irish females operated boardinghouses in their homes, and through their lodgers, they boosted the family income while simultaneously introducing another generation of Irish to the culture of the immigrant group.

Transportation

Prior to the Passenger Vessel Act of 1803 the transportation of emigrants overseas was unregulated. The worst aspects of the voyage – disease, overcrowding, poor food – were mitigated by the fact that the numbers were comparatively small. Even an outflow of five thousand per year did not unduly tax the capacity of shipping. The dramatic increase, however, in the volume of emigration in the nineteenth century required some state involvement in ensuring basic minimum conditions of safety and comfort. The 1803 Act imposed a ratio of one passenger to every two tons of the ship's register and required a surgeon to be provided on each ship. These conditions were not enforced, however, and a new Passenger Vessel Act of 1817 permitted one passenger per one and a half tons of the ship's register. A further Act of 1828 laid down stringent minimum requirements for food and water and made compulsory a five and a half foot clearance between decks. Subsequent British Acts of 1842 and 1847, and legal requirements demanded by Canadian and American jurisdiction, further regulated the traffic in passengers, but prior to the introduction of steam passenger ships in the mid-nineteenth century, the overall conditions of transport remained hazardous.

The harsh conditions under which most emigrants traveled were a function of the sheer scale of the migration and also a reflection of the fact that, prior to 1850, passengers were accommodated in temporarily-converted cargo boats. Thus, ships carrying cargoes of flaxseed to Ulster from Pennsylvania in the eighteenth century regularly advertized in Belfast, Newry, and Derry for passengers on the return leg of the voyage. In the nineteenth century the development of the Canadian timber trade generated a significant increase in the shipping capacity on the North Atlantic, prompting a fall in passenger fares from 16 to 3 pounds by 1845 and stimulating an upsurge in emigration.

A typical ship converted for the westward trip would have

contained a steerage of 75 feet long by 25 feet wide and 5 feet high. Double rows of berths made out of rough planks could accommodate upwards of three hundred passengers on such a ship. The importance to shippers of this passenger trade can be estimated on the basis that the timberboats typical of the North Atlantic trade cost approximately 1,500 pounds to build; a cargo of timber carried to Britain together with a westward complement of 200 passengers paying 3 pounds per head could pay for the ship within two or three seasons. Significant profit given the fact that the life expectancy of these ships was twelve to fifteen years. Emigration was therefore highly profitable for shippers and it is scarcely surprising that a large number of small firms and individuals operated in the business. In the 1830s more than twenty-five ports, large and small, in Ireland were engaged in the traffic; such a proliferation made enforcement of the Passenger Acts very difficult. These points of embarkation were linked to a series of North American destinations, although the bulk of them would have made their way to Quebec, Saint John, Halifax, Boston, New York, Philadelphia, and Delaware. As the nineteenth century progressed, the number of ports engaged in the trade dwindled. Within Ireland, improved internal communications by road, canal, and, later, railway directed emigrants to a few major ports. This refinement of a broad geographical pattern was further directed by the monopolistic position attained by the great steamship companies of the post-Famine period. By 1900 only Derry and Cobh (Queenstown) remained as the major emigration ports, and their importance was derived from their strategic location on shipping lanes linking Britain with Canada and the United States. British ships steaming westward had to navigate either to the south or to the north of Ireland, and thus, Derry and Queenstown in the northwest and southeast, respectively, asserted their prominence and overshadowed the much larger port cities of Dublin and Belfast.

The development of the regular passenger sailings of the Cunard and Allen lines permitted a greater policing of conditions on board and also led to an improvement in safety standards, the case of the Titanic notwithstanding. Passengers now crossed the Atlantic within seven days, whereas under sail the voyage had lasted seven to ten weeks. Comfort levels were much higher and mortality levels dropped to insignificance compared with the 1840s when the death rate among passengers going to Canada was 1.005 percent, rising to the tragic conditions of 1847 when out of ninety thousand Irish who embarked for Canada fifteen thousand died either on board or in quarantine or hospitals shortly after disembarking.

The majority of emigrants who crossed the Atlantic did so at their own expense or at the expense of family members who had preceded them. Landlord-assisted emigration, government-sponsored colonization schemes, and workhouse clearances only contributed a fraction – possibly five percent – of the outflow. It was largely a voluntary and independent movement, and the relatively short journey and comparatively low fares made the choice of emigration available to a very broad spectrum of Irish society. For those who could not obtain sufficient funds for the Atlantic voyage, the option of emigration to Britain remained. Regular steamships had plied the Irish Sea since 1820 and deckfares were as low as one shilling for the fourteen hour crossing. Even landless laborers could afford to avail of this facility and they did so in their thousands as seasonal and permanent emigrants. For those who were not attracted by the prospect of either Britain or America, the opportunity of emigration to Australia remained. The long distance and the tiresome voyage to the southern hemisphere was compensated for by government-subsidized passages, and probably a majority of the one-third of a million Irish settlers in nineteenth-century Australia were attracted there by the travel subvention; without it, Australia could not have competed with America and Canada.

Reception and Settlement

The reception accorded to Irish immigrants and the settlement preferences they exhibited were a function of the timing of their arrival, vis-à-vis the development stage attained by the country of reception, and also the social and religious composition of the immigrants themselves. No single model is applicable.

The eighteenth-century Protestant Irish in Colonial America were fortunate in that their arrival coincided with the early development phases of the colonies; consequently, they became identified with the process of frontier settlement. Although as a group they have sometimes been romanticized as the epitome of rootless and fearless pioneers forever operating at the very edge of civilization as "God's Frontiersmen", recent research has indicated that their settlement behavior was no different from that of their contemporary English, Scottish, or German neighbors. In rural areas and in urban settlements these Protestant Irish integrated easily into a society that in itself was new and of which they could justifiably claim to be a founding charter group. In this respect, their reception was greatly facilitated by their perceived conformity to an overall largely Protestant and English-speaking colonial ethos.

Anglo-conformity was the criterion applied most clearly to the immigrants of the colonies, and when the settlement frontier moved northward after American Independence, the established criteria remained in place. In the territory now known as Canada the arriving Irish found themselves in a familiar colonial situation. The trickle of immigrants to Nova Scotia and New Brunswick in the last third of the eighteenth century established Irish communities that were primarily Protestant; only in the isolated fishing outports of Newfoundland were there significant Catholic Irish communities. It was against this background that the upsurge of mass emigration in the nineteenth century was to operate. Although Protestants constituted only a quarter of the population of Ireland, they generated half of all those Irish who settled in Canada in the years 1815 – 55 and in the critical first few years the relative proportion of Protestants was even greater. They therefore took their place in the settlement process alongside American loyalists, English, and Scots, with whom they shared similar religious and colonial beliefs. Their integration was easy and made all the easier by the fact that the Protestant Irish were responsible for thirty percent of all immigrants into Canada before 1850. They outnumbered both the English and the Scots and so were in fact a dominant part of the charter group of Anglophone Canada. Their Catholic countrymen met a less accommodating reception and their presence was frequently the cause of heightened sectarian tensions. Their position within Canada has been identified as being that of a double minority – they were a religious minority among an English-speaking immigration that was seventy percent Protestant; within Canada they were a linguistic minority within a Catholic church dominated by French Canadians. In part, the Catholic Irish met these challenges by exhibiting a tendency to group, more readily than their Protestant countrymen, in urban centers, and in central Canada they also identified more closely with French Quebec than with Anglophone Ontario. The reception accorded the Irish in Canada was thus in part a function of their religious composition, but it was also equally a function of their time of arrival. The vast majority of the Canadian Irish arrived early enough to be counted among the founding fathers of the new country and were at an advantage in creating a niche for themselves. Their position was markedly different to that of the Irish who arrived during the Famine, 1845 to 52. Impoverished and diseased, the Famine immigrants – especially the 90,000 who arrived in 1847 – were pushed from community to community until eventually many of them either died or drifted southward to the United States. Their reception was shaped as much by fear as hostility, and their assimilation into Canadian society was further hampered by an obvious lack of casual jobs into which they could be inserted. Apart from Saint John, Quebec City, Montreal, and Toronto, which accommodated some few thousand of the refugees, the mass of the Famine victims simply bypassed the British North American colonies.

The Famine effectively marked the termination of mass Irish immigration into Canada; during the Famine, and henceforth, the vast bulk of the Irish crossing the Atlantic ended up in the United States. Unlike their fellow countrymen who had emigrated to Colonial America a century before, or to Canada in the previous generation, the Famine Irish were overwhelmingly Catholic. In addition, they were entering an already established society; they were not pioneers. Consequently, unlike their predecessors, their eventual settlement patterns displayed a marked urban preference; only a very few settled in rural areas. The American Irish preference for urbanism was all the more striking as the majority of the immigrants were derived from a predominantly agricultural society. Distinguished by religion, impoverishment, and lack of skills, the Irish became an urban proletariat, monopolizing the unskilled jobs and creating the first large-scale American urban ghettos. In 1855, for example, two-thirds of the gainfully employed Irish in Boston were either unskilled laborers or domestic servants. No other contemporary immigrant group exhibited such a narrow range of occupations, and fifteen years after the arrival of the first Famine immigrants the bulk of the Irish were still at the bottom of the occupational ladder. The ghetto situation welded the Irish together in a manner unprecedented in the annals of transatlantic migration, and their group consciousness was further reinforced by the bond of religion, which provided a community institutional structure but served also to exclude them from much of mainstream American life. Since the 1830s, a feature of American life had been the rise of Protestant nativism, fueled by a fear that American institutions were being threatened by the influx of (largely Irish) Catholics; in the 1850s this feeling culminated in the rise of the Know-Nothing party. These anti-immigrant groupings did not have the Catholic Irish as their sole target, but the scale of the Irish influx meant that they were the focus of much of the debate. Largely as a result of these animosities, the descendants of earlier, and Protestant, Irish settlers sought to distinguish themselves from the more recent arrivals by proclaiming their pre-Revolutionary origins through newly founded Scotch-Irish societies.

The role of the Famine was critical in shaping the character of the American Irish and that tragic watershed of Irish history serves also to distinguish the American from the essentially pre-Famine Canadian communities. Likewise, it serves to isolate the Australian Irish community which was predominantly post-Famine. Convict transportations and recruitment of a few hardy adventurers had created an Irish presence in Australia from the opening up of the colony in the late eighteenth century, but the rise of mass emigration from Ireland to Australia really belongs to the post-1850 period. Unlike America, the colony received very few Famine refugees, and its influx was initially prompted by the lure of gold, land, fortune, and adventure. In the decade 1851 to 60, a total of 100,000 Irish arrived and in the seventy years from 1851 to 1920, one-third of a million Irish settled in Australia and New Zealand. It has been argued recently that qualitatively the Australian Irish were superior to their American counterparts, less impoverished and more committed to progress, and consequently, they were assimilated with relative ease. Whatever the accuracy of this assertion, it is clear that the Australian Irish did tend to avoid urban ghettos, tending to exhibit a high degree of individualism. It must also be recognized that they tended to arrive in large numbers at an early stage in the colony's development and, therefore, as in Canada, they could claim some status as a charter group. Nonetheless, the Irish were not welcomed without reservation, they were frequently bestowed with an extrapolated convict image and were regarded as unruly, immoral, and lawless. Catholicism also distinguished two-thirds of them and raised further suspicion, but their widespread settlement pattern tended to dissipate much of the force of the hostility directed at them.

The suspicion and open hostility that was part of immigrant Irish life in Australia and in the United States in the second half of the nineteenth century, was also to be found in Irish emigrant groupings much closer to home. On the eve of the Famine, Britain contained almost half a million Irish-born, and this number was swollen during the Famine to such an extent that a quarter of the population of Liverpool could claim Ireland as a birthplace in 1860. Little Ireland in Manchester was described by Engels in his *The Condition of the Working Class in England in 1844*, and in the eyes of many other commentators, the Irish in Britain were synonymous with overcrowding, disease, urban ghettos, and unemployment.[7] Politically and socially the Irish were regarded as inferior and dangerous. The British view of the Irish was further heightened by the fact that the major British seaports were employed by the Irish as trans-shipment points on their way to destinations overseas. In the Famine year of 1847, for example, 300,000 Irish arrived in Liverpool, but half of them moved on very rapidly. For the British the arrival of the Irish represented what has been described as the first major invasion of the country since the arrival of the Normans. Britain, unlike her colonies, was not a society composed of immigrants, and the adjustments required to deal with the Irish were great. The assimilation of the sons and daughters of the immigrants proved relatively easy, but for most British, the immigrant Irish remained as objects of fear, suspicion, and symbols of the worst aspects of the new industrial cities.

Integration or Isolation: Return Migration

Apart from some movement to the continent of Europe in the seventeenth and early eighteenth centuries, Irish emigration was directed almost exclusively toward Britain and her overseas colonies. It was, therefore, a movement within an English-speaking world, and it was a world which offered also a familiar social, cultural, and legal context to the immigrants. It was a world into which the Irish should have integrated easily, for they, unlike immigrants from continental Europe, were possessed of several advantages as they entered a situation that demanded a high degree of Anglo-conformity. In the long run they did succeed: recent work has posed the question "what happened to the Irish" in relation to the virtual disappearance of a distinctive Irish identity in Canada; in Britain, Irish ethnicity is recognizable only as a label applicable to those born in Ireland – second, third and fourth generations of Irish descent have simply merged imperceptibly into mainstream British society; in Australia the Irish are now regarded as an enriching ingredient in a maturing society; in the United States a recent census has identified the Catholic Irish as being one of the top three most successful ethnic groups. The descendants of the original emigrants have therefore integrated into their host societies to the point that they have virtually lost their identity.

7. Engels, *Conditions of the Working Class.*

The process of integration proceeded most rapidly among the Protestant Irish because they possessed two distinct advantages. On the one hand, because they tended to adopt emigration as a solution to their socioeconomic problems more rapidly and earlier than their Catholic countrymen, they were numbered among the original founding groups of the transatlantic colonies. They, in fact, helped shape the societies into which they immigrated. Second, the Protestant Irish shared in all their destinations a common religious preference with the majority of the population. They took their place in Anglican, Presbyterian, and Methodist Churches alongside other ethnic groups derived from Britain, and as a result, intermarriage was facilitated, identities merged, and integration was expedited. Among the Catholic Irish these circumstances did not prevail. As a group they tended to be most prevalent in secondary waves of immigration; in only a few instances could they claim to be part of the founding fathers of the new society. They had to integrate into societies that were not of their construction. Furthermore, within Britain and its empire, their religion set them apart; it encouraged a group identity and attracted external hostility. In the long run, religion remained as their badge of distinctiveness, despite subsequent intermarriages with Italians, Poles, and other later arriving Catholic groups. Today in America, Canada, and Australia an Irish identity is held to be synonymous with Catholicism; the Protestant component of the exodus is now hidden and largely forgotten.

The integration of the Irish was accompanied by increased social and geographical mobility. As they moved up the social ladder, the Irish moved out of the urban ghettos of Canadian, American, and British cities and became part of the great assimilative process of suburbanization. In the case of the United States and Britain, however, the prolonged and continuous nature of the Irish emigration meant that every new generation witnessed a fresh influx, an influx that took its place in the inner city areas vacated by the suburbanizing second generation. Ghetto areas were thereby endowed with a prolonged life expectancy, and their continued existence as concentrations of recently arrived immigrants tended to exaggerate the absence of integrative forces and mask the assimilation of those who had moved socially and geographically into the mainstream of society.

In time, the successful integration of the Irish maintained an image of progress and achievement and few returned home. Indeed, the sustained outpouring of emigrants from Ireland offered little encouragement to those thinking about returning to their homeland.

The opportunities offered by life abroad were well known in eighteenth- and nineteenth-century Ireland, but that information was conveyed in emigrant letters and the popular emigration pamphlets that were read at public meetings and republished in the press. Returned migrants contributed little to this information flow. The cost of the journey, and its length in the case of Australia, were additional contributory reasons for the low numbers who returned to settle. So rare was the phenomenon that the "returned Yank" became an object of comment in nineteenth-century Ireland – his acquired mannerisms, his self-proclaimed success, made him an object of derision and envy among a population that had failed to emigrate. Some movement back across the Atlantic did, however, occur and particularly so after the advent of regular steam passenger ships. Local lore frequently recalls the movement of single women who emigrated to America to work for a few years in order to earn a dowry that they would bring back to Ireland in anticipation of marriage to a farmer's son. As yet, however, we know little about the scale of this phenomenon. Similarly, we cannot quantify the numbers of young children who were sent home to Ireland to be reared by grandparents. This group, whose most famous member was the Spanish American De Valera, may well have been more common than is generally recognized.

The one group that did return to Ireland was of course the seasonal migrants who annually went to work in the harvest fields of England and Scotland. Numbering more than 50,000 per annum before the Famine, and upward of 25,000 for the rest of the century, this group consisted mostly of young males aged 15 to 25 years. Their experience of seasonal migration was ultimately a preparation for permanent emigration, but in the short run, their seasonal earnings enabled them to delay their final departure.

Emigration was for most a final decision. Folk customs enshrined the departure in the celebration of an "American Wake," a funeral custom that likened emigration to death. In reality it did mark, for most, the last hours spent in Ireland by the intending emigrant.

Migration and Capital Movements

The Irish exodus moved a vast quantity of human capital but relatively little investment capital. The majority of the emigrants were at best but of modest means, and many had little more than their passage money. Records indicate that of 370 emigrants leaving

Country Antrim for Canada in the late 1830s, four carried more than 100 pounds, twenty-two carried more than 20 pounds, and the majority carried less than 10 pounds. Individual examples of educated and propertied emigrants conveying considerable sums of money to the colonies do exist, but it is fair to say that the Irish exodus was not associated with any large-scale cash transfers.

In fact, the nature of colonial relations often meant that mercantile interests tried to limit their expenditure of capital abroad. Wealthy Irish shippers and merchants invested in little more than warehouses in their foreign markets and their trade was centered upon the purchasing of raw materials abroad, their transfer to Britain, and the return export of goods with a high value-added component. Irish ship owners who ordered new ships to be built in New Brunswick, for example, merely paid for the construction of the hull; the high cost items such as sails, ropes, and iron hoops were prefabricated in Britain and transported to Canada for installation.

Migration, however, was associated with a capital flow in an easterly direction across the Atlantic. One of the most striking details of the Irish migration was the extent to which it was financed by emigrant remittances and prepaid passages provided by earlier emigrants. As early as 1830 it was estimated that one-third of the emigrants had their passage paid by family members on the other side of the Atlantic, and this proportion increased greatly during and after the Famine. In the early 1850s more than one million pounds per year was sent to British banks and shipping agents to pay for fares, and most of this money came from Irish communities in America. In 1850 emigration commissioners estimated that 75 percent of the emigrants had received their fares from North America in that year. This massive flow of money was, therefore, of critical importance in not only facilitating emigration but also in directing it to specific destinations. The flow of remittances was a crucial element in the chain migration process.

Migration and Political Movements

Eighteenth-, and especially nineteenth-century Irish emigration took place against a background in Ireland of intense political awareness and mass political involvement. Arguably, because of its status as a colonized society, Ireland tended to exhibit more than its share of social and political fissures: politics, class, and religion were interlinked variables upon which local and national identities were based and out of which came support for secret agrarian societies, sectarian outrages, and ultimately the development of a powerful nationalist movement. From the second decade of the nineteenth century, Daniel O'Connell's Catholic Emancipation and, later, Repeal of the Union movements had provided examples of the success of mass political movements. A more theoretical awakening had taken place a generation earlier through links with revolutionary France and the occurrence of the 1798 United Irishmen's rebellion. It was scarcely surprising, therefore, that emigrants should transplant much of their old-world political views into their new homelands. But in the new environments a mutation inevitably occurred, and in the long run the political activities of the emigrants represented fundamental adaptations to the realities of their adopted homeland.

The earliest political consciousness attributed to an Irish emigrant group is that associated with the Presbyterian or Scottish-Irish migration from Ulster to eighteenth-century colonial America. In popular lore this group had become the symbol of liberal individualism in America, a trait allegedly transferred along with their restless spirit from an Ulster that their families had helped colonize two to three generations before. More than any other immigrant group, the Scotch Irish are reputed to have solidly aligned themselves with the revolutionary side in the American War of Independence, a political stance that was celebrated and memorialized by the nineteenth-century Scotch-Irish Societies.

It is, however, to the mass migration of the nineteenth-century that we must turn to find the clearest evidence of transferred political movements. In Canada, particularly in New Brunswick and Ontario, the dominant Irish Protestant settlers brought with them the political sentiments of loyalty to the British Crown and Empire, and a heightened politico-religious view of a world in which Catholicism and disloyalty were equated. They came out of an Ireland that in 1795 had seen the formation of the Orange Order, and many of them were in fact first-generation Orangemen. In the colonies of British North America they sought to establish an ideological garrison of British, Protestant, and Imperial values, and they achieved a large measure of success. By 1870 one-third of all adult male Protestants in Canada were members of the Order, and through its membership it controlled municipal and provincial governments in Ontario and New Brunswick and continued to exert a strong influence on the Federal Conservative party until World War II. But increasingly this distinctive politico-religious organization was isolated from its spiritual hearth through the cessation of mass Irish emigration to Canada, and as a political force, its actions were almost entirely directed by a purely Canadian context in which a defensive stance against French Canadians, immigrant Catholics, and republican Americans was maintained.

The ideology of Orangeism was transferred to Canada at the same time as its identified Irish enemy, Republicanism, was being transferred to Australia in the form of transported rebels who had participated in the rebellions of 1798 and 1803. Approximately five hundred Irish political prisoners were transported to Australia prior to 1806. Upon this group, the image of wounded innocence and incipient terrorists was attributed by friends and foes respectively, but apart from the achievements of a few notable figures, this forced migration does not appear to have given rise to any long-lasting political movement. Australia was too far away from Ireland, and initially at least, the Irish were too few in number to sustain an emigré republican movement. The large-scale migrations of the post-1850s did produce a demographic base for Irish political movements and a growing nationalist movement emerged. In the 1890s this movement was taken over by the Catholic clergy, but for the most part, the issues with which it concerned itself pertained to the role and position of Catholics in Australia; its direct impact on Ireland was minimal.

The strongest expression of transferred political movements was to be found not in the British colonies, but in the United States. The Irish of America included within their demographic history the Famine episode, and this element was to color much of the thinking of emerging Irish organizations. Throughout the second half of the nineteenth century, a strong tradition of physical force was supported by American-based groups such as the Fenians, the Irish Republican Brotherhood, and, in the twentieth century, the I.R.A. and Noraid. In 1865 the American Fenians invaded Canada in a futile gesture of anti-British feeling, and at most times during the past 130 years, funds, and frequently arms, have been readily supplied for armed political activity in Ireland. Such groups were generally supported by Irish-born elements in America, and their links with Ireland were direct and specific. There was, however, also a tradition of nonviolent political groupings among the Irish in the cities of eastern America. Although clearly identified with the homeland these groups were fundamentally a reaction to American conditions. They were called into existence in response to anti-Catholic and nativist movements, and their central task was the creation and defense of a role for the Catholic Irish in the United States. At other, and more local, levels the Irish also maintained a high profile in political activity. Their facility with English, their tradition of mass political organization, and their virtual monopoly of some sectors of employment permitted the Irish to develop a strong grassroots movement. Their strength was seen in Tammany Hall, a byword for political manipulation, and also in the unions – particularly the Teamsters and Longshoremen Unions, which catered to a transport industry that was largely under Irish control. As union and ward bosses the Irish excelled, and in time, much of their power was directed into the Democratic party. But as in the other instances mentioned above, this participation in the political process was rooted in the context of the new environment; it was not powered by Irish nostalgia.

BIBLIOGRAPHY

Numbers

Dickson, R.J. *Ulster Emigration to Colonial America 1718–1775*. London, 1966.

Doyle, David. *Ireland, Irishmen and Revolutionary America (1760–1820)*. Cork, 1981.

Fitzpatrick, David. *Irish Emigration 1801–1921*. Dundalk, 1985.

Miller, Kirby. *Emigrants and Exile: Ireland and the Irish Exodus to North America*. Oxford, 1985.

O'Grada, Cormac. "A Note on Nineteenth-Century Irish Emigration Statistics." *Population Studies* 29 (1975) 143–149.

Push-Pull-Factors

Adams, William F. *Ireland and Irish Emigration to the New World from 1815 to the Famine*. New Haven, 1932.

Canny, Nicholas. *Kingdom and Colony: Ireland in the Atlantic World 1560–1800*. Baltimore, 1988.

Collins, Brenda. "Proto-industrialisation and Pre-Famine Emigration," *Social History* 7, 2 (1982) 127–146.

MacDonagh, Oliver. "The Irish Famine Emigration to the United States," *Perspectives In American History* 10 (1976) 357–446.

Mokyr, Joel. *Why Ireland Starved*. London, 1983.

Schrier, Arnold. *Ireland and the American Emigration, 1850–1900*. Minneapolis, 1958.

Migration and Demography of Sending Regions

Connell, K.H. *Population of Ireland, 1750–1845*. Oxford, 1950.

Cousens, S.H. "The Regional Variations in Emigration from Ireland between 1821 and 1841," *Transactions of the Institute of British Geographers* 37 (1965) 15–30.

Freeman, T.W. *Pre-Famine Ireland*. Manchester, 1957.

Goldstrom J.M. and L. Clarkson ed. *Irish Population, Economy and Society*. Oxford, 1981.

Robinson, Philip. *The Plantation of Ulster*. Dublin, 1984.

Female Emigration

Jackson, Pauline. "Women in 19th Century Irish Emigration," *International Migration Review* 18 (1984).

Kennedy, Robert E. *The Irish: Emigration, Marriage and Fertility*. Berkeley, 1973.

Parr, Joy. *Labouring Children*. London, 1980.

Robins, Joseph. *The Lost Children*. Dublin, 1980.

Vaughan W. and A.J. Fitzpatrick. *Irish Historical Statistics, Population, 1821–1971*. Dublin, 1978.

Transportation

Coleman, Terry. *Passage to America*. London, 1972.

Guillet, Edwin. *The Great Migration: The Atlantic Crossing by Sailing Ship 1770–1860*. Toronto, 1937.

MacDonagh, Oliver. *A Pattern of Government Growth 1800–60: The Passenger Acts and their Enforcement*. London, 1961.

Mannion, John. "Patrick Morris and Newfoundland Irish Immigration" in: C.J. Byrne and M. Harvey ed., *Talamh An Eire, Canadian and Irish Essays*. Halifax, 1986.

Reception and Settlement

Elliott, Bruce. *Irish Migrants in the Canadas*. Toronto, 1988.

Jackson, John. *The Irish in Britain*. London, 1963.

Lees, Lynn. *Exiles of Erin: Irish Migrants in Victorian London*. Manchester, 1979.

McCaffrey, L.J. *The Irish Diaspora in America*. Bloomington, 1976.

O'Farrell, Patrick. *The Irish in Australia*. Sydney, 1987.

Integration or Isolation

Akenson, Donald H. *The Irish in Ontario*. Montreal, 1984.

Leyburn, James. *The Scotch Irish*. Chapel Hill, 1962.
Mannion, John. *Irish Settlements in Eastern Canada*. Toronto, 1975.
O'Tuathaigh, M.A.G. "The Irish in Nineteenth Century Britain: Problems of Integration," *Transactions Royal Historical Society* 31 (1981) 149–173.
Ward, David. "The Ethnic Ghetto in the United States," *Transactions of the Institute of British Geographers* 7 (1982) 257–276.

Migration and Capital Movements

Houston, C. and W.J. Smyth. "New Brunswick Shipbuilding And Irish Shipping," *Acadiensis* (1987) 95–106.
Thomas, Brinley. *Migration and Economic Growth*. Cambridge, 1973.

Migration and Political Movements

Brown, T.N. *Irish American Nationalism*. Philadelphia, 1966.
Houston, C. and W.J. Smyth. *The Sash Canada Wore: A Historical Geography of the Orange Order in Canada*. Toronto, 1980.
MacDonagh, Oliver. *Irish Culture and Nationalism, 1750–1950*. Canberra, 1983.
McKeirnan, Colm. *Daniel Mannix and Ireland*. Melbourne, 1984.
O'Brain, Leon. "The Fenian Brotherhood" in: D. Doyle and O. Edwards ed., *America and Ireland 1776–1976*. Westport, 1980.
Engels, Frederick. *The Condition of the Working Class*. Trans. and ed. by W.O. Henderson and W.H. Chaloner. London, 1958.

4

The Push- and Pull-Factors Behind the Swedish Emigration to America, Canada, and Australia

LARS LJUNGMARK

Swedish historians were slow in beginning research on one of the greatest events in Swedish history: the emigration to the United States that turned one-fifth of all Swedes into Americans. After the statistician Gustaf Sundbärg had published his imposing Principal Report (*Betänkande*) of the Swedish Emigration Commission with twenty accompanying volumes (1907 to 1913), it lasted half a century until emigration became a topic for historical research. Then in 1963 a multimember project was started at Uppsala University entitled: "Sweden and America after 1860. Emigration, Remigration, Social and Political Debate." The project's final report was published in 1976.[1] There is no modern bibliography on Swedish emigration to the United States. Still indispensable, however, is O. Fritjof Ander's *The Cultural Heritage of the Swedish Immigration*, from 1956.[2] For current bibliographies, the *Swedish-American Historical Quarterly* is valuable. The latest bibliography is published in Hans Norman and Harald Runblom, *Transatlantic Connections*, which deals with the emigration to all three immigration countries that are in focus in this paper.[3]

Compared with the Swedish emigration to the United States, research about Swedish emigration to Australia and Canada is very insignificant. Against fifteen to twenty Swedish dissertations about the American emigration, there is only one about the emigration to Australia, and this has its focus not on Swedish immigration in

1. *From Sweden to America. A History of the Migration* (Minneapolis and Uppsala, 1976).

2. O. Fritjof Ander, *The Cultural Heritage of the Swedish Immigration. Selected References* (Rock Island, 1956).

3. Hans Norman and Harald Runblom, eds., *Transatlantic Connections. Nordic Migration to the New World after* 1800 (Oslo, 1988).

particular, but on the Scandinavian emigration as a whole.[4] Since Helge Nelson's monumental work on Swedish settlement in North America, in which some thirty pages deal with the Swedes in Canada, very little has been written in Sweden about the Swedish emigration to Canada.[5] In Canada, K.O. Bjork and W.C. Wonders have written about the Scandinavians' role in the settlement of Canada's prairie provinces.[6] Behind this lack of interest in the Australian and Canadian emigration is of course the fact that these emigration streams were tiny compared with the big flood to the United States. The poor statistics, owing to the immigration of seamen in Australia, which was impossible to control and the, for a long time, uncontrolled migration to and from Canada over the American border, also have offered big obstacles to researchers. During the last years, however, a growing interest in the emigration to Australia and Canada can be seen among the emigration scholars in Sweden. Behind this is probably the rising popularity of Australia and Canada among the Swedish younger generation that can be noted since the 1950s and has led to their growing emigration to both countries.

Sweden's new role as an immigration country has in a similar way focused the interest of the emigration scholars on a new topic: the assimilation of the Swedish emigrants. In a new project at the Center for Multiethnic Research at Uppsala University called "Ethnic Conflict and Cooperation in American Cities," the Swedish enclaves and the Swedes' confrontations with other ethnic groups are studied for four American cities and that of Winnipeg in Canada.

The Extent of the Swedish Emigration to the United States, Australia, and Canada

The extent of Swedish emigration to the United States is shown in Figure 4.1. Its growth curve is not strikingly different from that of other Scandinavian countries except that large-scale Swedish emigration began somewhat later. According to official statistics, a total

4. O. Koivukangas, *Scandinavian Immigration and Settlement in Australia before World War II* (Kokkola, 1974).

5. H. Nelson, *The Swedes and the Swedish Settlements in North America* (Lund, 1943).

6. Kenneth O. Bjork, "Scandinavian Migration to the Canadian Prairie Provinces 1893–1914," *Norwegian-American Studies* 26 (1974), 3–30 and William C. Wonders, "Pioneer Settlement by Scandinavians in Central Alberta," *Geografiska Annaler* 49B (1983), 129–152.

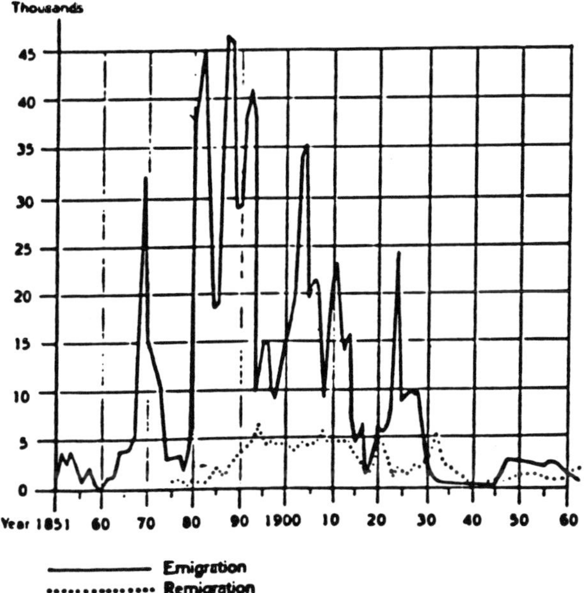

FIGURE 4.1 Emigration and Remigration between Sweden and the United States, 1851–1962, based on Official Swedish Emigration Statistics.

of 1,122,292 Swedes emigrated to America between 1851 and 1930. These statistics, however, are too low due to the high number of unregistered emigrants. Research has suggested (very tentatively) that unregistered emigration for the entire 1851 to 1930 period totaled 100,000 persons. This means that up to 1.25 million Swedes emigrated during that period. The greatest number of Swedish-born residents and their children in the United States was recorded in 1910 when about one-fifth of the world's Swedish population was living in the United States.

The first inkling of an emigration wave came in the early 1850s. An average of three thousand persons per year emigrated between 1852 and 1854. Emigration declined during the latter part of that decade but rose again steadily during the early 1860s, reaching a peak in 1869. Something akin to mass emigration began in 1868, and over the next five years, 103,000 Swedes left for America. Crop failures in Sweden, at a time when free land was available in America, and reports of great prosperity in the republic across the sea, inspired the exodus. These conditions were reversed later and led to a decline in emigration, but a new surge developed in 1879. Over the next fourteen years, up to 1894, an average of 34,000 Swedes emigrated annually. Fluctuating economic developments in Sweden and America were primarily responsible for this major emigration wave. While conditions were deteriorating, especially for farmers in Sweden, the United States was enjoying a tide of economic prosperity. At the same time, the American propaganda campaign, launched in the late 1860s to encourage emigration, began to bear fruit. Approximately forty percent of all Swedish emigrants left during the peak years of the 1880s.

Emigration declined at the very end of the nineteenth century, just as it did during the 1870s and for roughly the same reason: improved conditions in Sweden. From 1900 up to World War I, two minor peaks are recorded: one in 1902 to 1903 and another, smaller one, in 1910. Both were caused by crises affecting Swedish industry and the Swedish labor market. In 1909, Sweden experienced its only major labor conflict, the so-called Great Strike. After World War I, restrictive legislation in America began to affect emigration. A final peak came in 1923, when a record unemployment in Sweden caused close to 25,000 persons to leave for America. Emigration remained at a level of about 9,000 per year up to the stock market crash of 1929, when remigration surpassed emigration for the first time since World War I; this was to be the pattern for the coming years. During the 1940s, a total of 10,924 Swedes emigrated to the United States, the majority arriving after the end of World War II. Swedish emigration during the 1950s accounted for 25,500 persons. The annual average for the 1960s and 1970s has been in the vicinity of 1,700 persons. In general, immigration to Sweden from the United States has been higher.

Compared with the 1.2 million Swedes going to the United States, the Swedish emigration to Australia is very small. Even in the peak years in the 1960s and 1970s the Swedish emigration to the United States was three to four times larger. Exactly how many Swedes have gone to Australia is very hard to tell because so many entered Australia without address-change certificates or passports up to World War I. Examples of the very unreliable Swedish official statistics are easy to find: according to these statistics 152 persons emigrated from Sweden to Australia in 1888, but the statistics of the port of Melbourne state that in the same year 215 Swedes "jumped ship" in that port alone. During the period between 1882 and 1920 2,194 Swedes deserted their ships in Melbourne. According to the Swedish statistics, the total Swedish emigration to Australia during

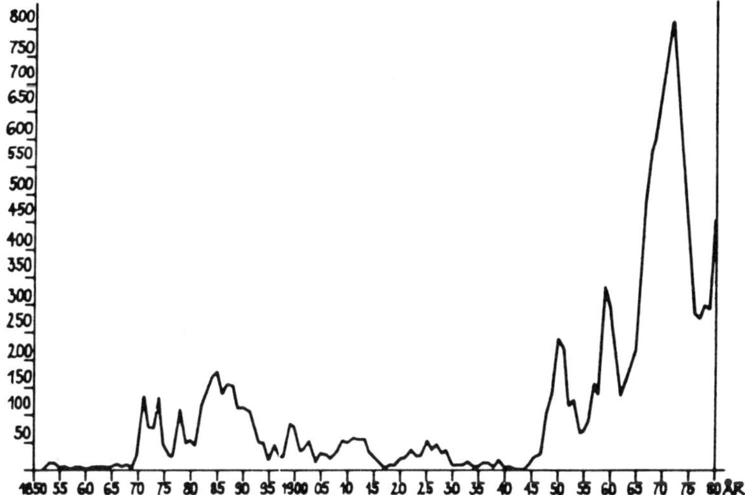

FIGURE 4.2 Swedish Emigration to Australia, 1851–1980

Source: Ulf Beÿbom, *Australienfararna. Vårt märkligaste utvandringsäventyr* (Stockholm 1983), 264.

the same period amounted to 2,447.

From naturalization records and census lists, historian Olavi Koivakangas estimates the total number of Swedish immigrants in Australia up to 1916 at about 12,500 – the Swedish statistics say 3,295. After 1915 the Swedish statistics are correct and, together with Koivokangas' estimation, the total number of Swedish immigrants up to 1980 could be estimated at 25,000.

The Swedish statistics form the basis of Figure 4.2. Even if the figures are much too low for the period up to World War I, the chart gives a fairly good impression of the ups and downs of the Swedish emigration to Australia. These changes mostly coincide with those of the Swedish emigration to the United States. From 1948, however, the Australian curve goes its own way to heights that undoubtedly – even if we had the proper figures for that decade – would surpass the heights of the 1880s. From 1970 the curve declines due to unemployment in Australia.

The Swedish emigration to Canada started with some Swedes traveling direct from Sweden in the 1870s and 1880s, joined by many Swedish Americans from the American border states. They obtained work in the railroad constructions, the mines, and building industry, first in Ontario, later in Manitoba and Saskatchewan. The prairies in the southern parts of the latter provinces also received Swedish farmers. By the late 1880s, free or cheap land ceased to be available in the United States, and up to World War I, large numbers of Swedish Americans moved to the western Canadian prairies. In turn, the new arrivals soon began to draw after them Swedes directly from the homeland.

From the 1880s and up to World War I, the Canadian Federal Government undertook a vigorous immigration campaign to get the "Last Best West" settled. This campaign also included Scandinavia, as the Scandinavians were considered by Canadian officials to be particularly desireable homesteaders. The immigration campaign was again intense in the 1920s, now primarily conducted by the Canadian Pacific Railroad, which wanted settlers along its line and farmer's products on the trains. During this decade, for many Swedes Canada became the new promising future.

In the 1930s, the depression hit wheat growers in the Canadian prairie provinces very hard. They also met natural disasters such as drought and grasshopper swarms, which caused very serious devastation. All this almost stopped the emigration and started a great remigration to Sweden. After World War II the emigration from Sweden to Canada rose again. Many of those who left Sweden were European war refugees who went further afield. Moreover, especially in the 1950s, many Swedes wanted to start a new postwar life in young, promising Canada.

Canadian immigration statistics have been described as a "statistical nightmare".[7] To a great extent, this nightmare is caused by the immigration from and emigration to the United States. First, until 1901, people entering Canadian ports and then going on to the United States were excluded from Canadian immigration statistics, and up to 1926, all Europeans entering Canada from the United States were not included in the statistics of European immigration to Canada. How wrong it is to base the immigration statistics on the number of people entering Canadian ports! The following provides an example: according to the Canadian census of 1871, there were 558 Scandinavians in Canada that year; ten years later, in 1881, there were 2,076. This means that only about 1,500 persons born in Scandinavian countries (plus the number needed to replace those dying during the period, say about 500) remained in Canada of the 65,000 who were reported as having arrived at Canadian ports

7. Harold Martin Troper, *Only Farmers Need Apply. Official Canadian Government Encouragement of Immigration from the United States, 1896–1911* (Toronto, 1972), 152.

during that decade. Another example is taken from Sten Aminoff's investigations of Scandinavians in the passenger lists in the port of Quebec: the S/S Sarmatian arrived in Quebec May 25, 1886 with 661 passengers. Of the 268 Scandinavians, six went to Canada and the rest to the United States. On April 21, 1887, there arrived the SS Oregon with 762 passengers. Of the 361 Scandinavians, 52 went to Canada and 309 to the United States.[8]

The fact that before 1926 the Swedes entering Canada via the United States-Canadian border are not recorded also affects the statistics, as most Swedes before 1920 came via the United States. Some idea of how many there were as compared with those coming directly from Sweden gives a comparison between the years of arrival of the Swedish-born in the census of 1931 and the Swedish emigration statistics for those going directly to Canada:

TABLE 4.1 Swedish Emigration to Canada via the United States

Year of Arrival	Census 1931	Swedish Emigration Statistics
1901–1910	11,860	3,150
1911–1920	8,056	2,970
1921–1930	11,215	11,858

From 1931, when the emigration of Swedes from the United States to Canada had ceased, the Swedish statistics give the following figures for the Swedish immigration to and immigration from Canada:

TABLE 4.2 Swedish Emigration to and Immigration from Canada

	Emigrants	Immigrants
1931–1940	349	2,887
1941–1950	4,327	501
1951–1960	10,171	2,061
1961–1970	3,636	2,824
1971–1980	4,092	2,075

Notable are the large remigration in the 1930s and the rather high emigration in the 1950s.

8. From manuscript through the courtesy of Sten Aminoff.

Early Emigration: Group Emigration to the United States, Deserted Seamen to Australia, and Swedish Americans to Canada

Prior to the first wave in 1868, Swedish emigration to the United States was largely characterized by movements of distinct groups of people. All of them have several features in common: they were led by a central figure, almost all of the members in each group came from the same general area of Sweden, and all of them founded colonies in the American Middle West. In fact, for the Swedish mass emigration, the early pioneers were of the utmost importance. The great exodus would never have materialized without their trailblazing example and their faithful contacts with people back home.

Noted among these pioneers are Gustaf Unonius, an Uppsala University student who left Sweden in 1841, together with his wife and two other students, and settled near Pine Lake, Wisconsin. Another was Peter Cassel, a 55-year-old farmer, miller, and master builder. Influenced by reports from Pine Lake, he left Kisa in southern Östergötland with a group of seventeen Kisa residents in 1845. His colony at Skunk river, Iowa, was named New Sweden. Unonius and his fellow settlers of the same social class soon failed, but Cassel's New Sweden had a brighter future and still exists as a Swedish settlement.

Another successful colony builder was Hans Mattson from Önnesta, outside Kristianstad in southern Sweden, who, after arriving in the United States in 1851, two years later founded a settlement, Vasa, along a tributary of the Mississippi west of Red Wing in Minnesota. Mattson left Vasa in 1856, but Vasa has preserved its Swedish flavor. This does not mean that all of the original settlers and their descendants remained in the area. Rather, Vasa is a typical example of frontier settlements functioning as "mother colonies" for Swedish settlements further west or "way stations" for travelers on the road west.

Direct group immigration from Sweden was the pattern until the American Civil War, while stage migration in groups occurred throughout the mass-emigration era. The fact that so many of the early settlements still exist is due to the so-called "stock effect": the pull from earlier emigrants upon their countrymen back home. Despite a continual loss of population, usually to states further west, the settlements managed to retain a distinctly ethnic flavor throughout the era of mass emigration.

At the same time as the Swedish group emigration to the United

States, the first Swedes arrived in Australia. They came together with the 200,000 free immigrants, mostly from the English lower classes, who arrived (lured by assisted passages) between 1830 and 1850. In 1830 only 7,000 out of Australia's 70,000 white inhabitants were free. By 1849, however, deportation had ceased. The Swedes did not get any assistance. They were seamen who paid their passage by working on British (but also on Swedish) ships and who had been dismissed or had deserted their ships in Australian ports. Most of them started to travel along the Australian coast or to work on the wharves of growing Sydney, Melbourne, or Adelaide. Some became masters or part-owners of small sailing ships. The development of whaling and sealing industries also brought some Swedish seamen to Australian waters and soon to Australian soil.

Once in Australia, the Swedes' contact with the old country was sparse, and they did not act as magnets for new immigrants as did the pioneers in the United States. They did not play a role, or just a small one, as trailblazing examples during the main emigration from Sweden to Australia, which occurred during the decades before and after the Australian economic depression of the 1890s. This emigration was characterized by assisted passage to Queensland and, as before, by immigration of seamen. The assisted immigrants were mostly poor people who would have gone to the United States if they had money for their tickets. They started their voyage from Hamburg where German sailing vessels chartered by the Queensland Government ferried them over the oceans. From the 1880s, this traffic was concentrated in Liverpool. The assistance was granted to Scandinavians during the years 1871 to 1886 and 1898 to 1901.

According to a recent estimate based on naturalization reports and on the assumption that only every third or fourth Swede took out Australian citizenship, the Swedes arriving at Queensland in the 1870s and 1880s numbered about 2,500 and by 1900 about 4,000. The other Australian colonies were not so anxious to get Scandinavian settlers as to extend their schemes of assisted passage or free land grants to them. Scandinavians, and among them the Swedes, did however come without the lure of assisted passage. Most of them were (as formerly) paid out or deserted seamen from Scandinavian ships, transporting timber to Australian ports, above all to Melbourne.

From the turn of the century to World War I the "stock effect" for the first time played a role in the Swedish immigration to Australia, as many of the arriving Swedes probably were lured by positive reports from friends and relatives already in Australia. The growing Swedish trade and shipping to Australia also contributed immigrants.

According to the Australian statistics, more than 10,000 Swedes and Norwegians arrived from the turn of the century up to World War I. But the departures from Australia were also considerable. A consular report of 1911 tells of 1,443 Swedes and Norwegians arriving during this year but also that of these, 953 left the country. The outbreak of World War I stopped the Swedish immigration. During the interwar period, the Swedish immigration to Australia was insignificant.

Two sets of factors are responsible for the development of a mass emigration. First are the push-factors, represented by the deplorable conditions in the homeland. The second are the pull-factors, the dreams and promises that the new country has to offer and that are made alive to European eyes by the promoters of emigration.

Push-Factors Behind the Swedish Emigration

Economic factors had a great deal of bearing on the development of Swedish mass emigration to the *United States*, in the beginning particularly in rural areas faced by overpopulation and insufficient acreage. The overpopulation can be explained by improved medical care, better food, and long periods of peace, which lowered the death rate but kept the birth rates at the same high level as before. The oversupply of manpower depreciated the wages of landless farm workers, and small-scale farmers struggled with insufficient acreage. For both groups the only solution was to leave the countryside, either by migrating to industrial centers and urban areas, or by emigration to open farmland in America, of which the early emigrant pioneers talked in their letters home.

The economic background of emigration from the Swedish countryside made this movement highly sensitive to business cycles and to the national economy. The effect of agricultural business cycles was best illustrated during the 1880s when Swedish emigration soared to record peaks. All of this movement reflected the impact of price crashes on the European grain market. Crop failures had nearly catastrophic consequences in rural areas caught between explosive population growth and sluggish land development. A succession of three crop failures from 1866 to 1868 made matters even more desperate. The flight from the countryside swelled to epidemic proportions in 1868 to 1869, giving rise to the first mass emigration wave. On the whole, however, famine and destitution were rarely the direct causes of Swedish emigration. What did have an impact on emigration was the general fear that crisis conditions would develop and the belief that too little progress was being made in Sweden to improve the lot of the agricultural proletariat.

The emigration wave from 1891 to 1893 marked a turning point in the development of Swedish emigration to the United States as it began to assume more of the character of an industrial and urban movement. By this time the supply of prime farmland in the United States was nearing exhaustion, which dampened the enthusiasm for emigration among Swedish farmers. A new emigrant category also emerged, dominated by job seekers. Although some of them still came from rural areas – farmers' sons, farmhands, maidservants, and children of small cottagers – increasing numbers were workers in urban industry, crafts, and domestic service. The flight from the Swedish countryside had turned into a march on the American job market.

Even if all emigration scholars are convinced that economic factors behind the Swedish emigration to the United States are the central push-factors, they also point at several other contributing factors. The most important ones are the following:

Religious Intolerance

Even though the Pietists and their followers were accorded equal status with the state church after 1858, they still considered themselves the object of official persecution. Hence, religious intolerance has often been cited as an important factor behind the Swedish emigration to the United States. Scholars, however, are sure that religion was no central factor and only played some role during the early period of Swedish emigration. On the other hand, there is some reason to point to the American revivalist movement as an attractive pull-force. Emigration thus became a natural extension of the village path leading to the prayer chapter. Probably more Swedes emigrated because of the religious freedom associated with the free-church movement than because of the religious intolerance of the state church.

Class Differences

It is true that the Swedish lower classes harbored feelings of inferiority that sometimes gave rise to resentment and hatred toward the upper, ruling classes. It is also true, however, that this lower-class consciousness lacked both a strong sense of class solidarity and conviction that class struggle was inevitable. An open show of protest against the established society was generally considered unnecessary; thus, social injustice alone did not create a need to emigrate.

Alternatively, it is obvious that many Swedes were convinced that the possibilities of moving up the social ladder were greater in America than at home. Furthermore, the hope of keeping one's social standing could also incite Swedes to emigrate during the nineteenth century. The shortage of farm acreage forced many farmers' sons to find work on other farms, in urban industries or with the railroad teams in northern Sweden. They then dropped to a lower social standing than that to which they had been accustomed. This led to feelings of discontent and, for many, to emigration to a new life as independent farmers in America.

Political Immaturity

The radical political press in Sweden, which, in its fight against the ruling classes and for sweeping voting reforms, thought emigration was an appropriate means of protesting the injustices in Sweden, played the most important role in linking emigration to political dissent. But real oppression, in whatever form, does not seem to have existed.

Military Service

Historical research has not supported the idea that opposition to military service was of decisive importance, but it is possible that the threat of military service played an indirect role. For instance, those who emigrated for economic reasons often made plans to leave the country near the time of induction. In other words, it was not the fear of military service in itself but rather the timing of induction that caused many men to emigrate.

News of America in the Swedish Press

On the whole, and especially prior to World War I, the Swedish press – with the exception of the radical papers – was strongly opposed to emigration. Newspapers' editorials denounced the exodus and branded all emigrants as traitors. But, at the same time, newspapers' enormous coverage of developments on the other side of the Atlantic revitalized the image of the New World and made it more familiar to thousands of readers. Moreover, the advertising sections were swamped with the glowing accounts of emigrant agents' operations. There is no doubt that the viewpoints expressed on the editorial pages carried very little weight.

In short, nearly all of the above-mentioned conditions that may have played some part in fostering Swedish emigration to the United States have one thing in common: while each of them had a role to play in this transatlantic movement none were primary determinants for the overall picture. In general, the only factors that induced people to emigrate were economic.

Swedish push-factors were not important in the emigration to *Australia*. During the "classic" Swedish emigration period in the late 1800s and early 1900s, the Swedish "push" naturally could turn Swedes to emigrants; not in the direction of Australia but to the United States. Only in the 1960s and 1970s could a Swedish "push" be said to be of some importance for the emigration to Australia. "Ideological" criticism against the "dull" Swedish society where the individual was under guardianship, as well as weariness of the long reign of the social-democratic party, were heard as reasons behind emigration to the supposedly freer Australian life.

In Sweden the push-factors behind the emigration to *Canada* were identical to those behind the emigration to the United States: economic reasons, based primarily on land hunger and later on the industrial workers' hope for better salaries and conditions. Among both rural and urban population lay the hope to get rich, move back, and start a new life in Sweden. Since the emigration of Swedish Americans is very important in the history of Swedish emigration to Canada, U.S. push-factors are of great importance. The lack of free homestead land and relatively inexpensive railway land in the states south of the Canadian border was the big push-factor. The solution to this problem was found north of the border in the Canadian prairie provinces. Another U.S. push-factor was the increased land values which resulted in significant increases in tenancy and mortgage rates.

Pull-Factors Behind the Swedish Emigration

The pull from America, the dreams and promises that America had to offer, were a necessary complement to the Swedish push-factors for the development of a Swedish mass emigration. They were made more attractive for Swedish eyes by those who "sold America." The chief "salesmen" were the federal government, state authorities, land companies, industry, railroads, steamship lines, and, last but not least, Swedes already there. The same factors worked for Australia and Canada and similar "salesmen," even if the pull-factors had different strength for the three immigrant countries and also the "salesmen" played different roles.

The Most Important Pull-Factor: The Land

By the time mass emigration began from Sweden, the American frontier had reached the Mississippi Valley. East of this frontier there was still private land for sale, but the asking price was usually more than the poor emigrant could afford. Up till 1890 then, the primary goals for land-hungry Swedes were government-land holdings along the frontier or further west. In 1862, just before the start of mass emigration from Sweden, came the "Homestead Act." This legislation offered 160 acres of free land to any American citizen of legal age or any immigrant who had notified the government of his decision to become a citizen. The purpose of the Homestead Act was to attract new settlers to the vast territory west of the Mississippi. Homestead land was available from the late 1860s up to around 1890, years which marked the beginning and the end of peak emigration from Sweden. Even today most of the larger Swedish settlements can be found in the Homestead Triangle between the upper reaches of the Mississippi and Missouri Rivers. Free government land was usually located in remote wilderness regions. Those who arrived with investment capital, the Swedish farmers, for example, who sold their homes and property, saw the advantages of buying private land in more populated areas. By far the most important sellers to Swedish immigrants were those railroad companies that had been given land by the government to finance railroad construction.

During the whole Swedish emigration to Canada up to World War II, land was the most important Canadian lure. When at the end of the nineteenth century the American government land ran out and the railroad land and other private land was too expensive for the Swedish emigrants, news of Canadian prairie land was brought to the Swedes in the United States and in Sweden in a vigorous campaign for the "Last Best West." Canada had a homestead law similar to that of the United States and also railroad land, which the Canadian Pacific Railroad Company offered to the land-hungry Swedes. The land was to be found on the prairies of Manitoba, Saskatchewan, and Alberta, where Swedish settlements are still visible. The last Canadian land propaganda was aimed during the 1920s at Swedes willing to start farming, especially at the northern frontier in the prairie provinces. The campaign, however, did not fulfill expectations as the Swedes now tended to go to the cities.

The fact that during the Swedish emigration up to World War II there was permanently land available, first in the United States and later in Canada, made the Australian land, so far away, a weak pull-factor, even if many Swedes did end up as Australian farmers. Australia had no homestead law and the land was rather expensive.

Good Wages, Plenty of Jobs

The start of mass Swedish emigration to the United States coincided with the demand for skilled and unskilled labor from the eastern seaboard to the plains of the Middle West. The eastern states were primarily interested in the better skilled industrial labor, while the Middle West attracted farmhands, lumberjacks, railroad workers, and unskilled labor. Their conditions also meant that the wages for unskilled labor were considerably higher in the Middle West than in the East or in Sweden itself. After 1890, the Swedish settlements in the Middle West still had need for farm workers and domestics. Railroad teams and lumberjacks, however, pushed westward as far as their jobs would take them, while a larger share of unskilled Swedish labor took jobs in factories and public service. The Swedish industrial working class began its march on the American job market settling primarily in the industrial cities in the eastern states.

The emigration of Swedes to the United States after World War II constituted a sort of "brain drain," for American jobs were in many cases offered to well-educated experts. For many of these emigrants the term "temporary emigrants" perhaps is the best way of describing their intentions. The opening of world markets to Swedish corporations, for example, has led to the transfer of business executives to American subsidiaries. To work in the United States they were required to have immigrant visas. The same held true with regard to university researchers, doctors, engineers, and other professional people, most of whom intended to stay only long enough in order to explore the possibilities of a career or permanent residence in America.

For Swedes going to Canada, job opportunities mostly meant the opportunity to earn money for a start as farmers. The Canadian immigration promoters were always eager to get Swedes as farmers rather than as labor in the cities. Propaganda brochures often stressed the poor opportunities for educated people and skilled labor in Canada. One important exception were the Swedish female domestic servants who were always wanted and where the demand was larger than the supply.

For emigrants to Australia, job opportunities per se were a real lure only during the last emigration period in the 1960s and 1970s. The federal Special Assistance Program then at work was offered especially to skilled labor and technicians.

Gold in the United States and Australia

In both the United States and Australia, gold sometimes was a very strong pull-factor. The gold discoveries in California attracted their share of Swedes at the end of the 1840s. There were Swedish "forty-niners", but the Californian gold played a quantitatively small role in Swedish emigration because the news arrived relatively late. Of course the news from California imparted to America a golden luster that was important in the years to come.

The gold discoveries in Australia in 1851 had a more direct impact on Swedish emigration. Many Swedes who had not succeeded in California went further west on American vessels, while others sailed from Hamburg or on English vessels directly from Europe. Most of the Swedes, however, came as seamen and were paid off or "jumped ship" in Australian harbors. The ships they left were usually Scandinavian vessels bringing Baltic timber. But Swedes employed as seamen in Australian waters or on the wharves were quick to go off to the gold fields. Most of the gold fields were in the colony of Victoria, with a population of 77,345 in 1851. As many as 94,644 immigrants came to this colony in 1852. Estimates have been made that about 1,500 Swedes arrived in the peak years of the Victoria gold rush. Extensive gold fields were also discovered in western Australia in 1892 to 1893; to these, many Swedish miners and seamen were attracted from the other colonies. Some also came direct from Sweden or the United States. After a period in the gold fields, many settled on available land. The developing western Australian shipping also attracted the Swedes and many worked in the port of Freemantle.

Assisted Passage

Assisted passage to contract labor, that is, economic support for the emigrant's voyage that he or she had to pay back through work, was forbidden in Sweden at an early stage. Nevertheless, there were some schemes of assisted passage to contract labor during the early years of Swedish emigration to the United States. Most notable was the import of farmhands from the parish of Barkeryd in the district of Småland to Texas led by S.M. Swenson, Texan millionaire from Barkeryd, in the 1850s and 1860s. They had to repay their tickets through work as farmhands on Swenson's and other farmers' estates for one to two years. This "import" was so successful that there still is a Swedish settlement in the vicinity of Austin, and the Swedish paper *Texas Posten* was published up to the early 1980s.

In the years thereafter, however, contract labor schemes like Swenson's disappeared from the Swedish emigration to the United States as the sponsors soon discovered how hard it was to get their transportation disbursals back from the emigrants, who often left their contracted work. Neither the federal nor the state authorities in the United States offered any assisted passage.

When the Canadian immigration promotion started at the end of the 1860s and the beginning of the 1870s, the Allan line, the leading private concern interested in increased immigration to Canada, worked out a system for providing acceptable immigrants, among them Swedes, with cheap transportation across the Atlantic. To conceal this low fare, which was against the rules of the international shipping cartel, it was called a "governmental subvention." A year later there was a real governmental subvention that reduced the fare by 25 percent for the Swedes going to Canada and also offered free transportation inside Canada. The lack of success, however, made the Canadian government withdraw its emigration agent in Sweden in 1876. When the new Swedish campaign started again at the beginning of the 1880s, there was no assisted passage scheme involved. From the 1890s up to World War I, however, there was a Canadian contract-labor scheme for import of Swedish servant girls. They went over on tickets prepaid by their employers in Canada who then gathered the transport costs out of their salaries.

Australia's big disadvantage, the long and expensive journey, made a reduction of the transport costs a necessity for success in the emigration market. There were only two solutions: first the seamen's free journey to Australian ports; second, assisted passage. The assisted passage offered by the colony of Queensland in 1871 to 1886 and 1898 to 1901 has already been mentioned. Many of the immigrants, and among them also the Swedes who took advantage of the assisted passage, soon left Queensland and went south to cooler climates in the colonies of New South Wales and Victoria. When in 1898 the assisted immigration to Queensland was revived, the immigrants were obliged to stay at least one year in Queensland to qualify for the assistance. Around 1,000 Scandinavians, among them some 400 Swedes, took advantage of the Queensland assisted scheme of 1898 to 1901.

After World War I, extensive plans were embarked upon to strengthen the "White Australia" politics through British-assisted immigrants. After 1929, the economic depression caused the schemes to be abandoned. The absence of assisted passage for the Scandinavians was no doubt the cause of their insignificant immigration in the 1920s.

In the 1950s, Australia again began to grant assisted passage to Scandinavians. This gave new impetus to Swedish emigration to the antipodes, especially in the 1960s and 1970s. According to the Special Assistance Programme, people between eighteen and forty-five years and accepted by the immigration officials at the Australian Embassy got free passage. They had to remain in Australia for at least two years. Thanks to this assistance and the Australian propaganda, 3,200 Swedes went to Australia in the 1960s and 4,885 in the 1970s. This is 58 percent of the total Swedish immigration to Australia since 1851, according to the official Swedish statistics. The peak years were 1971 to 1973 (together, 2,297 emigrants) when the Swedish economy was down and the press full of information from Australia, the "land of the future."

Organized Immigration Promotion

To present the immigration countries as offering many advantages to the prospective emigrants was the business of what I have previously called the "salesmen." When presenting these "salesmen" and the whole propaganda organization, it is natural to start with the United States because U.S. organizations, and sometimes even the U.S. salesmen, were used by Canada and, to a lesser degree, by Australia.

The federal government's role in selling America was primarily through the passing of the Homestead Act with its offer of free government land. The federal government did not wage any major propaganda compaign in support of emigration. Its Stockholm legation was instructed by Washington to proceed with caution and, at all costs, to avoid irritating the anti-emigration sentiments of the Swedish government.

In contrast to this caution, emigration was receiving encouragement from various state governments, particularly in and around the Upper Mississippi Valley, where the opening of homestead lands and new frontier settlements attracted scores of northern European immigrants. All of them established Boards of Immigration whose prime objectives were emigration propaganda and emigrant protection, both of which relied heavily on the contributions of resident immigrant groups.

From the 1850s up to the early 1870s the federal government allocated vast quantities of land for railroad construction west of Mississippi. These land grants varied in size from five to forty miles on both sides of the track. The railroads acquired ownership of their land sections with the laying of each new mile of track. For the railroads, the ideal worker was the individual who labored long hours for modest pay and eventually settled down on land-grant territory. They soon discovered that Scandinavian immigrants matched the ideal in almost all respects. It is no small coincidence that a Swedish-American heartland arose along the land-grant railroads west of Mississippi and in Michigan, Illinois, and Wisconsin.

The states' emigrant agents as well as the agents for the railroads' land departments always tried to locate "magnets," consisting of Swedish settlers out in the immigration area whose letters home and personal visits to the old country would bring new settlers to the area.

Throughout the mass emigration era, American and English steamship lines dominated the transport of Swedish emigrants over the North Sea and across the Atlantic. A total of ten different steamship companies were involved in the transport of the Swedes. In 1915, the *Swedish American Line* opened the first direct service route between Sweden and America. All of these companies established agencies in the leading port of embarkation, Gothenburg.

An impressive network of subagents connected the main office with field operations throughout Sweden. At least one or two subagents were stationed in every single parish of southern and central Sweden. American interests soon discovered that this network of agents and subagents provided an excellent means of promoting their own services. Aside from distributing the shipping lines' colorful brochures, subagents gradually acquired the role of salesmen for the glowing opportunities on the other side of the Atlantic (i.e., land, jobs, and the American way of life). In time, another group of people assumed greater importance in stimulating emigration, Swedish Americans who accepted offers of a roundtrip ticket in exchange for their services as visiting *Yankees*. American business interests made a special point of hiring "successful" immigrants for such purposes.

In recent years Swedish historians have taken a closer look at the emigrant agents to evaluate their significance in the emigration process. Their studies reach this conclusion: neither the agent nor their "product," transatlantic transport, had any independent impact on the extent of emigration. Once the transport market had been created, companies were largely dependent upon the pull- and push-factors in both countries as a means of maintaining their sales. The same is true of the shipping lines' ticketpricing policies. Public demand and emigrant volume alone determined what prices would be in effect, not the other way around. As a rule, prices increased during periods of peak emigration but decreased during periods of low emigration.

Much has been said here of the ways in which Swedish Americans came to the aid of American business interests in stimulating emigration. They also acted by themselves through their "America letters" and visits home. What motives did they have? On the surface, at least, their primary interests were both personal and emotional; to live together again with relatives and friends. Equally important, however, were the more materialistic considerations. The arrival of new Swedish settlers to land-grant regions in Minnesota, for example, had a positive effect on land values, provided a backbone for population growth, and stimulated the general economy. The pioneers won new customers for farm produce, household wares, and industrial crafts, and they found a ready supply of cheap and reliable manpower. The "stock effect," the attraction from Swedes already there, was – irrespective of whether Swedish Americans championed their own interests or those of the immigration industry – one of the most important pull-factors. The Swedish Americans were unexcelled as salesmen for America's open opportunities and as bearer of that inflammable disease known as "America fever."

Contrary to the American immigration promotion, the Canadian authorities played a central role in immigration policy. When Canada achieved dominion status in 1867, the new federal government undertook an active immigration policy, first directed toward Great Britain. In 1873 it also included the European continent in its campaign, but, as mentioned before, the Scandinavian emigrant agency was withdrawn in 1876 because of lack of success. In the beginning of the 1880s a new campaign was started on the continent and in the Scandinavian countries to get laborers to work on the Canadian Pacific Railroad and to attract settlers to the Canadian Northwest. In Scandinavia, as on the continent, the first and most important task was to get the New York steamship lines to work for Canada. The problem was that their agents were against the Canadian drive as they thought that the Canadian government would subsidize the Canadian lines so that they could cut the prices. To meet this problem, Canada offered the agents of the New York lines an extra commission for each emigrant to Canada. The agents promised to distribute the Canadian propaganda material.

Another big problem was the fact that the Canadian Northwest was an almost unknown and untried area for the presumptive Swedish emigrants. To overcome these difficulties, the Canadian campaign introduced Manitoba, Canada's foremost immigration area, not as a part of Canada, but as a northern part of the well-known American Middle West.

The early emigrants' interest in the immigration promotion, which had been so typical in the early American immigration history, is also seen in Canada. The leaders of the many Swedish colonies out in the prairies of Manitoba and Saskatchewan in the 1880s and 1890s distributed, with federal help, pamphlets and newspapers to Sweden and to Swedes in the United States. They also sent "return men" to do propaganda work in Sweden with federal backing. In 1896 the Laurier government started a very active immigration policy led by Clifford Sifton, the Minister of the Interior. One of the cornerstones of the new policy was a vigorous campaign in the United States to get farmers to the Canadian prairies. Here also a Swedish "Special Agent in the United States" worked; first with his office in New England, then in St. Paul, Minnesota. Through all this work, Canada, like the United States, at last got Swedish magnets from which the "stock effect" worked back in the old country.

In Sweden the propaganda distributed by the agents of the Atlantic lines was complemented by information from the "Canada Agency," a federal information center in Gothenburg. During the 1920s and 1930s the *Swedish American Line* maintained a close cooperation with Canadian immigration interests, especially the Canadian Pacific Railroad. The line's office in Gothenburg distributed news of jobs and land sent over from the SAL-agent in Winnipeg.

Australia needed a Swedish emigration-promoting organization of its own, if only because it had no chance to use the steamship lines' agents in Sweden. Until the turn of the century, the emigration promotion in Sweden was conducted variously by the different colonies, above all Queensland. In the 1890s an agent toured the Scandinavian countries. Thousands of booklets were circulated and advertisements were inserted in the press. Letters from successful colonists were printed and circulated. The lack of knowledge about Queensland was, however, a great disadvantage and false reports about the colony and the dangerous voyage were also spread by rival emigration or shipping agents working to attract Swedes to their own companies and lands.

From 1901 onward the Commonwealth Government handled the immigration promotion, for example during the Swedish drive in the 1960s and 1970s. The Canadian embassy and consulate then played the same role as the steamship agents had played for the American and Canadian propaganda.

Summary of the Pull-Factors

No special Swedish push-factor brought Swedes to any of the three immigration countries in particular. The different pull-factors, however, held different importance for the emigrants to the three receiving countries. Land was the most important factor for early emigrants to the United States and above all for the emigrants to Canada during the whole emigration period. Job opportunities were the most important factor to the Swedes going to the United States from 1890 and in a lesser degree to the emigrants to Canada during the interwar years. After World War II the possibility of employment was in the center for the emigrants to all three countries. Gold was an important pull-factor in Australia and for some early emigrants to the United States. Finally, assisted passage was in the center of the Australian immigration promotion and played an important role for the Swedish emigration to Australia in the 1960s and 1970s.

The organization of the emigration promotion was above all American, for both the United States and Canada. Up to World War I, they also used the same leading "salesmen," the steamship agents. As these lines did not sail to Australia, the Australian immigration promotors could not use their agents. Instead, the Australian promotion centered around its embassy and consulates. The stock effect from earlier emigrants played a big role for the U.S.

and Canadian immigration, while the longing for adventure perhaps was a stronger attraction of unknown, faraway Australia.

Transportation

The first emigrants who traveled in groups usually sailed directly to America from Sweden on sailing vessels. Passengers occupied the steerage section located directly above the cargo hold with its load of iron bars. Although there was no set time schedule, it usually took between one and a half to two months to reach America. From the middle of the 1860s steamship travel was the rule. The standard route for Swedish emigrants was by sea from Gothenburg to the English port city of Hull, by railroad from Hull to Liverpool and, after several days delay, by sea from Liverpool to the major immigrant harbors of New York, Boston, and Quebec. The voyage from Gothenburg to Hull lasted three days, the Atlantic crossing ten to twelve.

It was not until 1915 that the *Swedish American Line* opened a direct service route between Gothenburg and New York. From that time on the liners "Stockholm," "Kungsholm," and "Gripsholm" assumed major control of the Swedish emigrant traffic. A combination of canal boats, river steamers, and railroads carried the early immigrants from the east coast of the American continent to destinations farther west. From the mid-1860s, however, the railroads dominated, offering direct connections between New York and Chicago by special emigrant trains. For most Swedes, Chicago was the great transit station on the road west, but those who settled there soon transformed it into the world's second largest Swedish city.

Before World War I, most Swedish emigrants to Canada went on the steamers of the English and American New York lines and from New York by rail to Canada. Some Swedes – but not so many as the Norwegians – used the Canadian Allan line to Quebec. After World War I, the emigrants used the *Swedish American Line.* After World War II they went direct from Sweden by air. The Swedish Americans bound for the Canadian prairies went north by wagon trails, railway, and later by car.

That quite a lot of the Swedish immigrants worked for their passage over to Australia as seamen on Swedish or British ships is obvious, especially in the early days. During the goldrush, for instance, port authorities reported whole crews and captains leaving their ships. The immigrants who paid their voyages or got assisted passages went from Hamburg, later on from Liverpool. Up to the turn of the century the sailing vessels dominated. The normal route was Liverpool-Cape of Good Hope-Melbourne/Sydney. After having delivered the immigrants in Australia the ships took in new cargoes in East Asia, which they brought home via Cape Horn. Using the "Roaring Forties" the clippers made the trip to Australia in two to three months. In the 1880s emigrant steamers going through the Suez Canal lowered the time of the voyage to forty-five days. The Swedish emigrants with assisted passage in the 1970s went by chartered Boeing 707s which brought them to Sydney in less than twenty-four hours.

Remigration

Due to the rural and family-oriented character of early Swedish emigration to the United States there was little remigration to Sweden up until the 1880s. After that, the pattern changed and the steady influx of working-class immigrants to American industries and urban centers accelerated the pace of remigration during the 1900s. Although it cannot compare with the trend among southern European immigrants, Swedish remigration stabilized at a relatively high level and finally surpassed emigration during the 1930s, when conditions improved in Sweden. The first regular statistics on Swedish remigration date from 1875. From that year up to 1930, around 175,000 persons, or roughly 18 percent of the emigrants during that period, returned home.

Basically, there were two categories of remigrants. The first had never planned to stay in America for any length of time but simply used the move as a means of finding temporary and well-paid jobs. Must of them intended to invest their earnings in a farm back home. The second category of remigrants was dramatically different from the first, both in terms of prospects and end results. Statistics show that they left America almost as soon as they arrived. Obviously, something had gone wrong with the American experiment: the adjustment to a new language, a new society, and a new labor market placed far more demands on them than they had expected or were able to meet.

Whatever the motives for remigration, the timing was generally the same. Peak years of emigration were always followed by a surge of remigration, and the American economic picture weighed heavily in the balance. The recessions and panics of 1884, 1893, 1903, and

1907 had a leveling effect on emigrant labor and generated major waves of remigration. That urban wage earners had a greater tendency to remigrate than self-sufficient farmers is not surprising, especially when one considers their overall mobility in American society.

In Sweden the greatest impact of remigration was felt in farming districts, as former emigrants tended to settle in their old parishes. Despite their contacts with American urban environment, the majority chose not to become city dwellers after their return to Sweden. Over two-thirds of the remigrants were men. In most cases, then, the journey home was a return to ordinary, everyday living but with the added seasoning of a few insightful years as an immigrant on another shore.

According to Swedish statistics, the remigration from Canada between 1921 and 1980 was more than one-third of the total emigration. Most spectacular was the high remigration in the 1930s, caused by the depression and the hard times on the Canadian prairies; it was more than eight times the emigration ratio in the same period. The remigration in the 1960s was also high – more than three-fourths of the emigration. As in Australia, this provides a good illustration of the high degree of mobility among the modern emigrants.

More than half of the emigrants to Australia returned to Sweden according to official Swedish statistics. This is a very high percentage compared with the United States and Canada. A great part, however, of the returning Swedish-Australians had emigrated after 1930. The high percentage of return migrants is in agreement with the modern emigrants' high mobility and, if they are excluded, the result is that 25 percent of the emigrants before the 1930s returned. Thus, the remigration of Swedes from Australia during the "classic" emigration period did not dramatically exceed the American picture.

5

Icelandic Emigration

HELGI SKÚLI KJARTANSSON

Outline of Events

Emigration was a relatively short-lived feature in Icelandic history, occurring mainly during the 33-year period 1873 to 1905. It was, however, quite intense at its peak periods; a total of 20 to 25 percent of the population emigrated, a figure that is comparable with the emigration from Britain or Sweden.

General Background

Iceland was at the time a Danish dependency, which gained limited autonomy in 1874 and Home Rule in 1904. Its population grew from 70,000 in 1870 to 85,000 in 1910, the increase occurring mainly after 1890.

A majority of this small population lived on scattered farms in sparsely settled areas. Agriculture, almost exclusively livestock raising, still supported more than 50 percent of the population in 1910. The growth sector of the economy was fisheries. Traditionally a secondary occupation of farmers and farmhands, fishing was gradually becoming concentrated in seaside villages. This urbanization was fueled by changing technology: the curing of fish instead of drying, the advent of sailing vessels in addition to rowing boats, and later (from about 1904) the gradual replacement of both by motorboats and steam trawlers. Despite this, towns and villages of one hundred inhabitants or more did not comprise 25 percent of the total population until 1905. Reykjavik was the only sizeable town. In 1905 it had 9,000 inhabitants while three other towns had only recently passed the 1,000 mark.

Until approximately 1890 Iceland had been considered an underdeveloped and impoverished backwater of the Danish kingdom. By the turn of the century its economy had become more dynamic, both wages and employment were on the increase, and the combined potential of sea, land, and hydroelectric resources were thought to offer the country a bright future.

The Course of Icelandic Emigration

Prior to 1873, overseas emigration had been a mere trickle. The Mormon religion had led a small number of converts to emigrate to Utah in the late 1850s, and efforts to organize mass emigration to Brazil in the early 1860s, although largely a failure, resulted in a few Icelandic pioneers there. It could be argued that Brazil diverted Icelandic attention from the standard destination of Scandinavian emigrants: the American Midwest. Not until 1870 did the first few Icelanders go to Wisconsin, to be followed in subsequent years by slowly increasing numbers of immigrants.

In 1873 emigration quite suddenly reached mass proportions, 5 per thousand, and averaged almost 6 per thousand over the following six years. At first the emigrants settled in groups in several places in the United States and Canada. From 1875, however, the great majority headed for "New Iceland," a settlement later incorporated into the Canadian province of Manitoba.

A lull in 1880 to 1881 was followed by a sudden surge of emigration in 1882 and even more in 1883 (some 20 per thousand). There was a clear connection with hardships caused by the extremely cold year of 1882, which was aggravated by a measles epidemic. By then many of the former emigrants had abandoned New Iceland and established Icelandic communities elsewhere in the American Midwest and the Canadian Prairie Provinces. Nevertheless, Winnipeg was the only town to develop an appreciable Icelandic population and it functioned as a center for Icelandic immigrants in both countries.

After another lull, Icelandic emigration reached its most intense phase during the years 1886 to 1889, averaging approximately 16 per thousand. Once again agricultural distress, caused by cold climatic conditions, was obviously a causal factor, even if those were the years of an international upswing in transatlantic migration. Emigration from Iceland remained considerable during subsequent years, reaching a new peak in 1893. It then dwindled to next to nothing in 1895 to 1896, showing a somewhat delayed reaction to the 1893 slump and subsequent depression in North America.

The last phase of mass emigration from Iceland occurred during the years 1900 to 1905. Its volume is less accurately known than the earlier phases, but it may have reached an average of 5 to 7 per thousand, with peaks of some 10 per thousand in 1900 and 1903.

Icelandic emigration reacted promptly to the 1906 to 1907 economic slump and only recovered to a fraction of its previous level in 1910 to 1914. Compared with the British Isles and Scandinavia, Icelandic emigration not only started late but declined rather early.

Aspects of Emigration

The abrupt rise of emigration to high levels made it hotly disputed in Iceland at the time. In the intensely nationalistic atmosphere of the early 1870s, before Iceland was granted its own constitution in 1874, emigrants were blamed for deserting their country and nation. Their spokesmen in turn interpreted emigration as a reaction to Danish misrule and emphasized the new opportunities it offered for the development of Icelandic nationality in a new continent. During the peak years of emigration, 1886 to 1893, public discussion of the subject flared again with many influential people showing open hostility to emigration.

In 1876 a law, modeled on Danish and Norwegian legislation, came into effect that regulated the activities of emigration agents. After repeated attempts by parliamentarians, its provisions were greatly strengthened in 1895. The new law aimed, for instance, to curtail the recruiting activities of Canadian representatives. The basic freedom to emigrate remained undisputed. The resumed mass migration in the early 1900s went relatively unnoticed or it was at least no longer considered a threat to the country. In 1903 the emigration law was relaxed again in recognition of the fact that it had not been enforced.

The composition of the Icelandic emigrant population exhibits the familiar characteristics of family migration: a high proportion of married couples and children (with the concomitant two-topped age distribution), single persons often traveling together with families (as servants or relatives), and a relatively normal distribution by age and sex. The shift toward individual migration was remarkably slow until after 1905. The average age of adult emigrants and the proportion married were only slightly reduced and children were correspondingly fewer.

A shift in the social composition of the emigrant group was more pronounced. During the first decade of mass emigration, the typical emigrants were rural families of substantial means; they were replaced by those less well-off such as cottagers, servants, and even paupers. Wage laborers from villages and towns also made up an increasing proportion of the emigrants. Cheaper transport and the availability of assistance – from relatives who had already emigrated or even from local authorities anxious to get rid of their paupers – made emigration more easily available. At the same time it had lost some of its appeal for those of higher social status.

The geographical distribution of emigration was uneven. It was most intense in the northeast while the south and the northwest were more lightly affected by emigration. Proximity to fishing regions and urban centers tended, other things being equal, to keep emigration at a low level. The geographical disparity was most evident during the early phases of mass migration; many areas were practically unaffected until after 1885.

In North America, the Canadian prairies attracted the great majority (perhaps as high as 90 percent) of Icelandic immigrants throughout the entire period. Originally connected with the short-lived vision of New Iceland as a second and more prosperous national homeland, the tradition persisted, aided until the early 1890s by various forms of Canadian government subsidies. Winnipeg remained the interim destination for many Icelanders where they would first become acquainted with the ways of the New World before trying their luck as prairie farmers, either south or north of the border.

Themes

Push- and Pull-Factors

Icelandic emigration was part and parcel of European overseas emigration; the general explanations of the latter, it terms of push, pull and intervening obstacles, apply to Iceland as well. Specific explanations may be offered for the timing of mass emigration from Iceland (ca. 1873 to 1905) and its great intensity, as well as for the details of its geographical and temporal pattern.

Population pressure as a push-factor will be discussed in the section on demography. It may be seen as a symptom of economic stagnation and late urbanization. These same factors account for the lack of variety of economic and social opportunities, which in its own right contributed to the push to emigrate.

In this connection the small size of Icelandic society must be kept in mind. As previously stated, overseas emigration from Iceland reached relatively high, and for a while very high, proportions; high proportions, it must be added, in comparison to much larger societies. It would be easy to find in several countries local populations of similar size to the entire Icelandic nation with a higher emigration rate. And it would be easier still to find regions with a similar economic structure and a much higher total out-migration. In Iceland emigration served purposes that in a peripheral region of a larger country would be partly served by internal migration toward the central areas. If we consider Iceland as a part of the Danish kingdom, its geographical remoteness and cultural separateness reduced migration toward the center of the kingdom and thus increased the intercontinental emigration potential. In this respect Iceland fits into the general Scandinavian pattern: emigration tended to be greatest in areas that enjoyed neither local urbanization nor proximity to regional or national urban centers.

Push-factors like population pressure, simple employment structure, slow economic growth, etc., form the background to the onset of mass emigration from Iceland; however, they do not explain its timing.

Aller Anfang ist schwer. In a new recruiting country emigration had to contend with the paucity of information, the lack of an emigrant tradition, the unavailability of suitable transport, and the absence of useful contacts in the receiving country. Conversely, ongoing emigration had a self-sustaining effect. It was the overcoming of initial obstacles rather than any sudden increase in the push-factors that resulted in mass emigration in the early 1870s.

Mass emigration from remote Iceland would scarcely have been possible before the age of steam. Not only did emigration depend on ocean liners for the Atlantic passage, but also on the cheap steam-powered freighters, which around 1870 became available for transport between Iceland and Europe.

Some information about emigration to North America must have been available to Icelanders through contact with Scandinavia and even Britain, although the Danes, with whom Icelanders had closest ties, were relatively late participants in the mass migration. Increasing trade with Norway in the 1860s and 1870s may have brought the prospect of emigration closer to the people of Iceland. The early preoccupation with Brazil acquainted people with the idea of emigration while diverting attention from North America. The early emigration to Utah was too distinct from ordinary emigration to be of much importance, but small-scale emigration to the United States from 1870 to 1872 was immediately followed by an increased flow of information through letters and newspapers.

It was perhaps only a matter of time before Icelandic emigration would reach mass proportions. That question was decided by the Allan Line when it started to offer organized transport from Iceland to North America in 1873. Transportation (see the following separate section) was subsequently a key factor in the emigration history of Iceland.

To judge from the overall number of immigrants, the "pull" of North America, and Canada in particular, was at a low ebb in the mid-1870s due to the economic depression. Why should the Icelanders, previously so immune to emigration, take to it so easily at such a time? And why did Canada, so unpopular with immigrants in general, become their preferred destination? The depression may be interpreted as an indirect cause of Icelandic emigration. The failure of ordinary emigrant traffic made shipping lines all the more interested in new recruiting grounds. And the young Dominion of Canada, with its newly acquired western lands and chronic population drain to the south, was desperate for immigrants. In those circumstances, the Canadian Allan Line cooperated with its government in a recruiting effort, including promotion campaigns and price cutting.[1] The Scandinavian market was given special attention, which led to the successful Icelandic venture.

With the Allan Line the Icelandic emigrants had to travel via Quebec and in 1873 their guide, the Allan agent, dissuaded most of them from continuing their journey to the United States. If they settled in Canada, at least for the time being, they could take advantage of subsidized fares, free inland transport, and a more generous homestead offer than was available in the United States. The prospect of a separate settlement in Nova Scotia or New Iceland soon became a specific "pull"-factor in favor of Canada. The Canadian incentives were mostly of a temporary nature, but they succeeded in establishing a tradition of emigration to Canada, unlike the tradition of emigration to the United States, which Canada had to struggle against in order to attract emigrants from most other countries. The Icelandic-Canadian population became a pull-factor in its own right. Canadian authorities, the province of Manitoba as well as the central government, later supported promotion activities in Iceland. In 1893 Manitoba backed a transport offer that definitely increased emigration from Iceland (see the section on transportation

1. Norman Macdonald, *Canada: Immigration and Colonization* 1841–1903 (Aberdeen 1966), 31ff, 46ff, 108, 110ff, 125; Kristian Hvidt, *Flugten til Amerika eller Drivkraefter i masseudvandringen fram Danmark 1868–1914* (Aarhus 1971), 366ff, 386ff, 461–467.

below). This happened during a downturn of the business cycle and thus recalls the conditions in 1873.

At its outset, emigration from Iceland had been less sensitive to the business cycle than emigration in general, not only because the inexperienced Icelanders lacked information and understanding but also because they did not intend to seek employment in the towns. They planned to take up farming in more or less self-sufficient settlements where they would be less concerned with business conditions. They discovered soon enough the importance of paid employment for newly arrived immigrants. Immigration from Iceland did, however, remain rurally oriented to a large extent, making Canada better suited for Icelanders than for most other immigrant groups.

In Icelandic historiography, emigration is traditionally explained with reference to push-factors only. One factor often mentioned is the opposition to Danish rule. This is attested to by contemporary evidence but mainly in a polemical context, which makes apologetic explanations rather suspect. Political frustrations may have had some effect at the beginning of emigration from Iceland but scarcely after 1874, when a new constitution for Iceland ushered in a decade of political calm. An attempt to make the Canadian constitution a model for the Icelandic Home Rule movement met with electoral disaster in 1890, indicating that Canada appealed to Icelandic emigrants for reasons other than political.

Natural adversity, especially climatic conditions, are more definitely connected with emigration from Iceland. The 1860s were a difficult decade in Iceland. The climate was unusually cold, the country was plagued by a sheep epidemic, and cod catches were rather low. Around 1870 things took a turn for the better and mass emigration began during a generally favorable period. There were localized exceptions: a cold spring in 1872 brought hardship to farmers in a region that contributed many of the emigrants in subsequent years, and a volcanic eruption in 1875 damaged many farms in the northeast, with an unmistakable effect upon the record emigration of the following year. After the eruption, many families fled from the afflicted area to the adjoining region of Vopnafjördur. The displaced families triggered the mass emigration from the region in 1876, which would become a local tradition; for decades Vopnafjördur had the highest emigration rate in the country.

During the 1880s hardship inflicted by severe cold and the repeated encroachment of sea ice, as well as the measles epidemic of 1882, were undoubtedly important causes of the high level of emigration. In the late 1880s agricultural distress in Iceland coincided with favorable economic conditions in North America and a period of cheap fares from Iceland (see the section on transportation below), resulting in record emigration.

The accelerating development of Icelandic fisheries and increasing urbanization after the turn of the century reduced the push to emigrate, and a climate of optimism following Home Rule in 1904 doubtless contributed to the sharp reduction in emigration after 1905.

Demography[2]

Population growth in Iceland from the eighteenth century was characterized by a pronounced cyclical pattern. Around 1830 a period of growth coincided with favorable agricultural conditions. From 1847 to 1858, when large cohorts were coming of age, there was again considerable population growth, followed by a period of stagnation.

Population pressure is evident in the increasing size of households (to a maximum of 7.5 in 1870) and decreasing nuptiality. Thus, the proportion of married women twenty-five to twenty-nine years old fell from 46 percent in 1850 to 33 percent in 1880. Mass emigration began as large cohorts were once more reaching marriageable age. Such an age distribution may be regarded as one of the push-factors in Icelandic emigration.

There is an interesting contrast between the agricultural regions of southern Iceland and of the northeast. The former, already densely populated, had a history of slow population growth, late marriage, and a negative migration balance. Here the response to population pressure after about 1850 was a further reduction of nuptiality and its emigration rate remained consistently low (with the exception of the Westman Islands where a successful Mormon mission caused considerable emigration). In contrast, the northeastern parts of Iceland, more sparsely settled in the early decades of the century, had an established pattern of positive migration balance, early marriage, and considerable population growth. When agricultural expansion reached its limits (in the late 1850s, the 1880s brought pronounced contraction) the inhabitants of this region

2. For a more detailed discussion see appendix to Helgi Skůli Kjartansson, "Emigrant Fares and Emigration from Iceland to North America, 1874–1893", *The Scandinavian Economic History Review* 27, no. 1 (1980).

persisted in relatively early marriage. It would subsequently prove to be the most emigration-prone part of the country.

Female Emigration

Contrary to what amounts almost to a law of long-distance migration, women form the majority of the recorded Icelandic emigrants. A register of 13,821 emigrants from 1870 to 1925 – including perhaps 85 percent of total emigration – shows 50.8 percent as being female. For the pioneering period 1870 to 1880 the proportion is slightly lower, only 49.5 percent, but rises to 51.3 percent during the years 1881 to 1895, the period of emigration at its most intense. From 1896 to 1910, when emigration was in its receding phase and one might expect a preponderance of young single men, it is still 51.2 percent. One may suspect a sampling error here, as the figures for the third period rely only on parish registers with imperfect coverage. Towns and fishing regions are only minimally covered and migrant laborers tend to be omitted. It must be accepted, nevertheless, that women were as numerous as men among rural emigrants up until the end of mass emigration, even though other signs of family migration, such as the proportion of married people and the number of children, were less pronounced than they had been during the earlier periods.

Children, as might be expected, are equally divided between the sexes. In fact, girls comprise exactly 50 percent of emigrants zero to fourteen years of age. It was quite common in Iceland, especially among the poorer classes, for children to leave their parents at a young age, and some were left behind permanently when the parents emigrated. This does not, however, seem to have caused any imbalance between the sexes. In the age group fifteen to nineteen, the boys are slightly in a majority with only 49.1 percent female. This is caused by a marked imbalance during the years 1870 to 1880 (44 percent female) and thus not connected with the familiar preponderance of young men in the later stages of emigration.

Among adult emigrants the proportion of women increases in older age groups: twenty to twenty-nine years old, 50.4 percent; thirty to forty-nine years old, 51.3 percent; and fifty and over, 54.7 percent. The corresponding percentages for the population as a whole are even higher. Men have, in other words, been marginally more prone to emigrate, but the unequal sex ratio in the country gives women the majority among the emigrants.

Perhaps the limited degree of urbanization can explain the high and stable proportion of women among Icelandic emigrants. In short distance, rural-urban migration women, especially younger women, tend to be overrepresented. This was the case in Iceland as well, with the exception that Icelandic towns were so few and their capacity for absorption so limited prior to 1910 that emigration, in some respects, usurped the demographic role of urbanization.

Transportation

Plans to emigrate to Brazil depended on assisted passage (via Hamburg) and failed because of transportation problems.

Prior to 1873 emigrants to North America traveled as ordinary passengers to Scandinavia or Britain where they could buy tickets as emigrants, and a small number continued to travel in this fashion. In order to evade the strict legal controls imposed on them in 1895, emigration agencies ostensibly sent their customers to Britain as ordinary passengers.

In late 1872 the Canadian Allan Line established the first emigration agency in Iceland. This must be seen as an important cause of the sudden onset of mass emigration the following year.[3] Emigration became cheaper, more convenient, more easily accessible, and, of course, better promoted. For the period 1876 to 1893 ticket copies – together with other archival material, advertisement, and newspaper coverage – give a relatively complete picture of the operations of emigrant agencies.[4] The Allan Line was the only one with an agent in Iceland until 1878, when the Anchor Line registered an agent. He seems to have done little if any business, but a more vigorous successor managed to secure a majority of the 1884 emigrants for Anchor. During the years 1885 to 1889 Allan again carried the majority of Icelandic emigrants, and Anchor closed down its agency in 1890. It was soon replaced by an agency for the Dominion Line, which held a minor share of the market from 1891 to 1894. Finally, the small Beaver Line entered the market and dominated it in 1893 and, probably, 1894. Thereafter, Beaver and Dominion withdrew, leaving to Allan the few passengers that were still emigrating. In the early 1900s Allan was still the only emigrant line visibly operating in the country.

3. Cf. Helgi Skúli Kjartansson, "The Onset of Emigration from Iceland" in *Nordic Population Mobility: Comparative Studies of selected Parishes in the Nordic Countries* 1850–1900, Bo Kronborg, et al., eds., American Studies in Scandinavia 9, nos. 1–2 (Oslo, etc. 1977).

4. The following discussion is mostly summarized from Kjartansson, 1980.

The passengers of the Allan Line traveled via Glasgow and Quebec; Anchor's via Glasgow and New York, and Dominion's via Liverpool and Quebec. Beaver, on the other hand, provided direct passage from Iceland to Quebec in 1893. Allan had twice (1874 and 1876) sent its own ships to Iceland but only for the journey to Scotland. Ordinarily, agents would arrange for their customers to be carried to Leith or Granton as steerage (third class) passengers, either by the scheduled packetboat or by freighter or cattle boat. Although the ocean fare was decided by competition and cartel agreements between the shipping lines, it seems that the Icelandic agencies could adjust the Iceland-Scotland fare to local market conditions, keep it high in the absence of competition, and reduce it when necessary, as the Allan agency did after 1885 under pressure from Anchor's lower prices. Thus, the record emigration of the late 1880s was encouraged by fare reductions, which lasted longer in Iceland than elsewhere. Allan's Quebec fare, for instance, came down from 128 crowns from 1877 to 1883 to 90 crowns from 1887 to 1888.

The boost given to emigration in 1893 was again prompted by competition between shipping lines. The Beaver Line, not a member of the prevailing European shipping cartel, undersold its competitors and offered a highly convenient direct passage to Quebec. Not only did it offer the cheapest fare on record (Quebec 80 crowns), it also offered poor emigrants tickets on credit, the prompt payment of which was guaranteed by the province of Manitoba. The province also sent a recruiting officer, who naturally promoted Beaver, to Iceland. The Dominion of Canada had since 1886 employed a recruiting officer in Iceland who cooperated with the Allan agency until 1891, then tried Dominion with little success in 1892, and now turned to Beaver.

Emigration from Iceland was mainly limited to a short summer season in June and July. Each agency sent its customers in one or two main parties led by a guide and interpreter. The emigrant groups were collected by a ship that called at a number of ports along the coast. The fare was the same from all ports of call. In 1884 emigration agencies in Iceland started to sell rail tickets to Canadian destinations. After that, most of the tickets preserved are to Winnipeg. In 1884 and 1885 Anchor managed to offer Winnipeg tickets cheaper than Allan, despite the inland journey from New York, which was slightly more expensive than from Quebec.

The Icelandic Immigrants

Settlement The first Icelandic emigrants intended to establish their own rural settlements where they would be able to keep their language and customs and live in relative isolation from the host society. They soon realized that the American Middle West offered no scope for such settlements, nor did the Canadian province of Ontario, which received most of the Icelandic immigrants of 1873 and 1874. The alternatives were either integration – for reasons of language and religion, preferably in existing communities of Norwegian or other Scandinavian immigrants – or exclusive settlements in less-developed regions.

One such region was the newly purchased Alaska, which President Grant seriously considered colonizing with Icelandic immigrants.[5] The plan foundered due to a lack of funds. The province of Nova Scotia provided assistance to establish an Icelandic settlement, which was soon abandoned as unsuitable. The successful one was "New Iceland," established in 1875 with assistance from the Government of Canada on Dominion land and later incorporated into the province of Manitoba. The site was considered suitable for livestock raising, with fishing as a sideline as in the Icelandic tradition. Immigrants who had already settled elsewhere flocked to New Iceland, and for the next few years, most newcomers headed there. The colony was, however, beset by calamities (an epidemic, floods) and around 1880 it was, for a while, largely abandoned. The Icelandic immigrants subsequently formed several less exclusive rural communities in the grain-growing regions north and south of the U.S. border. At the same time, it was becoming increasingly common for immigrants to settle, at least temporarily, as urban wage earners.[6]

Integration As other Scandinavians (definitely white and Protestant), Icelandic immigrants were relatively well received in North America. Despite their early tendency to settle in groups, or even to form exclusive settlements, they adapted easily to an English-speaking educational system, perhaps aided by a tradition of literacy. Icelandic Canadians of the second and third generations were considered well-integrated; they spoke good English and a high

5. Hjörtur Pálsson, *Alaskaför Jóns Ólafssonar 1874* (Reykjavik 1974) (with a summary in English).
6. See a more detailed description in Kjartansson, 1977, 90ff.

proportion of them married a partner of British background or applied for Canadian citizenship.

If Icelandic Canadians and Americans did preserve their ethnic identity remarkably well, considering their small numbers, it may be interpreted as a sign of pride by a successfully integrated ethnic group rather than as a compensation for maladjustment.

Return Migration No direct statistics are available on Icelandic remigration. Registration of births and deaths, together with decennial population censuses, allow reasonable estimates of net migration. Yet, the unknown balance of migration to and from Scandinavia (perhaps turning from negative to positive) and the uncertain emigration figures after 1893, make it risky to estimate the level of remigration. It appears to have been minimal prior to 1880, but during the decade 1880 to 1890 there is a surplus equivalent to around 15 percent of emigration. This ought to show the combined effect of transatlantic return migration and net immigration from Scandinavia (Norway?). It is also possible that the coverage of the census was better in the latter year. The 1901 census shows a much smaller discrepancy, 10 to 15 percent of the now reduced emigration, although the actual return migration should have increased from the previous decade. Finally, a census in 1910 suggests a large increase in return migration. Annual population estimates, although less reliable than the decennial censuses, indicate that return migration reached a peak during the 1906 to 1908 depression.

Emigrants and Capital There were no wealthy people among the Icelandic emigrants. Well-to-do farmers took some funds with them to America, especially in the early stages of emigration; yet, most Icelandic farmers were tenants, with only their livestock to sell, and an increasing portion of the emigrants were poor people. All things considered, Icelandic emigrants must have left with much less than their proportional share of the national wealth.

Return migrants can scarcely have brought back much capital either, as the less fortunate immigrants would be most likely to give up and go back, provided they could raise money for their fares.

The more prosperous ones might have sent back money, either to provide for poor relations in Iceland or to pay their fares to America. Contemporary sources regarded this money flow as significant, but quantified estimates are few and unreliable. Prepaid tickets were illegal in Iceland as they were not issued by licensed emigration agencies. Benefactors would therefore send money rather than tickets and, thus, leave no traces in our sources.

Scholarship and Literature

In the previous discussion, mention was made primarily of works in English, or that include a summary in English, omitting important works in Icelandic. Even the history of Icelandic immigrants in North America, which has been the subject of more extensive writing than Icelandic emigration, has mostly been written in Icelandic.[7]

The pioneering work on the history of Icelandic emigration was written by an Icelandic-Canadian author, Borsteinn B. Borsteinsson, and published (in Icelandic) in 1940.[8] Among Icelandic academic historians the subject has attracted attention since the 1970s. Docent Bergsteinn Jònsson of the University of Iceland has done research in North America and contributed to the history of Icelandic emigration and Icelandic immigrants in America.[9] Professor Bòrhallur Vilmundarson directed the Icelandic contribution to the Nordic Emigration Research Project 1970 to 1977.[10] Two of his students participated in the project. The late Jùnìus Kristinsson wrote his graduate thesis in history in 1972 on emigration from the district of Vopnafjördur in northeastern Iceland.[11] He later published a unique work, a nominal register of 14,268 Icelandic emigrants.[12] A preliminary register (of 13,821 emigrants), compiled

7. Icelandic immigration receives a considerable treatment in Macdonald. Some authors of Icelandic origin have been able to draw upon the extensive literature in the ethnic language; see Wilhelm Kristjansson, *The Icelandic People in Manitoba: A Manitoba Saga* (Winnipeg 1965); Thorstina Walters, *Modern Sagas: The Story of the Icelanders in North America* (Fargo 1953); and V.J. Eylands, *Lutherans in Canada* (Winnipeg 1945). Pålsson, *Alaskaför Jòns Olafssonar* describes the attempt in 1874 to make Alaska a "New Iceland."

8. Borsteinn B. Borsteinsson, *Saga Islendinga ì* Vesturheimi I (Reykjavik 1940).

9. See, for example, his articles (with summaries in English) in *Saga* 13 (1975), 15 (1977) and 18 (1980).

10. See Sune Åkerman, "A Brief History of a Research Project" in Kronborg, et al. eds., *Nordic Population Mobility*.

11. Unpublished. An unpublished abridged translation, "Emigration from Vopnafjördur 1873–93" (Reykjavik 1973) is utilized by Andreas A. Svalestuen, "Five Local Studies of Nordic Emigration and Migration" in Kronborg, et al., eds., *Nordic Population Mobility*.

12. Jùnìus Kristinsson, *Vesturfaraskrà 1870–1914: A Record of Emigrants from Iceland to America 1870–1914* (Reykjavik 1983), published posthumously with an introduction in Icelandic and English by Professor Sveinbjörn Rafnsson.

for the Nordic Emigration Research Project, provided the statistical basis for my own graduate work on Icelandic emigration.[13]

Statistics quoted in the previous discussion are derived from the earlier register. It is based upon two sets of sources: parochial registers, which in principle should state the destination of everyone permanently leaving the parish, and passenger lists, partly supported by preserved copies of the actual tickets. After 1893 only parochial registration is available and its coverage becomes less and less comprehensive. As a consequence, the last phase of mass migration is the one most imperfectly documented. Canadian immigration statistics, which from 1900 count Icelanders separately from Danes, now replace Icelandic sources as the main records on Icelandic emigration.

13. Unpublished thesis (1976). See further Kjartansson, "Onset of Emigration"; Idem, "Emigrant Fares."

6

German Transatlantic Emigration in the Nineteenth and Twentieth Centuries

KLAUS J. BADE

Courses of Historical Development

Emigration before the Mass Exodus

In 1983 a German-American tricentenary was celebrated on both sides of the Atlantic: the United States and the Federal Republic of Germany put on extravagant events to commemorate the arrival of the thirteen Krefeld families, a total of 33 people, in Philadelphia in October 1683.[1] They had gone in search of a homeland that would allow the unhindered development of their religious beliefs, having taken up William Penn's offer to join the colony later known as Pennsylvania. There they founded the settlement "Germantown," which is now a part of the city of Philadelphia.[2]

The significance of this German-American celebration in 1983 was first and foremost a political symbol of transatlantic partnership. On both sides there had been conscious efforts to overcome contemporary irritations in German-American relations through this well-known historical event, celebrated for the first time in the

1. For comprehensive surveys and research reports see K.J. Bade, "Trends and Issues of Historical Migration Research in the Federal Republic of Germany," *Migration. A European Journal of International Migration and Ethnic Relations* 6 (1989) 7–27, n. 1. I thank Walter D. Kamphoefner who had a critical look through these lines. German and American historians met at two conferences in Krefeld and Philadelphia. While the proceedings of the Krefeld conference remain unpublished, the revised version of the papers presented in Philadelphia has been published as F. Trommler and J. McVeigh, eds., *America and the Germans: An Assessment of a 300-Year-History*, 2 vols. (Philadelphia 1985); German edition: F. Trommler, ed., *Amerika und die Deutsche Bestandsaufnahme einer 300-jährigen Geschichte* (Opladen 1986).

2. F. Nieper, *Die ersten deutschen Auswanderer von Krefeld nach Pennsylvanien. Ein Bild aus der religiösen Ideengeschichte des 17. und 18. Jahrhunderts* (Neukirchen 1940).

United States in 1833 as "Deutscher Tag."[3] In fact, the year 1683 was not the correct date for the 300-year anniversary of German emigration to America as the Krefeld families were not the first Germans in North America. The year 1681 however, was a relevant point in the history of German emigration to North America for another reason: the emigration of the Krefeld families marked the start of German group migration and community settlement in the New World.

Estimates of the number of Germans who may have immigrated during the colonial period range from about 65,000 to about 100,000. At the time of the American Revolution, approximately 225,000 German-Americans made up about 8 to 9 percent of the total population in the colonies and, according to the first U.S. census in 1790, about a twelfth of the U.S. population was of German descent.[4]

The bond uniting these groups of immigrants was their essentially religious or utopian social outlook. It was mainly as a result of William Penn's campaign in Germany that Pennsylvania (where about half of all German-Americans settled in the eighteenth century) became the main destination point for group migrations of religious dissidents and separatists of the most varied persuasions; from there they spread further afield. This was, for example, true of the Westphalian "Tunkers," a separatist group related to the Mennonites who immigrated in 1719 and 1729. They founded communities first in Pennsylvania and later in Maryland, Virginia, Ohio, Indiana, Kansas, Missouri, and Texas. Roots of such religious group migrations can be traced well into the nineteenth century: in 1805, some of Georg Rapp's supporters ("Rappists") founded Harmony in Pennsylvania, then settled in Indiana (New Harmony), and finally moved back to Pennsylvania (Economy). Under the leadership of Joseph Bäumler, Swabian separatists came to Ohio (Zoar) in 1817, while in 1843 the Amanites settled near Buffalo and later in

3. See for example G. Moltmann, "Antiamerikanismus in der Bundesrepublik: Eine Legende?," *Amerikastudien/American Studies* 31 (1986), 363–70; idem., "Deutscher Anti-Amerikanismus heute und früher" in *Vom Sinn der Geschichte*, O. Franz, ed. (Stuttgart 1976) 85–105; idem, "Der 'Deutsche Tag' in Amerika: Geschichte und Gegenwart" in *The Transit of Civilization from Europe to America. Essays in Honor of Hans Galinsky*, W. Herget and K. Ortseifen, eds. (Tübingen 1986), 231–48; cf. the essays of K. Sontheimer, T. Sommer, and F. Stern in Trommler, eds., *Amerika und die Deutschen*, 437–90.

4. W. Helbich, W.D. Kamphoefner, and U. Sommer, eds., *Briefe aus Amerika. Deutsche Auswanderer schreiben aus der Neuen Welt, 1830–1930* (München 1988), 11; G. Moltmann, "300 Years of German Emigration to North America" in *Germans to America: 300 Years of Immigration, 1683–1983*, idem, ed. (Stuttgart 1982), 9.

Iowa (Amana). As late as 1854, Ambrosius Oschwald and 113 of his separatistic supporters finally left Germany and founded St. Nazianz in the "wilderness" between Milwaukee and Green Bay. Group migrations faded away and were replaced by chain migrations after the rise of the social mass movement that became characteristic of German transatlantic migration in the second half of the nineteenth century.[5]

The primarily religiously oriented group migrations leading to community settlements were without doubt of significance in the German emigration to North America in the colonial era. Overinterpretation of religious motives should, however, be avoided: "The motives for emigration were always complex, economic and social problems were always important, and often decisive." In fact, growing numbers of emigrants without any perceivable religious motivation or even any group membership had already found their way to the New World in the eighteenth century. That was above all true of those for whom the "Redemptioner" system, which can be traced from 1728 through the American Revolution and into the 1820s, opened the way across the Atlantic. According to reliable estimates, a half to two-thirds of the German immigrants in British North America were "Redemptioners." There were even cases of mass migration leading thousands of Germans to North America in the eighteenth century (1709, 1749 to 1752, 1757, 1759, 1782). It was not until the first half of the nineteenth century that this level was to any great extent exceeded.[6]

In the early nineteenth century, however, the United States was still not the principal country of immigration for Germans. Not until

5. G. Moltmann, "German Migration to America in the Colonial Period and the Redemptioner System" in idem, ed., *Germans to America*, 26–35; H. Wellenreuther, "Vorstellungen, Traditionen, Erwartungen. Die deutschen Einwanderer in der englischen Kolonialgesellschaft in Pennsylvanien 1700–1765" in Trommler, ed., *Amerika und die Deutschen*, 107–26; H. Schempp, *Gemeinschaftssiedlungen auf religiöser und weltanschaulicher Grundlage* (Tübingen 1969); H. Lehmann, "Endzeiterwartung und Auswanderung. Der württembergische Pietist Johann Michael Hahn und Amerika" in *Geschichte und Gegenwart. Festschrift für K.D. Erdmann*, H. Boockmann, J. Jürgensen, and G. Stoltenberg, eds. (Neumünster 1980), 177–94; F.S. Beck, *Christian Communists in America. A History of the Colony of Saint Nazianz, Wisconsin, during the Pastorate of its Founder, Father Ambros Oschwald, 1854–1873* (St. Paul 1959); H. Treiber, "'Wie man wird, was man ist'. Lebensweg und Lebenswerk des badischen Landpfarrers Ambros Oschwald (1801–1873) im Erwartungshorizont chiliastischer Prophezeiungen," *Zeitschrift für die Geschichte des Oberrheins* 136 (1988), 293–348; Helbich, Kamphoefner, and Sommer, eds., *Briefe aus Amerika*, 15ff.

6. Helbich, Kamphoefner, and Sommer, eds., *Briefe aus Amerika*, 29 (quotation), 32; Moltmann, "300 Years," 10; G. Moltmann, "The Migration of German Redemptioners to North America, 1720–1820" in *Colonialism and Migration. Indentured*

the 1830s did continental emigration from Germany (especially to Russia and into the countries of the Habsburg monarchy) fade in importance compared with the growing transatlantic mass emigration, mainly directed to the United States. As G. Moltmann pointed out, in fact another, more important date in the history of German emigration could have been commemorated in 1983: the defeat of the Turks near Vienna (Battle of Kahlenberg 1683), which reopened Hungary for the big stream of German settlers. This continental emigration to eastern and southeastern Europe was to dominate the history of German emigration until the time of transatlantic mass emigration.[7]

The "Proletarian Mass Migration"

German transatlantic migration was part of the "old" immigration from western, central, and northern Europe, which decreased in importance compared with the new immigration from southern, southeastern and eastern Europe starting in the early 1890s and reaching its climax in 1910. As Figure 6.1 clearly shows, within transatlantic emigration from early nineteenth- to early twentieth-century Germany, four distinct "emigration waves" can be distinguished: the first, from 1846 to 1857, reaching its climax in 1854; the second lasted from 1864 to 1873; the third from 1880 to 1893; and the final one took place in 1923.[8] The principal destination of German transatlantic

---

Labour before and after Slavery, P.C. Emmer, ed. (Dordrecht 1986), 105–22; cf. W. v. Hippel, *Auswanderung aus Südwestdeutschland. Studien zur württembergischen Auswanderung und Auswanderungspolitik im 18. und 19. Jahrhundert* (Stuttgart 1984), 35ff., 41, 132; H. Fenske, "International Migration: Germany in the 18th Century," *CEH* 13, 4 (1980), 332–47.

7. Moltmann, "300 Years," 10; cf. v. Hippel, *Auswanderung*, 38ff.

8. K.J. Bade, "German Emigration to the United States and Continental Immigration to Germany in the Late 19th and Early 20th Centuries," *CEH* 13, 4 (1980), 348–77 (table p. 354); for the following see also: K.J. Bade, "Die deutsche überseeische Massenauswanderung im 19. und frühen 20. Jahrhundert: Bestimmungsfaktoren und Entwicklungslinien" in *Auswanderer – Wanderarbeiter – Gastarbeiter: Bevölkerung, Arbeitsmarkt und Wanderung in Deutschland seit der Mitte des 19. Jahrhunderts*, idem, ed., 2 vols., 2d ed. (Ostfildern 1986) 1: 259–99.

The substantial fluctuations in the emigration curve may be fitted into the popular and current picture of "emigration waves." This picture may be misleading, however, and has already led to miscalculations. Among these are tendencies to explain the abrupt rise of such a wave as caused by a putative intensification of constellations of push and pull at the same time. This is problematic, because emigration is not an event but is often a medium, if not a long-term process. It began with the stimulation of latent interest in emigration. The subsequent decision to emigrate was often determined by the turn of events. It was, furthermore, not unusual for a period of time, perhaps several years, to elapse before the decision was finally acted upon.

emigration was North America, constituting about 85 percent of the first emigration wave, 98 percent of the second, and 92 percent of the third. Canada, Brazil, Argentina, and Australia followed at great distance. Statistical evidence estimates German transatlantic emigration between 1847 and 1914 to have been barely 4.5 million people; of these, nearly 4 million (89 percent) went to the United States, about 86,500 (1.9 percent) to Canada, about 56,000 (1.3 percent) to Australia, and about 89,000 (2 percent) to Brazil. From 1871 to 1914 about 24,400 (0.9 percent) of the 2.9 million emigrants of these decades went to Argentina (no data available for 1847 to 1870).

Between 1816 and 1914 about 5.5 million and after 1914 another 1.5 million Germans emigrated to the United States. From 1820 to 1860, Americans of German descent formed the second largest ethnic group in the United States after the Irish, and from 1861 to 1890 even the largest group. As to overall figures of European immigrants since 1820 (over 46 million to date) the Germans have constituted the largest proportion with about 15 percent.[9] Apart from the rapid increase in the number of emigrants to about 20,000 in 1816 to 17, as a result of a poor harvest and a famine, numbers remained relatively low until the mid-1830s.[10] After the sharp rise in emigration figures between the mid-1830s and the mid-1840s, transatlantic emigration can be characterized as a "proletarian mass migration," conditioned primarily by socioeconomic factors.[11] As a mass movement, it must be seen against a background of population growth, profound changes in the social institutions, and a rapid economic transformation.

Population growth, rationalization of agriculture, and laissez-

---

There was, in fact, only one large "emigration wave" from the rise of transatlantic mass emigration during the 1840s until its final decline in the early 1890s'; this "wave" comprised various peaks and sudden breaks caused by disruptive events, which – to stay with this common picture – could be classified as "thoughts." The clearance of such a congestion of the emigration stream could provoke a boom in emigration appearing as a "wave," upon which decisions made years before could have an effect.

The ups and downs of the curve during the second emigration wave are due to statistical problems; see G. Moltmann, ed., *Deutsche Amerikaauswanderung. Sozialgeschichtliche Beiträge* (Stuttgart 1976), 201.

9. Moltmann, "300 Years," 9.

10. See G. Moltmann, ed., *Aufbruch nach Amerika. Friedrich List und die Auswanderung aus Baden und Württemberg 1816/17. Dokumentation einer sozialen Bewegung* (Tübingen 1979); cf. H. Focke, "Friedrich List und die südwestdeutsche Amerikaauswanderung 1817–1846" in Moltmann, ed., *Deutsche Amerikaauswanderung*, 63–100.

11. I. Ferenczi, "Proletarian Mass Migrations, 19th and 20th Centuries" in *International Migrations* I, F.W. Willcox, ed. (New York 1929), 81ff.

faire economics, during and after the Napoleonic wars, worked together to turn peasants into farm laborers, to overcrowd the towns, and to effect chronic underemployment. The still largely pre-industrial labor market could not absorb the jobless, and industry, still in its infancy, provided far too few opportunities. These long-term processes were highlighted by hunger crises in about 1830 and before 1848. The combined result was relative overpopulation, albeit with regional differences, and a steep rise in emigration. The main demo-economic push-factor derived from the difference between population increase and economic growth during the change from an agrarian to an industrial society. Hence, the million-fold emigration from nineteenth-century Germany can be seen as serving to relieve widespread social tensions in the home country, with the effect of exporting social problems.[12]

This became particularly clear during the first emigration wave (1846 to 1857). The latter was initiated by Germany's last pre-industrial crisis of the disastrous *type ancien* (E. Labrousse) in 1846 to 1847, striking agriculture as well as the crafts.[13] This crisis pushed the emigration curve up above the level of the revolution period to that of 1852 (176,402). From there, figures rose sharply to the 1854 peak of 239,246, while emigration increasingly took on the nature of a mass flight to the New World. The mass movement lowered the threshold of individual decision-making and developed its own momentum ("emigration fever"). Between the last crisis of the *type ancien* and the start of the "first world economic crisis" (H. Rosenberg) in 1857 to 1859, nearly 1.3 million Germans emigrated overseas – more than half a million of them moving in 1854 to 1857 alone.[14] The defeat of the 1848/49 revolution and the subsequent period of political reaction reinforced the tendency to emigrate but did not change emigration into a mass political movement, except for the small group of Forty-Eighters.[15]

12. H. Fenske, "Die deutsche Auswanderung in der Mitte des 19. Jahrhunderts: öffentliche Meinung und amtliche Politik," *GWU* (1973), 221–36; C. Hansen, "Die deutsche Auswanderung im 19. Jahrhundert – ein Mittel zur Lösung sozialer und sozialpolitischer Probleme?" in Moltmann, ed., *Deutsche Amerikaauswanderung*, 8–61; M. Kuckhoff, "Die Auswanderungsdiskussion während der Revolution von 1848/49" in Moltmann, ed., *Deutsche Amerikaauswanderung*, 102–45.

13. E. Labrousse, *Esquisse du mouvement des prix et les revenus en France au XVIIe siècle* (Paris *1933*); idem, *La crise française à la fin de l'Ancien Règime et au début de la Révolution* (Paris 1944); cf. W. Abel, *Massenarmut und Hungerkrisen im vorindustriellen Europa. Versuch einer Synopsis* (Hamburg 1974), 302–396.

14. H. Rosenberg, *Die Weltwirtschaftskrise 1857–1859* 2d ed. (Göttingen 1974).

15. A.E. Zucker, ed., *The Forty-Eighters. Political Refugees of the German Revolution of 1848* (New York 1950); C. Wittke, *Refugees of Revolution. The German Forty-Eighters in*

The outbreak of the American Civil War in 1861 led to a short-term congestion of the emigration stream, but by 1864, before the end of the war, the second emigration wave began to swell. During the economic recession from 1873 to 1879, which equally affected both the German and the American economies, emigration figures again fell sharply. Immediately after the end of the recession, the third and largest emigration wave of the nineteenth century started abruptly in 1880, involving almost 1.8 million emigrants until the American economic crisis in 1893.

After the "panic of 1893" in the United States, the last emigration wave from nineteenth-century Germany came to an end. During the period of rapid industrialization in Germany, population pressure was counterbalanced by economic growth and by the employment opportunities that had increased in leaps and bounds. Hence, in that phase of rapid economic growth since the mid-1890s, the attraction of the United States declined, in view of the sharply increasing prospects on the industrial labor market in Germany. Instead of transatlantic emigration, there was a rising internal migration from rural to urban-industrial employment. From the beginning of the 1890s (new immigration), transit migrations from east and south-east Europe through Germany to German seaports replaced the strongly diminishing German transatlantic passages.[16]

Emigration After the Mass Exodus

From the mid-1890s to the eve of World War I, German transatlantic emigration remained a trickle and was practically nonexistent after the outbreak of the war. After the war, and especially after the Treaty of Versailles, a new, tremendous emigration wave should have been expected; however, this was deceptive: in 1919 to 1920, emigration remained insignificant. It increased with the gradual dismantling of the wartime curbs, but reached its peak only in 1923, forming the last but rapid and short wave, as is shown in Figure 6.1.

This last short-lived emigration wave was influenced by four

America (Philadelphia 1952); E.W. Dobbert, *Deutsche Demokraten in Amerika* (Göttingen 1958); W.D. Kamphoefner, "Dreissiger and Forty-Eighters: The Political Influence of Two Generations of German Political Exiles" in *Germany and America. Essays on Problems of International Relations and Immigrations*, Hans L. Trefousse, ed. (Brooklyn 1980), 89–102.

16. M. Just, *Ost- und südosteuropäische Amerikaauswanderung 1881–1914. Transitprobleme in Deutschland und Aufnahme in den Vereinigten Staaten* (Stuttgart 1988).

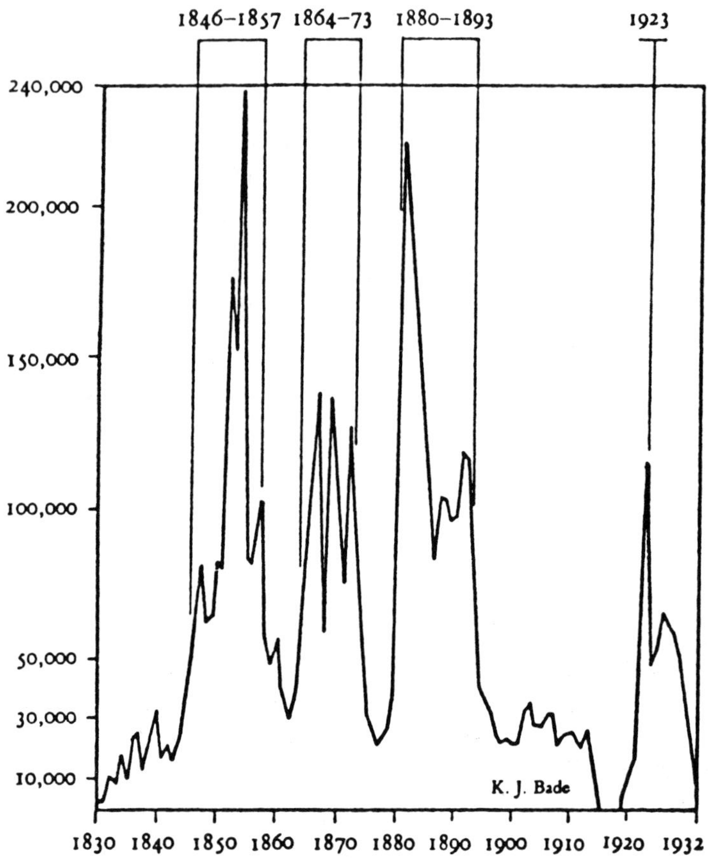

FIGURE 6.1 Transatlantic Emigration from Germany, 1830–1932

Source: F. Burgdörfer, Die Wanderungen über die deutschen Reichsgrenzen im letzten Jahrhundert, in: *Allgemeines Statistisches Archiv* 20. 93, 161–196, 383–419, 536–551 (189, 192); *Statistisches Jahrbuch für das deutsche Reich*, 52, 93, 49. The second dip in the second emigration wave at the end of the 1860 results from a shortened fiscal year (see n. 9).

principal factors: (1) the realization of aspirations having been forcibly thwarted by the First World War and the difficulties of the immediate postwar years; (2) feelings of alienation arising from defeat, the Versailles Treaty, the loss of territories, and the fall of the monarchy, coupled with fears generated by the revolution and the founding of the Republic; (3) the flight of capital together with financial insecurity in the postwar economic crisis; and (4) the emigration of people who had already planned to leave but brought their departure forward for fear that inflation would wipe out the value of savings they had built up to start a new life overseas.

During the period of economic stabilization in the mid-1920s, transatlantic emigration decreased steadily and fell again abruptly from the beginning of the world economic crisis, a development similar to that seen in the crisis years of the mid-1870s. In the early 1930s, the extent of German-American return migration outnumbered that of German emigration. On America's part, this was due to the problems arising from the economic crisis, while in Germany it was because of the National Socialist "Home to the Empire" (*Heim ins Reich*) campaign.[17]

The United States, still the main overseas destination for Germans during the Weimar Republic, was able to indirectly determine the direction, volume, and structure of transatlantic emigration with its restrictive immigration policy, to an extent hitherto unknown. The proportion of German transatlantic emigration to the United States between 1921 and 1933 sank to about 71 percent, while German immigration into South America increased all the more. This was due to the attractive immigration policy of the various countries in Latin America and to the developing idea of German-South American pioneer settlement, the attraction of which also grew among the middle classes and was determined to a certain extent by tendencies of alienation from the political culture of the new Republic. Above all, it was a result of the restrictive imposition of U.S. immigration quotas such as the Quota Act (1921) and its intensification with the Johnson Bill (1924) and the National Origin Law (1927). However, it was not the laws as such that had restrictive effects, as quota levels were not even reached at this time in German-U.S. immigration. Rather, these restrictions were based on the complicated legal requirements for their execution, which were both restrictive and open to diverse interpretations and constituted a great deterrent.

Futhermore, the American immigration restrictions and prohibitions for whole occupational groups completely altered the occupational makeup of German emigration to the United States and, thus, of the greater part of German transatlantic emigration: entry regulations for farmers and farm laborers in the United States, for example, pushed the number of emigrants employed in agriculture,

17. H. Bickelmann, *Deutsche Überseeauswanderung in der Weimarer Zeit* (Wiesbaden 1980).

as a proportion of all German emigrant employees, back from 23.1 percent in 1930 to 11.3 percent in 1931.

The North American immigration requirements even considerably influenced the male-female ratio of German emigration. Although emigration from the Weimar Republic saw a great increase in single working women, the noticeable dwindling of the proportion of men, from 53.5 percent in 1929 to 1930 to just 44.6 percent in 1931, resulted from another factor; namely, the preference of the American authorities, on account of the world economic crisis, for female applications for immigration permits.[18]

The emigration from Nazi Germany marked the beginning of a new period in the history of German emigration. Leaving out of account the emigration of the "Forty-Eighters," of Catholics at the time of the *Kulturkampf* (1871 to 1887), and of Socialists during the time when the anti-Socialist law (1878 to 1890) was in force, the flight from Nazi Germany could not be compared to the transatlantic emigration of the preceding century. Its volume can only be estimated as a large proportion of emigrants were compelled to cross the borders illegally or as tourists, leaving no traces. From 1933 to 1945, the total number of emigrants from German-speaking countries, who were of Jewish descent in the broadest sense of the term, amounted to more than half a million. The flight from Nazi Germany was predominantly due to the anti-Semitic laws and their attendant measures, to persecution on religious, ideological, and political grounds, and to the banning of critical authors and journalists, scientists and academics, as well as representatives of the "degenerate arts" (*entartete Kunst*) from their professions.

Customary emigration from Nazi Germany did not begin with a definite intention to leave the home country permanently. Often the road to exile began with the notion of a temporary flight, only to end in a permanent residence abroad. Moreover, in most cases the road did not even lead directly into the new country of permanent settlement. All in all, the traces of flight and refuge, exile and emigration led to seventy-five countries worldwide. It is true that the United States was the predominant country of final destination for these refugees, totaling 48 percent of the emigration from Nazi Germany. But half of these emigrants did not arrive there before

18. K.J. Bade, "Arbeitsmarkt, Bevölkerung und Wanderung in der Weimarer Republik" in *Die Weimarer Republik. Belagerte Civitas*, M. Stürmer, ed. (Königstein 1980), 160–87; cf. M.S. Seller, "Historical Perspectives on American Immigration Policy: Case Studies and Current Implications" in *U.S. Immigration Policy*, R.R. Hofstetter, ed. (Durham 1984), 137–62.

1938 to 1941, for they had fled first into neighboring European countries and headed for the United States only when the German expansion during the war progressed.[19]

An even greater mass emigration was expected from West Germany after the Second World War than after the First, because the country was mutilated, economically ruined, as well as overpopulated, due to the immense influx of expellees and refugees. Among those who still entertained the idea of emigrating after the war's end, the term "emigration" still involved the nineteenth-century notion of leaving the country of origin without any preconceived purpose of ever returning permanently. That was especially true for a significant number of displaced persons and refugees from the East: West German emigration statistics of the 1950s clearly show that for some years their emigration share was twice as high as their population share in the Federal Republic.[20]

However, the transatlantic emigration, which has only been able to develop fully since the late 1940s, did not even approach the dimensions fearfully expected in the post-war years. It reached its maximum in 1952 with a total of about 90,000 emigrants. In 1956 it receded to 82,000 and has dwindled continuously, amounting to 48,000 in 1960, the first year of full employment in West Germany. Among the most important countries of final destination, the United States still came first, Canada second, Australia third, and Brazil fourth. With the increasing opening-up of labor markets worldwide, "emigration" has been merely a "nineteenth-century term" to most of the Germans who moved abroad since the 1960s. The deliberate decisions to emigrate were replaced by simply seeking employment in foreign countries for an indefinite period of time or by working abroad for German firms. Depending on the length of the stay abroad, quite a large part of this temporary employment migration

19. W. Frühwald and W. Schieder, eds., *Leben im Exil. Probleme der Integration deutscher Flüchtlinge im Ausland 1933–1945* (Hamburg 1981); E. Lacina, *Emigration 1933–1945. Sozialhistorische Darstellung der deutschsprachigen Emigration und einiger ihrer Asylländer auf Grund ausgewählter zeitgenössischer Selbstzeugnisse* (Stuttgart 1982); *Biographisches Handbuch der deutschsprachigen Emigration nach 1933*, 3 vols. (Munich 1980–1983); H. Möller, *Exodus der Kultur. Schriftsteller, Wissenschaftler und Künstler in der Emigration nach 1933* (Munich 1984).

20. For the following see: S. Bethlehem, *Heimatvertreibung, DDR-Flucht, Gastarbeiterzuwanderung: Wanderungsströme und Wanderungspolitik in der Bundesrepublik Deutschland* (Stuttgart 1982), 210–323, K.J. Bade, *Vom Auswanderungsland zum Einwanderungsland? Deutschland 1880–1980* (Berlin 1983), 59–124; idem, "Transatlantic Emigration and Continental Immigration: The German Experience Past and Present" in idem, ed., *Population, Labour and Migration in 19th and 20th Century Germany* (Leamington Spa 1987), 135–62.

did, however, end up as definite emigration. On this basis, the proportion of "true" emigrations in the annual figures for "removals abroad" (1980: 53,728) is difficult to assess.

In the late 1970s, the inclination to emigrate overseas increased, especially among the younger generation, once again in the sense of a definite departure from the country of origin. Besides the United States, other countries of final destination gained in importance in this "new emigration," as indicated by the hundreds of thousands of inquiries addressed to Australian and New Zealand information centers. The figure of actual "new emigrations," however, was by far lower than the number of inquiries made and increased, for example, in 1980 by a mere 1.8 percent. The reason for this is that such inquiries and intentions to emigrate were in many cases provoked by cultural pessimism, critique and despair of industrial civilization, by fears of political crises, and by the search for an overseas country that can offer a freer lifestyle – ideas that in most cases are bound to remain dreams.

Looking at the estimated figures of annual "actual" emigrations, it becomes apparent that West Germany has ceased to be a country of emigration in the conventional sense. Nevertheless, in thinking of all the hundreds of thousands who indicate the desire to emigrate, and who would perhaps even do so if their dreams had any earthly chance of being realized, it could be said that the long tradition of transatlantic emigration may not yet have reached its end.

Special Issues and Research Questions

Push- and Pull-Constellations and the Sending Regions

With the exception of flight and expulsion (merely push-factors), an interrelation exists between push- and pull-factors that may either cause migrations or at least trigger them. Taken by itself, however, this trivial basic assumption only leads to superficial models of explaining migration movements, in particular when thinking primarily of simultaneously-operating economic push- pull- constellations, which as such do not exist, as the Homo sapiens is neither a *homo oeconomicus* nor an *animal rationale migrans*.

Economic explanations of migration only allow for partial explanations, even in cases where one primarily has to deal with labor migrations. As a rule, the "purer" an exclusively or predominantly economic or econometric push-pull model, the more constrained its explanatory power, for several reasons: the scenario of indicators stipulated within an economic push-pull model may vary both qualitatively and quantitatively throughout an extensive period of time, just as the volume, course, and structure of the investigated migration movement may vary. Moreover, the sociohistorical validity of these models depends on whether and to what extent non-economic (social, psychological, cultural, mental, ideological, and others) factors are taken into account. This provides a clear explanation for the tendency of various populations, classes, groups, and individuals living in comparable economic situations at the same time to react in different ways – or even not at all – to related or even identical economic push-pull-constellations.

Only by these means can one assure that a seemingly significant relationship between economic factors and simultaneous migrations does not merely conceal a historical nonsense correlation. This applies for example to insufficient accounts of the dynamic character of the migration process, and the interrelated problem of when decisions to migrate are made and when they are actually realized, whereby this may take place at two different points in time.[21] Once obstacles to emigration, either due to economic (e.g., the depression of 1873 to 1879) or to noneconomic factors (e.g., the American Civil War), have been removed, a migration stream may abruptly swell to become an "emigration wave."[22] In this wave, however, decisions to migrate are belatedly put into practice and no longer are the result of the prevalent economic factors.

All this also applies to the question of how push-pull-constellations operated behind the curves of transatlantic emigration from nineteenth-century Germany as shown in Figures 6.2 and 6.3.[23] As is mentioned above, demographic and socioeconomic causes definitively came to the fore after the rise of "proletarian mass migration" in the 1840s. At that time the push-factors were clearly decisive, which fact, to a certain extent, was also verified by a positive correlation of food prices with the number of emigrants (see Figure 6.2). In the emigration from late nineteenth-century Germany to the United States, the pull-factor became more noticeable. There was more and more individual labor migration, dependent above all on the economic opportunities that the labor market in the United States had to offer (see Figure 6.3).

21. See Bade, "Trends and Issues," 3.
22. See n. 8.
23. Helbich, Kamphoefner, and Sommer, eds., *Briefe aus Amerika*, 18.

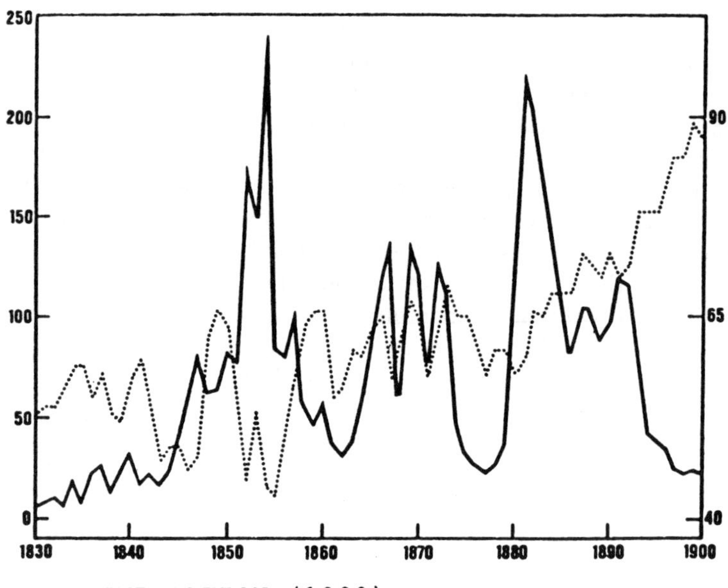

FIGURE 6.2 Transatlantic Emigration from Germany and Real Wages in Germany, 1830–1900

Source: P. Marschalck, *Deutsche Überseewanderung im 19. Jahrhundert. Ein Beitrag zur soziologischen Theorie der Bevölkerung*, (Stuttgart 1973), 35–37; R. Gömmel, *Realeinkommen in Deutschland. Ein internationaler Vergleich (1910–1914)*, (Nürnberg 1979), 27–29 (see n. 24).

For the period during which the transition took place, however, the alternative of push- or pull-factors is too unsophisticated as to serve as a basis for our analysis, given the many time lags and disparities within Germany, as M. Walker has shown so convincingly.[24] The question of what could have been either a push- or a pull-factor or both, and when, under which conditions, and for which groups, can be answered only by the very concrete investigation of group-specific emigration conditions in the sending regions.[25]

24. M. Walker, *Germany and the Emigration, 1816–1885* (Cambridge Mass. 1964), 175–194; cg. S. Faltin, *Die Auswanderung aus der Pfalz nach Nordamerika im 19. Jahrhundert* (Frankfurt 1986), 131–37, 148–63.

25. For a regional case study on collective motivations behind transatlantic emigration and internal out-migration see K.J. Bade, "Massenwanderung und

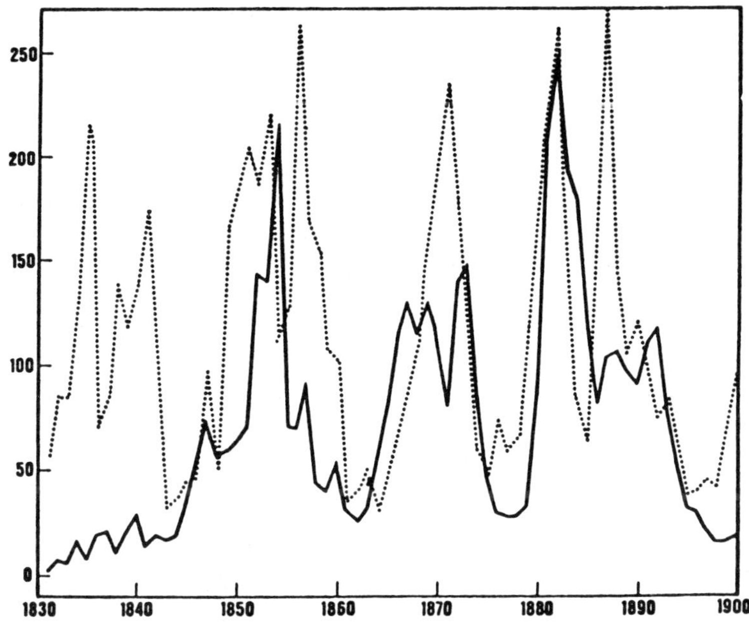

FIGURE 6.3 German Immigration to the United States and U.S. Business Cycles, 1830–1900

Source: B. Thomas, *Migration and Economic Growth*, (Cambridge 1973), 397, 402 (see n. 24).

It is exactly for such extensively data-based regional studies on the history of German transatlantic mass emigration that a great demand still exists. Moreover, to quantify such analyses more closely, one needs to rename the nameless data of emigration and immigration statistics. There is much emphasis on preparing data collections of that kind on both sides of the Atlantic, but there is still a long way to go.[26]

Arbeitsmarkt im deutschen Nordosten von 1880 bis zum Ersten Weltkrieg: überseeische Auswanderung, interne Abwanderung und kontinentale Zuwanderung," *Archiv für Sozialgeschichte (AfS)* 20 (1980), 265–323.

26. Outstanding data-based regional studies on background and motivating factors of transatlantic emigration are, for the German northwest: W.D. Kamphoefner, *Westfalen in der Neuen Welt. Eine Sozialgeschichte der Auswanderung im 19. Jahrhundert* (Münster 1982), 22–85 (revised and enlarged American edition under the title: *The Westfalians. From Germany to Missouri* (Princeton 1987); for the German southwest: v. Hippel, *Auswanderung*, 58–94, 148–211; for a comprehensive survey on respective

This is all the more true for the converse question of how and to what extent transatlantic emigration was of importance for the country of emigration as a whole and, more specifically, for the main sending regions. If there were demographic-economic push-factors that, along with the pull-factors, pushed emigration ahead, then one could generally assume that transatlantic mass emigration may have led to a decline in population pressure. Moreover, from several sending regions, for example in the Prussian East of Imperial Germany, we know that the oversupply of manpower in agriculture, which once had caused transatlantic emigration as well as internal out-migration, was reversed as early as the late 1880s into its opposite; that is, into an acute shortage of manpower in agriculture. Hence, many and, at the turn of the century, most owners of large estates in the Prussian East were urged to recruit foreign migrant workers from across the eastern borders of Prussia to bridge the gaps in the labor supply caused by transatlantic emigration and by internal out-migration. Living, working, and earning conditions that "pushed" German workers out of the country, or at least out of agriculture, were obviously attractive enough to "pull" foreign migrant workers from the east.[27] There is also a more speculative question involved as to how Germany's population, its economy and society, would have developed during the critical transition from an agrarian to an industrial state in the nineteenth century if about five million Germans had not emigrated to the United States, and in view of the fact that those who stayed had at least been able to avail themselves of this opportunity.[28]

---

data problems see Helbich, Kamphoefner, and Sommer, eds., *Briefe aus Amerika*, 39–45; collection: I.A. Glazier and P.W. Filby, eds., *Germans to America. Lists of Passengers arriving at U.S. ports, 1850–1855*, I, 2 partial vols., Jan. 1850–May 1851 (Wilmington 1988); for a German regional collection see e.g. F. Müller, "Westfälische Auswanderer im 19. Jahrhundert" (Regierungsbezirke Münster, Minden), *Beiträge zur Westfälischen Familienforschung* 22–24 (1964–66) and 38–39 (1980/81).

27. K.J. Bade, "Politik und Ökonomie der Ausländerbeschäftigung im preußischen Osten 1885–1914: Die Internationalisierung des Arbeitsmarkts im 'Rahmen der preußischen Abwehrpolitik'" in *Preußen im Rückblick*, H.J. Puhle and H.U. Wehler, eds., *Geschichte und Gesellschaft*, special issue 6 (Göttingen 1980), 273–99; K.J. Bade "'Preußengänger' und 'Abwehrpolitik': Ausländerbeschäftigung, Ausländerpolitik und Ausländerkontrolle auf dem Arbeitsmarkt in Preußen vor dem Ersten Weltkrieg," *AfS* 24 (1984), 91–283.

28. G. Moltmann, "German Emigration to the United States During the First Half of the Nineteenth Century as a Social Protest Movement" in *Germany and America. Essays on Problems of International Relations and Immigration*, H.L. Trefousse ed. (New York 1980), 104–10; G. Moltmann, "Nordamerikanische Frontier und deutsche Auswanderung – soziale 'Sicherheitsventile' im 19. Jahrhundert?" in *Industrielle Gesellschaft und politisches System. Festschrift für Fritz Fischer* (Bonn 1978), 279–96;

On a regional and local level, there is the question of how, and to what extent, transatlantic emigration provided a learning process for those who did not emigrate but were closely connected to certain German-American settlement districts in the New World through transatlantic communication formed for generations by continuous chain migrations. This implied that those who stayed at home participated in the learning process of their German-American relatives. There are scattered hints that such "emigrant letters" and "visits from America," by which information on agricultural economy and techniques in the United States was spread in the sending regions, caused significant changes in these regions. So far, these issues concerning the effects of emigration on those who stayed at home have scarcely been studied.

Such questions demonstrate both the need to intensify quantitative analyses and, at the same time, to give up the notion that it would suffice for migration research to put statistical data through some kind of a heuristic circulating plant. Migration research has to view itself more as part of – in the best sense of the term – "conventional" historical research, and in particular, it needs to relearn how to dig for the many treasures still buried in the archives on both sides of the Atlantic.

Transportation

Until mid-nineteenth century, the adventure of traveling from Germany to the New World consisted of three often separate stages: the journey to the port, the sea-crossing, and the continuation of the journey to the area of destination. Although numerous commercial emigration agencies with a widespread network of subagents were able to offer fully organized emigration routes from the mid-nineteenth century onward, many emigrants were still "going to America" independently and only entered into passage contracts during their journey or at the port.[29]

G. Moltmann, "Auswanderung als Revolutionsersatz?" in *Die Deutschen und die Revolution*, M. Salewski, ed. (Göttingen 1984), 272–297; cf. Hansen, "Deutsche Auswanderung;" P. Marschalck, *Deutsche Überseewanderung im 19. Jahrhundert. Ein Beitrag zur soziologischen Theorie der Bevölkerung* (Stuttgart 1973), 85–95; v. Hippel, *Auswanderung*, 276–80; Faltin, *Auswanderung aus der Pfalz*, 272–75.

29. A. Bretting, *Die Auswanderungsagenturen in Deutschland im 19. und 20. Jahrhundert: Ihre Funktion im Gesamtauswanderungsprozeß* (forthcoming in the series "Von Deutschland nach Amerika," ed. by G. Moltmann). H. Bickelmann, "The Venture of Travel" in Moltmann, ed., *Germans to America*, 134–42; cf. G. Moltmann, "Das Risiko der Seereise. Auswanderungsbedingungen im Europa-Amerika-Verkehr um die

In the eighteenth century, the journey to the port took several weeks. First, the Rhine had to be reached on foot or horse-drawn vehicle. Then there followed a break, often of several days, while the occasion was awaited for traveling with a freight barge. The ensuing trip meant passing through numerous customs points; twenty-nine on the stretch between Mainz and Rotterdam alone. Finally, there was the waiting time at the ports, in the 1820s very often still amounting to weeks. This, however, meant running the risk of losing the savings intended for beginning a new life overseas – or at least for supporting life during the first weeks in the New World – through idle waiting or some form of deceit. In addition to all this, the crossing itself usually took six to eight weeks. According to a reputable travel report of 1756, the journey from Enzweihingen near Vaihingen on the Enz to Philadelphia could take up to five months: seven weeks were needed for the inland journey to Heilbronn and the subsequent boat trip up the Neckar and the Rhine to Rotterdam, passing through thirty-six customs points. Then came the Atlantic crossing, lasting a total of fifteen weeks. Even the obligatory stopover in an English port – in accordance with the regulations concerning the traffic to and from the British colonies – lasted nine days.[30]

In the first decades of the nineteenth century the large majority of German emigrants still traveled via foreign ports, particularly Antwerpen, Rotterdam, and Le Havre. There were two reasons for this: first, emigration routes followed the paths of rivers, especially the Rhine. Second, French ports were important for emigrants from southwestern Germany. In the 1840s and the 1850s, combined travel by steamer and rail came to dominate the scene. From the mid-1850s rail travel took on greater importance: the journey to German ports by special emigrant trains took just a day, so that Hamburg and especially Bremen (with its direct rail connection with Leipzig and Cologne) became the predominant points of departure for overseas.[31] Nevertheless, the proportion of German emi-

---

Mitte des 19. Jahrhunderts" in *Festschrift für Eberhard Kessel zum 75. Geburtstag*, H. Duchardt and M. Schlencke, eds. (Munich 1982), 182–211; Moltmann, ed., *Aufbruch nach Amerika*, 188–303, 335–62; M. Wokeck, "Deutsche Einwanderung in die nordamerikanischen Kolonien. Prototyp einer transatlantischen Massenwanderung" in Trommler, ed., *Amerika und die Deutschen*, 29–39, esp. 33–39; J. Mikoletzky, *Die deutsche Amerika-Auswanderung des 19. Jahrhunderts in der zeitgenössischen fiktionalen Literatur* (Tübingen 1988), 199–221.

30. v. Hippel, *Auswanderung*, 34ff.

31. E. Engelsing, *Bremen als Auswandererhafen, 1683–1880* (Bremen 1961); B. Gelberg, *Auswanderung nach Übersee. Soziale Folgen der Auswandererbeförderung in Hamburg und*

grants departing from foreign ports (only approximately registered even in the statistics of Imperial Germany, if at all) remained high, amounting to around 20 percent in 1880 to 1910.

The main reason for the enormous increase in transatlantic traffic from the Hanseatic ports at the peak of German transatlantic emigration was the profitable combination of exporting people and importing goods. This was noticeable first of all in the internal spatial division of the emigration ships themselves, particularly in the form of the notorious "tween deck." The second half, and particularly the last third of the century saw an increasing improvement in the quality of transatlantic traveling. Finally, the complete replacement of the sailing ships by steamships toward the end of the 1870s offered those emigrants leaving within the third emigration wave (1880 to 1893) fundamentally different conditions. Sea travel had become better, cheaper, and more frequent. The time of travel was reduced to two and a half weeks or even to one and a half weeks in the 1890s on fast ships. At the same time, the continuous expansion of the rail network made the continuation of the journey from the seaports within the country of immigration easier and shorter.

Indeed, the cost of emigration fell constantly, especially during the period when the shipping giants were competing for control and domination of the market, resulting in dumping prices for transatlantic passages. Nevertheless, the costs were still too high to entice the poor to emigrate. There were, however, a number of possibilities for those who could not finance the crossing themselves. First of all, there existed the above mentioned "Redemptioner" system, which remained in operation until the 1820s, whereby those poor willing to emigrate were offered the chance to reimburse the costs of their crossing through their "indentured servitude" in America.[32] On the other hand, there existed the possibility of being exported as a social problem: at their own costs, communities sent their poorest citizens, often also convicts, to the New World.[33] When chain migrations

---

Bremen von der Mitte des 19. Jahrhunderts bis zum Ersten Weltkrieg (Hamburg 1973); G. Weißenberg, "Die Bedeutung der Auswanderung für die Hamburger Schiffahrt" in ". . . *nach Amerika*," G. Moltmann, ed., Museum für Hamburgische Geschichte, issue 5 (Hamburg 1976), 29–32; G. Moltmann, "Hamburg als Auswanderungshafen" in *Stadt und Hafen. Hamburger Beiträge zur Geschichte von Handel und Schiffahrt* (Hamburg 1986), 166–79.

32. Moltmann, "German Migration to America."

33. G. Moltmann, "Die Transportation von Sträflingen im Rahmen der deutschen Amerikaauswanderung des 19. Jahrhunderts" in idem, ed., *Amerikaauswanderung*, 147–96; K.J. Bade, ed., *Friedrich Fabri und der Imperialismus in der Bismarckzeit: Revolution*

increased in the nineteenth century, another way of obtaining free travel was to have a "prepaid ticket" sent by friends or relatives in America.[34] A fourth possibility was offered after the American Civil War in the form of the recruitment of contract workers by American firms in Europe, paying for the crossing in return for subsequent contract labor. This contract-labor system was attacked by the American labor movement and outlawed by Congress in 1885.[35]

The more German transatlantic emigration declined from the early 1890s, the more important east European emigration became for the Hanseatic transatlantic lines. This migration stream, part of the new immigration to the United States, crossed German territory only in the form of transit migration to the ports. Until 1880, fewer than 150,000 immigrants arrived in the United States from countries of the Habsburg monarchy and of Russia. In the following decade the statistics looked different: 354,000 immigrants came from Austria-Hungary alone and 265,000 from Russia, while in the 1890s 593,000 and 602,000, respectively, were counted. When the new immigration reached its peak in 1919, 2,145,000 immigrants came from Austria-Hungary and 1,597,000 from Russia, of whom 976,000 were Jews and 874,000 Poles. In comparison to the high tide of east European transit migration via German ports, German transatlantic emigration dwindled to a runlet: the 1,437,934 German emigrants traveling via German ports in 1880 to 1893 constituted about 81 percent of all German transatlantic emigration and still accounted for 51 percent of the total emigration via German ports (2,831,058). Between 1894 and 1910, on the other hand, German emigrants made up a mere 11 percent (380,907) of the total (3,133,163).[36]

In order to fill the German emigration ships, agents of German shipping lines in eastern and southeastern Europe took over the role played in mid-nineteenth-century Germany by American agents; frequently, they were prosecuted and hunted by the police. The German agents were treated with equal suspicion by east and southeast European governments, on account of both their success

– *Depression – Expansion* (Freiburg i. Br. 1975), 91–94; cf. G. Raiss, "Erfelden schickte seine Armen nach Amerika" in *Erfelden – Geschichte und Geschichten* (Trebun 1980), 349–57.

34. Kamphoefner, *Westfalen*, 86–122; idem, "'Entwurzelt' oder 'verpflanzt'? Zur Bedeutung der Kettenwanderung für die Einwandererakkulturation in Amerika" in Bade, ed., *Auswanderer* I, 321–49; Helbich, Kamphoefner, and Sommer, eds., *Briefe aus Amerika*, 16ff.

35. Ph.S. Foner, *History of the Labor Movement in the United States* II, 2d ed. (New York 1975), 407.

36. Bade, "Die deutsche überseeische Massenauswanderung," 274.

and their often reckless methods. Agents of transatlantic shipping lines fought tooth and nail to get emigrants at all costs, applying all available means. Thus, the director of the North German Lloyd, Wiegand, was compelled to confess that in Galicia one worked with the "scum of the earth."[37] This competition for transatlantic passengers in southeastern and eastern Europe escalated even more when German, and particularly Prussian, agents recruited for seasonal migration farmhands in the same areas, in order to lessen the labor shortage in agriculture caused by transatlantic emigration and internal out-migration. A certain number of these seasonal migrants may have used their savings, built up during their stay in Germany, to finance their own transatlantic emigration. Altogether, this compelled large-scale agrarian producers in Galicia, for instance, to recruit by themselves foreign labor in order to compensate for the shortages caused by the seasonal labor migrations and transatlantic emigrations.[38]

Structural Changes in the Pattern of Migration: the Regional, Social, and Occupational Makeup, the Age Structure and Sex Ratio

Transatlantic emigration from nineteenth- and early twentieth-century Germany underwent a multifaceted structural change. This encompassed a shift in sending regions and, thus, a change in the social and occupational makeup of the migration streams, as well as the long-term change from family to individual migration and from rural settlement migration to industrial labor migration. These changes are also reflected by alterations in the employment and settlement patterns of the German-born population in the United States.[39]

Changes in Emigration The continuous domination of southwest German sending regions remained unbroken from the eighteenth right to the second half of the nineteenth century, although western

37. *Verhandlungen der Budapester Konferenz betreffs Organisation des Arbeitsmarkts, 7. und 8. Oktober 1910* (Leipzig 1911), 89.

38. K.J. Bade, "Arbeitsmarkt, Ausländerbeschäftigung und Interessenkonflikt" in *Fremdarbeiterpolitik des Imperialismus* 10 (Rostock 1981), 27–47.

39. For the following see Bade, "Die deutsche überseeische Massenauswanderung," 275–84; Marschalck, *Deutsche Überseewanderung*, 72–84; P. Marschalck and W. Köllmann, "German Emigration to the United States," *Perspectives in American History* 7 (1974), 499–554; Kamphoefner, *Westfalen*, 22–85; v. Hippel, *Auswanderung*,

sending regions gained in significance during the 1850s. In the mid-1860s there was a shift in emphasis from the southwest, via the central to the northeast German regions. By the time of the third emigration wave (1880 to 1893), the northeast German regions had become dominant. The abrupt end of this wave was tantamount to the sharp fall in emigration from these areas.

The aforementioned shift in the sending regions corresponded with alterations in the social and occupational makeup of the emigration movement. As a result of the constant splitting of farms due to custom of equal division among heirs (*Realerbteilung*) in the German southwest, small peasants on the verge of poverty made up the most significant professional group of emigrants until well into the 1860s, followed by small tradesmen and craftsmen. It must be pointed out, however, that visible regional discrepancies in the occupational and social makeup of the emigration stream also arose from variations in the economic, agricultural, and social constitution of the sending regions. For example, self-employed, small-scale farmers dominated the scene in the southwest, while most emigrants from central Germany worked in the home industries or as craftsmen. Those from rural Mecklenburg-Schwerin, on the other hand, were principally day laborers and farmhands.

The gradual shift in the main sending regions from the southwest to the northeast increasingly altered the occupational and social structure of the emigration movement from the mid-1860s onward. During the second (1864 to 1873) and especially during the third emigration wave (1880 to 1893), free farm laborers, farm contract workers (*Insten*), and sons of farmers not entitled to inherit from the rural northeast became prevalent. The proportion of workers employed in the urban secondary and tertiary sectors, however, slowly increased in the 1880s and at the beginning of the 1890s and noticeably predominated, as the third emigration wave from the rural northeast rapidly tailed off. The shift in emphasis to the secondary and tertiary sectors was complete by 1899, when the occupational makeup of transatlantic emigration was for the first time included in the German Emigration Statistics. By the turn of the century, the agricultural sector accounted for less than one-third of German emigrants (1900 to 1904: 30.6 percent). In the five years before World War I, it was barely more than a quarter (1910 to 1914: 26.4 percent), and at the start of the 1920s, it shrank to less than one-fifth

211–50; Faltin, *Auswanderung aus der Pfalz*, 163–73; Helbich, Kamphoefner, and Sommer, eds., *Briefe aus Amerika*, 19ff.; Mikoletzky, *Deutsche Amerika-Auswanderung*, 111–34.

(1921 to 1923: 17.8 percent). The fact that the figure rose slightly in the mid-1920s (1924 to 1928: 21.5 percent) was essentially a result of the restrictive American immigration policy and of the increased pioneer settlement in South America.

A visible change in the emigrants' social status accompanied the changes in the occupational makeup of the migration streams during Germany's transition from an agrarian to an industrial state. At the beginning of the twentieth century, those from the agricultural, the secondary, and tertiary employment areas were predominantly dependent on others for employment, while the number of self-employed was falling steadily. Farm laborers, workers, and employees replaced emigrating peasants and artisans. At this point, 6.4 percent of those employable emigrants from the agricultural sector and 7.3 percent of those from the trades and industries were self-employed. This was to remain so until the end of the 1920s. From 1921 to 1928 farm laborers and farmhands accounted for 93.4 percent of emigrants engaged in agriculture, while workers and assistants made up 93.9 percent of those from the secondary sector and employees and assistants 91.4 percent of those from the tertiary sector.

Changes in the regional, occupational, and social makeup corresponded to the development from family to individual migration, as well as to changes in the age and sex ratio. Until the mid-1860s, the emigration of farming and craftsmen's families from combined agricultural and commercial areas were predominant, particularly from the southwest. The fact that family emigration was still far greater than the fast-increasing individual migration during the third emigration wave can be explained mainly by the shift in emphasis to the agricultural areas of northeast Germany. The sharp drop in emigration figures from these areas in the first half of the 1890s, led in turn to a sudden acceleration in individual emigration, which had already risen to over 40 percent in the 1880s. Paradoxically, the ratio was reversed by the end of the Weimar era, so that instead of the 57.8 percent family emigrants and 42.2 percent individual emigrants of the period 1881 to 1890, family emigration was down to just 33.8 percent in the period 1921 to 1928 while individual emigration came to 66.2 percent.

Declining family emigration was accompanied by a continual fall in the size of emigrant families. The average declined from 3.7 members in 1880 to 2.6 in 1928. At the same time, the alteration in the age structure of the migration movement as a whole showed itself in the increase in the number of emigrants of employable age and the decrease in the emigration of nonworking family members. The share of emigrants under fourteen years of age fell from 25.4 percent in 1884 to 1890 to 12.3 percent in 1921 to 1928, and the proportion of those aged fourteen to twenty-one decreased from 21 percent to 18.9 percent during this time. The share of emigrants over fifty years of age, which had in any case been small, fell steadily from 6.1 percent in 1884 to 1890 to 4.4 percent in 1921 to 1928. On the other hand, there was at the same time a rapid rise in the proportion of emigrants of the most employable age (twenty-one to fifty), from 47.7 percent in 1884 to 1890 to 64.4 percent in 1921 to 1928.

As yet, it has only been possible to provide a very general answer to the poignant question of the development of female emigration as there is a lack of in-depth study in this field. W.D. Kamphoefner came to the following conclusion, based on the state of the research: from the mid-1830s onward, the proportion of German female migration – on average 40 percent – was higher than most of the other ethnic groups. Most female migrants, however, either emigrated with their families or were subsequent migrants, following either their parents or their husbands and fiancés. These had emigrated first and, having established a firm basis for family life, had asked their daughters, wives, or fiancés to follow. Only a relatively small proportion of women emigrated alone. Unfortunately, there are only sporadic regional statistics to support these assumptions. For example, it is known that women accounted for about 30 percent of individual emigrations from Württemberg in 1855 to 1870 and for about 34 percent in Osnabrück in 1832 to 1859. For most women, the only chance of finding work in the United States was to become a domestic servant, a definite "immigrant profession." A large number of them had already worked in this field in Germany.[40] The Germans were surpassed only by the Irish in some medium-sized and large American cities as an ethnic group with a high concentration of female domestic servants.[41]

40. T. Pierenkemper, "'Dienstbotenfrage' und Dienstmädchenarbeitsmarkt am Ende des 19. Jahrhunderts," *AfS* 28 (1988), 173–201.

41. Helbich, Kamphoefner, and Sommer, eds., *Briefe aus Amerika*, 19ff., 493–501; cf. C. Harzig, "Frauenarbeit und Familienstrategien: Immigrantinnen in den USA um die Jahrhundertwende," *Gulliver. Deutsch-englische Jahrbücher* 18 (1985), 44–57; D. Schneider, "'For Whom Are All the Good Things in Life?' German-American Housewives Discuss Their Budgets" in *German Workers in Industrial Chicago, 1850–1910: A Comparative Perspective*, H. Keil and J.B. Jentz, eds. (DeKalb Ill. 1983), 145–60; H. Keil, ed., *Deutsche Arbeiterkultur in Chicago von 1850 bis zum Ersten Weltkrieg. Eine Anthologie* (Ostfildern 1984), 80–87, 291–300; D. Hoerder, "Arbeitswanderung und Arbeiterbewußtsein im atlantischen Wirtschaftsraum: Forschungsansätze und -hypothesen," *AfS* 28 (1988), 391–425, 415–18.

The visible increase in individual migrations since the 1880s, and the increased importance of professional groups from the secondary and tertiary sectors in the occupational makeup of transatlantic emigration, marked the shift from the "old", that is, "agrarian," settlement migration to the "new," or "industrial" labor migration, prevalent among advanced industrial societies. This economically speculative type of migration was determined to a much greater degree by fluctuations in the economy and in the labor market. This mitigated the fundamental nature of the decision to emigrate and in the late nineteenth century even provoked the first German temporary transatlantic migrations. It is hard, however, to distinguish these temporary migrations in the statistical data from the supposedly "genuine" emigration and return migration.[42]

Changes in Immigration The shift to the "new," "industrial" labor migration is also reflected in the American census statistics on the employment and settlement structure of the German-born population in the United States.[43]

The proportion of the German-born population employed in agriculture in the United States was 31.5 percent in 1880 and 31.1 percent in 1890; thus still the highest among the foreign-born population. From then on, it fell constantly, until in 1920 it was less than the Norwegian, Danish, Dutch, Swiss, Finnish, and Swedish populations in the United States, at barely 20 percent.

The share of the German-born population in the United States in the primary sector who were self-employed (mainly "farmers" and "planters") and employed by others (mainly "agricultural laborers" and "farm and plantation overseers"), accounted for 26.8 percent in 1870. This was already about 10 percent less than those in the secondary sector (36.9 percent working in "manufacturing, mechanical and mining industries") and those in the tertiary sector

42. See n. 6.

43. It is extremely difficult to analyze the occupational makeup of the German-born population on the basis of these data, and even more to compare these data with those of Germany. The formation of the "German-born" within the "foreign-born population" in the nineteenth century United States' Census data causes particular problems, because the distinctive criterion was not nationality but "mother tongue." Furthermore, the American census data do not count emigrants of the respective decade but the whole "German-born population." The same is true for the data of the employment structure. Moreover, there is the problem of fluctuations of the group organization of "gainfully employed" citizens by professions from one survey to another. Finally, this organization corresponds only in a very limited way to the allocation of individual professions and branches to the firm set of the three employment sectors in the statistics of the German *Reich*.

(36.3 percent working in "domestic and personal service," "trade and transportation," and "professional service"). In 1870 to 1890 the primary sector recorded an increase of just 155,597 German-born people "engaged in gainful occupations," while the secondary, and the particularly fast-growing tertiary sector, on the other hand, registered a total increase of 509,298. Thus, the growth of the secondary and tertiary sectors was more than three times stronger than that of the agricultural sector.

Consideration of the settlement structure of the German-born population in the United States confirms these tendencies: unlike the situation in the country of origin, about 48 percent of the German-born population lived in towns and cities of over 25,000 in 1890 and by 1900 more than 51 percent. Moreover, only a part of the German-born population living in rural communities of less than 2,500 inhabitants (whose share fell from 33.3 percent to 26.8 percent in 1910 to 1930) can be classified strictly as "population living on farms." According to the line of distinction as drawn by the data of 1930 between "rural-farm" and "rural-nonfarm communities" (26.8 percent), only half (13.4 percent) can be shown to have been living in "rural-farm" areas. Although a relatively large proportion of the German-born population remained employed in agriculture for a considerable length of time, the employment in the secondary, and particularly in the tertiary, sectors grew much earlier and quicker than in Germany. At the same time, the share of the German-born population employed in "gainful occupations" rose from 49.5 percent to 54 percent and the employment of women, from 7.6 percent to 10.9 percent.

Thus, the German-born population in the United States was engaged to a much greater extent in urban and industrial employment than the population in the home country. It can therefore be assumed that the majority of German immigrants of the period 1870 to 1890, and especially in the decade 1880 to 1890, intended to find and actually found a living in urban and industrial employment. This happened in spite of a romantic, utopian vision of obtaining a family farm in the New World. During the third emigration wave, many German emigrants from agricultural areas may have boarded the transatlantic liners in the conservative hope of regaining their old world, which was lost or threatened, by founding a small farm in the New World. However, for many this transatlantic migration was in fact to be the very transit to modernity, which they had believed they could avoid by emigrating. Many of them had to face the choice of remaining what they had been in Germany – namely agricultural laborers – or of joining the urban industrial job market. This choice, however, existed in the homeland too: in Imperial Germany, rapid economic expansion from the 1890s onward offered opportunities for rural-urban migration as an internal alternative to transatlantic emigration, even stimulating the idea among an incalculable number of German-Americans of return migration to Imperial Germany.

Reception, Settlement, Integration, and Isolation in the Receiving Areas

As pointed out by A.B. Faust, the census report of 1900 showed clearly, "that the German population is not only widespread, but is more equally distributed over the territory of the United States than any other foreign element."[44] There were, however, large German settlement zones, especially in the "German belt", stretching from New York across Pennsylvania, Ohio, Indiana, and Illinois to Wisconsin, Minnesota, Iowa, Nebraska, Missouri, and Kansas. Early settlement migrations of closed groups often provided the basis for settlement in these mainly rural areas, which were later stabilized and expanded by chain migrations.

It was in these rural settlements that newcomers, from equally rural sending regions in nineteenth-century Germany, found communities of relatives and acquaintances that still bore the mark of the German way of life, in religion, education, or language (even regional dialects).[45] This is why these German immigrants were not so much "uprooted" as "transplanted."[46] Scepticism soon arose toward German settlements where English was visibly being relegated to the status of a foreign language. Facing the increasing German element in Pennsylvania (where in 1790 about 30 percent of the population was of German descent), Benjamin Franklin, for example, as early as 1751 demanded the abolition of German

44. A.B. Faust, *The German Element in the United States* 2 vols. (Boston 1909) I: 574. For the following see A. Bretting, "Little Germanies in the United States" and "The Old Home and the New: The Problem of Americanization" in Moltmann, ed., *Germans to America*, 144–51 and 152–59; cf. Helbich, Kamphoefner, and Sommer, eds., *Briefe aus Amerika*, 21–31; K. Conzen, "Germans" in *Harvard Encyclopedia of American Ethnic Groups* (Cambridge, Mass. 1980), 405–25.

45. K. Conzen, "Die deutsche Amerikaeinwanderung im ländlichen Kontext: Problemfelder und Forschungsergebnisse" in Bade, ed., *Auswanderer* I, 350–77; idem, "Historical Approaches to the Study of Rural Ethnic Communities" in *Ethnicity on the Great Plains*, F. Luebke, ed. (Lincoln 1980), 3–18.

46. O. Handlin, *The Uprooted. The Epic Study of the Great Migration that Made the American People* (Boston 1951); Kamphoefner, "'Entwurzelt' oder 'verpflanzt'?"

schools and an increased Americanization of the Germans. His fear was that Pennsylvania "could become a colony of aliens who will shortly be so numerous as to Germanize us instead of our Anglifying them."[47]

Different from German rural settlement districts were the background and the conseqences of the formation of "Little Germanies" in countless nineteenth-century American cities, from New York to San Francisco and from St. Louis to Minneapolis.[48] The formation of these urban communities was first and foremost a result of the special acculturization problems facing Germans from the start of the transatlantic mass migration. The growing, soon overwhelming, stream of German immigrants into the explosively expanding cities, led to a heavy pressure to assimilate into a world with a foreign language and a strange way of life.

These urban "Little Germanies" were, therefore, a kind of cultural halfway house. The greater the gap between the way of life in the old and new world, and the greater, therefore, the danger of progressive alienation, the more important these stages became. As a rule, German newcomers in town first of all joined this American-German world of urban colonies, and only after successful acclimatization did they move on into the surrounding "real" American world.[49]

The defensive delimitation of the "Little Germanies" from the American outside world resulted from an interdependence of action and reaction. On the one hand, the urban German colonies were seen by nativist circles, from the 1840s and 1850s, as deliberately promoting isolationism, and these colonies were not understood for

47. *The Papers of Benjamin Franklin*, Leonard W. Labaree ed., 14 vols. (New Haven 1961), 234, quoted from: Bretting, "Old Home," 154; cf. Helbich, Kamphoefner, and Sommer, eds., *Briefe aus Amerika*, 11.

48. J.F. Nau, *The German People of New Orleans, 1850–1900* (Leiden 1958); K. Conzen, *Immigrant Milwaukee, 1836–1860*: *Accommodation and Community in a Frontier City* (Cambridge, Mass. 1976); idem, "Immigrants, Immigrant Neighborhoods, and Ethnic Identity: Historical Issues," *JAH* 66, 3 (1979), 603–15; G.D. Dobbert, *The Disintegration of an Immigrant Community: The Cincinnati Germans, 1870–1920* (New York 1980); A.L. Olsen, *St. Louis Germans 1850–1920: The Nature of an Immigrant Community in its Relation to the Assimilation Process* (New York 1980); A. Bretting, *Soziale Probleme deutscher Einwanderer in New York City, 1800–1860* (Wiesbaden 1981); R.R. Doerries, *Iren und Deutsche in der Neuen Welt. Akkulturationsprozesse in der amerikanischen Gesellschaft des späten 19. Jahrhunderts* (Stuttgart 1986).

49. H. Keil, "Die deutsche Amerikaeinwanderung im städtisch-industriellen Kontext: Das Beispiel Chicago, 1880–1910" in Bade, ed., *Auswanderer* I, 378–405; idem, "Einwandererviertel und amerikanische Gesellschaft. Zur Integration deutscher Einwanderer in die amerikanische städtisch-industrielle Umwelt des ausgehenden 19. Jahrhunderts am Beispiel Chicagos," *AfS* 24 (1984), 47–89.

what they really were: a refuge from the crisis of cultural identity caused by the immigration process itself. The nativists did not realize that these American-German urban colonies were, in many respects, much more American than German, at least from the viewpoint of a German newcomer from the old world. From the outside, it was impossible to see the regional, social, confessional, and political fragmentation of these "Little Germanies". Attitudinal differences were particularly noticeable in the field of political activities: in Milwaukee and Cincinnati, German-Americans were consistently active in local politics, while in New York they "generally became involved in political activities only when their interests were threatened."[50]

The impetus for tensions and conflicts between German-Americans and American nativists, which were even known sometimes to lead to violent confrontations, was the social and political divide: "With regard to social life, nativists often took exception to certain customs of the Germans. The widely-subdivided, secular world of clubs, sociability and boisterous behavior or on the holy sabbath, beer-parlors, where women and children also foregathered, were things which appeared foreign to the stricter, ecclesiastically-minded American. In the domain of politics, the nativists criticized the radical, socialist Germans, who, they thought, were endangering American democracy." While the criticism of German sociability practices was aimed at the large majority of German Americans, the accusation of political radicalism applied to a small minority of German-Americans "most of whom were either uninterested in politics or conformist."[51]

Nativist pressure led to an increased delimitation of the "Little Germanies" from their American environment, creating a greater barrier to the assimilation process. These pressures furthermore provoked and stimulated a deliberate cultural Germanism: "Belief in the superiority of German culture was present, though latent, among Germans; but it was the politically sensitive "Forty-Eighters" who gave expression to the corresponding doctrines and used them in the struggle against nativism. Most German immigrants had

50. Bretting, "Little Germanies," 148. See for Milwaukee: Conzen, *Immigrant Milwaukee*; for Cincinnati: Dobbert, *Disintegration*; for New York: Bretting, *Soziale Probleme*; cf. F. Luebke, "The Germans" in *Ethnic Leadership in America*, J. Higham, ed. (Baltimore 1978), 64–90.

51. Bretting, "Old Home," 156; cf. Doerries, *Iren und Deutsche*, 189–200; Keil, ed., *Deutsche Arbeiterkultur*, 161–300; G. Moltmann, "Roots in Germany: Immigration and Acculturation of German-Americans" in *Eagle in the New World. German Immigration to Texas and America*, T. Gish and R. Spuler, eds. (Texas A & M UP 1986), 3–25.

made the effort to become Americans, without denying their German origin. If this origin was spurned, however, they were quickly ready to produce their German heritage and present it as superior."[52]

With the New Immigration from eastern, southeastern, and southern Europe increasing around the turn of the century, American nativism found new grounds and objects for animosity.[53] German nationalism, reinforced by this nativism and strengthened by the foundation of the German Reich in 1871, certainly continued to exist in the "Little Germanies." During the assimilation process, however, the German element itself slowly began to diminish, particularly as subsequent reinforcement of those communities decreased after the end of German mass immigration in the early 1890s. In fact, it was for this very reason that German ethnic leaders founded the German-American *National-Bund* in 1901, a pan-German holding with a corporate membership of numerous German-American clubs, amounting to about two million members on the eve of the First World War.[54]

The German-American conflict was thereby put on a set course, constituting the decisive factor in the decay of "Little Germany" in the United States: the old and the new world met as enemies during World War I. Demonstrative pride in German tradition, or even nationalism, became dangerous for German-Americans, especially as their leaders had originally identified themselves expressly with Imperial Germany. This resulted in a severe conflict of loyalties for German-Americans once the United States had entered the war. The outcome was a breakdown of the German-American "hyphenated culture." German ways of life faded away. German-Americans definitively became Americans of German descent.[55] National Socialism and World War II, in which Germans and Americans of German descent found themselves once again face to face, served to conclude the disintegration of "Little Germany." This time there

52. Bretting, "Old Home," 57.

53. W.P. Adams, "Die Assimilationsfrage in der amerikanischen Einwanderungsdiskussion, 1890–1930" in Bade, ed., *Auswanderer* I, 300–20; D. Hoerder, "Akkulturationsprobleme in den USA: die 'New Immigration' zwischen Einwanderung und Arbeitsmigration" in Bade, ed., *Auswanderer*, 406–28.

54. H.L. Trefousse, "Die deutschamerikanischen Einwanderer und das neugegründete Reich" in Trommler, ed., *Amerika und die Deutschen*, 177–91; Bretting, "Old Home," 157ff.; cf. Keil, ed., *Deutsche Arbeiterkultur*, 393–401.

55. F. Luebke, *Bonds of Loyalty. German Americans and World War* I (DeKalb, Ill. 1974); L.J. Rippley, "Erleichterte Amerikanisierung: Die Wirkung des Ersten Weltkriegs auf die Deutschamerikaner in den zwanziger Jahren" in Trommler, ed., *Amerika und die Deutschen*, 558–71.

was no conflict of loyalties; for most Americans of German descent, Nazi Germany had nothing in common with the "good old Germany" that they or their ancestors had once left.

Return Migration

In nineteenth-century Germany, American-German return migration certainly played a significant role in public debate and in fiction – mainly as the story of the remigration of the disappointed, the defeated migrant, only rarely of the successful one, returning alone or with their families, but never in large groups.[56] Our historical knowledge of return migration, however, is, even today, for the most part nonexistent.[57]

The reason for this is, above all, the lack of data. According to G. Moltmann's definition, one could demand that return migration "should include only those Germans who intended to immigrate permanently to America, not visitors or those seeking temporary work or exile. Only those should be counted as remigrants who had the definite intention of resettling permanently in Germany, not German-Americans returning from visits, business purposes, or as tourists."[58] But how are we to know which of the remigrants had originally been genuine emigrants? As far as American data are concerned, there have only been harbor lists regarding return migration from the United States since 1908; that is, long after German transatlantic migration had ceased to be a mass movement.[59] The only German sources of information are the reports of the Norddeutsche Lloyd in Bremen, starting in 1868, and of the Hamburg

56. See also Bade, "Trends and Issues," 2.2. Mikoletzky, *Deutsche Amerika-Auswanderung*, 181–87, 247–52.

57. Essentially biographically-oriented and focusing on outstanding personalities. A. Vagts, *Deutsch-amerikanische Rückwanderung: Probleme, Statistik, Politik, Soziologie, Biographie* (Heidelberg 1960); for regional studies see G. Kortum, "Untersuchungen zur Integration und Rückwanderung nordfriesischer Amerikaauswanderer," *Nordfriesisches Jahrbuch* 14 (1978), 45–91; idem, "Migrationstheoretische und bevölkerungsgeographische Probleme der nordfriesischen Amerikarückwanderung" in *Die deutsche und skandinavische Amerikaauswanderung im 19. und 20. Jahrhundert*, K.D. Sievers, ed. (Neumünster 1981), 111–201; research report: D. Hoerder, "Immigration and the Working Class: The Remigration Factor," *International Labor and Working Class History* 21 (1982), 28–41; for the following see G. Moltmann, "German-American Return Migration in the 19th and Early 20th Centuries," *CEH* 13, 4 (1980), 378–92.

58. Ibid., 380.

59. For estimations based on an extrapolation from these 1908 to 1914 data back into the nineteenth century see: Willcox, ed., *International Migrations* 2: 87–99; cf. M. Curti and K. Birr, "The Immigrant and the American Image in Europe, 1860–1914," *Mississippi Valley Historical Review* 37, 2 (1950), 203–30, esp. 213ff.

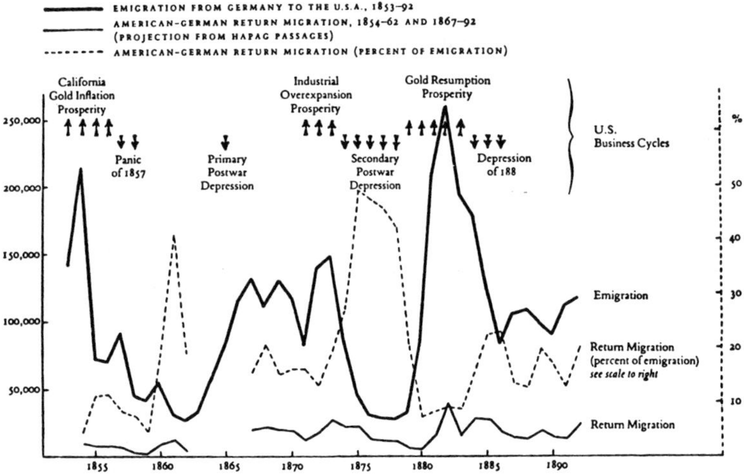

FIGURE 6.4 German Transatlantic Migration and U.S. Business Cycles, 1800s–1890s

Source: Moltmann, *Return Migration*, 382, 384f. (see n. 61)
Note: The data on U.S. business cycles are based on a graph in Harold Underwood Faulkner, *American Economic History*, 7th ed., (New York 1954), 641–42.

Americanische Packetfahrt-Actiengesellschaft (HAPAG) in Hamburg after 1854. Even the HAPAG data, however, which Moltmann evaluated in Figure 6.4, is problematic: "The HAPAG figures make no distinction between emigrants and remigrants on the one hand and visitors, businessmen, tourists, etc. on the other." Moreover, they "do not distinguish between German and non-German travelers." Finally, the extent to which "from the 1880s a growing number of transient workers influenced the course of emigration and return migration" cannot be deduced from these data.[60]

For this reason, G. Moltmann has commented with great reservation on his tentative results shown in Figure 6.4: in absolute figures, the curve of return migration appears to correspond to that of emigration on a low level. Return migration, however, seems to be more continuous and, therefore, less dependent on American business cycles. The curve of the annual percentage of return migration

60. Moltmann, "Return Migration," 382, 384f (data) and 386 (table).

shows, on the other hand, a trend contradictory to that of emigration. The trend could be interpreted as a reaction to the disturbances in the country of immigration; however, theoretically it could also be seen simply as a result of the percentage of return migration having been exaggerated on the basis of the fluctuating emigration curve.

The nonquantitative sources seem to testify that fluctuations in the return migration percentage were by no means only due to miscalculations. The estimates as made in the new investigation by Mikoletzky of the portrayal of migration in fiction, while of an equally tentative nature, support Moltmann's results: a relatively low-level return migration percentage in the mid-nineteenth century (4.7 percent, a slight increase in the 1850s –6.6 percent–, and a sharp increase in the 1860s and 1870s –18.4 percent and 23.3 percent). The climax was reached during the period of economic crisis in the mid-1870s (49.4 percent). Return migration receded in the 1880s (14.2 percent) and it finally rose again at the start of the 1890s. This pattern also corresponds to our own results concerning the currents, patterns, and structural changes in German transatlantic migration in the late nineteenth century.[61]

Migration and Related Capital and Political Movements

A few regional studies aside, economic or even econometric analyses of capital movements, as related to transatlantic mass emigration from nineteenth-century Germany, do not exist.[62] As a rule, capital export through emigration was low where and when emigration was high: in the mid-nineteenth century, the property of an unmarried male emigrant from the areas around Osnabrück, Münster, and from Württemberg ranged from 60 to 85 Talers, an unimportant sum out of which even the passage (about 30 Talers) still had to be paid.[63] One of the most crucial arguments in the nineteenth-century public discussion in Germany about the pros and cons of transatlantic emigration, however, was the complaint about the loss of "human," of "educational capital" (*Erziehungskapital*), and of capital as such. In the discussion, the arguments ranged from the boldest arithmetic calculations on the loss of capital as caused by

61. Ibid., 383, 387; Mikoletzky, *Deutsche Amerika-Auswanderung*, 188; see section Structural Changes.

62. See e.g. Kamphoefner, *Westfalen*, 57–66; v. Hippel, *Auswanderung*, 236–50.

63. Helbich, Kamphoefner, and Sommer, eds., *Briefe aus Amerika*, 14ff.; cf. Faltin, *Auswanderung aus der Pfalz*, 104–7.

emigration, to considerations of how this loss could be turned into a profit for Germany.[64]

With regard to transatlantic migration and related political movements, it is necessary to distinguish between immigration and emigration. As far as the social and economic history of German immigration is concerned, we are now well informed by American studies, as well as by West German research, which has recently been strongly intensified, providing a few outstanding case studies.[65] Research on German-American ethnic leadership – if there was something like that – is only in its initial stages.[66] As regards political participation as such, it can in general be assumed that the political activities attracting the attention of, and often being criticized by, nativist circles were in fact practiced only by a small but radical, and therefore striking, minority:

> Composed for the most part of refugees from the German 'Vormärz,' the 1848 revolution, and Bismarck's anti-socialist policy, it supplied the leaders, in the large cities such as New York or Chicago, of the Communist and Socialist wings of the working-class movement. Even freethinkers and anarchists in the United States often proved to be citizens who had emigrated from Germany. They were a favourite target of the nativist. How far anti-foreign feelings, directed against these groups, had spread, became clear in the proceedings against and verdicts upon the suspected terrorists in the Chicago Haymarket demonstration of 1886.[67]

As regards emigration from Germany and related political movements, as well as policies, one needs primarily to address three fields of research. On the one hand, there is the history of emigration as a "social protest movement" and, at the same time, as a "social safety valve." In this field we so far have some good answers; however, there still are more questions than answers, particularly due to the lack of adequate regional studies.[68] In addition, there are the above-mentioned concepts regarding the "redirecting" of transatlantic emigration, which have been extensively discussed by the

64. See n. 8.

65. See e.g. Bretting, *Soziale Probleme*; Doerries, *Iren und Deutsche*; Kamphoefner, *Westfalen*; Keil and Jentz, eds., *German Workers*.

66. K. Conzen, "Deutschamerikaner und die Erfindung der Ethnizität" and W.P. Adams, "Ethnische Führungsrollen und die Deutschamerikaner" in Trommler, ed., *Amerika und die Deutschen*, 149–64 and 165–76.

67. Bretting, "Old Home," 156; cf. C. Poore, "Wessen Feier? Die Hundertjahrfeier von 1876 und die deutschamerikanische sozialistische Kultur" in Trommler, ed., *Amerika und die Deutschen*, 192–203; Keil, *Deutsche Arbeiterkultur*, 256–81; H. Überhorst, *The German Element in the US Labor Movement* (Bonn 1983); D. Hoerder, ed., *The Immigrant Labor Press in North America, 1840s–1970s* (Westport 1986).

68. See n. 8.

contemporary public from mid-nineteenth-century Germany until the German colonial movement of the 1880s. Respective illusions ranged from the idea of founding a German state in the United States to founding the German "Federal States of South America" by informal expansion through "organized" settlement migration. The line of illusions ended as late as the early 1880s with ideas to redirect transatlantic emigration into the dreamed-of German colonial Empire, which was completely unsuitable for a mass settlement migration; however, this became evident in 1884/85.[69]

Finally, there is the history of German "emigration policy": the secular transatlantic mass movement from nineteenth-century Germany was to a great extent left to itself.[70] No restricting laws as yet existed in the United States. In Germany, restrictions with a deterrent effect no longer existed, apart from the prosecution of commercial emigration agents from abroad and of emigrants about to be drafted for military service. The latter measure was, however, mostly of no avail because the offenders had in most cases already emigrated via foreign seaports. The emigration laws of the German Federal States were for the most part relatively liberal. Their emigration policies – to the extent that they had any – were occasionally linked to the above-mentioned idea of purposely exporting social problems by means of transatlantic emigration. This central idea pervaded the entire nineteenth century, admittedly without culminating in large official programs, because migration also caused national and cultural losses.[71] On the Reich level, the first German emigration law of 1897 only provided indirect measures for controlling migration and was introduced too late anyway. When it came into effect, transatlantic mass emigration from Germany was already on the brink of disappearing.[72]

69. E. Schnitzer, *Der Nationalgedanke und die deutsche Auswanderung nach den Vereinigten Staaten von Amerika in der ersten Hälfte des 19. Jahrhunderts* (Dresden 1935); G. Moltmann, "Überseeische Siedlungen und weltpolitische Spekulationen: Friedrich Gerstäcker und die Frankfurter Zentralgewalt 1849," *Frankfurter Historische Abhandlungen* 17 (1978), 56–72; Fenske, "Deutsche Auswanderung"; Bade, *Friedrich Fabri*, 64–120, 191–200, 354–68.

70. A. Bretting, "Der Staat und die deutsche Massenauswanderung. Gesetzgeberische Maßnahmen in Deutschland und Amerika" in Trommler, ed., *Amerika und die Deutschen*, 50–63.

71. E.v. Philippovich, ed., *Auswanderung und Auswanderungspolitik in Deutschland. Berichte über die Entwicklung und den gegenwärtigen Zustand des Auswanderungswesens in den Einzelstaaten und im Reich* (Leipzig 1892); W. Mönckmeier, *Die deutsche überseeische Auswanderung. Ein Beitrag zur deutschen Wanderungsgeschichte* (Jena 1912), 228–52; Bade, *Friedrich Fabri*; v. Hippel, *Auswanderung*, 94–112, 133–37.

72. P. Goetsch, *Das Reichsgesetz über das Auswanderungswesen vom 9.6.1897* 2d ed. (Berlin 1907); cf. Mönckmeier, *Deutsche überseeische Auswanderung*, 252–69.

7

Italian Emigration in the Post-Unification Period, 1861–1971

LUIGI DE ROSA

The Periodization of Italian Emigration

Emigration has been a constant feature of Italian population movements. Even if we limit our study to the post-unification period, that is, from 1861 onward, we can say that, save for the difficult years of the First (1917 to 1918) and Second (1941 to 1942) World Wars (when emigration fell to a negligible level) Italian migratory movements were never insignificant.[1]

During the entire period under study, a flood of men, women, and children, with fluctuating degrees of intensity, left their native country to move abroad, to Europe or elsewhere, in search of better working and living conditions. Between 1861 and 1971, about 25 million people emigrated from Italy, and even though the greater part subsequently returned to their home country, about 9 million individuals settled elsewhere.[2]

The constancy of the phenomenon can perhaps partly be explained by the entrepreneurial legacy bequeathed by the Italian merchants of the Middle Ages – those of Amalfi, Pisa, Genoa, Siena, Venice, etc. – who widely ranged the Mediterranean and traded to and from North Europe; or by the spirit of adventure and curiosity of countrymen such as Marco Polo and the Vivaldi brothers, who, as Dante recalls, became lost in the Atlantic while searching for new sea routes; or to the likes of Christopher Columbus, the Cabots, Amerigo Vespucci, and Pigafetta, who went in search of new routes to the Indies. All this may well have exerted an influence.

1. The number of emigrants fell from 142,364 in 1916 to 46,496 in 1917 and 28,311 in 1918; and from 51,817 in 1940 to 8,809 in 1941 and 8,246 in 1942. Cf. *Sommario di statistiche storiche italiane, 1861–1955*. ISTAT (Roma 1958) 65.

2. Cf. M. Livi Bacci, *La trasformazione demografica delle società europee* (Torino 1977), 251–256.

A decisive role, however, was undoubtedly played by the imbalance between population and resources, which was to become more acute in time. For Italy is the European country where, notwithstanding the constant migratory movements just mentioned, the population grew at a rhythm in the last century second only to that of Great Britain; moreover, this occurred without Italy's economic resources developing, at least up to the last war, at the same rate as Britain. From about 22 million inhabitants in 1861, at the moment of unification, the resident Italian population rose to 35 million in 1911, to about 47 million in 1951, and to more than 54 million in 1971; thereby almost trebling in the period 1861 to 1971.[3]

It is important to appreciate that the continual rise in the population was not accompanied by a corresponding rise in the rate of emigration, a sign that the country was able, and has been able, to absorb a not insignificant part of the demographic surplus, thanks to the progressive creation of job opportunities. There have been, however, three periods when, above and beyond the normal phases of rise and fall in the migratory cycle – related in some way, even if inversely, to the Italian economic cycle – emigration has reached such notable levels as to be considered remarkable.

Two of these periods embrace respectively the years following the First and the Second World Wars. During the period 1919 to 1923 the economic, social, and political crisis that Italy underwent can be taken as the principal cause of a renewed increase in emigration, which would have been even greater if the United States had not put a limit to the migratory flow. Emigration, which had risen from 253, 224 units in 1919 to 614, 611 in 1920, fell, in fact, to 201, 291 in 1921, thereafter to increase gradually to 389, 957 in 1923.[4] In reality, even if the imposition of national immigration quotas in the United States had the effect of increasing emigration from Italy to France and Argentina, it seems to have led to the overall reduction of Italian migration. Post-war emigration continued to decrease rapidly, with a final boost at the beginning of the 1929 economic crisis, when between 1929 and 1931 about 596,000 people emigrated, the majority going to France.[5]

While the period 1919 to 1923 followed a war from which Italy, together with the Allied Powers, had emerged victorious, the period 1945 to 1960 followed in the wake of a harsh and heavy defeat. Italy had been the theater of military operations throughout her territory,

3. See Appendix Table 1.
4. See Appendix Table 2.
5. See Appendix Table 3.

from Sicily to the Po Valley, and had suffered wide-scale destruction both to her infrastructure and to her industries and cities. Therefore, in the aftermath of the war, she did not appear to offer great hopes for the unemployed masses. Consequently, emigration began to rise again, with an expatriation of more than 308,000 Italians already in 1948. This migratory flow continued in the following years, and 2,937,406 Italians emigrated during the decade 1951 to 1960. After slowing down for a short while, emigration started to increase again rapidly, and during the decade 1961 to 1970 the number of expatriations reached 2,646,994.[6] In the following years, however, not only did expatriation progressively decrease, but an increasing number of emigrants returned to their homeland.[7]

If in the period following World War I the United States and Argentina attracted about 50 percent of Italian emigration, in the post-Second World War years, the flow was principally orientated toward Europe.[8] France, demographically impoverished by her neo-Malthusian policies, continued to be one of the favorite countries of Italian emigrants. Later, however, she was overtaken by Switzerland.[9] There also began to be substantial Italian emigration to Belgium and, above all, to Germany.[10] Outside Europe, Argentina continued to attract a certain number of Italian emigrants, as did Brazil.[11] Emigration to Canada and Australia, on the other hand, which had been virtually insignificant up till then, intensified, while emigration to the United States continued at a modest level.[12]

In contrast to post-First World War emigration, when peasants formed the principal nuclei of migrants, emigration in the period following World War II favored industrial laborers; moreover, whenever the supply of the latter was insufficient, peasants were expected to, and did, turn into factory workers, miners, etc. It is necessary to add that, while in the period following World War I, emigration affected above all northern Italy, in the post-Second World War period the regions of northeast Italy (the Veneto, Friuli, Emilia), and especially the south of Italy and the islands, were mostly affected. While the southern regions had not begun to close the gap separating them from the north, in spite of government intervention, the regions of northern Italy had not only managed to

6. See Appendix Table 4.
7. See Appendix Table 5.
8. See Appendix Table 6.
9. See Appendix Table 7.
10. See Appendix Table 8.
11. See Appendix Table 9.
12. See Appendix Table 10.

protect their industries during the war, but they had embarked upon a rapid and intense process of industrialization immediately after the end of the conflict, absorbing a large part of the population surplus that had been created in agriculture, then undergoing total mechanization.[13]

Yet, however significant the migratory flow of the aforementioned period was, undoubtedly the great era of Italian emigration must be considered the period between the 1880s and the eve of World War I. Between 1881 and 1910 alone, 10,720,527 Italians emigrated, at a rhythm that progressively intensified with the passing of every decade: 1,879,201 in the period 1881 to 1890; 2,834,726 in the period 1891 to 1900; and 6,026,690 in the period 1901 to 1910.[14] This era of grand exodus was determined on the one hand, by the extraordinary economic progress taking place in several countries in Europe and the New World; on the other hand, by economic changes occurring during the same period for Italian workers abroad, lured largely by the prospects of high wages, stability, and the general improvement of the standard of living, both for themselves and for their children. We must remember that this was also the period of the Italian "take-off." Moreover, it should be underlined that such a "take-off" had been preceded by a radical transformation of the model of Italian economic development. Between the end of the 1870s and the end of the 1880s, Italian economic policy radically altered. From a period of free-trade policies in which the State assumed a largely neutral position in industrial questions, there was a change to a period of protectionist tariffs and of increasing State intervention in the economy.[15]

This State intervention was determined by the need to protect the interests of the domestic industries in the sectors of iron and steel, naval-mechanical, and military defense.[16] The instruments were government orders and the granting of special subsidies. During the period 1881 to 1888, as has been shown, the greatest progress was made essentially in four sectors: metallurgical, mechanical, chemical, and textiles, with growth rates that, at least until 1913, were never again attained, except for the mechanical and textile sectors.[17]

13. L. De Rosa, *La rivoluzione industriale in Italia* (Bari 1981) 77ff.

14. Livi Bacci, *Trasformazione*, 253.

15. De Rosa, *Rivoluzione industriale*, 17.

16. L. De Rosa, *Iniziativa e capitale straniero nell'industria metalmeccanica del Mezzogiorno* (Napoli 1968), 136ff.; De Rosa, *Rivoluzione industriale*, 158ff.

17. A. Gershenkron, *Economic Backwardness in Historical Perspective* (Cambridge, Mass. 1962), in translation *Il problema storico dell'arretratezza economica* (Torino 1965), 84.

The magnitude of the industrial progress and of the technical modernization that had taken place emerges clearly from the information we have about the consumption of energy in that period.[18]

The crisis that exploded in 1888 with the intensifying of protectionism, with the application of the new customs tariff, and with the breakdown in commercial relations with France, caused by the early rescinding of the trade treaty binding the latter country to Italy, signaled a temporary arrest for the industrial growth of the country. This growth, however, was to return around the middle of the 1890s with even greater vigor than before. Progress was made in all the industrial sectors, as was demonstrated not only by the increase in both the number of boilers employed in industry and the amount of horsepower they were able to generate, but also by the multiplication of the number of joint-stock companies operating in industry and the increase of their capital. After 1898 the electrical and electromechanical industries also rapidly developed.[19]

The Geographical Origins of Italian Emigrants

This industrial development, which led to the urbanization of great masses of peasants, especially in the Genoa-Turin-Milan triangle, not only modified the town-countryside relationship, but it also brought about a notable development in the building, food, furniture, and clothing industries. On the one hand, this widened the country's industrial base; on the other, it reduced the agricultural work force.

The consequent rise in wages had the effect of reducing, rather than increasing, the number of employed as the landowners set about replacing manual labor with agricultural machinery, which was undergoing continual perfection and was now being turned out at continually lower costs by the country's advancing mechanical industry.

In reality, even though the phenomenon was more widespread in the north, agriculture lost workers all over Italy. Later on we will consider the main reasons contributing to the expulsion of the population from southern agriculture. In the meanwhile, it should be kept in mind that so far as the active population is concerned, the

18. De Rosa, *Rivoluzione industriale*, 32ff.
19. Ibid., 42.

TABLE 7.1 Emigration from Italy's Major Regions

	1876–1880	1881–1890	1891–1900	1901–1910
Northwest	250,060	589,340	506,753	1,139,550
Northeast	186,140	635,441	1,166,947	1,313,127
Central	37,821	130,253	216,783	757,702
Total	474,021	1,374,990	1,383,730	3,210,379

TABLE 7.2 Emigration from Northwestern Regions

	1876–1880	1881–1890	1891–1900	1901–1910
Piedmont	137,718	311,393	259,965	556,289
Lombardy	90,198	221,128	207,774	513,936
Liguria	22,144	56,783	39,014	69,325
Total	250,060	589,304	506,753	1,139,550

percentage of agricultural workers fell in the northern regions from 34.8 percent to 26 percent between 1871 and 1911, while the percentage of industrial workers rose from 12.2 percent (1871) to 14.7 percent (1911).[20] For those who found themselves expelled from agricultural work, and for whom the towns were unable to offer an adequate alternative, emigration appeared as the only concrete and convenient prospect. In short, the industrialization of northern Italy produced an emigration incentive.

The phenomenon is evident not only for the regions of northeast, but also for those of northwest and central Italy. The following figures speak for themselves.[21]

Of course, not every region made an equal contribution to emigration. If we also take into account the population sizes of the respective regions, we can see that the northwest of Italy, Piedmont and Lombardy, were the regions with the greatest rate of emigration. Above all, it was the populations of the pre-Alpine and Alpine areas that provided the biggest contingents of emigrants.

As far as the northeast of Italy is concerned, the region with the highest emigration rate was the Veneto, especially in the pre-Alpine and Alpine areas of this territory, as the following figures reveal:

20. Ibid., 82.
21. Livi Bacci, *Trasformazione*, 254.

TABLE 7.3 Emigration from Northeastern Regions

	1876–1880	1881–1890	1891–1900	1901–1910
Veneto	77,555	286,798	576,358	597,816
Friuli-Venezia Giulia	88,466	301,063	457,543	383,771
Emilia	20,119	67,580	133,046	331,540
Total	186,140	655,441	1,166,947	1,313,127

TABLE 7.4 Emigration from the Central Regions of Italy

	1876–1880	1881–1890	1891–1900	1901–1910
Tuscany	35,909	109,850	144,397	312,014
Umbria	141	870	7,855	101,301
The Marches	1,481	19,369	49,200	221,519
Latium	290	209	15,331	122,868
Total	37,821	130,253	216,783	757,702

With regard to central Italy, it was Tuscany that provided the greatest number of emigrants, above all her Apennine zones.

The greatest contribution, however, came from the southern regions. The *agrarian inquest* of the 1880s had already brought to the fore the precarious conditions of the life of the peasants, together with the backwardness of the type of agriculture that prevailed there. Impoverished by excessive taxation, lacking sufficient capital for the purchase of state-owned land and of the land confiscated from the church and offered for sale by the State, and lacking adequate infrastructures, south Italian agriculture remained in a depressed state. It consisted on the one hand of small peasant holdings that, in the majority of cases, did not go beyond a subsistence economy, and on the other hand, of the latifundia, for the most part given over to extensive farming, particularly to the cultivation of cereals. Nevertheless, part of the south's agricultural classes had made great efforts to take advantage of the free-trade policies adopted by the central government. A restricted group of small and medium landowners – made up for the most part of lawyers, doctors, magistrates, engineers, high-ranking civil servants, etc. – had dedicated themselves to replacing the unproductive cultivation of wheat with horticulture, fruit-farming, and vine-growing; the latter stimulated by the pressing demand for wine suitable for mixing in France, where the vineyards had been devastated by phylloxera.

This transformation stimulated considerable industrial development and brought notable benefits to several southern regions, such as Puglia, Basilicata, Calabria, and Sicily. It came to a sudden halt with the adoption of the protectionist tariff of 1887 and above all – so it is presumed – because of the customs rupture with France, following the early cancellation by Italy of the commercial treaty between the two countries.

Deprived of a market for its most lucrative agricultural products, and unable to recover the capital invested in that sector (capital that had been procured thanks to the contracting of very large bank loans), the south of Italy relapsed into a terrible crisis that was not only agrarian in nature but also financial. Public demonstrations and clashes with the police typified popular reaction to the decline in employment and to the bankruptcies of landowners and banks. The industrial tariff of 1887 set a high duty on imported cereals in order to deal with the competition of American grains, safeguarding the interests of extensive farming to the detriment of intensive farming (represented by market gardening and fruit farming). This policy took every prospect of economic and occupational improvement away from the southern peasantry. In the following years it became increasingly apparent that emigrants from the south of Italy, who in the past had left their native country to work temporarily abroad, were now leaving in growing numbers and with no intention of returning. The banking and farming crisis of 1888 provided the impetus for a massive exodus to foreign countries, depopulating entire villages and agricultural centers, especially in the hilly and mountainous inland regions. To grasp fully the dimensions of this movement, a glance at the following data will suffice.[22]

A more detailed examination of this phenomenon in terms of specific regions reveals that Campania, Calabria, the Abruzzi, and Puglia (in that respective order) supplied the largest number of emigrants. It is important to note, however, that the lesser figure that emerges for Basilicata is misleading. In fact, considering its population size, the rate of emigration (and also that of the Abruzzi and Molise) by percentage is even higher than that of the other regions.[23]

In all, Italian emigration increased more than tenfold between the years 1876 to 1880 and 1901 to 1910 (from 543,248 to 6,026,690).

22. Ibid.
23. Ibid.

TABLE 7.5 Emigration from the Southern Regions

	1876–1880	1881–1890	1891–1900	1901–1910
South	65,028	451,811	766,986	1,985,643
Sicily	4,832	50,955	170,662	774,096
Total	69,860	502,766	937,648	2,759,739

TABLE 7.6 Emigration from the Regions of Mainland Southern Italy

	1876–1880	1881–1890	1891–1900	1901–1910
Total	65,028	451,811	766,986	1,985,643

The Destinations of Italian Emigrants

The enormous number of emigrants headed for numerous destinations in every continent; however, 90 percent of them preferred Europe and North and South America. Until 1883, Europe assimilated more than 50 percent of Italian emigrants, a figure that, except for the years between 1898 to 1900, was never reached again, even though Europe continued to play an important role by assimilating more than 33 percent of Italian emigrants during that period. This percentage, however, is related to a total migratory movement, which during this same period increased from 157,103 (1885) to 872,508 (1913): in other words, emigrants to Europe increased from 78,232 (1885) to 307,627 (1913).[24] A substantial part of this emigration was not of a permanent nature. Some workers changed locations temporarily, often because of seasonal employment or because of the construction of public works. Nearly all European countries were involved. Although there was no dearth of Italian emigrants to Russia, Sweden, Norway, Denmark, Great Britain, Ireland, Portugal, Spain, and the Benelux countries, and to eastern Mediterranean and Balkan countries such as Greece, Montenegro, Serbia, Bulgaria, Rumania, and Turkey, the vast majority went to Central European countries such as Austria-Hungary, Germany, Switzerland, and to France.

In the period immediately following the unification of Italy, most

24. *Annuario statistico della emigrazione italiana dal 1876 al 1925*, Commissariato generale dell'emigrazione (Roma 1926), 8.

emigrants went to France. From the end of the 1880s, however, this preference switched to Austria and Hungary. By the end of the century, Germany, and especially Switzerland, began to attract a growing number of Italian workers, whereas their influx into Austria-Hungary decreased.[25]

As mentioned above, most of this emigration was temporary. Nevertheless, it was not rare that emigrants successfully adapted to their new countries and remained there permanently. One thing is certain in that the censuses of Italians abroad showed an increase: from 155,278, resulting from the censuses of Italians in European countries for the year 1871, to 380,352 in 1881, 470,118 in 1891, 649,095 in 1901, and 910,568 in 1911. In the central empires of Germany and Austria-Hungary, the Italian immigrant residents increased from 30,862 in 1871 to 192,301 in 1911.[26] Furthermore, in France the increase went from 244,170 in 1881 to 426,434 in 1911.[27]

From the end of the last century, Italian emigration to the Americas intensified; even before that, large numbers of emigrants had been heading for the New World. In 1879, for example, 30.04 percent emigrated to the New World: the largest part (11.01 percent) went to Argentina, 6.67 percent to Brazil, while the remainder went to the United States (2.60 percent), Central America (3.91 percent), and Uruguay, Paraguay, etc. It is important to emphasize the fact that, from 1881 onward, there began to be a sizeable increase in emigration to the Americas. The major destinations for Italian emigrants were the United States, Brazil, and Argentina.

Until 1889, before the beginning of its economic crisis, Argentina assimilated the largest number of Italian emigrants, even as many as half of all emigrants to the Americas. From 1887 onward, however, Brazil emerged as the main destination, also absorbing over half of the total Italian emigration to the Americas. After 1897, this interest in Brazil decreased due to both the working conditions of the Italian immigrant and to the fall in coffee prices. The coffee industry was then the primary factor in the rapid colonization of the country.

Italian emigration to Brazil never again attained noteworthy levels, and although emigration to Argentina showed an upward trend after 1903, it was the United States that began to receive the majority of Italian emigrants when emigration to the Americas was rapidly increasing.[28] The phenomenon becomes evident if one com-

25. Ibid., 89ff.
26. Ibid., 1533.
27. Ibid., 1534.
28. For Italian emigration to Brazil, see L. De Rosa, "Emigrazione italiana in

pares the data of the migratory flow toward the Americas and the United States during the same period.[29]

Censuses of Italians residing abroad indicate an extraordinary increase in the Italian population in the Americas, from 87,026 in 1871 to 579,335 in 1881, 1,426,446 in 1891, 2,782,225 in 1901, and 4,698,793 in 1911.[30] It is worth noting that this Italian presence was considerable in Brazil, Argentina, and Uruguay, not negligible in Canada, Chile, Peru, Mexico, etc., and massive in the United States, where it increased from 170,000 in 1881 to over 2,000,000 in 1911.

The migratory phenomenon involved all the regions of Italy, and all the above-cited continents and countries received Italians from all regions, especially from the south and the central north. It has been ascertained, however, that emigration to America was primarily characteristic of the southern regions of Italy. Only Argentina and Brazil had a noteworthy percentage of emigrants from the north of Italy, which itself was nevertheless overshadowed by emigration from the south. More specifically, the largest groups of emigrants to the United States and Canada came from Sicily, Calabria, and the Marches. Most of the emigrants to Brazil came from the Veneto, Campania, and Calabria.[31]

After Migrating from Italy: Economic Achievements

The majority of adult males who emigrated came from agricultural centers and villages and were essentially employed in jobs related to agriculture. Skilled workers, artisans, and merchants were in the minority, as were professionals, artists, and domestics.[32] As to emigrant females, the majority of these were also employed in agriculture at the beginning; thereafter, the number employed as domestics increased.[33]

Brasile: un bilancio" in *Emigrazioni europee e popolo brasiliano*, G. Rosoli ed. (Roma 1987), 153–167; for Italian emigration to Argentina, see L. De Rosa, "L'emigrazione italiana in Argentina: un bilancio," *Rassegna Economica* no. 6 (1986), 1213. See Appendix Table 11.

Italian emigration to Argentina:

1907	107,227
1908	104,718
1913	111,500

Source: *Annuario Statistico*, 88.

29. See Appendix Table 12.
30. Ibid., 1535.
31. Ibid.,148.
32. See Appendix Table 13.
33. See Appendix Table 14.

When this extraordinary migratory movement was directed toward transoceanic destinations, and not toward European countries, which could be reached by train, the departure points were several large Italian ports. Of the three major embarkation ports (Genoa, Naples, and Palermo), Naples was the most important in terms of the number of emigrant departures. All the major shipping companies, both national and foreign (English, German, French, Spanish, etc.), that transported emigrants, were based in Naples. Many emigrants, however, left from ports such as Le Havre, or other French or German ports, in order to avoid Italian police control or perhaps under the illusion that leaving from a foreign port facilitated entrance into the United States.

In the Americas the principal landing ports of Italian emigrants were New York (which received 90 percent of Italians migrating to the United States), Boston, and Philadelphia. As most immigrants only possessed limited financial resources, they generally settled around these port areas. Thus, there soon arose conspicuous Italian communities in coastal cities of states such as Pennsylvania, New York, Massachusetts, Connecticut, and Rhode Island. At the turn of the century, for instance, New York could almost be considered one of the largest Italian cities, with several hundred thousands of Italian residents. Many Italians subsequently were attracted by the employment opportunities generated by industrial development in Chicago, by the mining industry in Denver, Colorado, by the sugar industry in Louisiana, and by the rapid urban growth of San Francisco, both before and after the 1908 earthquake. Italians were eventually to be found in nearly every state of the Union.

In Brazil, there were two principal ports of entry for immigrants: Rio de Janeiro and Santos; Porto Alegre was less important. Italian communities of considerable size sprung up along the coast, but the majority of Italian immigrants went to the southern states (Espirito Santo and Minas Gerais) and chiefly to the capital of São Paulo, a city characterized by a prevalently Italian population.[34] The main ports of arrival in Argentina were Buenos Aires and Rosario, and many Italians settled there permanently. A sizeable portion of the population of the capital was Italian, and considerable numbers of Italians were also residing in Rosario, Cordoba, Mendoza, and even in Salta and Jujuy.[35]

34. De Rosa, "Emigrazione italiana in Brasile."
35. De Rosa, "Emigrazione italiana in Argentina."

In general, although most immigrants were of peasant origin, they preferred to settle in the cities (as was the case in Brazil), even if their initial destination had been the countryside. City neighborhoods thus acquired an Italian or even regional Italian flavor. If there were no industrial jobs available in the cities, the Italian immigrants generally preferred commerce, especially the kinds more closely related to their farming origins. In the United States, selling vegetables became a typically Italian occupation: often beginning with a simple stand, with luck one could hope to open a shop, then a chain of stores, and finally to control a share of the fruit and vegetable market.

The hotel and restaurant business also employed a large number of Italians. In both North and South America it was not rare, however, to find Italians involved in higher-level commerce (e.g., jewelry, textiles, mechanical products, import-export, etc.). It was also common, especially in South America, to find Italians in industry (mechanical and textile), farming (mills, macaroni, and biscuits manufacturing), as well as in banking. In Argentina and Brazil, Italian immigrants, in fact, participated in the creation of banks, which were quite successful.

One of the most characteristic, and constant, aspects of Italian emigration was the fact that the emigrants sent financial help to family members left behind.[36] The volume of this aid increased along with the volume of emigration. The statistical data (although controversial because of the criteria with which these were elaborated or interpreted) are sufficient proof that these remittances increased rapidly after the beginning of the century, from 9 million lire in 1902 to approximately 85 million lire in 1914. Obviously, the major contributions came from the United States, followed by Argentina, Brazil, Canada, and other countries; the order of which confirms the geographical distribution of the Italian diaspora.

The constant and increasing flow of funds, while ameliorating conditions for family members left behind, was also an important factor in the balance of payments, and this was a vital contribution to the strengthening of the lire. This enabled the Italian Government, at the beginning of this century, to abandon the forced currency regime, which had until then been imposed on the lire, and to restore its convertibility to gold.

Indirectly, then, emigration contributed to improving the Italian

36. L. De Rosa, *Emigranti, capitali e banche* (Napoli 1981); L. De Rosa, "Emigrantes italianos, Bancos y remesas: El caso argentino" in *La Inmigración italiana en la Argentina*, F. Devoto and G. Rosoli, eds., (Buenos Aires 1985), 241–70.

monetary system. Moreover, as many emigrants returned home after several years of having worked in foreign factories and other sectors, it is hardly necessary to point out that they brought back considerable "know-how," new initiatives, and, most important, an open outlook providing a general stimulus for progress. The repatriated emigrant was usually called "the American," and in his native town he or she became a source of experience and knowledge. On the one hand, the returned emigrant contributed to the promotion of the myth of America as the land of opportunity, wealth, and work – a myth that became even more fascinating and attractive at the end of World War II when thousands of Italians emigrated. On the other hand, the returned emigrant also contributed to providing those who had remained in Italy with new stimuli and conceptions of products and techniques, which were inevitably useful to national progress.

It is necessary to add that the Italian State hardly remained indifferent toward the migratory phenomenon in the case of the countries receiving Italian emigrants, and subsequently passed emigration legislation imposing restrictions and setting hygiene, health, moral, and economic requirements for these immigrants. Up until the last decade of the last century, in fact, the attitude of Italy's government was on the whole unfavorable toward emigration. This was prompted by the landowners, representing the principal electoral base of the democratic government set up in 1861. The central government was sensitive to the worries of these landowners about a possible depauperization of the labor market. Thus, the State sought to discourage emigration, creating difficulties in issuing passports.

The intensification of emigration, however, appeared to benefit the Italian economy, and a lively political debate arose regarding this issue. Emigration began to be considered less of an evil and more of a benefit. Toward the end of the nineteenth century, there was a general feeling that the State could no longer remain insensitive to this issue and that it should not abandon the emigrants, particularly in the light of the growing number of cases of abuse against emigrants, being recorded both in Italy and abroad. In 1901 a law was passed setting up the General Commissariate of Emigration ("Commissariato Generale dell'Emigrazione"), charged with assisting the emigrants at the ports of departure, during their journey as well as in the country of arrival. The Commissariate was authorized to exercise control over the navigation companies and their agents, only authorizing the transport of emigrants on ships that satisfied the necessary requirements and offered guarantees with regard to accommodation of the passengers, to hygiene and sanitary conditions, and to the diet and the quality of food prepared. A representative of the Commissariate, and a doctor employed by the same, were to travel with the emigrants in order to ensure that the navigation company observed these conditions and to make a report for the Commissariate. At the embarkation ports, the Commissariate arranged for the setting up of offices, for the purpose of giving assistance to the emigrants and, at Naples and Palermo, for the setting up of an emigrants' hospice, where emigrants could stay at little expense while they were awaiting embarkation and could thereby avoid falling victim to the speculation of hoteliers and roomletters. At the main landing ports, the same Commissariate organized other assistance offices, as well as offices that acted as job agencies. It also sent its own inspectors to the prospective countries of Italian emigration in order to gather information about opportunities and working conditions.

The State also concerned itself with the protection of the emigrants' savings and safeguarding the transfer of these savings to Italy. This had become necessary as the emigrants had become victims of numerous cases of abuse and fraud. With another law of 1901, one of the Italian note-issuing institutes, the Banco di Napoli, was empowered to see to the safeguarding, or to the remission at low expense, of the emigrant's savings through the issuing of a special certificate, the "emigrants' voucher" (*vaglia dell'emigrante*). Correspondents and representatives were appointed in those countries with a considerable number of Italian emigrants.

In view of its operations in the south of Italy (the area with the greatest rate of emigration), the Banco di Napoli was subsequently induced to open its own branch in New York – the first Italian bank in the United States – and later, also one in Chicago. In addition, it opened a branch in Buenos Aires for the same reasons.

When Italian emigrants later improved their economic position and began to embark on their own industrial and commercial enterprises, other Italian credit institutions were induced to open branches in the various countries of Italian emigration, or to acquire shares in local banks. Before World War I, such banks included the Banca Italiana di Sconto, the Banca Commerciale Italiana, and the Banco di Roma. In this way, it is possible to say without exaggerating that the Italian migratory flow carried with it a financial flow, controlled by the emigrants, which was not only based on the emigrants' remittances, but also resulted from the importations demanded by the emigrants from Italy, as well as from the emigrant's gradual involvement in more substantial and advantageous economic activities abroad. In the year following World War I, with the slowing of Italian emigration, the General Commissariate of Emigration ceased to exist, and the Banco di Napoli no longer enjoyed a monopoly over the safeguarding and transfer of the Italian emigrants' remittances. Moreover, the second and third generation of emigrants no longer had the same interest in assisting relatives left behind in Italy as their fathers and grandfathers once had. Thus, the Banco di Napoli began to take on the same function as the other Italian banks abroad, little by little widening its activity beyond the limited scope of the Italian overseas communities and extending it to the entire local financial market. At least from the beginning of 1901, another migratory flow began to interest Italians: the flow of capital.

APPENDIX

TABLE 1 Population At Each Census (figures rounded off to the thousand)

1861	22,182,000
1871	27,303,000
1881	28,953,000
1901	32,965,000
1911	35,845,000
1921	38,449,000
1931	41,652,000
1936	42,994,000
1951	47,516,000
1961	50,624,000
1971	54,137,000

Source: *Sommario di statistiche storiche dell'Italia, 1861–1975* ISTAT (Roma 1976), 11.

TABLE 2 Emigration from Italy

1918	28,311
1919	253,224
1920	614,611
1921	201,291
1922	281,270
1923	389,957
1924	364,614
1925	280,081
1926	262,396
1927	218,934
1928	149,967

Source: *Sommario, 1861–1955*, 65.

TABLE 3 Emigration from Italy

1930	280,097
1931	165,860
1932	83,343

Source: *Sommario, 1861–1955*, 65.

TABLE 4 Emigration from Italy

1946	110,286
1947	254,144
1948	308,515
1949	254,469
1950	200,306
1951	293,057
1952	277,535
1953	224,671
1954	250,925
1955	196,826
1956	344,802
1957	341,733
1958	255,459
1959	268,490
1960	383,908
1961	387,123
1962	365,611
1963	277,611
1964	258,482
1965	282,643
1966	296,494
1967	229,264
1968	215,713
1969	182,199
1970	151,854
1971	167,721
1972	141,852
1973	123,802
1974	112,020
1975	92,666

Source: *Sommario, 1861–1975*, 34.

TABLE 5 Emigration from Italy

	Expatriations	Repatriations
1971	167,721	128,572
1972	141,852	138,246
1973	123,802	125,168
1974	112,020	116,708
1975	92,666	122,774

Source: *Sommario, 1861–1975*, 34.

TABLE 6 Expatriations to:

	France	Switzerland	Un. States	Argentina	Total
1919	98,281	20,838	82,492	12,834	253,224
1920	157,025	24,277	349,042	37,431	614,611
1921	44,782	8,753	67,495	33,277	201,291
1922	99,464	7,464	41,637	63,582	281,270

Source: *Sommario, 1861–1955*, 66.

	France	Switzerl.	U. States	Argentina	Canada	Total
1946	28,135	48,808	5,442	749	–	110,286
1947	53,245	105,112	23,471	23,379	58	254,144
1948	40,231	102,241	16,677	69,602	2,406	308,515
1949	52,345	29,726	11,486	98,262	5,991	254,469
1950	18,083	27,144	8,998	78,531	7,135	200,306
1951	35,099	66,040	10,225	56,630	21,467	293,057

Source: *Sommario, 1861–1975*, 34–35.

TABLE 7 Italian Emigration to France and Switzerland

	France	Switzerland
1952	53,810	61,593
1953	36,687	57,236
1954	28,305	65,671
1955	40,713	71,735
1956	87,552	75,632
1957	114,974	78,882
1958	72,469	57,453
1959	64,259	82,532
1960	58,624	128,257
1961	49,188	142,114
1962	34,911	143,054
1963	20,264	122,018
1964	15,782	111,863
1965	20,050	103,159
1966	18,370	104,899
1967	15,517	89,407
1968	13,100	81,200
1969	10,741	69,655
1970	8,764	53,658

Source: *Sommario, 1861–1975*, 35.

TABLE 8 Italian Emigration to Belgium and West Germany

	Belgium	West Germany
1941–50	110,440	15,217
1951–60	118,824	160,513
1961–70	33,760	748,848

cf. Livi Bacci, *Transformazione*, 252.

TABLE 9 Italian Emigration to Argentina and Brazil

	Argentina	Brazil
1952	33,366	17,026
1953	21,350	14,328
1954	33,866	12,049
1955	18,276	8,523
1956	10,652	6,022
1957	14,928	6,157
1958	9,523	4,528
1959	7,549	3,874
1960	4,406	2,976
1961	2,483	2,223
1962	1,817	1,205
1963	945	548
1964	621	233

Source: *Sommario, 1861–1975*, 35.

TABLE 10 Italian Emigration to the United States, Canada, and Australia

	United States	Canada	Australia
1946	5,442		4
1947	23,471	58	50
1948	16,677	2,406	2,047
1949	11,480	5,991	10,939
1950	8,998	7,135	13,516
1951	10,225	21,467	17,453
1952	7,525	18,742	26,802
1953	9,996	22,610	12,865
1954	26,231	23,440	16,960
1955	34,975	19,282	27,689
1956	36,386	28,008	25,631
1957	16,805	24,536	17,003
1958	25,302	28,502	12,375
1959	10,806	23,734	14,149
1960	15,208	19,011	19,606
1961	16,293	13,461	16,351
1962	15,348	12,528	14,406
1963	13,580	12,912	11,535
1964	6,866	17,600	10,888
1965	11,087	24,213	10,320
1966	31,238	28,541	12,523
1967	17,896	26,102	13,733
1968	21,693	16,745	14,505
1969	15,470	9,441	8,740
1970	15,490	7,249	6,362

Source: *Sommario, 1861–1975*, 35.

TABLE 11 Italian Emigration to Argentina

1907	107,227
1908	104,718
1913	111,500

Source: *Annuario Statistico*, 88.

TABLE 12 Italian Emigration to the Americas and to the United States

1886	82,166	12,485
1896	192,908	37,851
1902	282,586	121,139
1905	444,724	316,797
1913	556,325	376,776

Source: *Annuario Statistico*, 89.

TABLE 13 Employment (Percentage of Males)

Years	Agricultural Workers	Landless Laborers Day-Workers	Workmen Employed in Building	Skilled Workers and Artisans	Tradesmen	Professional People	Domestics
1878	38.70	19.05	16.88	13.40	6.04	1.60	2.06
1888	56.75	19.09	9.64	6.04	2.15	0.76	0.92
1898	32.52	28.40	18.70	7.78	2.65	1.08	0.79
1913	34.03	31.21	14.43	12.55	3.54	0.84	1.82

Source: *Annuario Statistico*, 207.

TABLE 14 Employment of Females (For Every 100 Female Emigrants)

Years	Agricultural Workers	Landless Laborers Day-Workers	Workmen Employed in Building	Skilled Workers and Artisans	Tradesmen	Professional People	Domestics
1878	55.61	8.60	0.58	13.04	4.02	2.24	9.95
1888	72.51	19.94	1.25	5.54	1.49	0.74	4.37
1898	58.04	14.73	1.46	7.53	2.13	1.49	7.29
1913	26.83	13.61	0.77	16.17	2.96	0.85	37.33

Source: *Annuario Statistico*, 208.

8

British Immigration into India in the Nineteenth Century

P.J. MARSHALL

Migration and Nineteenth-century Colonialism

In a by-now classic definition, European expansion in the nineteenth century has been characterized as the integration of large tracts of the earth's surface into a world economy dominated by Britain. Distinctions are conventionally drawn between two processes of integration: on the one hand, the creation of new economies by European settlement in "empty" lands of temperate climate, from which a thinly scattered indigenous population had been displaced, and, on the other, the subordination and partial development of existing economic systems in densely populated tropical areas. Migration from Europe clearly had a role in both processes. It was crucial to the first: economic integration of "new" lands could hardly take place without it, or at least historically it has not done so. The role of European migration in the second process would appear to be more limited. Whites were only likely to be involved in productive processes of agriculture or manufacturing at the highest managerial levels or as technical experts, and much of the military and administrative underpinning deemed necessary for economic domination could be provided by Asian or African clerks and soldiers.

While conventional distinctions of this sort clearly have their value, the history of particular societies suggests that the relationship between migration and expansion in the nineteenth century was in fact a very complex one. There is, of course, much scholarly debate about the precise connections between migration and economic growth in the new societies of mass European settlement. This paper is intended to stimulate debate about the deployment of white man- and woman-power in the European tropical empires of the nineteenth century. Patterns are likely to prove diverse. Certain obvious variables can be suggested. The nature of the indigenous society and its capacity to produce commodities and to generate capital and labor, both skilled and unskilled, were certainly of great importance. But any assumption that imperial powers carefully regulated the input of whites, by neat calculations of the minimum needed to remedy deficiencies in what the indigenous society could provide, thereby ensuring the cheapest possible collaborative mechanism, would be unrealistic. For various reasons, which might include racism and considerations of military power, colonial regimes sometimes seem to have employed a much larger number of whites than could be justified on functional grounds. In such cases, the extent of white migration is likely to have been determined by the level of resources that could be extracted from the colony; the wealth of the colonial state could be more important than the needs of the colonial economy. Colonial governments might also be subject to pressures, from within their own metropolitan societies, to provide outlets for white migrants; if not for masses of the poor or displaced, then for those of potential substance who sought affluence, status, or a scope for their talents that they could not find at home. In short, the movements of Europeans to the tropical empires of the nineteenth century, if minuscule in scale by comparison with movements to North America, Australasia, or temperate South America, still reflected a complex interaction between pressures emanating from the metropolitan society and opportunities available overseas.

At first sight, British India in the nineteenth century might seem to have been a colonial enterprise requiring a minimum of white migration to sustain it. The Indian economy was already a sophisticated one, abundantly supplied with labor and mechanical and entrepreneurial skill. It was an extremely difficult one for Europeans to penetrate and provided very few opportunities for the deployment of European capital and technology before the late nineteenth century. The British administration found no shortage of collaborators or well-qualified candidates for its service, while large armies of Indian sepoys were recruited by the end of the eighteenth century. Nevertheless, India received significant inputs of British manpower throughout the nineteenth century. From an early stage the colonial state chose, or was required by its masters in London, to spend a considerable proportion of what were very large resources, by the standard of any other colonial regime, on the services of Europeans. Most of these Europeans had little direct connection with the economic exploitation of India. The mass of them were the rank and file of the formidable British army, which imperial strategic priorities allocated to India in addition to the Indian soldiers in British pay. The elite consisted of army officers, civilian administrators, and professional men; no doubt few in absolute numbers, but a significant element in British upper class employment.

At any time in the nineteenth century, soldiers were the largest part of the British population of India. A large contingent of the regular British army from home was kept in India. During the first half of the century the number rose to nearly 30,000. They were supplemented by a rather smaller number of European soldiers directly recruited by the East India Company. After the 1857 mutiny, the Company's European forces were merged with those of the crown, while the number of British troops in India was greatly increased, both as a consequence of the mutiny and of perceived external threats to India, above all from Russia. The British garrison in India at full strength at the end of the century consisted of some 75,000 British soldiers.

While the forces of the crown in India were officered by those who held the royal commission, the East India Company had its own officer corps, serving with its Europeans and its huge force of Indian soldiers. With the winding up of the Company, the Indian troops were transferred to the service of the crown, and their British officers were granted the Queen's commission as officers of the Indian army. Commissioned ranks in the various Indian forces attracted men from Britain of good social standing. Others were attracted to the civil administration created by the East India Company and taken over by the crown in 1858. The East India Company quickly developed an ambitious administrative structure, by nineteenth-century standards, staffed by an elaborate bureaucracy. At the top of the hierarchy was the very prestigious "covenanted" service of the Company or the crown, supported by uncovenanted assistants and, later in the century, by an increasing number of Europeans serving in the Special Departments, such as the police, the engineers of the Public Works Department, or the education service.

A "private" or "unofficial" British community of persons not employed by the Company had existed in India from the early days of the East India Company. In its origins it consisted mainly of seamen and merchants pursuing their own trade. As the Company's own commercial operations contracted and then ceased altogether, British private commercial enterprise in India expanded very greatly. Private plantations, merchant houses, and industrial concerns recruited most of their managers and other senior staff from Britain. A professional community of lawyers, doctors, and teachers from Britain also established itself in India; Missionary clergy also went there. European labor was not recruited to India on any large scale, but British skilled craftsmen and foremen were thought to be necessary for the railways and the new factories in the later nineteenth century. Small numbers of relatively poor whites were also to be found as shopkeepers, domestic servants, or even as vagrants.

Precision in estimating the size of the European population in India during the nineteenth century is hard to attain. Figures from the Government of India's own censuses are only available from 1871. Even in 1871, the census report reflected that "it is a little remarkable that the census of the European population appears to be the least satisfactory of the whole inquiry."[1] What appears to have caused the late nineteenth-century enumerators the most vexation was the difficulty they experienced in preventing people of mixed race from passing themselves off as "Europeans." By the end of the century, however, they believed that they had attained "a great degree of success in counteracting this source of error." The enumerators of the British censuses for 1851 and 1861 collected material on the European population of India, some of which was printed in their reports. Estimates for any year before 1851 have to be based on attempts to aggregate tentative totals for the main categories of Europeans: the soldiers, those employed by the Company, and the "unofficials."

In 1830, for instance, the strength of the European troops in India, both King's and Company's, was reported at 36,409; a statement for the Company's civil establishments, including its marine, for 1827 put its European complement at approximately 3,550; and a very suspect statement of "private settlers" for 1830 gave a total of 2,149.[2] Women and children appear to be omitted from these figures, which might, however, support an estimate of a European population of between 40,000 and 50,000 at the end of the third decade of the nineteenth century. Twenty years later, the British census of 1851 gave the strength of the royal army as 20,096, with 39,631 for the civil and military employees of the Company with their families. A further 10,006 can be added for "unofficial" European men, women, and children.[3] Thus, the total British

1. *Parliamentary Papers* (hereafter *PP*) *1875* LIV, 407.
2. *PP 1830* XXVIII; *PP 1831–32* IX, 316.
3. *PP 1852* X, 351.

population was probably over 80,000. The 1861 census reported that there were 70,962 British military personnel in India (including their families) and gave a total of 40,379 civilians. If these figures are accurate, the European population in India amounted to 111,341 in all. The totals for Europeans recorded by the Indian censuses are as follows:

1871: 121,147, 1881: 141,473, 1891: 166,428, 1901: 169,677.

A European population dominated by soldiers (even in 1901 they amounted to 60,695 out of 169,677, and they constituted the overwhelming majority in the early part of the century) inevitably had a highly unbalanced ratio between the sexes and an unusual age profile. Young adult males were by far the largest element at all times. Until relatively late in the century, the British army was reluctant to encourage or even to recognize marriage by private soldiers or noncommissioned officers.[4] For Indian service, only 12 percent of any regiment were permitted to take their wives with them from Britain. It was reported that in 1861 only 6.5 percent of the Queen's troops in India consisted of married men with wives with them. The figure for the Company's troops was much higher – 28.8 percent for 1861 – but it seems likely that most of these marriages were not to European women.[5] Only senior officers in the royal regiments were likely to have brought out wives with them on their first appointment to India. Virtually none of the cadets beginning service with the Company's army, or the subalterns joining the later India army, were married.

This would also be true of the civil servants either under the Company or the crown. Nearly all first appointments to India were made to very young men or to boys. Early marriage was very much discouraged. Men in prestigious positions in India were not expected to marry until they were able to support their wives in a proper style. At the end of the eighteenth century, it was stated that "nine-tenths of the Company's servants abroad" were unable to "enter into matrimonial connections of a suitable kind."[6] The *Cadet's Guide* of 1820 explained that the "expenses attending the married state in India are so inconvenient, that to a young officer it is death to all prospects of ever attaining a competency to return

4. M. Trustram, *Women of the Regiment* (Cambridge 1984).
5. *PP 1863* XIX, i, 101.
6. S.C. Ghose, *Social Condition of the British Community in Bengal 1787–1800* (Leiden 1970), 71.

home with."[7] Once an officer or a civil servant had attained some seniority, he might return home on leave in search of a wife and bring her back with him to India, or he might seek a wife from among the sisters or other female relatives who had come out to live in the household of a member of service. Such female migrants were the victims of ill-natured jests throughout the entire history of British India, the assumption being that they came to India for the sole purpose of obtaining an eligible husband. Early in the century, newly arrived females were indeed subjected to degrading rituals, at which they submitted to the inspection of potential suitors. With improved communications, more British females ventured to India, and the married element of the male population increased. In 1861 19 percent of the royal officers and 45 percent of the British civilian population were recorded as being married.[8] The proportion of females to males in the European population as a whole was 384 to 1000 in 1901. By 1901 a few of the women had come to India on a basis that would have been inconceivable for most of the century: they were pursuing careers comparable to those of men, as teachers, missionaries, or nurses.

Migration and Return Migration

By far, the largest part of the European population in India at any time in the nineteenth century were first-generation migrants. All the higher ranks of the civil service and commissioned ranks in the Company's army were filled by appointments made in Britain. Royal regiments were posted to India from Britain or from other parts of the empire. They were reinforced by drafts from home. The Company's European units were kept up to strength by annual parties of recruits sent out from Britain. The majority of the unofficial residents were probably also migrants from Britain. A European community resident in India for more than one generation only, slowly established itself. The 1881 census recorded that one-third of the European population had been born in India, but a considerable number of these were young children. If children were not counted, the proportion fell to one-quarter.

Virtually all those who left Britain did so with the expectation of returning. It was established wisdom that India, apart from its hills,

7. *The Cadet's Guide to India by a Lieutenant of the Bengal Establishment* (London 1820), 46.

8. *PP 1863* XIX, i, 28, 101.

was an unhealthy environment, which would ultimately debilitate and destroy those Europeans who tried to live out their lives there. At least until 1833, the East India Company was hostile to any concept of European settlement and was prepared to use its formidable powers to discourage it. Later schemes of "colonization" came to very little.[9] The expectation was that royal regiments would eventually be posted elsewhere, while time-expired men would be repatriated to Britain. Army officers, civil servants, and the more aspiring members of the "unofficial" community, whatever other motives may have brought them to India, hoped to leave it with a "competence" or an "independence," which would enable them to live out the latter part of their lives in respectable circumstances.

Return migration may have been the almost universal expectation, but for most, until late in the century, the reality was otherwise. A few chose to "stay on" or felt compelled to do so (even at the end of the nineteenth century only 5 percent of the European male population in India was over fifty); most died in India. Relatively few British soldiers left India in the first half of the nineteenth century. Their tours of duty were very long: the Company's soldiers enlisted virtually for the whole of their active lives, while royal regiments could serve for twenty years in India before being posted elsewhere. When the regiments finally left India, very few of those who had first come out were likely to go back. Men with long Indian experience were encouraged to transfer out of departing regiments into newly arrived ones. A significant number did so. Others bought their discharge in order to enter civilian employment in India or chose to be pensioned there. Transfers and discharges may have accounted for some of those who never returned, but death took the great majority. Figures published for a British regiment that spent sixteen years in India in the first half of the nineteenth century, illustrate what happened to soldiers in the service of the empire. The regiment had arrived with 705 men and received a further 1,475 men as transfers and recruits; Yet, it left India with only 671. Of the 2,170 men who had served in it, 633 had died from natural causes, 165 had been killed in action, 153 had bought themselves out, 197 had completed their service and earned their pensions, 229 had transferred into other regiments, and 10 had committed suicide.[10] A report on the sanitary condition of the army in India of 1863 confirmed that it was death from diseases that

9. D. Arnold, "White Colonisation and Labour in Nineteenth-Century India," *Journal of Imperial and Commonwealth History* 11 (1983).

10. *A Handbook of Useful Information for . . . Bengal, the Punjab* (Maidstone 1853), 22.

above all other reasons prevented the British soldier from leaving India. The report estimated that while men of the same age group as the soldiers died in Britain at the rate of 0.9 percent a year, those of the royal troops in India had died at the rate of 7 percent between 1817 and 1855, and the Company's Europeans had died at the rate of 6.9 percent over a comparable period. "A company out of every regiment has been sacrificed every 20 months" to "fevers, dysentery, diseases of the liver, and the epidemic cholera." The report estimated that over a period of twenty years in India, only 9 percent of a body of British troops could be expected to return to Britain, a further 16.6 percent being "invalided," which could mean remaining in India on a pensions.[11] In the late nineteenth century the death rate dropped sharply; in 1882 it was down to 1.7 percent.[12] Although men were still paid bounties to remain longer in India, the standard term for the infantry was reduced to six years. Under these conditions, a very large number of men with experience in India returned to Britain.

Expectations of eventual return to Britain were much better founded for members of the elite than for the mass of soldiers. Civil servants and army officers also did long tours of duty in India. When pensions for the civil service were instituted on a regular basis, they required twenty-five years' service to qualify. The East India Company's officers were also entitled to a pension after twenty-five years, but many of them served longer in order to obtain promotion, with a correspondingly higher pension. Promotion was notoriously slow in the Company's army. In the post-1858 Indian army it was less so, but officers still had to expect over twenty years' service. Prolonged exposure to India was, however, considerably less lethal to the officers and civil servants than it was to the soldiers. In 1863 civil servants were dying at the rate of 2 percent a year and officers in the royal and Indian's service at 3.8 percent and 3.4 percent, respectively.[13]

The prospects for European women and children of returning to Britain probably depended largely on their social position. It seems most unlikely that many European women, who had been brave enough early in the century to go to India with their husband's regiment, ever saw their native land. Although the 1863 report found that soldiers' wives died at half the rate of the soldiers

11. *PP 1863* XIX, 2 vols..
12. T.A. Heathcote, *The Indian Army* (Newton Abbot 1974), 161.
13. *PP 1863* XIX, i, 23.

themselves, most widows seem to have chosen to remarry within the regiment, rather than return on their own to Britain. The fate of their children is also obscure. A witness told a parliamentary inquiry in 1831 that a "great number" of children of "pure European blood" were born in the regimental lines, but that all his inquiries showed "how very few are living in proportion to the great numbers that have been born there."[14] Most of such children as did survive their earliest years, were removed to orphanages run by the East India Company in the presidency towns and later in the hills.[15] Soldiers' children who survived the orphanage remained for the rest of their lives in India. Only the orphans of officers might be sent with official support to Britain.

Departure for Britain was the usual fate of any child of the British-Indian elite. Children over a certain age were thought to be particularly vulnerable in India. In 1825 it was said that children were not usually kept in India beyond their third or fourth year.[16] At the end of the century it was still believed that "European children demonstrate most forcibly the unfavourable effects of hot climates, and in India it is generally thought desirable to bring them at an early age to a cold climate like that of this country to escape the effects of the tropical heat, and few sights are more pleasing than to see these puny, pallid, skinny, fretful little ones converted by British food and British meteorology, into fat and happy English children."[17]

Push-Pull

The bulk of British migrants to India in the nineteenth century, the soldiers of the royal regiments, were most unlikely to have been responding to any kind of "pull" exerted by service in the subcontinent. They went to India, not because they chose to do so, but because their regiments were posted there. The moment of choice for most soldiers was when they chose to join the British army in the first place. Contemporary military opinion had no illusions about the army's attraction for most of its recruits. A royal commission in 1861 concluded that "few enlist from any real inclination for military

14. *PP 1831–32* XIII, 9.
15. D. Arnold, "European Orphans and Vagrants in India in the Nineteenth Century," *Journal of Imperial and Commonwealth History* 7 (1979).
16. J.B. Gilchrist, *The General East India Guide and Vade Mecum* (London 1825), 212.
17. "J.P.," *The Care of Infants in India*, 6th ed. (London 1907), 88.

life;" recruits responded to the "push" of "want of work," or "difficulties of a private nature."[18] Pay was no inducement. Throughout the century the army recognized that it could not offer adequate rewards. An inquiry of 1892 concluded bleakly that: "The inducements at present offered by the service do not attract those who are capable of earning men's wages in the labour market."[19] The tone of those charged with recruiting the much smaller number of men into the Company's European forces was generally more optimistic. For some of them at least, India seems to have exerted some "pull." The Company's service was said to be a "favourite" one, "chiefly as holding out prospects to deserving men of obtaining promotion in various departments of the government of India."[20]

The "pull" of posts in the civil service, under the Company or under the crown, or of commissioned rank in the Indian armies was such that candidates competed eagerly for them, either by deploying the influence of their families and connections or, after 1854 for the civil service, by submitting themselves to written examinations. There were, however, limits to the "pull" exerted by even the most prestigious posts in India. Young men from the highest tiers of the British social system, or those who were confident that they could make a successful career in Britain, rarely went to India. When a royal regiment was posted to India in the first half of the nineteenth century, up to the half of its officers were likely to ask for a transfer.[21] Throughout the century there were complaints that men of the very highest caliber were not being attracted to the civil service. Open competition was intended to secure the highest flyers from Oxford or Cambridge. It rarely did so, even though the rules of the competition were modified at intervals in order to exclude the products of "crammers" or of the Irish universities. By the 1890s Oxford was beginning to win a large number of places, but men with olympian standards of judgment, like Lord Curzon, still considered the overall level of the service to be irredeemably mediocre.[22] By contrast with the royal army, the East India Company's forces never attracted more than a sprinkling of aristocratic officers, nor did the Indian army of the crown.[23]

18. Cited in E.M. Spiers, *The Army and Society 1815–1914* (London 1980), 44.
19. *PP 1892* XIX, 10.
20. *PP 1859* V, 404.
21. Heathcote, *Indian Army*, 119.
22. B. Spangenberg, *British Bureaucracy in India* (New Delhi 1976); C.J. Dewey, "The Education of a Ruling Caste: the Indian Civil Service in the Era of Competitive Examination," *English Historical Review* 88 (1973).
23. P.E. Razzell, "Social Origins of Officers in the Indian and the British Home

Those attracted to Indian service seem to have been drawn from a broad band of British families who regarded themselves as aspiring to genteel status and the occupations appropriate to it: professions, such as the church, the law, or medicine, government employment in Britain, finance, and certain branches of trade. Such families were socially below the aristocracy and most of the landed gentry. They might live in the countryside and affect a rural style of life, but their income was likely to come from other sources. Few of such families had any significant involvement with manufacturing industry. They were heavily recruited from the south of England, strongly reinforced from Scotland (especially for the army), and from some largely Protestant Irish. In the first half of the nineteenth century the education of many of them may not have been very distinguished, consisting of attendance at "cheap proprietary schools."[24] Later in the century, most civil servants and army officers were recruited from the new or reformed public schools, which were establishing an increasingly standardized pattern for genteel education.[25] In general it seems appropriate to describe them as members of a "service middle class" or a "professional middle class."[26]

The disadvantages of Indian service were obvious to such people. It separated them for long periods from their families and connections and exposed them to the risks of diseases and early death. Its advantages were also palpable. Generous salaries were attained relatively quickly by the civil service, very much more slowly by the army officers. Promotion was according to seniority or merit, not according to influence. Pensions were attached. Social status was assured. Army officers and civil servants were treated as "gentlemen" by their peers and maintained a style of life in India more elaborate than would have been available to most of them at home. What has been written of the twentieth century was also true of the nineteenth: "However elevated or humble their social origins, all I.C.S. men moved into the top of the service class."[27]

Real as these advantages were, Indian service seems to have been regarded as second best to comparable employment at home for most of those who competed for it. There were of course many

Armies 1750–1862," *British Journal of Sociology* 14 (1963), 249; Heathcote, *Indian Army*, 135.

24. J.H. Bourne, *Patronage and Society in Nineteenth-Century England* (London 1986), 102–103.

25. For the civil service, see Dewey, "Education of a Ruling Caste," 284–285.

26. Bourne, *Patronage*, 105; Spangenberg, *Bureaucracy*, 19.

27. D.C. Potter, *India's Political Administrators 1919–83* (Oxford 1986), 58.

exceptions, such as the offspring of certain families who sent their children to India for generation after generation. Most of the others, however, seem to have found themselves in India because they lacked the family influence, the financial resources, or the intellectual prowess to win places in the British army or the home civil service. The huge armed forces and the elaborate bureaucracy created in British India had greatly extended the range of public employment. Yet, those who took advantage of this extension seem often to have been, in the words of a recent assessment of them, the "second eleven" or the "genteel middle class," seeking a "change to secure the level of social status and economic security which they were denied at home."[28] Against the "pull" of office in India needs to be set the "push" of too little employment in Britain deemed appropriate to the aspirations of "the genteel middle class."

Generalizations about the motives that brought officers and civil servants to India can also be applied to the higher echelons of the "unofficial" British community in India. Merchants, financiers, and professional men were usually drawn from the same social strata as the officials. Indeed, in the first half of the century they had often begun their careers with the Company, later resigning to concentrate on their business affairs. By the end of the nineteenth century, the career of an "East India merchant" was recognized to be a genteel one, which attracted men from the public schools and the universities. Less obviously genteel were those who organized the manufacture of indigo, ran tea gardens, or acted as managers of jute or cotton mills or of coal mines. The Scottish element among such men seems to have been very high. For them, Indian service must have been a very welcome road to material well-being and social advancement. Below them was a very limited white labor aristocracy. It was strongly entrenched in the railways, where by the end of the century more than 6,000 Europeans were employed as drivers or foremen, and in those sections of the government, such as the police, where a premium was paid for the presumed loyalty of whites.[29] The "pull" of India for such men must have been very powerful indeed. Many of them appear to have joined the army or enlisted as seamen on ships going to India with the express purpose of obtaining their discharge or even deserting once they had gotten there. They at least were neither involuntary migrants, like most of the royal regiments, nor people for whom India was second best to a career at home, like so many of their social superiors.

28. Bourne, *Patronage*, 181.
29. Arnold, "European Orphans," 151.

Integration or Isolation

As is notorious, British migrants to India isolated themselves from the indigenous population to a very high degree. With their hearts set on returning home and with India for most of them little more than the means to a satisfactory life at home, most British migrants absorbed very little of their surroundings.They lived in isolation, in the "white towns" and later in the European suburbs of the port cities, or "up-country" in separate civil lines and cantonments and in hill stations, which were exclusively European creations.[30] Intermarriage was very infrequent. Acculturation was very superficial, usually being limited to some adoption of new dietary and dress habits.

The seclusion from their surroundings of most of the British-Indian elite was very marked indeed. It is widely supposed that this aloofness became more accentuated during the nineteenth century, although there is not much evidence that suggests significant integration in earlier periods. In their early settlements, the East India Company's servants lived in the manner of other trading groups, as a separate community in the Indian ports. As the number of British people in Madras and Calcutta increased, so did their self-sufficiency and their ability to reproduce something like a European environment. From the outset, the Company tried to discourage its "young gentlemen" from mixed marriages that would scandalize "good families in England."[31] Late in the eighteenth century a few mixed marriages, usually to Muslim ladies, were openly acknowledged. This is an indication that a small number of Europeans could make themselves at home in the courts of cities like Hyderabad or Lucknow. For most Europeans, however, relations were much less equal. Many civil servants and army officers kept Indian women and fathered children by them. Such relationships were openly discussed in publications. The *Cadet's Guide* of 1820, for instance, argued that what may be "inexcusable in one situation, may be allowable in another" and went on to consider the rival merits of "keeping a native girl" or of resorting to prostitutes. It ended on a harsh note of racism, warning the young men that they would not receive from children born in India "the full satisfaction that he would have done, had their features been freer from the Asiatic tinge of their mother."[32] This seems to have been characteristic of an

30. A.D. King, *Colonial Urban Development* (London 1976).
31. Cited in T. Wilkinson, *Two Monsoons*, 2d ed. (London 1987), 99.
32. *The Cadet's Guide to India*, 47–50.

essentially exploitative relationship, unduly glamourized by later critics of the Victorians.

What changed most by mid-century was probably the tone, rather than the practice, of race relations. The aloofness of the ruling class came to be regarded as a political imperative, as well as a matter of taste. Emphasis on racial difference became more pronounced. Mixed marriages were no longer acceptable, nor was it acceptable openly to keep Indian women. As the number of Europeans increased, European society became more self-sufficient, and in more places it became possible to reproduce something like the rituals, entertainments, and institutions of home life. On their own terms, Europeans began to make new kinds of contacts with Indians, who could move toward them by learning English and by joining with them in educational, scientific, or sporting activities. On their own terms too, Europeans moved towards Indians in the acquisition of knowledge about Indian languages, art and history. It was, however, a rare occurrence for a member of the European elite to move toward an Indian way of life.

The prejudices of the British elite are material for satire and novels. The ability of the mass of British migrants, the soldiers, to keep themselves largely aloof from the population of India is of great historical importance: it ensured that the immigration of British people into India, as opposed to the immigration of British institutions, British ideas, or even British capital, would be a phenomenon with remarkably few long-term effects.

In the 1830s some of the most influential Englishmen in India, notably Lord William Bentinck, hoped that British migration would eventually produce a society as marked by racial intermixture as Mexico or Brazil.[33] Such expectations did not of course rest on any realistic calculation as to how many migrants would be needed to have an impact on a population the size of India's. Nevertheless, the outcome of more than a century of British immigration into India was still remarkably meager by 1900. The 1901 census reckoned that only a quarter of the adult population of Europeans had been born in India and that the "Eurasian" population was only approximately half that of the Europeans (87,030 to 169,677). Not only was the population of mixed race a small one, but a large part of it was poor and disadvantaged. An inquiry undertaken in Calcutta, the Anglo-Indians' main stronghold, in 1892 considered that 22 percent

33. J. Rosselli, "Lord William Bentinck and his Age," *Bengal Past and Present* 94 (1975), 68, 71–72.

of them should be classified as "paupers."[34]

Nearly all Bentinck's successors abhorred his vision of a racially mixed India. That their view prevailed, rather than his, was presumably due to the fact that waves of British soldiers lived out considerable portions of their lives and often met their deaths in India with minimal contact with its population. The seclusion imposed on the royal troops was particularly rigorous. In 1832 they were said to be "cooped up in barracks and fortresses."[35] From 1864 a series of regulations were enacted, strictly controlling access to the cantonments in order to protect the soldiers from disease. At times the army tried to regulate sexual relations through its own brothels.[36] Recollections of army life in the twentieth century still stressed "the great segregation" from Indian society.[37]

Some royal soldiers and considerable numbers of the Company's Europeans appear to have broken through this segregation, especially in the period of long spells of service in the first half of the nineteenth century. Marriages were entered into, and it was said that those who did this "never leave India, or very few of them do, because they are almost natives in their habits; they associate with natives and live with natives." Two to three thousand European soldiers were said in 1863 to have been invalided in India and to be living there on their pensions. Most of them were thought to be married.[38] An earlier committee had been told of "old soldiers with a native family and half-native habits."[39] Such examples of "going native" can never have been demographically significant and with the coming of short-service and the disbanding of the Company's army, always more inclined to settle in India than the Queen's troops, the number seems to have dwindled to very few indeed.

Migration and Capital Movements

Movements of people and movements of capital into India during the nineteenth century were rarely closely connected. Indeed, with most Europeans aiming to repatriate their savings on their return home, an increased inflow of migrants was likely to produce an increased outflow of capital.

34. L.B. Varma, *Anglo-Indians* (Delhi 1979), 122–123.
35. *PP 1831–32* XIII, 397.
36. K.A. Ballhatchet, *Race, Sex and Class under the Raj* (London 1980).
37. C. Allen, ed., *Plain Tales from the Raj* (London 1977), 184ff.
38. *PP 1863* XIX, i, 288.
39. *PP 1859* V, 364.

In the period of the East India Company's monopoly, transfers of private capital from Britain were negligible. Early European enterprise was financed either by borrowing from Indians or by drawing on the accumulated savings of the Company's civil and military servants. It was confidently expected that after the easing of the restrictions on migration and access to land by Europeans in 1833, India would attract numerous new settlers with capital. Such expectations were disappointed. Large movements of capital from Britain did not occur until the 1850s, and when they did occur, the investors in the great extension of railways, or in the government of India's mounting public borrowing, remained in Britain. By comparison with the railways or public securities, much smaller sums were invested in European-owned plantations, mines or factories. For the most part these enterprises appear to have been financed by the traditional means of borrowing in India.[40]

Comparative Dimensions

The pattern of British immigration into India during the nineteenth century was a very distinctive one. Its character seems to have been determined by the elaborate colonial state that the British were able to construct very early in their rule. By comparison with other European colonial regimes of the period, the British Indian state was not only unusual in its size and resources but also in the degree to which it followed British models. The higher ranks in its service were filled by members of an already formed British service class. Throughout the history of the Raj, the social origins and the outlook of Indian civil servants and army officers were very much those of their peers who had remained in Britain. Their service in India marked most of them relatively lightly, and the extent of their identification with India was limited. Unlike the European soldiers in the armies of the other colonial powers, the great majority of British soldiers in India also remained very un-Indianized. India was required to pay for very large contingents of the regular British army, which generally lived in carefully regulated seclusion from Indian society. Numerically this dispatch of royal regiments to India was a considerable migratory movement, which certainly deserves a place in the history of labor migrations within the orbit of European imperialism. Members of the poorest strata of British society were

40. A.K. Bagchi, *Private Investment in India 1900–39* (Cambridge 1972), 159; see also R.S. Rungta, *Rise of Business Corporations in India* (Cambridge 1970), 265.

shipped out to India to die, at least until the 1870s, at a rate markedly higher than that of indentured Indian labor in the Caribbean. But with very few European women accompanying the soldiers, with restricted access to Indian women, and (it would seem) with very low fertility from such access, it was a wave of migration that left little behind it. British immigration into India was little more than an oil slick on the surface of the deep waters over which it briefly spread.

BIBLIOGRAPHIC NOTE

The printed sources used for this report have been drawn from the British censuses of 1851 and 1861 and the Indian censuses of 1871, 1881, 1891, and 1901. Use has also been made of the huge collections of material on nineteenth-century India in the British *Parliamentary Papers*.

The quantity of scholarly secondary work on the elements that made up the British population in India is very uneven. The civil servants have been intensively studied. The most important works on their recruitment and social origins are: B.S. Cohn, "Recruitment and Training of British Civil Servants in India" in *Asian Bureaucratic Systems Emergent from the British Tradition*, R. Braibanti ed. (Durham, N.C. 1966); J.M. Compton, "Open Competition and the Indian Civil Service 1854–76," *English Historical Review* 83 (1968); C.J. Dewey, "The Education of a Ruling Caste: The Indian Civil Service in the Era of Competitive Examination," *English Historical Review* 88 (1973); B. Spangenberg, *British Bureaucracy in India* (New Delhi 1976).

Less has been written on the army officers. T.A. Heathcote, *The Indian Army* (Newton Abbot 1974) is a useful survey. There is also much relevant material in J.M. Bourne, *Patronage and Society in Nineteenth-Century England* (London 1986). See also P.E. Razzell, "The Social Origins of Officers in the Indian and British Home Armies 1750–1862," *British Journal of Sociology* 14 (1963), 249.

Very little is available on the British soldiers in India during the nineteenth century beyond the material in the *Parliamentary Papers*, such as the superb "Report of Commissioners to inquire into the Sanitary State of the Army in India" of 1863 (*PP 1863* XIX [2 vols.]). P. Burroughs, "The Human Cost of Imperial Defence in the Early Victorian Age," *Victorian Studies* 24 (1980) provides an interesting comparison. See also K.A. Ballhatchet, *Race, Sex and Class under the Raj* (London 1980).

The unofficial community has recently been studied in R.K. Renford, *The Non-Official British in India to 1920* (Delhi 1987). D. Arnold has written valuable articles on "European Orphans and Vagrants in India in the

Nineteenth Century" and "White Colonisation and Labour in Nineteenth-Century India," *Journal of Imperial and Commonwealth History* 7 (1979) and 11 (1983). The economic framework of private enterprise in India is analyzed in R.S. Rungta, *The Rise of Business Corporations in India* (Cambridge 1970).

Work on European women in India in the nineteenth century is still largely anecdotal, see for instance, P. Barr, *The Memsahibs* (London 1976). M. Trustram, *Women of the Regiment: Marriage and the Victorian Army* (Cambridge 1984) is an important study of the background to soldiers' wives in India.

9

Emigration from Western Africa, 1807–1940

W.G. CLARENCE-SMITH

When the abolitionists achieved the suppression of the British slave trade in 1807, they believed that a brave new world of free labor was opening up for Africa. Although they thought mainly in terms of ex-slaves providing the labor for plantation areas, they hoped that any shortfall could in part be met by free emigration from Africa.[1] The reality was to be cruelly different from these dreams. Emigration continued, but overwhelmingly in the form of coerced labor, and most attempts at stimulating free emigration failed. Labor exports across the Atlantic remained close to the late eighteenth-century high point for about four decades, and then fell away steeply to almost nothing by World War I, as the long, halting, and often contradictory European campaign to abolish coerced labor slowly bore its fruits. In the interests of comparison with other areas of emigration, this report will devote a little space at the end to analyzing why a small current of free emigration developed and why it remained so limited. The bulk of the report will focus on large exports of coerced labor.

General Patterns of Coerced Labor Exports

The precise effects of abolition measures on the slave trade have been hotly debated. It would seem that exports of slaves continued at high levels until about 1850 but that they would have been much higher in the absence of abolition measures. Far from being a

1. For a general discussion of abolitionism, see David Eltis, *Economic Growth and the Ending of the Transatlantic Slave Trade* (New York and Oxford 1987), which is also by far the best general book to consult for the whole of this report. See also David B. Davis, *Slavery and Human Progress* (New York and Oxford 1984); Seymour Drescher, *Econocide: British Slavery in the Era of Abolition* (Pittsburg 1977).

moribund system, plantation slavery was alive and well and was boosted by the surge in demand from the industrializing economies of the West. The first serious fall in transatlantic slave exports resulted from the enforcement of Brazilian import restrictions from 1850, and the deathblow came from similar Spanish measures in Cuba in the late 1860s. Altogether, Eltis estimates that about 2.35 million slaves were exported to the New World from western Africa between 1811 and 1867.[2]

As restrictions on the illegal export of slaves tightened, it became common to attempt to convert slavery into a pretense at an indentured labor system. Labor was nearly always coerced in some way, and most of this was nothing but a thinly disguised slave trade. There were slight differences, in that the laborers were usually paid some kind of a wage, but in most cases the workers were bought as slaves and were never repatriated. This was clearly so for the *libres engagés*, of whom about 20,000 were sent to the French Caribbean possessions from 1854 to 1862.[3] The Portuguese ran an almost identical system, sending some 100,000 *serviçães* to the cocoa islands of São Tomé and Principe in the Gulf of Guinea from the mid-1870s to the early 1910s.[4] The Spaniards in neighboring Fernando Po also imported this kind of labor, although in much smaller numbers and with the British enforcing some degree of repatriation.[5] The British for their part did not purchase slaves, but they captured them on illegal slave ships and put considerable pressure on them to go to plantation colonies, from which they never returned. A little over 30,000 laborers of this kind were sent from Sierra Leone and Saint Helena to the British Caribbean between 1841 and 1867.[6]

By 1914, British antislavery campaigners had put an end to the straight purchasing of slaves for use as nonrepatriated "indentured labor," but some administratively-coerced labor continued to flow

2. Eltis, *Economic Growth*, Appendix A. See also P. Lovejoy, "The Volume of the Atlantic Slave Trade: a Synthesis," *Journal of African History* 23, 4 (1982), 473–501; J. Rawley, *The Transatlantic Slave Trade; a History* (New York 1981).

3. François Renault, *Libération d'esclaves et nouvelle servitude* (Abidjan and Dakar 1976), 158 and passim.

4. James Duffy, *A Question of Slavery* (Oxford 1967); G. Clarence-Smith, *The Third Portuguese Empire, 1825–1975* (Manchester 1985), 107–108.

5. Ibrahim K. Sundiata, "Prelude to Scandal: Liberia and Fernando Po, 1880–1930," *Journal of African History* 15, 1 (1974), 97–112.

6. Monica Schuler, "The Recruitment of African Indentured Labourers for European Colonies in the 19th Century" in *Colonialism and Migration; Indentured Labour before and after Slavery*, P.C. Emmer, ed. (Dordrecht, 1986), 136. See also Monica Schuler, *Alas, Alas, Kongo: a Social History of Indentured African Immigration into Jamaica* (Baltimore 1980).

to the Portuguese and Spanish cocoa islands of the Gulf of Guinea until well into the 1950s. Exact numbers are not available, but this trade probably involved no more than some three thousand laborers per year on average.[7] It is thus clear that the flow of "pseudo-indentured laborers" never came anywhere near equaling the great illegal exports of slaves.

Geographical Origins and Demographic Impact

If abolition saw little immediate change in overall volumes of exports, it did provoke quite marked changes in supplies of coerced labor. These changes depended on four main variables: the ease with which different stretches of the coast could be patrolled by naval forces, particularly the British navy; the degree of cooperation encountered by abolitionist forces among local authorities on the coast, both African and European; the ability of merchants and producers to switch to other export commodities and other uses for slaves; and endogenous factors affecting the supply of slaves. It was rare that a single factor determined the supply of slaves, so that one generally has to look for the specific combination obtained in any given region of western Africa.[8]

In Upper Guinea, roughly from modern Mauritania to Ghana, the slave trade rapidly contracted and came to be heavily concentrated in the area from modern Guinea-Bissau to Liberia. Even in this core zone, the trade declined rapidly from the 1840s. This happened before the major growth in demand for slave labor to produce groundnuts for export and does not seem to be explained by it. Effective policing by Western naval forces was probably the main cause for decline. Demand for slaves from further inland was also a factor: Manding traders coming to the coast were more likely to buy than to sell slaves. This reinforced the tendency for slaves to be drawn from closer to the coast than in the eighteenth century, often from no more than a hundred miles inland. From 1811 to 1867, the whole of Upper Guinea exported less than 300,000 coerced laborers.[9] The slave trade lingered on right into the interwar years

7. Sundiata, "Prelude to Scandal"; Ronald W. Davis, *Ethnohistorical Studies on the Kru Coast* (Newark 1976), 56–64; Alvaro de Freitas Morna, *Angola, um ano no governo geral, 1942–1943* (Lisbon 1944), 240.
8. Eltis, *Economic Growth*, ch. 10.
9. Ibid., 165–168, 252; A. Jones, *From Slaves to Palm Kernels: a History of the Galinhas Country, 1730–1890* (Wiesbaden 1983).

in the independent republic of Liberia, under the guise of "contract labor," with the Spaniards in Fernando Po and the French in Gabon as the main customers.[10]

In the much smaller Bight of Benin, roughly from modern Togo to southwestern Nigeria, the slave trade was far more intense and lasted into the 1860s. Moreover, slaves came from a wider catchment area, and the whole trade was strongly supply driven. The predatory expansion of the kingdom of Dahomey, the internecine wars between the Yoruba states, and the great islamic *jihads* of the far interior, all provided the slavers with an inexhaustible source of human captives. Given the generally dense population of this vast area, the demographic impact was probably slight, and the greater willingness to export women may have reflected a lack of concern over the demographic effects of the trade. The growth of slave-worked palm oil plantations did not compete with the export trade of slaves, given this abundant servile population, and the two forms of enterprise cohabited harmoniously. The greater domestic use, however, of servile labor probably pushed up the relative export price of slaves, for they came to be about twice as expensive as those from the Congo by the 1860s. Between 1811 and 1867, the Bight of Benin exported over 400,000 coerced laborers.[11]

The Bight of Biafra exported nearly as many slaves over the same period, some 350,000, but they came overwhelmingly from what is today southeastern Nigeria, and the traffic contracted sharply from the 1840s. The combination of British threats and bribery, together with the huge increase in revenue from exporting palm oil, appear to have convinced the city-states of the Niger delta that it was not worth continuing the export traffic in human beings. In this area, slaves were hardly used in palm oil production itself, but they played a vital role in transporting the oil and in cultivating foodstuffs for specialized producers. Unlike the neighboring Bight of Benin, slaves came from very close to the coast, from the extremely densely populated Igbo and Ibibio zones, and were mainly obtained by internal social means, rather than by war. The demographic impact in this well-populated area appears to have been nil.[12] It is possible, however, that the much smaller exports from the Gabon coast had

10. Davis, *Ethnohistorical Studies*, 56–64.

11. Eltis, *Economic Growth*, 168–171, 252; Patrick Manning, *Slavery, Colonialism and Economic Growth in Dahomey, 1640–1960* (Cambridge 1982); Pierre Verger, *Flux et reflux de la traite des nègres entre le Golfe de Bénin et Bahia de Todos os Santos du XVIIe au XIXe siècle* (Paris and The Hague 1968).

12. Eltis, *Economic Growth*, 171–173, 252; David Northrup, *Trade without Rulers: Pre-Colonial Economic Development in South-Eastern Nigeria* (Oxford 1978).

more deleterious demographic effects, as this was one of the least densely populated parts of the continent.[13]

The largest exporter of slaves was the area covering the Congo estuary and Angola, which sent an astonishing 1.3 million slaves and coerced laborers across the Atlantic between 1811 and 1867. The Congo estuary, like the Bight of Benin, was one of the areas where the transatlantic trade lingered on the longest. Slaves in this thinly populated area were drawn from a huge catchment zone, stretching right into the trading hinterland of the east coast. Endogenous supply factors of the type operating in the hinterland of the Bight of Benin were not so prominent, and most of the capturing and enslaving of peoples was a direct response to demand on the coast. Nor were alternative sources of employment of slave labor anything like as developed as further north, a fact which may have encouraged the continuation of the trade, and which certainly appears to have made the Congo chiefs and the Portuguese in Angola far less cooperative with the Royal Navy than the city-states of the Niger delta.[14] Angolan slaves were the main source of São Tomé *serviçães* up to 1911, and many of the forced laborers who continued to be sent to the islands after the war still came from this colony.[15] If any region in Africa can claim to have sustained severe demographic damage from the slave trade, Angola is probably the best candidate.

Prices and Sex/Age Ratios

Push-pull phenomena and the differentiation of emigrants by gender and age were partly determined by the price of slaves. The evolution of prices varied greatly according to whether one looks at sending or receiving areas. In Africa prices remained generally steady and considerably below the high point reached in the late eighteenth century. Eltis argues that this reflects the fact that restrictions on exports were not compensated by alternative employment in Africa.[16] It could also have been, however, that the particularly disturbed conditions in much of the continent in the nineteenth

13. K. David Patterson, *The Northern Gabon Coast to 1875* (London 1975), passim.
14. Eltis, *Economic Growth*, 173–177, 252; Phyllis Martin, *The External Trade of the Loango Coast, 1576–1870* (Oxford 1972); Joseph C. Miller, *Way of Death. Merchant Capitalism and the Angolan Slave Trade, 1730–1830* (London 1988).
15. Duffy, *Question of Slavery*; Morna, *Angola*, 228–229, 240–247.
16. Eltis, *Economic Growth*, 230, 260–264.

century were producing a larger supply of slaves.

What is certain is that prices on the other side of the Atlantic rose spectacularly from the 1840s to the late 1850s, before falling back again in the last years of the trade. In the late 1850s, the price of a prime male African slave actually rose to over $1,000 in Cuba (in constant 1821 to 1825 dollars), at a time when the average cost on the African coast was under $50. A combination of rising commodity prices, technical innovations of a labor-saving kind, and a lack of alternative sources of labor made the planters willing to pay over the odds for slaves.

The effects of this great price disparity between continents were that after 1850 payments in Africa represented only between 8 and 15 percent of the cost of slaves in Cuba. Distribution costs in Cuba and Brazil – basically the bribing of officials – came to constitute an ever-increasing proportion of slave prices in the New World. Moreover, it was these rising costs that were gradually reducing the Cuban trade before the Spaniards moved decisively against it.[17] Much the same could be said about the neoslave trade to São Tomé up to 1911, for by the 1900s the cost of a slave on the cocoa islands was around 36 pounds, six times higher than in Angola, and the continuing steep increase was worrying planters and causing them to think of alternative sources of labor.[18]

In terms of sex ratios, the predominance of males over females continued. On average from 1811 to 1867, there were between six and seven males to three to four females in intercepted cargoes. Although New World planters generally preferred males, and were prepared to pay a slight premium, the price differential was insufficient to explain this imbalance, which was due rather to preferences in exporting societies. It was noticeable that the proportion of females was higher in exports from west Africa than in those from the Congo-Angola region, suggesting that women were more highly valued in west-central Africa, with its sparse population and demographic problems. It should also be noted that a high proportion of the females exported were girls, and it was generally the case that less than 15 percent of slaves exported were women of child-bearing age. The only exception was the Bight of Benin, where at one point nearly 30 percent of exports consisted of adult females. Moreover,

17. Ibid., chs. 11 and 13.

18. Duffy, *Question of Slavery*, 196; Francisco Mantero, *A mão d'obra em S. Thomé e Principe* (Lisbon 1910).

there were no barriers to lactating women being exported from this region, in contrast to other regions.[19]

That African suppliers determined sex ratios seems confirmed by the experience of São Tomé. The cocoa planters were extremely keen to import women and breed a future labor supply, as increasing British pressure foreshadowed the ending of the trade. But in the early 1900s, they were receiving roughly six males for four females, not enough to right the considerable sex imbalance already existing on the islands.[20] The Spanish and German imports of labor for their cocoa plantations in the Gulf of Guinea appear to have been almost entirely masculine.[21]

One of the striking features of the nineteenth-century Atlantic trade was the overall rise in the proportion of children, which went from roughly two out of ten at the beginning of the period to nearly half in some cases by the end of the trade. Children were especially numerous in cargoes sent from the Congo-Angola region, for reasons that remain unclear. The growth in the numbers of children may have been connected to the desire to prevent uprisings on board ship, which certainly declined in this period, but it remains something of a puzzle.[22] It could be that rocketing prices for prime male slaves led some planters to go for children. In this context, it is worth noting that in the 1890s, juvenile slaves were generally retained by the poorly capitalized and struggling planters within Angola, while prime adult slaves were reserved for the booming cocoa plantation of São Tomé; this said, some children were also exported to the cocoa islands.[23]

The "Middle Passage"

Nothing created more emotional furor in the nineteenth century than the conditions under which slaves were illegally transported to the New World. Opponents of naval patrols argued that British attempts at abolition simply made the shippers even more inhumane and encouraged "tight packing." But the evidence on transportation

19. Eltis, *Economic Growth*, 165–177, 255–259.
20. Duffy, *Question of Slavery*, 181 n.24; Mantero, *A mão d'obra*, passim.
21. Archives Nationales du Cameroun, Yaoundé, FA 1/806, 216, Fickendey article 1912; José Antonio Moreno Moreno, *Reseña historica de la presencia de España en el Golfo de Guinea* (Madrid 1952), 85.
22. Eltis, *Economic Growth*, 69–70, 132, 175, 255–259.
23. Manoel J.M. Contreiras, *A provincia de Angola* (Lisbon 1894), 90 n.2; Duffy, *Question of Slavery*, 168.

scarcely bears this out. The average space of four square feet per slave remained stable and virtually identical to eighteenth-century figures; thus, it was much less than the average twelve square feet for free emigrants from Europe across the Atlantic.

Abolition had no immediate effects on ship sizes. The very intense naval measures of the late 1830s and early 1840s led to a temporary recourse to smaller boats and greater numbers of slaves carried per ton. But the general trend was to employ larger and faster ships, with clippers and then steamers coming into use, although the latter never featured very prominently. Turnaround times on the coast fell greatly, as slavers employed factors to guarantee a full complement of slaves immediately ready on arrival, and voyage times were slightly reduced.

Mortality rates, which had been falling in the eighteenth century, tended to rise once again in spite of shorter voyages. These rates stayed higher than mortality for other forms of long-distance travel, and as the latter fell during the century, differentials between slave and nonslave mortality widened. The higher proportion of children carried in the nineteenth-century slave trade probably supplies one of the keys to rising mortality rates. High mortality rates appear to have been due to the hostile epidemiological environment in Africa, together with conditions of enslavement and travel to the coast. The months showing the highest mortality tended to coincide with the hungry period before harvest and with the times of heaviest rainfall. Neither tight packing nor provisioning appear to explain the phenomenon.[24]

Conditions of Settlement and Return Migration

The question of slave conditions is a vast one, but it seems clear that the nineteenth century was a period of reform. Threatened in their supplies of labor, the masters reacted by trying to defuse abolitionist criticism of servile conditions. Governments harassed by the British would in any case lean heavily on entrepreneurs to ensure these kinds of reform. Moreover, as slave prices rose steeply in receiving areas, slaves became ever more valuable capital assets, and slave breeding became a veritable industry in the "Old South" regions of the United States. Eltis shows that American-born slaves were generally taller than their African-born peers on either side of the

24. Eltis, *Economic Growth*, ch. 8 and Appendix D.

Atlantic, indicating better diets in the New World.[25] Even the fiercest critics of the São Tomé plantations would praise the Portuguese for their efforts in raising the standards of services on the plantations by the beginning of the twentieth century.[26]

It would be quite wrong to deduce from this that plantations became little paradises, but it does seem to have affected rates of return migration. Returns to Africa after the abolition of the institution of slavery were on a minuscule scale, especially when contrasted with free migratory flows.[27] It is true that the two phenomena are not strictly comparable, given the very long periods that some ex-slaves had spent away from their homes. It should also be borne in mind that many Africans enslaved within their own societies would have been treated as slaves had they returned home. In this sense, the more rapid and complete abolition of the institution of slavery in the plantation areas than in mainland Africa militated against return flows.[28]

Migration and Related Capital Movements

One of the myths associated with the nineteenth-century slave trade is that it was an archaic hangover from an earlier age, whereas in reality slave traders were often in the vanguard of technical and organizational progress. Already referred to was the use of new forms of ships, and the slave traders were also quick to set themselves up as joint-stock ventures and companies, in order to spread risk. As risks and insurance rates rose because of abolition, firms also became more concentrated, and there was much greater use of specie, bills of exchange, and rudimentary futures markets.

Profits and losses were both considerable, with average profits rising somewhat compared to the previous century and standing at around 20 percent before 1850. These were high compared to other

25. Ibid., 239, ch. 11 and passim; Arthur F. Corwin, *Spain and the Abolition of Slavery in Cuba* (Austin 1967); Franklin W. Knight, *Slave Society in Cuba during the 19th Century* (Madison 1970); Manuel Moreno Fraginals, *El ingenio* 2d ed. (Havana 1978) (English version New York 1976); Robert Conrad, *The Destruction of Brazilian Slavery* (Berkeley 1972); Mauricio Goulart, *Escravidão africana no Brasil* (Sao Paulo 1950); Mary Karasch, *Slave Life in Rio de Janeiro, 1808–1850* (Princeton 1987).

26. For a summary of British attitudes, see *Sao Thomé and Principe*, Great Britain, Foreign Office, Historical Section (London 1920).

27. Eltis, *Economic Growth*, 239.

28. Paul Lovejoy, *Transformations in Slavery: a History of Slavery in Africa* (Cambridge 1983); Suzanne Miers and Igor Kopytoff, eds., *Slavery in Africa* (Madison 1977); Claude Meillasoux, ed., *L'esclavage en Afrique* (Paris 1975).

ventures, reflecting the risky nature of the business, but they were much lower than the inflated estimates put out in abolitionist writings. The most successful firms and entrepreneurs were generally those who spread their operations much wider than slave trading and used their profits to buy into safer businesses. Slaving operators came to be overwhelmingly Spanish and Portuguese after abolition, with a scattering of French, Italians, and Americans, but with very few native Brazilians or Cubans; however, much of the credit and trade goods with which they operated, continued to come from British sources.[29]

In Africa, the continued slave trade was especially profitable for areas excluded from the "cash crop revolution." Cash crops were limited to specific ecological zones and, because of their high bulk-to-value ratio, had to be grown close to the sea or the few stretches of navigable river. In contrast, slaves could be drawn from all over the continent, thus preventing regional economic differentials from growing. Moreover, the repression of the trade forced it out of the great commercial centers and into what were often poor, backward, and remote stretches of the coast. The effects of this phenomenon on regional capital accumulation still need to be investigated. This said, Eltis reminds us that both cash crop and slave exports remained marginal to overall African production in the nineteenth century.[30]

Migration and Related Political Movements

The slave trade and exports of forced labor gave rise in the Western world to one of the greatest political crusades of modern times, the nature of which is still hotly debated. This is a vast topic, on which entire volumes could be written. Briefly summarized, Eric Williams's thesis that slavery had become unprofitable for the new capitalist system, is now rarely believed. Plantation slavery was going from strength to strength when first the slave trade and then slavery were abolished. Abolition does appear to have been linked to the rise of capitalism, but in indirect ways. The ideological belief that free labor was always superior, the political stress on the free individual as the basis of society, and the evangelical revival that was in part linked to social upheavals, all meshed in complex ways with political

29. Eltis, *Economic Growth*, ch. 9 and Appendix E.

30. Ibid., ch. 13; Anthony Hopkins, *Economic History of West Africa* (London 1973), chs. 3 and 4.

struggles in the metropolis – the campaign for the franchise in Britain, or republicanism in France, for example – to produce the abolitionist crusade.[31]

In receiving societies, the continued slave trade had some unexpected political effects. In Cuba, and to a lesser extent in Puerto Rico, the Spaniards acquiesced in the continuing trade for many decades, in an effort to keep the loyalty of the planter elite and thus hang on to the last and highly profitable vestiges of their American empire. Consequently, opposition movements to Spanish rule often adopted antislavery elements in their program.[32] In Brazil, the defense of the slave trade kept the huge country together, at times when fragmentation on Hispanic lines threatened, and preserved the privileged position of Portuguese expatriate traders. Xenophobic anti-Portuguese rioting thus became closely linked to antislave-trade protest. In both Cuba and Brazil, the general British liberal ideology linked with abolition gradually progressed within the elites and contributed to slowly growing abolitionist sentiment within the receiving zones.[33]

As for Africa, decisions as to whether to collaborate with abolition or oppose it could have significant political effects. At times, the British resorted to open and illegal violence against slave trading societies. More important were the changing opportunities for building state power on the basis of an export trade in slaves; the growing internal market for slaves within Africa considerably attenuated the impact of such changes. Political effects in Africa, in this way, depended on a combination of vulnerability to European attacks and alternative markets for slaves. One has to be very cautious in attributing the rise or fall of any particular state to changes in slave trading.[34]

31. Davis, *Slavery*; Drescher, *Econocide*; Eric Williams, *Capitalism and Slavery* (Chapel Hill 1944); Roger Anstey, *The Atlantic Slave Trade and British Abolition, 1760–1810* (London 1975).

32. Eltis, *Economic Growth*, ch. 12; David Murray, *Odious Commerce; Britain, Spain and the Abolition of Slavery in Cuba* (Cambridge 1980); Corwin, *Spain*.

33. Eltis, *Economic Growth*, ch. 12; Leslie Bethell, *The Abolition of the Brazilian Slave Trade* (Cambridge 1970); Luiz-Felipe de Alencastro, "La traite négrière et l'unité nationale brésilienne," *Revue Française d'Histoire d'Outremer* 66, no. 244–245 (1979), 395–419.

34. Eltis, *Economic Growth*, ch. 13 and passim.

Free Emigration

Free emigration from western Africa was both very small and restricted to three main areas. One of these, the Cape Verde Islands, exhibited European conditions typical of the other Atlantic archipelagos, with private freehold tenure, renting and sharecropping of land, and serious overpopulation, to which was added the particular problem of terrible droughts and famines. This example of emigration is best left to be integrated with studies of European emigration, although those interested may consult Carreira's informative book.[35]

The other two areas of free emigration were the Kru coast, in modern eastern Liberia and the western Ivory Coast, and Cabinda, the northern enclave of present-day Angola. From about the late eighteenth century, if not earlier, these two regions began to provide European ships with crew, stevedores, and lightermen. The Cabindans also emerged as important builders, owners, and operators of ships in their own right, sometimes crossing the Atlantic with loads of slaves. Having established this nautical niche for themselves, the Kru and Cabindans spread along the coast and tended to monopolize naval employment wherever it was to be had. The Kru-Cabinda "frontier" lay roughly between modern Cameroun and Gabon, although there was much overlap. Having acquired an excellent reputation as ship labor, it was natural that they should have been solicited for other work overseas, notably in general urban employment, plantations, and public works. Thus, Ferdinand de Lesseps employed some Kru in both his Suez and his Panama Canal projects.[36]

The extent, however, of employment of free emigrants in plantations had often been exaggerated, especially in regard to the Kru. Although some free Kru labor was recruited for the British and French Caribbean in the 1840s and 1850s, together with some free Sierra Leone residents, the laborers quickly found that wages were too low, conditions were too harsh, and repatriation was hampered by poor communications. Hence, this flow of labor remained small and did not persist for long.[37] Attempts to replace slaves with Kru in

35. António Carreira, *The People of the Cape Verde Islands; Exploitation and Emigration* (London 1982 [tr. from Portuguese ed. 1977]).

36. Davis, *Ethnohistorical Studies*; George E. Brooks Jr., *The Kru Mariner in the 19th Century* (Newark 1972); Martin, *External Trade*; Phyllis M. Martin, "Cabinda and Cabindans: Some Aspects of an African Maritime Society" in *Africa and the Sea*, Jeffrey Stone, ed (Aberdeen 1985); João de Mattos e Silva, *Contribuição para o estudo da região de Cabinda* (Lisbon 1904).

37. Schuler, "Recruitment of African Indentured Labour," 129–135, 149–151;

São Tomé, after the formal abolition of slavery in 1875, foundered for the same reasons and were given up within a few years.[38] German cocoa planters round Mount Cameroun briefly employed Kru in the 1890s but found them too expensive.[39] The longest record of employing such labor was ostensibly by the Spaniards in Fernando Po, from the 1890s to 1930. A closer examination of these "Kru," however, reveals that they were generally slaves and forced laborers from the interior of Liberia, sold by the Kru and the Vai or rounded up by the Liberian Frontier Force.[40] Although it is impossible to give exact numbers, it would appear that free labor from western Africa was extremely rare in plantation work and that the numbers involved in nautical and general urban occupations were not all that great.

The Kru and the Cabindans shared many characteristics: they were both unusually dependent on activities to do with the sea, whereas many African peoples seemed in some sense to turn their backs on the ocean, and they therefore had skills that were essential to European shippers. As the slave trade was slowly repressed, the Kru and the Cabindans found themselves with few alternative possibilities for earning money but involved in social relations where young men needed important financial resources to marry and achieve political office. It must be stressed, however, that emigration was rarely permanent, even along the African coast, and that it mainly involved short-term recurrent migrancy by young men.[41]

Conclusion

The reasons for the limited extent of free emigration from Africa mirror the reasons for the persistence of coerced labor exports. Africans did not come from densely populated regions, where access to land was blocked by institutions of private property. On the

---

Monica Schuler, "Kru Emigrants to British and French Guiana, 1841–1857" in *Africans in Bondage*, Paul Lovejoy, ed. (Madison 1986), 155–201.

38. Banco Nacional Ultramarino, *Relatórios*, 1875–1883.

39. Adolf Rüger, "Die Entstehung und Lage der Arbeiterklasse unter dem deutschen Kolonialregime in Kamerun, 1895–1905" in *Kamerun unter deutscher Kolonialherrschaft* I, Helmuth Stoecker, ed. (Berlin 1960), 193–197, 208–211.

40. Sundiata, "Prelude to Scandal;" Davis, *Ethnohistorical Studies*, 56–64.

41. Davis, *Ethnohistorical Studies*, ch. 2; Brooks, *Kru Mariner*; Andreas Massing, *The Economic Anthropology of the Kru* (Wiesbaden 1980); Martin, *External Trade* and "Cabinda"; Joaquim Martins, *Cabindas: história, crença, usos e costumes* (Cabinda 1972); José Martins Vaz, *No mundo dos Cabindas* (Lisbon 1970).

contrary, they came from land-abundant but resource-poor societies, where the main advantage of emigrating to work was to bring back goods into one's society of origin. This meant that voluntary emigration would take the form of temporary movement to high-wage zones. It also meant that an alternative, and generally preferable, way to attract resources was forcibly to sell off your reluctant neighbors or dependents into servitude overseas.

10

Immigration into Latin America, Especially Argentina and Chile*

MAGNUS MÖRNER

Colonial Antecedents

Numbers

On principle, immigration to Spanish America was reserved for Spanish subjects of the monarch, and out-migration to the Americas was also strictly supervised. Consequently, control procedures produced an extensive source material, which facilitates the evaluation of the extent and composition of legal emigration. Thanks to the studies of Peter Boyd-Bowman, the foremost student of the subject so far, and the data of Pierre and Huguette Chaunu on navigation from Seville to the New World, 1506 to 1650, I was able, in 1976, to elaborate an estimate of a total of almost 450,000 Spanish emigrants until 1650 (see Table 10.1). On the other hand, as yet, we cannot

* This report is based on my book *Adventurers and Proletarians. The Story of Migrants in Latin America* (Pittsburgh 1985) and my article "Spanish migrations to the New World prior to 1810. A report on the state of research" in *First Images of the New World on the Old* I, Fred Chiappelli ed. (Berkeley 1976), 737–82, 797–804. From them the graphs and maps have all been taken. Both works carry extensive bibliographies; therefore, bibliographical references are only made to the sources for these illustrations or to studies more recent than 1984 or omitted in the two contributions. The graphs were drawn by Mrs. Retsuko Sims, Pittsburgh. Statistical data were gathered by Mr. George Calafut and Mr. Laird Bergad, my research assistants in 1976 to 1977 at the University of Pittsburgh.

At the fourth Meeting of European Latin Americanist Historians in Cologne, West Germany, in 1975, the European background of Latin American immigration was thoroughly studied. For the numerous reports and papers, see *La emigración europea a la América Latina: fuentes y estado de investigación: informes presentados a la IV. Reunión de Historiadores latinoamericanistas europeos.* Bibliotheca Ibero-americana 26 (West Berlin 1979) and *Jahrbuch für die Geschichte von Staat, Wirtschaft und Gesellschaft Lateinamerikas* 13 (Cologne and Vienna 1976). At the sixth meeting of the same group in Stockholm in 1981 the transfer of both European labor, entrepreneurs, and capital was on the agenda. See *Capitales, empresarios y obreros europeos en América Latina. Actas del VI° Congreso de AHILA, Estocolmo, 25–28 de mayo de 1981* 2 vols. (Stockholm 1983).

TABLE 10.1 Spanish Migration to the Americas, 1500–1650

	Average tonnage per ship[a]	Average crew per ship[b]	Average passengers per ship[c]	Average total westbound passages[d]	Average total passengers[e]	Westbound passages in excess of eastbound	Average sailors remaining in the Americas[f]	Estimated total overseas migrants[g]
1506–1560	100	30	15	1,781	26,715	689	16,536	43,251
1541–1560	150	40	20	1,511	30,220	305	12,200	42,420
Total, 1506–1560								85,671
1561–1600	230	60	30	3,497	104,910	1,089	52,272	157,182
Total, 1506–1600								242,853
1601–1625	230	60	30	2,480	74,400	769	35,912	111,312
1626–1650	300	80	40	1,366	54,640	451	28,864	88,504
Total, 1601–1650								194,816
Total, 1506–1650								436,669

Source: Magnus Mörner, "Spanish Migration to the New World prior to 1810. A Report on the State of Research" in *First Images of America. The Impact of the New World on the Old* I, F. Chiapelli, ed. (Berkeley 1976), 737–82, 797–804, especially 766–67.

a. Based on Huguette and Pierre Chaunu, *Séville et l'Atlantique* (1504–1650) 8 vols. (Paris 1955–1959), I 4:6, 168.

b. Ramón Carande, *Carlos V y sus banqueros. La vida económica de España en una fase de su hegemonía* (Madrid 1943), 274–75, who gives minimum crews required for various units of tonnage. See also Huguette and Chaunu, *Séville et l'Atlantique* 6:6, 305–6 and John H. Parry, *The Age of the Reconnaisance* (London 1964).

c. Our estimate for 1506–1560 is somewhat lower than that of Juan Friede, "Algunas obervaciones sobre la realidad de la emigración española a América en la primera mitad del siglo XVI," *Revista de Indias* 12, 49 (1952), 467–96, especially 471–72; however, we maintain his crew/passenger ratio for later periods. Our conjectures in this highly uncertain matter should be conservative.

d. Huguette and Chaunu, *Séville et l'Atlantique* I 6:6, 337. Total for 1506–1650 is 10,635 westbound passages.

e. This estimate is based on passengers × voyages; see Ibid., 337.

f. The deduction should account for mortality during westbound passages and for those returning on other ships. On losses of ships going west, see Ibid., 861–64.

average sailors remaining in the Americas.

possibly estimate, even vaguely, Spanish emigration to America from 1650 to 1810, or rather, 1821. A figure sometimes referred to in literature for the eighteenth century, is devoid of scientific value.[1]

Of all immigrants until 1640, by far most settled in Mexico and Peru. Chile only received some 4 percent, the River Plate even less. For 1595 to 1598 we know the destinations of 2,283 emigrants of whom 26 (1.7 percent) went to Chile, 10 (0.4 percent) to the River Plate.[2] These were poor, peripheral areas, exposed to constant Indian warfare. Toward the end of the colonial period, their share of the total white population had increased. According to Alexander von Humboldt, in 1823, there were about 3.3 million whites (native born *criollos* and peninsulars) in Spanish America. The division he makes between the two groups (300,000 Europeans) is of doubtful value however. Of the total white population, that of the River Plate now constituted about a tenth. There were always some non-Spanish foreigners who, legal prohibition notwithstanding, settled and remained in Spanish America, but they probably never constituted more than a tiny percentage of the total.[3]

On Portuguese emigration to Brazil prior to 1808, we have very little quantitative information. As different from the restrictive Spanish policy, immigration was free to individuals from all nationalities, provided that they were Catholics. The gold rush in the interior around 1700, raised the level of immigration considerably. Historical demographer Maria Luiza Marcílio estimates an inflow of about 400,000 people in the course of the eighteenth century.[4]

By comparison, according to Philip Curtin's well-known estimate, Brazil between 1500 and 1810 was reached by a total of 2.5 million African slaves; Spanish America by a little less than 950,000.[5]

1. Mario Hernández Sánchez-Barba, *La sociedad colonial americana en el siglo XVIII. Historia de España y America* IV, J. Vicens Vices, ed. (Barcelona 1958), 326, who calculated a total of 52,500 emigrants on the basis of three scattered years. This conjecture is inexplicably used by Nicolas Sanchez-Albornoz in his recent survey: "The Population of Colonial Spanish America" in *The Cambridge History of Latin America* II (Cambridge 1984), 3–35, esp. 31 (but without mention of the source). See also David Eltis, "Free and Coerced Transatlantic Migrations: Some Comparisons," *American Historical Review* 88, 2 (1983), 251–80, esp. 254.

2. Boyd-Bowman, "Spanish Emigrants," 723–35, esp. 726. For the entire sixteenth century, the same author assigns 5.1 percent to the River Plate, 3.6 percent to Chile, see Boyd-Bowman, "Pattern of Spanish Emigration," 580–604, esp. 602.

3. This immigration, with respect to eighteenth-century Mexico, has been studied by Charles F. Nunn, *Foreign Immigrants to Early Bourbon Mexico, 1700–60* (Cambridge 1979).

4. Maria Luiza Marcílio, "The Population of Colonial Brazil" in *The Cambridge History of Latin America* II, Leslie Bethell, ed. (Cambridge 1984), 37–63, esp. 47.

5. Philip D. Curtin, *The Atlantic Slave Trade: A Census* (Madison 1969), 268.

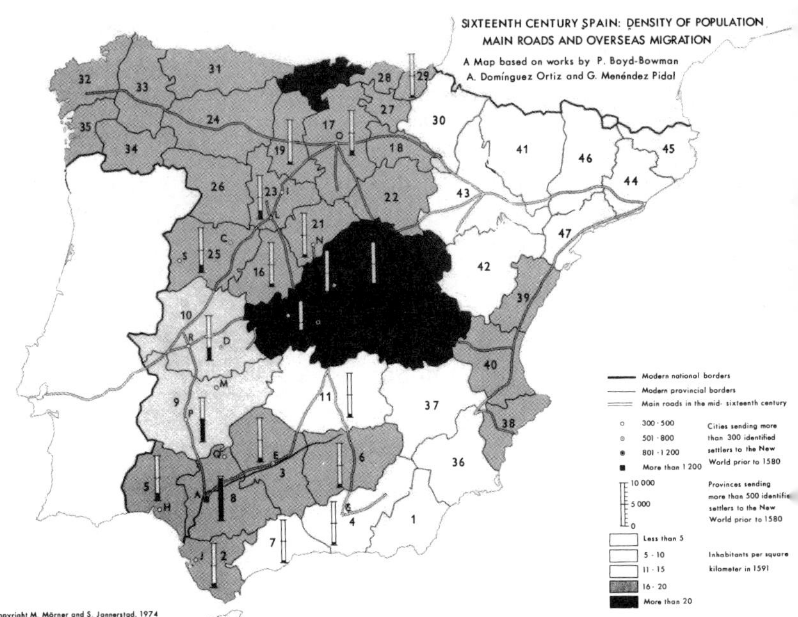

FIGURE 10.1 Sixteenth-Century Spain: Density of Population and Overseas Migration

Push and Pull

Thanks to Boyd-Bowman we have a fair idea about the regional/local patterns of Spanish out-migration during the sixteenth century (see Figure 10.1). Two regions, Andalusia and Extremadura, dominated strongly. Moreover, until 1580, a total of 31 cities, with Seville ranked first, provided no less than 45 percent of total overseas emigration prior to 1580. Also, a more detailed map than ours would show that districts of high frequency of emigration clustered along the main roads of central and western Spain. This spatial pattern strongly suggests that pull- rather than push-factors were responsible for overseas migration until at least 1580. In the course of the deepening crisis of seventeenth-century Castile, however, the role of push-factors probably increased. To judge from various samples, such as a list of a thousand Spaniards in Mexico City in 1689, and later ones, the largest migrant groups now came from the northern and eastern Spanish seaboards. In the first case, we know that population pressure and lack of land caused internal migration, and probably did so with respect to external out-migration as well. In the case of the eastern seaboard, on the other hand, out-migration is in line with the notable economic and demographic expansion of Catalonia and Valencia from the late seventeenth century onward. If merchants and others went from here to the Americas, it was probably the case of pull rather than push.

Immigration into Brazil during the early 1700s, was clearly above all a question of pull. At the same time, the continuous predominance of people from Minho and the Atlantic islands, both overpopulated regions, also suggest the structural importance of push-factors in Portuguese out-migration.

Demography of Sending Regions

Around 1590, Spain had, we may assume, a total population of 7.9 million. Granted that the yearly overseas migration reached 4,000 people, this outflow implied a yearly loss of 0.5 per thousand, that is a rather insignificant impact. If, however, only the four provinces with the highest overseas migration (Seville, Badajoz, Toledo, Cáceres), with a population of 1.4 million and 2,000 out-migrants yearly, are included, 1.43 per thousand (instead of 0.5) is reached. In the case of a stagnant population, the impact of migration on a regional level would then be rather noticeable.

Passing to Portugal, Marcílio's estimate of 400,000 out-migrants during the eighteenth century should be related to a total population of probably 2 million, that is approximately 0.2 per thousand. It was by then surely higher in northern Portugal from which most emigrants came.

Female Emigration

Boyd-Bowman's figures on Spanish overseas migrants cover about 20 percent of the total outflow, until 1598. A basis of this size should warrant the general validity of the percentage of female participation in the transatlantic migratory movement as given in Table 10.2. This means that the traditional view of an overwhelmingly male settlement in Spanish America, as opposed to the North American family pattern, no longer holds. On the other hand, a large female participation in immigration from mid-sixteenth century onward helps to explain the striking speed with which a new society with a white upper stratum took shape in Spanish America long before that century had come to an end.[6]

6. Boyd-Bowman underscores the fact that more than half of the female emigrants

TABLE 10.2 Approximate Percentage of Women of Total Spanish Overseas Emigration, 1509–1598

1509–1519	1520–1539	1540–1559	1560–1579	1580–1600	1595–1598
5.6	6.3	16.4	28.5	26.0	35.3

Sources: Peter Boyd-Bowman, "Pattern of Spanish Emigration to the Indies until 1600," *The Hispanic American Historical Review* 56, 4 (1976), 580–604; Idem., "Spanish Emigrants to the Indies, 1595–98: A Profile" in *First Images of America: The Impact of the New World on the Old* I, Fred Chiapelli, ed. (Berkeley 1976), 723–35.

Transportation

In Table 10.1 we estimated the average tonnage of the ships of the Spanish fleets, carrying both merchandise and passengers, to be 100 tons in 1506 to 1540, increasing little by little to 300 tons in 1626 to 1650. Similarly, the average number of passengers and crew seem to have increased from 15 and 30 to 40 and 80, respectively. Like the Chaunus, Antonio García-Baquero Gonzalez, in his study concerning Cádiz and the Atlantic during the period 1717 to 1778, does not even mention the passengers, although he shows that 47 percent of the crossings were made by ships which held between 200 and 500 tons. The average crew of such a ship was 71 men. In the eighteenth century, the voyage from the Andalusian harbor to Vera Cruz took an average of 85 days; during the period of 1506 to 1650, the average duration was 10 days shorter.[7]

Out of 1909 passengers listed by Boyd-Bowman for 1595 to 1598, 238 were married couples, with a total of 522 children, at least 118 of who were 5 years old or younger. There were also 30 wives, who went to join their husbands, and 48 widows. Very few single women, for reasons of honor, traveled alone. Nothing is known about the mortality rate during the passage, but the trip could hardly be called a pleasant one. "The cabins are closed, obscure and smell so horribly that they look like the tombs of the dead," exclaims a Spaniard

---

until 1600 came from Andalusia with its specific cultural characteristics. In Seville, emigrant women even outnumbered men. Boyd-Bowman, "Pattern of Spanish Emigration," 596–600.

7. Antonio García-Baquero González, *Cádiz y el Atlántico (1717–78)* 2 vols. (Seville 1976), 1:255, 276, 388. For a more detailed and lively account of life on board with nutrition problems and sickness, with respect to the traffic between Portugal and Brazil, see Frédéric Mauro, *Le Portugal et l'Atlantique au XVIIe siècle, 1570–1670* (Paris 1960), 71–85.

who made the crossing with his wife in 1573.[8] A huge number of letters from sixteenth- and seventeenth-century settlers in Spanish America to relatives back home, uncovered in the 1960s, has shown that travel money was very often advanced by the former.

Other Aspects

In both Spanish and Portuguese America, the immigration taking place during the colonial period was, indeed, of fundamental importance for every aspect of the later historical development. Therefore, in this part of my report it would hardly make sense to take up single aspects such as reception/settlement, integration/isolation, capital transfer, and politics.[9] Return migration certainly took place but, unfortunately, we have no basis for even the crudest of an estimate of its extent. As always, some of the returnees simply were able to fulfill their original intention to spend their last years leisurely at home, while others returned because of disappointment but still with money enough to purchase the passage.

Immigration until the Depression

Independence meant a radical change from colonial to national government attitudes toward non-Iberian immigration. Everywhere, measures were taken to encourage immigration. Even in Cuba, still a Spanish possession, non-Hispanic immigration was permitted in 1817 to help counterbalance the swelling influx of black slaves. While, in the various Latin American countries, the conservatives and the Church insisted that immigrants profess the Roman Catholic faith, liberals wanted to suppress that condition, as was done, for example, in Argentina in 1825.

8. Guillermo Céspedes del Castillo ed., *Textos y Documentos de la América Hispánica (1492–1898)* Historia de España dirigda por M. Tuñón de Lara 14 (Madrid 1986), 178.

9. Recent research made increasingly clear, however, that the white skin did not automatically confer upper stratum positions. There were many poor people among *criollos* and *peninsulares* alike. According to J.E. Kicza, in the eighteenth century the "'Diario de Mexico' often carried advertisements by jobless Spaniards soliciting any sort of low level supervisory post, whether in the city or the countryside." See his *Colonial Entrepreneurs: Families and Business in Colonial Mexico City* (Albuquerque 1983), 14.

Numbers

In the course of four generations, between 1824 and 1924, some 52 million Europeans emigrated overseas. While 72 percent set out for the United States, 21 percent opted for Latin America, that is, 11 million. As is well known, the backdrop of this enormous population movement was European demographical growth, the need for raw materials, for industrial products as well as for food from overseas, and improved transportation. In the case of Latin America, however, mass immigration set in relatively late, compared with the United States. Admittedly, statistics for the first part of the nineteenth century are rather uncertain, but we know, for example, that during the transition to Independence, 1810 to 1822, some 4,000 non–Portuguese entered Brazil, a quarter of them merchants. Also, some 7,000 British and Irish enlisted in the armies of Simón Bolívar; of the thousand survivors, many settled down. Various colonization projects brought more or less numerous groups to the various countries, but most plans failed miserably for being badly prepared by the leaders and/or by the national authorities. One such project, of 2,000 Swiss who settled down in Novo Friburgo in Brazil in 1819, has been the subject of an excellent monograph.[10] Another colonization project, however, would prove both lasting and successful. Some 3,000 Germans settled in the forests of Valdivia and Llanquihue in southern Chile between 1846 and 1858.[11] Most Europeans, however, among them many from France, preferred Brazil, Argentina, and Uruguay. It has been estimated that these countries were reached by a total of 200,000 immigrants from 1816 to 1850.

Total migration to Latin America, as is shown by Figure 10.2, according to the invaluable work of Ferenczi and Willcox, took a clear upward turn in 1861 to 1865, reaching an even higher level in 1876 to 1890. After a low in the 1890s, in both Argentina and Brazil, the culmination of European immigration took place in 1901 to 1909. At that time, World War I caused a drastic downward trend, like the Depression of 1929 would also do and in a more lasting fashion.

Figures 10.3 and 10.4 show the origins and destinies of mass emigration respectively. Development over time from 1854 onward is traced in Figures 10.2, 10.5, and 10.6. In southern and eastern Europe, the imports of cheap cereals, cultivated particularly by

10. Martin Nicoulin, *La genèse de Nova Friburgo. Emigration et colonisation suisse au Brésil 1817–27* (Fribourg 1973).

11. See the impressive standard work by Blancpain, *Les allemands au Chili.*

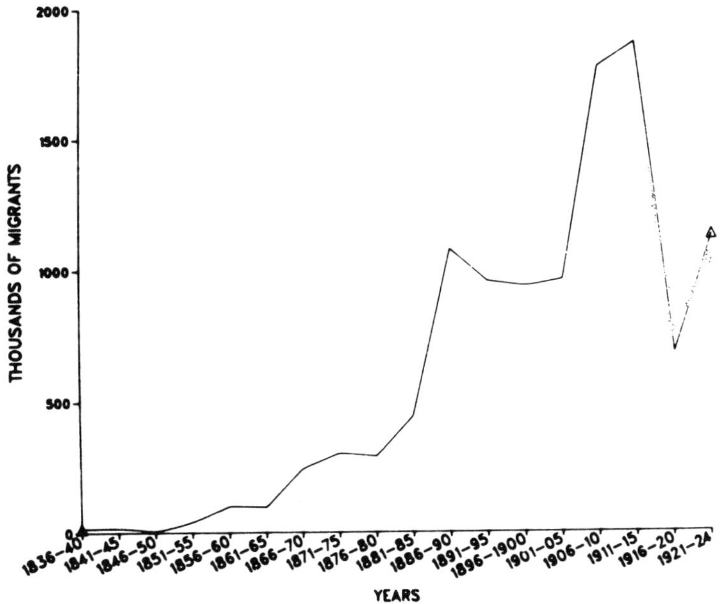

FIGURE 10.2 Total Migration to Latin America, 1836–1924

Source: Ferenczi and Willcox, *International Migrations* 1:263–37.

European immigrants in the United States' Midwest, would provoke a genuine agricultural crisis from the 1880s onward; this explains the forceful rise of Italian out-migration at that time (see Figure 10.2). Out-migration from Spain and Portugal, as from eastern Europe, only reached higher levels around 1900.

Argentina and Brazil vied with each other for the Italian migrants, as shown by Figure 10.7. Argentina held the lead until the crisis of 1890 when it had to suspend the subsidized passages that since 1888 had brought 130,000 immigrants to the country. In Brazil, on the other hand, the São Paulo coffee boom and the final abolition of slavery in 1888 facilitated immigration. Moreover, the State of São Paulo subsidized passages for immigrants between 1887 and 1902; thereby, almost 700,000 immigrants, mostly Italians, were attracted to that state. By 1910, the Portuguese took over the lead in Brazil, the Spaniards in Argentina. In 1924, it was clear that Argentina had received practically half of the total inflow of European immigrants to Latin America since the mid-century.

Chile received no more than 0.5 percent of total European

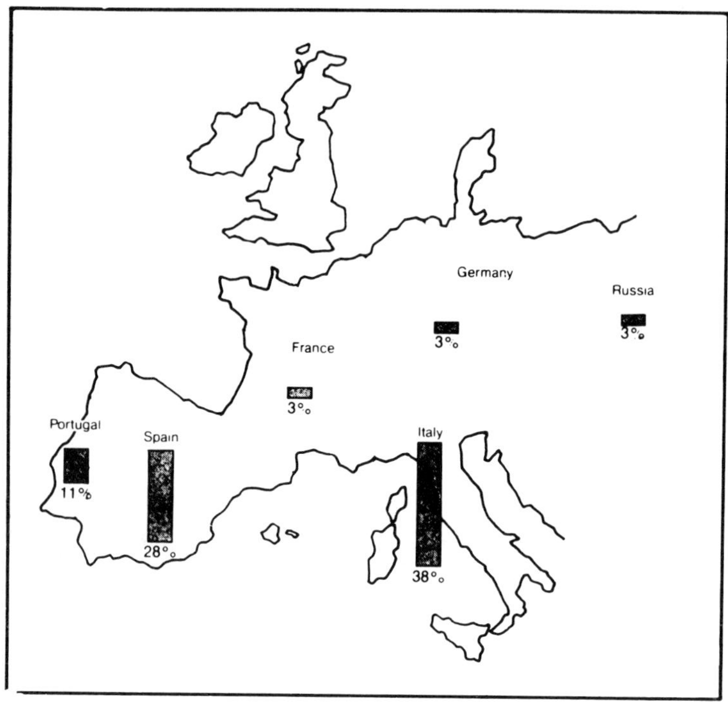

FIGURE 10.3 Emigration from Europe to Latin America, 1854–1924

Source: Magnus Mörner, *Adventurers and Proletarians. The Story of the Migrants in Latin America* (Pittsburgh, PA and Paris 1985).

immigration during the same period. As is shown by Figure 10.9, in the 1880 to 1890s Spaniards, French, and Italians were the largest immigrant groups. The substantial number of Germans in southern Chile (like in southernmost Brazil) owed much more to the rapid indigenous growth of isolated population centers than to continuous immigration. The settlers totaled, 4,250 immigrants from 1846 to 1880. A secret census carried out by the Germans themselves in 1916 gave a total of 25,000 German-speaking people in southern Chile.

To give some idea of the total human influx to Latin America in the course of the nineteenth century, we should keep in mind that 600,000 to 700,000 African slaves reached Spanish America and that almost twice as many reached Brazil between 1811 and 1870, when the slave trade was finally suppressed. For the Caribbean, Pieter Emmer, in his contribution to this volume, gives the relevant data on the influx of Asiatic and other indentured laborers who were

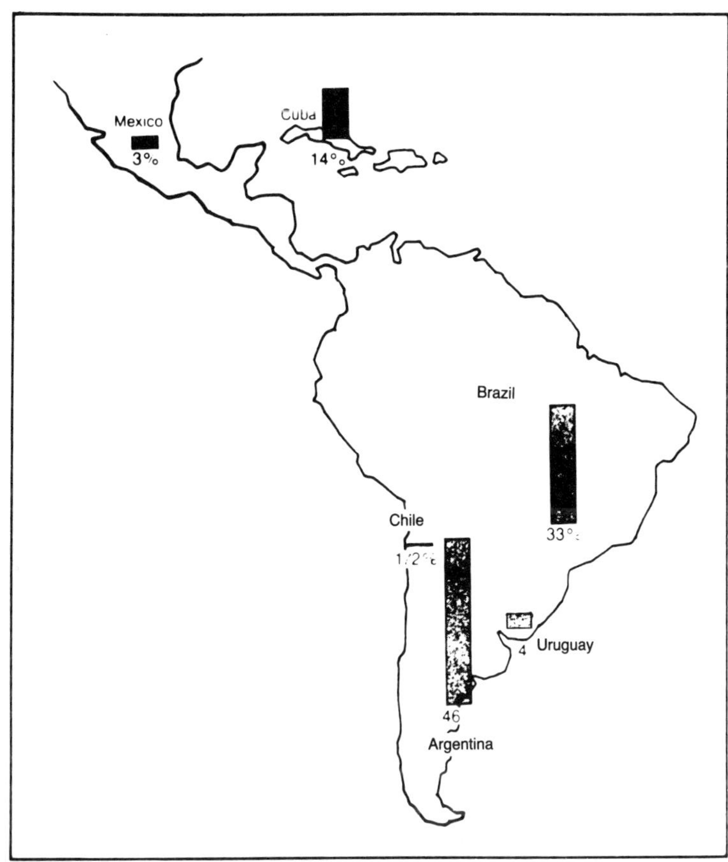

FIGURE 10.4 Total Migration to Latin America, by Major Countries of Destination, 1851–1924

Source: Imre Ferenczi and Walter F. Willcox eds., *International Migrations* 2 vols. (New York 1929), 1:262–73.

imported to the Caribbean from 1839 to 1917. To these should be added a total of 75,000 Chinese contract laborers, who entered Peru between 1849 and 1874.[12]

The demographic impact of immigration, notwithstanding a very

12. An attempt at integrated analysis of transatlantic migrations, both free and coerced, has been made by Eltis, "Free and Coerced Transatlantic Migrations." "Not until 1840 did arrivals from Europe permanently surpass those from Africa," he maintains, 255.

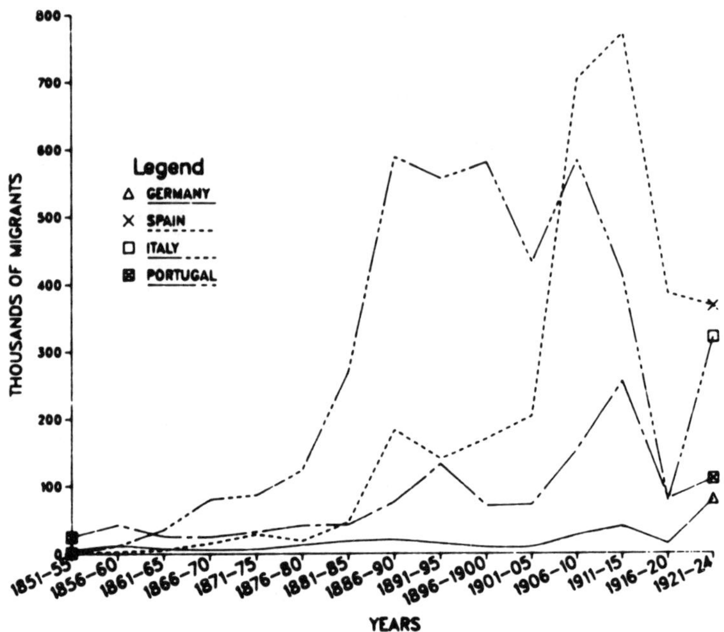

FIGURE 10.5 Total Migration to Latin America, by Country of Origin, 1856–1924

Source: Ferenczi and Willcox, *International Migrations*, 1:262–73.

high remigration rate (see below) from some of the receiving countries and regions, was extraordinarily strong. In 1940, no less than 30 percent of Argentina's population was born abroad. In the United States, by contrast, the foreign born never passed the 1910 figure of 14.7 percent. Immigrants and their children were responsible for 57 percent of the growth of Argentina's population, from 800,000 in 1841 to 14 million in 1940. In the state of São Paulo, Brazil, by 1934, immigrants and their children constituted more than half of the population.

Push- and Pull-Factors

Latin America's attraction for European migrants was very limited and selective during, and for some decades after, the wars of independence. At first many European merchants went to Latin America, but the London crash of 1825, the impossibility of reviving the colonial mining economy, and the political turmoil curtailed that

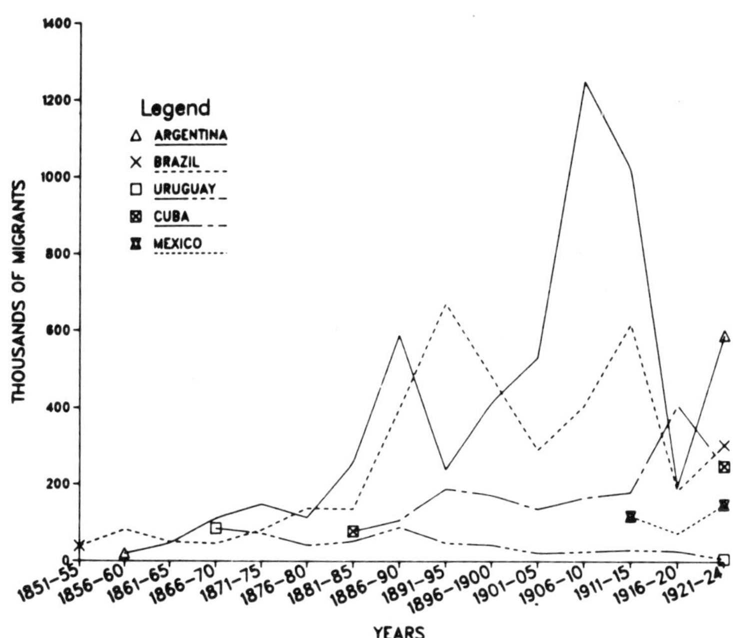

FIGURE 10.6 Total Migration to Latin America, by Major Countries of Destination, 1851–1924

Source: Ferenczi and Willcox, *International Migrations*, 1:262–73.

current. Instead, soldiers and adventurers were attracted by that very turmoil, once Europe attained peace in 1815. The natives of the overpopulated Canary Islands took up once more their curiously selective emigration to Uruguay, Venezuela, and Cuba, already under way during the late colonial times.[13] Some of the participants in the defeated European revolutions of 1830 and 1848, such as Garibaldi, went as refugees to Latin America.

The general push-factors promoting European out-migration on a large scale toward the mid-nineteenth century have been alluded to already. The process of demographic growth and related phenomena, however, began in the northeast of Europe. To begin with, both cultural affinity and various pull-factors to be discerned in the dynamic United States, made it the main goal for the migratory

13. For a survey of Canarian emigration over time, see James J. Parsons, "The Migration of Canary Islanders to the America: An Unbroken Current since Columbus," *The Americas* 39, 4 (1983), 447–81. This case should exemplify the "stock effects" on a large spatial level.

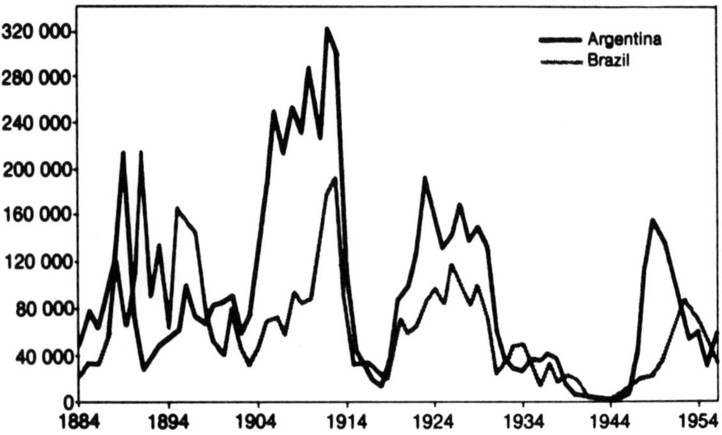

FIGURE 10.7 Italian Immigration to Argentina and Brazil, 1884–1954, Including Subsidized Passages

waves composed by North Europeans. Latin America only entered the scene as an important option when the combination of demographic growth and agricultural crisis had reached southern and eastern Europe. Workers' wages in Spain, Portugal, Italy, and Russia were the lowest ones in Europe. Only in Italy had they improved by 1900. In the Russian empire, the persecutions of the Jews were also intensified in the 1880s and after 1900. In Italy and Spain/Portugal, cultural affinity this time helped to direct the outflow toward Latin America.

The importance of the cultural factor, however, should not be exaggerated. One-fourth of the total immigration into Brazil and one-seventh of that into Argentina came from non-Latin countries. The basic wish of the out-migrants was to improve their material conditions, while the receiving countries were looking to obtain a larger and "better" labor force in order to satisfy the growing European demand for Latin American products. Argentina, a sparsely populated temperate country, was dominated by a ranching oligarchy linked to the exportation of hides. The country remained an importer of wheat until the 1870s. A few European colonies in the northeastern part of the Pampa became the pioneers in the cultivation of wheat. Toward the end of the 1880s, the local market for grain had been satisfied, and exportation on a massive scale had set in. At this juncture, the government started its short-lived, but effective, program of subsidizing immigrants' fares. Around

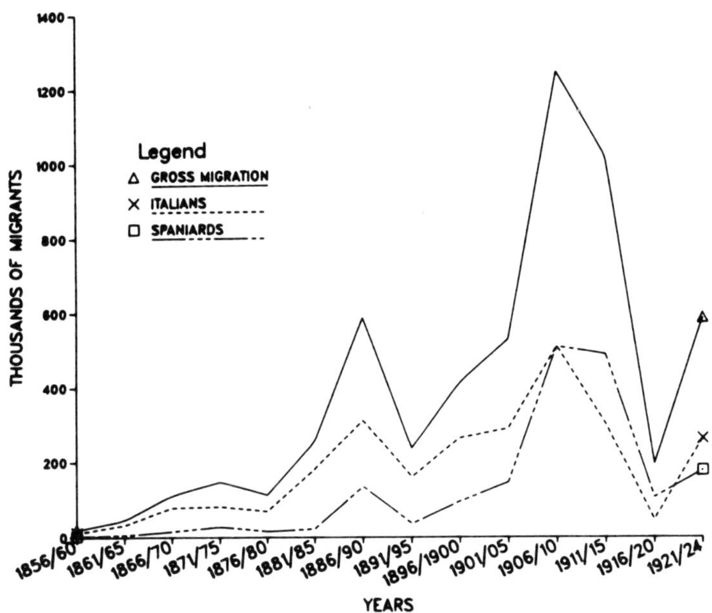

FIGURE 10.8 Total Migration to Argentina, the Italian and Spanish Shares, 1856–1924

1900, in Argentina food absorbed only 25 percent of a worker's wages, as compared to 60 percent in Italy and Spain, 33 percent in the United States, and 28 percent in Australia. Also, an agricultural laborer coming from the Mediterranean could recover his travel costs with only two weeks' work in Argentina. This gave rise to the phenomenon of Spanish and Italian workers, called *golondrinas* ("swallows"), going to the River Plate in October and November to assist in the harvests of wheat and fruits. In May, perhaps after another brief stay in the coffee districts of São Paulo, they returned to Europe in time for the harvest season there. The *golondrinas* were hardly true immigrants, but naturally figure in the statistics.

On the other hand, there are also examples of very stable foreign colonies, such as Pigüe in the Pampa, inhabited by people from Aveyron in France (a good example of the "stock effect") or the nationalist Welsh colony in Chubut in southern Argentina.[14] In

14. See Bartolome Benassar, *Les Aveyronnais dans la pampa: Fondation, développement et la vie de la colonie aveyronnaise de Pigue, Argentina 1884–1974* (Toulouse 1977) and Glyn Williams, *The Desert and the Dream. A Study of Welsh Colonization in Chubut, 1865–1915* (Cardiff 1975).

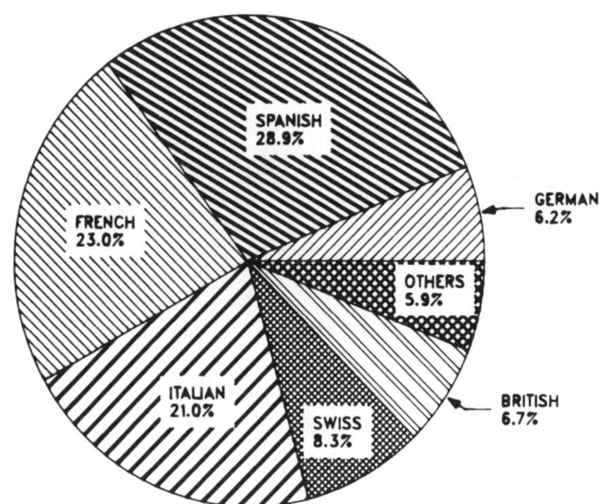

FIGURE 10.9 Total Migration to Chile, by Nationality, 1882–1897 (total 36,510)

Source: Jean-Pierre Blancpain, *Les allemands au Chili (1816–1945)* (Cologne and Vienna 1974), 481.

such cases, the pull effect was strengthened by continuous contact with friends and relatives back home.

Business cycles on both sides of the Atlantic naturally influenced the migratory movement. In Argentina, immigration and wheat exports, between 1871 and 1910, presented at the least a Pearson correlation coefficient of 0.8072 (see Figure 10.10), but politics also played a role. In Chile, a decline in immigration between 1891 and 1908 was related to the civil war of 1891, as well as to an economic crisis.

The Demography of Sending Regions

Even in the European country sending the largest number of emigrants to Latin America, Italy, these constituted merely 30.5 percent of total out-migration from 1876 to 1900. Other European countries received 48.5 percent of the Italian outflow (see Figure 10.11). Of the Italians arriving in Argentina in the years 1876 to 1913, about 60 percent came from the north. Later on, Italians in the United States mostly came from the south, but there was also a large share of southerners in Argentina.

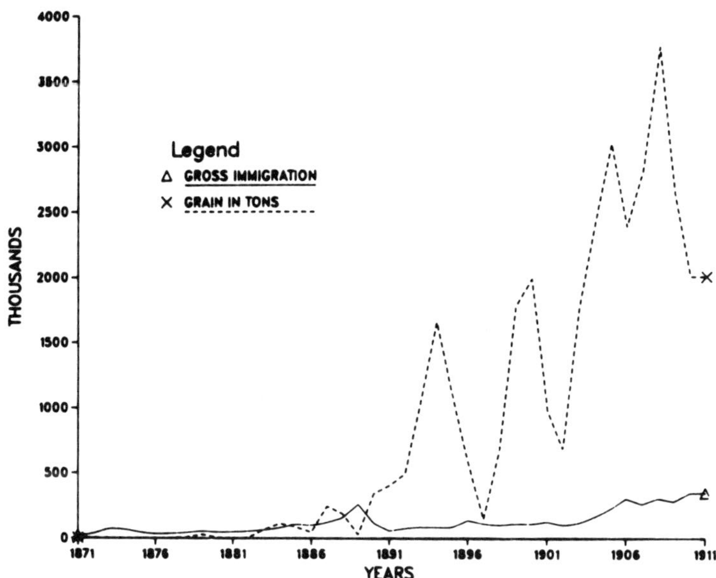

FIGURE 10.10 Export of Wheat and Flour from Argentina and Total Immigration, 1871–1910

Source: James R. Scobie, *Revolution on the Pampas: A Social History of Argentine Wheat, 1860–1910* (Austin 1964), 169–79.
Note: r = 0.8072; r2 = 0.6516.

In Spain, annual overseas emigration per thousand rose from 2.16 in 1881 to 1990 to 4.48 in 1901 to 1908. On the provincial level, however, the impact was much stronger. In 1885 to 1886 the Canaries took the lead with 18.0 per thousand, followed by Pontevedra and La Coruña (Galicia) with 13.3 per thousand and 12.7 per thousand, respectively. In the Canaries, no doubt, emigration helped to balance a yearly demographic growth rate of as much as 1.18 per thousand (1878 to 1884).[15] On the whole, however, Spain's population growth between 1860 and 1900 was rather slow (from 15.6 to 18.5 million) as was Italy's (25.1 to 32.4 million). Spain's net migratory "loss," between 1890 and 1930, of 1.5 million should, however, be compared with an internal migration of twice that size.[16]

15. Ann-Sofie Kälvemark, *Reaktionen mot utvandringen. Emigrationsfrågan i svensk debatt och politik 1901–04* (Stockholm 1972), 16; Jorge Nadal, *La población española (siglos XVI a XX)* 3d ed. (Barcelona 1973), 192ff.

16. Miguel Martínez Cuadrado, *La burguesía conservadora (1874–1931)* Historia de España Alfaguara 6 (Madrid 1978), 114–17 and passim.

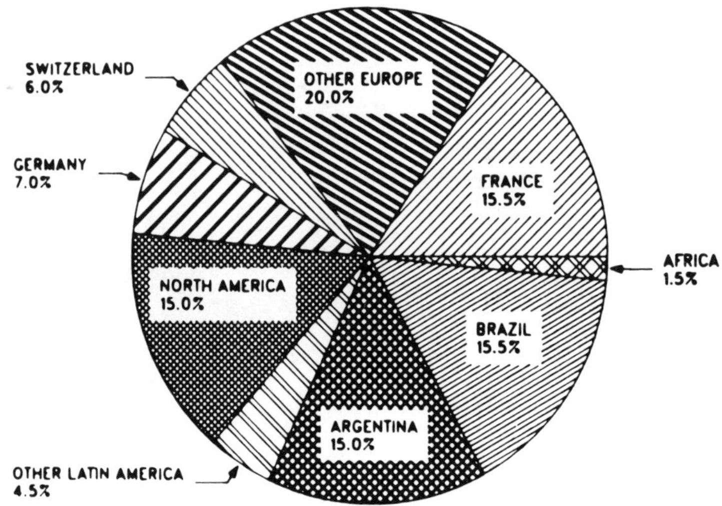

FIGURE 10.11 Worldwide Distribution of Italian Out-migrants, 1876–1900

Source: G. Rosoli, ed., *Un secolo di emigrazione italiana (1876–1976)* (Rome 1978), 22, table 3.

Portuguese emigration to Brazil constituted 93 percent of the total out-migration from 1901 to 1911, but the share dropped to 67 percent in the 1920s. The country's population grew from 3.6 million in 1857 to 5.6 in 1911. Even so, Portuguese students of these migratory movements tend to take a somber view of out-migration.[17]

Female Migration

As is normally the case, young adults formed the bulk of the migratory current from Europe to Latin America; also, men outnumbered women. Of the total Italian out-migration across the Atlantic in 1901, 26.9 percent were women; in 1903, 21.3 percent. In Argentina, the sex ratio of Italian immigrants between 1893 and

17. Joel Serrão, *A emigração portuguesa. Sondagem historica* 2d ed. (Lisbon 1974); see also the articles by Serrão and Jose-Gentil da Silva in *Jahrbuch für die Geschichte von Staat, Wirtschaft und Gesellschaft Lateinamerikas* (herafter *JGLA*) 13 (Cologne and Vienna 1976), 84–131. For lack of space I have not taken up in this report the complex problems of source criticism and methodology that mass migration poses. A valuable contribution is that of George Calafut, "Analysis of Italian Emigration Statistics, 1876–1914," *JGLA* 14 (1977), 310–31.

1909 was 267.8 as compared to that of 366.5 in the United States in the years 1899 to 1910.[18]

Of all immigrants arriving in Argentina between 1857 and 1926, only 29 percent were female. Interesting national differences may be observed, however. Among the French living in Buenos Aires in 1914, women were clearly in the majority. This may have reflected a demand for French governesses, seamstresses, and prostitutes. The distribution of both age, sex, and marital status would no doubt have suffered considerable changes over time.

Transportation

Mass migration was clearly conditioned by improved and more economic transportation.[19] Sailing crafts were gradually replaced by large steamships. By 1888, three-quarters of the ocean-going vessels arriving in Argentine ports were powered by steam. It is likely, however, that by the 1870s steamships were already carrying more immigrants than were sailing ships.

At that time, the price of the passage of Genoa-Rio de Janeiro fluctuated between 100 and 150 lire. In just three years, from 1903 to 1906, fares fell from 165 to 80 lire on the Italy-River Plate route. Moreover, voyages became less and less risky. During the 1903 to 1925 period, the mortality rate on voyages between Italy and South America was only 4 per thousand. To these circumstances one should add that, as already mentioned, travel was subsidized during certain periods, by both the São Paulo and the Argentine governments. As a result, from the 1870s onward, the transatlantic movement to Latin America would include members of the poorest strata of the countries of origin, which during the previous period had hardly been the case. Also, in fact, shipping companies allied to Latin American authorities and emigration agents, helped to channel many prospective emigrants to precisely a Latin American destiny.

18. Antonio Francheschini, *L'emigrazione italiana nell'America del Sud* (Rome 1908), 97; Herbert S. Klein, "The Integration of Italian Immigrants into the United States and Argentina: A Comparative Analysis," *American Historical Review* 88, 2 (1983), 306–46, esp. 316ff. (including comments by J. Balan, J.D. Gould, and T. Halperin-Donghi).

19. For a strict comparison between slave and north Atlantic migration traffic during the first half of the nineteenth century in terms of passenger-per-ton ratio and mortality, see Eltis, "Free and Coerced Transatlantic Migrations," 270–77.

Reception and Settlement

More than 90 percent of the total migration to Latin America prior to the Depression was absorbed by three countries only: Argentina, Brazil, and Uruguay. This concentration can be explained in terms of relatively stable political conditions, low population densities, temperate climate, and the economic development largely achieved as a result of immigration itself. The three countries wanted immigrants mainly in order to develop their agricultural resources. Most of the early waves, no doubt, came from European rural areas. But occupational figures derived from sources in the receiving countries are not overly reliable, based as they were upon the declarations of the immigrants themselves. The immigrants were very well aware of the fact that by declaring themselves to be "farmers," they would be better received.

As time went by, more and more immigrants were poor members of the urban proletariat in Italy and Spain or city dwellers from eastern European ghettos. According to Mulhall's *Dictionary of Statistics* (1899), 43 percent of immigrants in Latin America were urban workers and artisans, 12 percent servants and 39 percent agricultural workers. Merely 6 percent were educated people.[20] As a matter of fact, out of all immigrants arriving in Santos, Brazil, between 1908 and 1936, above the age of seven years, only 37 percent were able to read and write; of all the emigrants leaving the Canaries, fewer than 10 percent could.

By contrast to this trend toward proletarianization of the masses, there was also a trend toward professionalization within the small group of "educated" people. It included a great many technicians and professionals from northern and western Europe who deliberately opted for Latin America, either because they could not find appropriate jobs in their own countries or by special invitation of some Latin American governments. Given the antiquated character of most Latin American educational systems, they easily filled an acute need.[21]

Upon their arrival, the bulk of the immigrants settled down in the countryside as they were expected to do, as renter producers of wheat in Argentina, or as salaried laborers on the coffee plantations of São Paulo. In contrast, however, to the United States with its

20. Michael G. Mulhall, *The Dictionary of Statistics* 4th ed. (London 1899).

21. At the Cologne conference on migration in 1975, engineer migration was especially taken up by the Norwegian Gudmund Stang and the Belgian Eddy Stols. See *JGLA* 13, 320–30, 361–85.

Homestead Act (1862), in Argentina, Brazil, and Uruguay, with certain local or regional exceptions, cultivable land, prior to their arrival, had already been divided among large landowners, and farms were, on the whole, hard to buy. Moreover, the conditions of rural labor and tenants were often exceedingly harsh. Thus, disappointed immigrants in the countryside tended either to re-emigrate or to move into the great cities, a clear case of "push."

As a result, immigration into Latin America soon acquired a mainly urban character. In Argentina, by 1895, merely 16 percent of the immigrants were employed in agriculture, whereas 17 percent were artisans or skilled workers and 14 percent were involved in commerce and transportation. All of these percentages were much higher for immigrants than for the native born who were instead more likely to be domestic servants, day laborers, or marginalized. In 1914, the share of immigrants in Argentine agriculture had been further reduced to 10 percent. Instead, in 1905 to 1915, foreign immigrants formed by far the largest group contributing to the growth of Buenos Aires during that period (see Figure 10.12).

Integration/Isolation and Return Migration

Assimilation or integration is related to: (1) the reason for emigration; (2) family ties in the country of origin, as well as in that of reception; (3) the collective and/or individual conditions of settlement in the new country; and (4) national or ethnic origins of the migrant.

Many migrants bound for Latin America surely departed with the commitment of returning some day, rich enough to ensure themselves a comfortable old age. These were the "Indianos" of the Mediterranean countries, who were looked upon with a mixture of envy, ridicule, and astonishment.[22] Others who had left Europe with the same intention, failed to return because death intervened or they simply lacked money to buy the ticket or instead had a change of heart because they met with unexpected success. On the other hand, some emigrants returned, though they had not originally intended to do so. This might reflect either personal failure or a failure on the part of the host country or, perhaps, some event in their native country.

The overall return-migration rate from Latin America came to be quite high, almost 50 percent. According to economist W. Arthur

22. According to James Parsons: "At every turn one encounters *indianos* . . . in the Canaries of today, and virtually every *campesino* has relatives or friends *allá*." "Migration of Canary Islanders," 451.

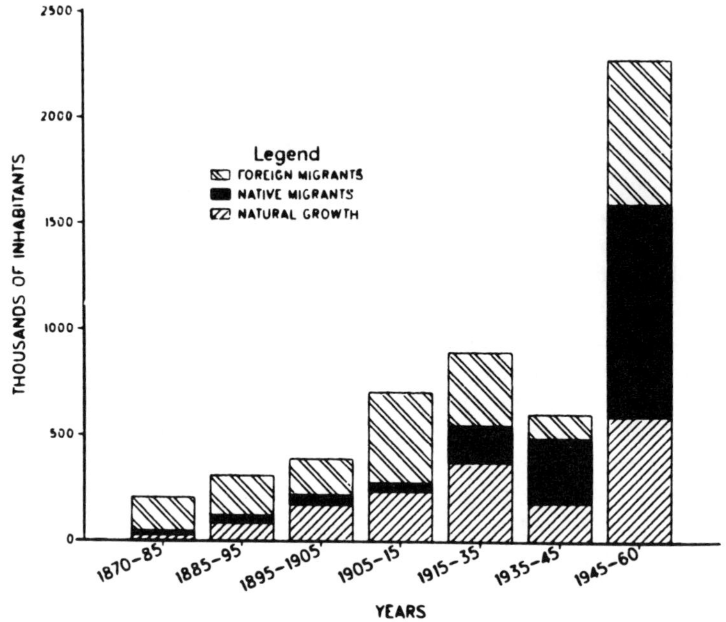

FIGURE 10.12 Growth of Buenos Aires, 1869–1960 (1869 = 250,000 inhabitants)

Source: Zulima Recchini de Lattes, *La población de Buenos Aires: componentes demográficos de crecimiento entre 1855 y* 1960 (Buenos Aires 1971), 130.

Lewis thus net migration to Argentina, 1871 to 1915, was only 2.5 million people; to Brazil, 1.4 million. In his view, gross immigration had simply been "beyond the absorptive capacity" of Argentina and Brazil, as well as of Canada and Australia reflecting a similar experience.[23] To slow down re-emigration, the Argentine authorities in 1911 forced shipping companies to double the price of passages to Europe. Whatever the proportions were between "successful" and "disappointed" returnees (which we shall never be able to determine), from the point of view of Latin America, the high re-emigration rate compares unfavorably with other continents. It should be kept in mind, however, that also from the United States as much as a third of the immigrants sooner or later opted for the return to their home country.

I already mentioned one of the factors behind re-emigration from Latin America, that is, the scarcity of land to buy. For a worker who

23. W. Arthur Lewis, *Growth and Fluctuations, 1870–1913* (London 1978), 181–85 (quotation on 183).

had immigrated with his family in São Paulo's coffee districts, it proved easier to save 300 milreis for the family's return trip, than 6,000 milreis to acquire a modest farm. Other adverse circumstances should also be kept in mind, such as a primitive environment, diseases, a deficient administration of justice, or the callous behavior of landlords used to slavery.

I believe these "objective" factors, however, do not suffice as an explanation. Emigration agencies, encouraged by Latin American governments and shipping companies, had often used misleading, over-optimistic propaganda to entice migrants to Latin American countries. When confronted with a harsh reality in the promised paradise, the disappointment of the immigrants was bound to be particularly bitter and acute. Such "subjective" factors should receive the attention they surely deserve.

The incidence of re-emigration among the various national or ethnic groups, however, varied widely, as indicated by Figure 10.13, which shows the rates for some of them from Argentina, 1857 to 1924. An even more depressing example can be taken from Brazil. Between 1908 and 1932, a total of 198,000 Italians arrived at the port of Santos. By the latter date, however, only 26,000 (13 percent) remained.[24]

The Russians seem to have exhibited the lowest re-emigration rate, the English the highest one. Then it has to be observed that the Russians were largely Jews, who had no wish to return to their ghettos; in fact they could be considered as refugees. The English, on the other hand, almost always had the intention of returning. Ever since the wars of independence, they had formed the most important part of the merchant communities. As soon as they had gathered some money, the majority went back to Britain, even if some opted to remain and even to marry a "native" woman.[25]

Also, the marital status of the immigrant on his arrival was highly relevant to both re-emigration and integration. An immigrant remaining single would be able to return easily, if he so wished. On the

24. Nicolás Sánchez-Albornoz, *The Population of Latin America. A History* (Berkeley and London 1974), 161.

25. Eugene W. Ridings, "Foreign Predominance Among Overseas Traders in Nineteenth-Century Latin America," *Latin American Research Review* 20, 2 (1985), 3–27. See also the debate about his article in *Latin American Research Review* 21, 3 (1986), 145–55. For a closer view of the British community in Chile prior to 1880, see John Mayo, "The British Community in Chile Before the Nitrate Age," *Historia* 22 (Santiago de Chile 1987), 135–150. Some merchants did remain. Diana Balmori and Robert Oppenheimer have studied a sample of eighteen Argentine and twenty-four Chilean elite families in the nineteenth century. They found similar three-generation sequences in both countries that normally started with a late colonial or early

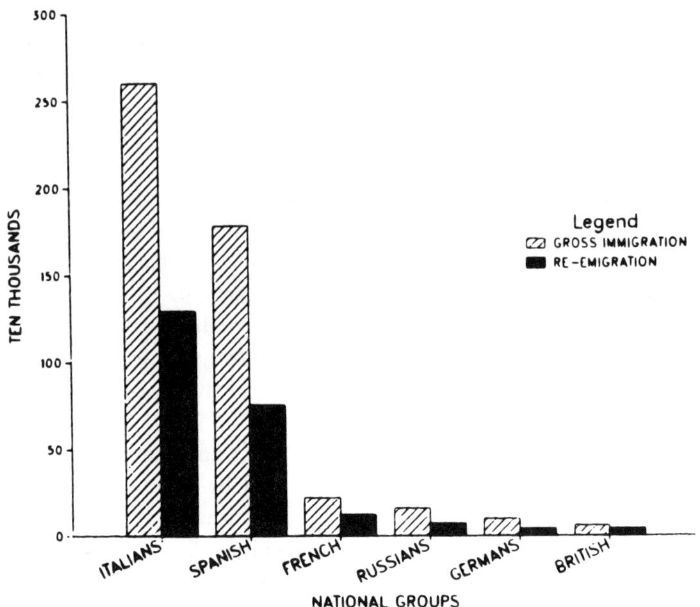

FIGURE 10.13 Total Immigration and Re-emigration, Argentina, 1857–1924

Source: Ferenczi and Willcox, *International Migrations*, 1:543–46.

other hand, marrying a native would favor his or her assimilation. The re-emigration of entire families was rather costly and complicated. If, however, such families settled down together in an isolated rural environment, as did the Germans in southern Chile, they would perhaps retain a separate culture, as well as their old language, for generations. It is interesting to notice that, out of the groups shown in Figure 10.13, in 1910 no less than 41 percent of the Russians were married, compared to 38 percent of the Spaniards and 37 percent of the Italians, but merely 32 percent of the English.

Cultural affinity did not only help many "Latins" to opt for a Latin American destiny, but it also facilitated their assimilation, although the speed of this process should not be exaggerated. Research on an Argentine provincial city, Córdoba, has shown that the reality was far from the "melting pot" model.[26] Yet, as Herbert

---

nineteenth-century merchant immigrant. "Family Clusters: Generational Nucleation in 19th Century Argentina and Chile," *Comparative Studies in Society and History* 21 (1979), 230–63.

26. Mark D. Szuchman, *Mobility and Integration in Urban Argentina: Cordoba in the*

Klein argues, Italians were clearly more successful in terms of upward social mobility in Latin America (more precisely, Argentina) than they were in the United States. The rate of Italian re-emigration from the United States was also slightly higher than that of Italians from Argentina. The Italians in Argentina invested more money in their new country.[27]

Immigrants from eastern Europe were assimilated slowly but steadily, as exemplified by the Yugoslavs who settled in the frigid Magallanes in southernmost Chile. Polish peasants who had escaped from the extreme misery of their home country, found the harsh rural conditions to be superior to those in their homeland. Their integration was hampered by prejudice against them but facilitated thanks to their Catholic faith.

On the other hand, in the German area in southern Chile, the antiquity of the settlement, the strength of the immigrants' social and cultural institutions, as well as their high rate of endogamy, made their integration a very slow process. During the two world wars, the propaganda of the governments in Germany tried to exploit that fact to their advantage. Also in a very different environment, Buenos Aires, the assimilation of the Germans was a complex process. The German colony had increased from 4,000 in the 1880s to 30,000 in 1914 (see Figure 10.14). By 1939 another 15,000 had been added. Until World War II, these largely middle-class elements resisted assimilation vigorously, while their once considerable economic power and social status declined. Politically, Nazi

---

Liberal Era (Austin 1977). The complexity of the linguistic assimilation of immigrants speaking an Italian dialect in a village in the southeast of the Buenos Aires province is well presented by Isabel Blanco, Elizabeth Rigatuso, and Silvia Suardiaz, "Asimilación linguística de los immigrantes italianos en Aldea Romana," *Cuadernos del Sur* 15 (Bahia Blanca 1982), 99–114. On the other hand, the assimilation of otherwise similar non-Latin groups tended to be even more slow. Compare a Danish community in the same area, Elizabeth Rigatuso, "Algunos aspectos del mantenimiento y cambio de lengua en la colectividad dinamarquesa de la provincia de Buenos Aires," *Cuadernos del Sur* 15 (1982), 117–42.

27. Klein, "Integration of Italian Immigrants," 319. Between 1880 and 1920, the return ratio was 51 for Italians in Argentina, 54 for those in the United States. When comparing, more specifically, Italian "adjustment" in Buenos Aires and New York City, Samuel L. Baily concludes that, above all, the "multiclass" structure of the Italian community in Buenos Aires made the process easier and quicker. Also, Italian-born in New York were only 2.6 percent of the city's population in 1890, when mass immigration set in, and did not reach but 7.1 percent in 1910. In Buenos Aires they were 12 percent in 1856 already and would attain as much as 31.8 percent after mass immigration had set in (1887). Samuel L. Baily, "The Adjustment of Italian Immigrants in Buenos Aires and New York, 1870–1914," *American Historical Review* 88, 2 (1983), 281–305.

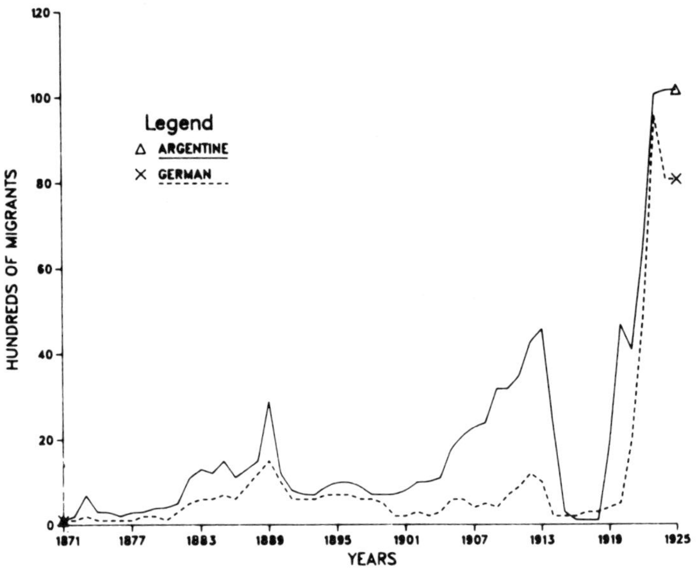

FIGURE 10.14 German Migration to Argentina, 1871–1924

infiltration was naturally opposed by the socialists and Jews among them.

The so-called "Turks" (from Syria and Lebanon) were assimilated rather easily, in part due to their resemblance to southern Europeans and because they were often economically successful. In Cuba and Peru, the Chinese "coolies" imported by the mid-nineteenth century, had virtually all been male. To some degree, they later intermarried, and their descendants often merged with the urban middle strata. On the other hand, Japanese immigration into Latin America, from 1899 onward, and especially important in the case of Brazil, was usually composed of families. Their assimilation often took three generations.

Naturally, the integration of the immigrants did not only reflect the attitudes of the migrants but also those of the host country. Originally, immigration policy in Latin America had been very positive, even if often poorly carried out. It expressed the desire on the part of both governments and elites to achieve economic expansion without altering the respective country's sociopolitical status quo.[28] When immigrants were "too" successful, however, they

28. Immigration schemes and the political debates they triggered in Chile are

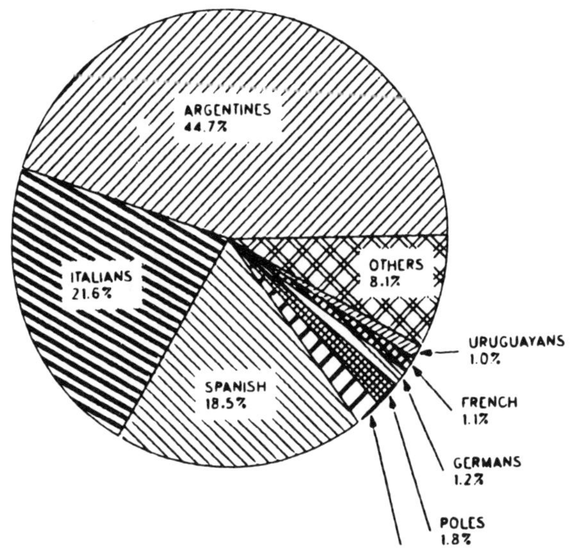

FIGURE 10.15 Citizenship of Owners of Industrial Establishments in Argentina, 1935 (total 52,317)

Source: Oscar Cornblit, "European Immigrants in Argentine Industry and Politics" in *The Politics of Conformity in Latin America*, Claudio Veliz, ed. (Oxford 1967), 231.

raised the suspicion and fears of the same elites who defamed, above all, the most vulnerable immigrant groups. In 1919 the Jews in Argentina suffered a virtual pogrom. In Brazil, a virulent anti-Portuguese movement sprang up among the middle class in the 1890s.

Whatever the feelings of the observer, the presence of the immigrants sometimes became very conspicuous. In 1895, in Argentina 81 percent of the industrial proprietors, 74 percent of the owners of businesses, and 60 percent of blue-collar workers and other industrial employees were foreigners. These still owned more than half of the industrial plants in 1935 (see Figure 10.15). In Chile, in 1914, only 4 percent of the population had been born abroad. Yet, immigrants

exemplified by the short studies of William F. Sater, "Race and Immigration During the War of the Pacific," *Historia* 22 (Santiago de Chile 1987), 313–23, and Pedro Santos Martínez, "La inmigración en Chile: el caso de los colonos vascos (1882–83)," *Historia* 22 (Santiago de Chile 1987), 287–311.

made up 32 percent of business owners and 49 percent of the owners of industrial plants. While in both countries the immigrants' share of rural landowning remained rather small, they acquired a huge part of the urban rural estate; two-thirds in Buenos Aires in 1909. In Chile, although few in number, the immigrants owned as much as 13 percent of the urban rural estate in 1907.[29]

Related Capital Movements

In general, immigrants tended to save more of their earnings than did natives. No less than 79 percent of the depositors in the Bank of the Province of Buenos Aires in 1887 were foreigners. The crucial question is, of course, which share of such immigrant savings was forwarded later on to the depositor's homeland (something negative for the host country however laudable per se). Between 1905 and 1912 the sums sent from Argentina by Spanish and Portuguese immigrants totaled 50 to 80 million gold pesos. To show the magnitude, it may be mentioned that the value of Argentine exports in 1900 totaled 157 million.

Still, on the average, remissions received in Italy from Argentina, Uruguay, and Brazil appear to have been much lower than those from the United States, notwithstanding the fact that most Italians had a lower living standard in the United States. Thus, Italians in Latin America seem to have invested the largest part of their savings in the host country. We do not know, however, whether this was due to the profitable opportunities for investment or because they had reached a higher level of integration and identification with the new country.

Political Aspects

What were the political consequences of mass immigration? The question has usually been answered with reference to the role of immigrants in political parties, as well as in the political activities of trade unions. In Chile, certainly, the famous statesmen Arturo Alessandri was the son of an immigrant, but otherwise, descendants of immigrants did not appear to have exercised much weight in party politics. In Argentina, immigrants were well represented within the socialist party; however, for that very reason, they were

29. Carl Solberg, *Immigration and Nationalism: Argentina and Chile, 1890–1914* (Austin 1970), 57ff.

far from popular with the more important Civic Radical Union party.[30] In southern South America, the process of trade union formation was largely due to the efforts of Italian or Spanish leaders (or to natives influenced by them). Mediterranean anarchism was introduced by immigrants. Publications written and read by the immigrants, such as the socialist *Vorwärts* and the anarchist *La questione sociale*, spread a radical ideology. In order to deny activists entrance or to even expel them, the Argentine government substantially restricted the country's traditionally liberal immigration policy through the Laws of Residence (1902) and the Law of Social Defense (1910).[31]

Yet, the tardiness and irresolution that characterized immigrant participation in the political life of their new countries, seem much more important than were their active contributions. By 1914, only 2 percent of the immigrants in Argentina had bothered to take out citizenship, and in Chile, in 1895, the percentage of those naturalized was even lower. By comparison, in the United States 46 percent of the foreign born had been naturalized as of 1910. Naturally, most immigrants everywhere, in all times, have concentrated on improving their own material well-being, without concerning themselves very much with politics, but the Latin American case seems to be an extreme one. It has to be kept in mind then that involvement in politics was often dangerous. Moreover, well into the twentieth century, political power remained the monopoly of a small elite. This surely helps to explain the immigrants' apathy.

Any general assessment of the immigrants' role in the political evolution of their host countries, depends not only on the values and criteria of the observer but also on the moment at which the assessment is being made. During the 1930s through 1960s, countries

30. Immigrants in the Argentine province of Santa Fe, however, did join the Radicals in armed insurrection in 1893 against what they considered as exploitation on the part of the authorities. For these "revoluciones gringas," see Ezequiel Gallo, *La pampa gringa. La colonizacion agricola en Santa Fe (1870–95)* (Buenos Aires 1983), ch. 9.

31. As Eric J. Hobsbawm sees it in, for instance, Argentina, "Highly unified working classes with a powerful class consciousness have been forged out of a mixture of natives *and* various immigrant groups." This in contrast to the division along ethnic/national lines that so often occurs. See Dick Hoerder, ed., *Labour Migration in the Atlantic Economies. The European and North American Working Classes During the Period of Industrialization* (Westport 1985), 439. However, a specialist on Latin American labor history, Hobart A. Spalding, Jr., emphasizes, rather, that employers often used ethnic/national differences in the labor forces "as a wedge" between immigrants and the native-born or between different immigrant groups; see his *Organized Labour in Latin America. Historical Case Studies of Workers in Dependent Societies* (New York 1977), 15.

like Argentina and Uruguay, as well as Chile and Brazil (where the share of immigrants was lower but their importance nevertheless great), appeared to be moving toward a better and democratic future. Had mass immigration helped to promote that process? During the following two decades, however, dictatorships and brutal repressions became the order of the day in all of these four countries. It was accompanied by economic and social decline. A soul-searching analysis of the roots of these disasters has set in. To what extent was a lack of identity and of national purpose responsible? Did these, perhaps, have some of their roots in mass immigration? During the nineteen-eighties, Argentina, Uruguay, and Brazil have attained constitutional rule once again, but are still beset by severe structural economic and social problems. In Chile, a descendant of immigrants, General Pinochet, and his colleague in Paraguay, General Stroessner, both personified the most retrograde characteristics of Latin American political life. Against this whole backdrop, social scientists today cannot possibly take for granted that mass immigration promoted progress and change, rather than reinforcing the existing skewed political, social, and economic structures of the receiving countries. It is not a question of "fault," naturally, but of long-term effects.

Later Developments

The impact of the Depression of 1929 to 1930 on Latin America was very severe. Admittedly, it did not produce unemployment of the same proportions as in West Europe and North America; yet, it was clearly no longer meaningful to stimulate mass immigration. Argentina tried to close its ports to urban immigration in 1930 to 1931, and Brazil introduced a strict system of national quotas. Everywhere, selective immigration, at best, was imposed. Return migration increased. In Brazil, however, a positive immigration saldo was maintained thanks to Japanese farmers, who in 1931 to 1935 formed 31 percent of a total of 271,000 immigrants admitted.

In the 1930s, like a hundred years earlier, many of the Europeans who arrived were refugees. Argentina received a total of 120,000 Jews from 1920 to 1947, but only 15,000 during the crucial years of 1936 to 1942. From 1939 to 1942, Mexico received 12,000 refugees after Franco's triumph. Of the hundreds of thousands of "displaced persons" in Central Europe after World War II, Latin America only took care of a minor part (1947 to 1950, 73,000 or 12 percent,

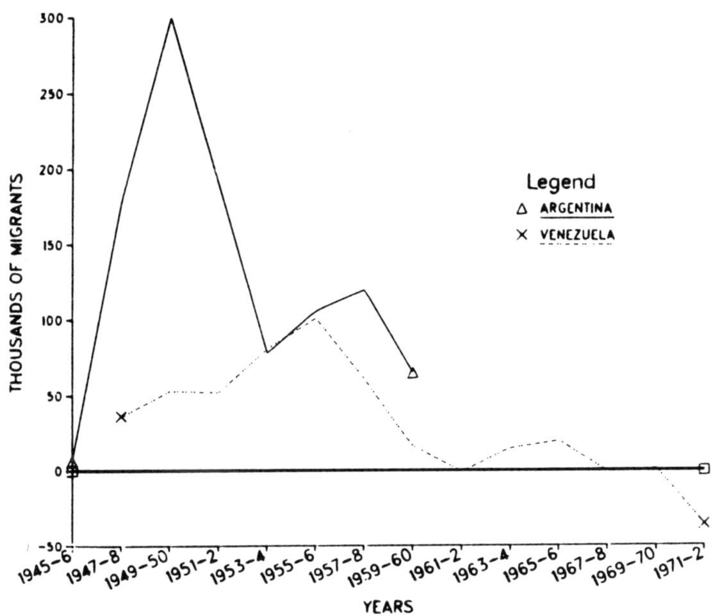

FIGURE 10.16 Net Migration to Argentina and Venezuela after the Second World War

Source: Argentina: Zulima Recchini de Lattes, *Migraciones en la Argentina: estudio de migraciones internas e internacionales* . . . (Buenos Aires 1969), 78; Venezuela: Santiago-Gerardo Suarez, *Inmigración y naturalización* (Caracas 1975), 13, 17.
Note: Argentine data cover only movement to and from overseas and Montevideo.

including 37,000 Jews; 1952 to 1965, 264,000 or 4.3 percent). As is well known, Nazis like Eichmann and Barbie joined the same current as their surviving victims.

From the end of the war onward, there was also a certain renewal of mass migration, mainly from Italy, Spain, and Portugal, to Argentina and Venezuela, as is shown in Figure 10.16. From 1946 to 1957 Argentina received a net total of 608,700 immigrants. The dip in 1955 reflected the economic deterioration at the time of Perón's downfall. With its oil boom and low population density, Venezuela received 374,000 immigrants from 1948 to 1957. By 1961, foreigners constituted 15 percent of its active population. 51 percent of the managers of businesses were foreigners. Yet, the fall of the dictator

Marcos Pérez Jiménez and an acute economic crisis and xenophobia led to a massive net outflow in 1961 to 1962.[32] In the 1970s a more liberal immigration policy was once again pursued. In 1976 resident Europeans formed 6 to 7 percent of the population.

By contrast to the era of mass immigration, 1870 to 1930, European post-war immigrants in Latin America were largely educated, skilled, and provided with funds. Their contributions might be very valuable, but they were also very sensible to adverse conditions, economic and otherwise, and followed closely European economic trends. Thus, their re-emigration ratio has been very high, indeed.

In Brazil, Japanese immigration recommenced in 1952. During the next decade, some 43,000 Japanese went there, mostly thrifty and productive farmers. Yet, in the 1960s, push-factors in Japan with its economic boom ceased to exist. Something similar occurred in western Europe at the same time. From the Mediterranean, labor migration directed itself toward the countries to the north, being much more advantageous in terms of wages and distances to cover.

At the present time, migration from Europe to Latin America has become insignificant in numbers. Mighty counter-currents, such as the Caribbean migrants to England and France and the Latin American political refugees, have crossed the Atlantic. Migrations on a much larger scale, however, are those that – largely illegally – carry hundreds of thousands of Latin Americans every year to the United States and, also, great numbers of unemployed workers from the very poor Latin American countries to the somewhat better-off neighbors. On an even larger scale, rural-to-urban internal migration has above all led to the dramatic increase of the large multimillion cities.

Rural-to-urban migration reveals parallels, as well as differences, with the mass immigration of the period 1870 to 1930. In both cases, push-factors were at work in backward rural environments. In Latin America, such conditions also redirected many European settlers from the countryside to the cities. During the period of mass immigration this resulted in the Europeanization, or "whitening" of the urban population. Today, on the contrary, internal migration gives that population a darker appearance. In the early twentieth century, the urban labor market seemed to offer almost unlimited job opportunities as long as industrialization maintained a rapid pace. In

32. For a synthesis of mass immigration in Venezuela between 1945 and 1961, see Susan Berglund, " . . . Y los últimos serán los primeros. La inmigración masiva en Venezuela, 1945–61" in *Población y mano de obra en América Latina*, Nicolás Sánchez-Albornoz ed. (Madrid 1985), 313–26.

more recent times, industrial development slowed down and its labor intensity decreased; thus, the service sector is where most job opportunities can now be found. While European immigrants once merely spent a generation in the slums (like the Argentine *conventillos*), today's internal migrants continue to populate the urban slums for a much longer time. At the same time, the large cities suffer from unmanageable traffic and air pollution, apparently inevitable companions of urban "progress." What can be done to resolve, once and for all, the twin problems of "underdevelopment" and over-development?" So far the poor internal migrants in the cities have hardly been more "revolutionary" than their cousins who came from the Old World at the turn of the century. Neither have been able to overcome the combination of forces that successfully oppose any thorough going change in the Latin American reality. Thus, we are forced to conclude that it was not so much the collective "virtues" and "weaknesses" of the immigrants themselves that have determined the range and impact of their contribution; rather, the limits were set by pre-existing power structures and prevailing sets of values.

11

Immigration into the Caribbean: The Introduction of Chinese and East Indian Indentured Laborers Between 1839 and 1917

P.C. EMMER

The Need for Immigration in the Caribbean

It seems no exaggeration to say that the Caribbean used to "eat" people. The autochthonous inhabitants of the region, the Amerindians, estimated to have numbered about one million before Columbus, quickly embarked on a course of rapid demographic decline after the intrusion of the Europeans. Around 1700, all Amerindians had virtually disappeared from the islands and only a fraction of them remained in the hinterland of the Guianas.[1]

On the other hand, the Europeans also paid dearly for their invasion into the Caribbean. It has been estimated that between 1500 and 1800, around 600,000 Europeans immigrated into the Caribbean, of whom the British Caribbean received 300,000, the French Caribbean 150,000, the Dutch and Danish Caribbean 100,000, and the Spanish Caribbean 40,000.[2] At the end of these first three centuries, actually about 920,000 lived in the region, but their distribution was completely different: the British Caribbean

1. David Watts, *The West Indies, Patterns of Development, Culture and Environmental Change since 1492* (Cambridge 1987), 73–74, 93, 101, 122, and 126. Franklin W. Knight, *The Caribbean; the Genesis of a Fragmented Nationalism* (Oxford 1978), 3–22.

2. The figures are derived from: Henry A. Gemery, "Markets for Migrants: English Indentured Servitude and Emigration in the Seventeenth and Eighteenth Centuries" in Emmer, *Colonialism and Migration*, 40 (British Caribbean); P. Pluchon, "Le peuplement blanc" in *Histoire des Antilles et de la Guyane*, P. Pluchon, ed. (Toulouse 1982), 167, 168 (French Caribbean); Stanley L. Engerman, "Servants to Slaves to Servants; Contract Labour and European Expansion" in Emmer, *Colonialism and Migration*, 271 (Dutch and Danish Caribbean). The number of Spanish migrating to the Caribbean has not been calculated at all. B.H. Slicher van Bath, "The Absence of White Contract Labour in Spanish America during the Colonial Period," in Emmer

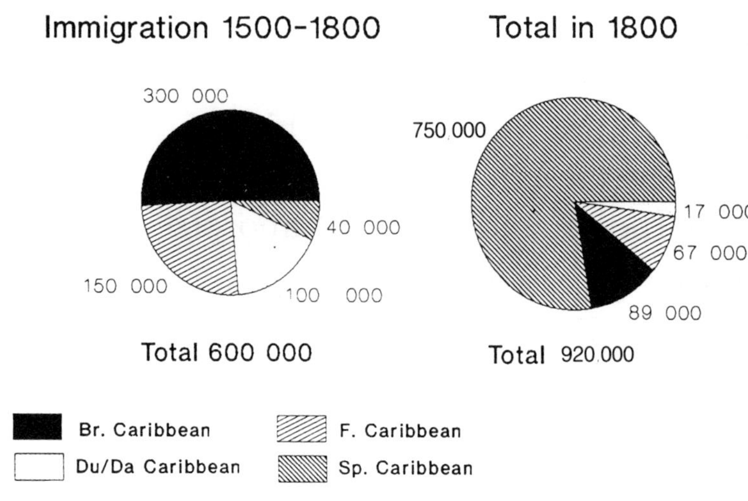

FIGURE 11.1 Europeans

counted 88,752 Europeans and their descendants, the French Caribbean around 67,000, the Danish and Dutch Caribbean around 17,000, and the Spanish Caribbean around 750,000. The conclusion must be that only the Europeans in the Spanish Antilles escaped demographic decline and that only Cuba, Puerto Rico, and Santo Domingo had been able to imitate the growth in population of the European settlement colonies in the temperate zones of North and South America.[3]

Colonialism and Migration, 25, mentions 200,000 migrants to Spanish America as a whole until 1600. Mörner, *Adventurers and Proletarians*, 14 mentions that there is only one, very unlikely, estimate of 52,000 for the eighteenth century. If we assume that another 50,000 Spanish migrated to the New World during the seventeenth century, we arrive at a grand total of 300,000 migrants for the whole of Spanish America between 1500 and 1800. Watts, *West Indies*, 122, mentions that during the sixteenth century about 10 percent of the migrants to Spanish America went to the Caribbean. If we assume that this percentage did not change during the subsequent two centuries, we arrive at a total of about 30,000 immigrants coming to the Spanish Caribbean between 1500 and 1800. In private correspondence, Magnus Mörner has urged me to increase the number of Spanish immigrants for the seventeenth and eighteenth centuries. If we double their numbers (seventeenth century, 100,000; eighteenth century, 100,000), the total number of Spanish migrants coming to the Americas would amount to 400,000, and the emigration to Cuba between 1500 and 1800 would then come to 40,000.

3. These figures are taken from Knight, *Caribbean*, 238–239 (table 4). Added to the number of whites are half the number of mulattoes. In comparing the immigration figures and the population figures of the Europeans and their descendants in the Caribbean, it should be noted that there existed a return migration to Europe. Its

The extremely high mortality among both the Amerindians, as well as among the Europeans, made it virtually impossible to cultivate those labor intensive cash crops for which the Caribbean had a geographical advantage: sugar, coffee, and – toward the end of the eighteenth century – cotton. The only realistic option in getting more laborers to come to the Caribbean was the slave trade from West Africa. Until 1870 around 5.5 million slaves had been forcibly migrated to the Caribbean, of whom 2,443,000 arrived in the British Caribbean, 1,655,000 in the French Caribbean, 550,000 in the Dutch and Danish Caribbean, and 934,000 in the Spanish Caribbean. As in the case of the Europeans, we have to compare these numbers with the number of blacks actually resident in the Caribbean after the ending of the Atlantic slave trade in order to compare the African demographic development in the Caribbean with that of other ethnicities in the region. As had been the case with the Amerindians we can speak again of a demographic catastrophe. In total there were about 2.1 million slaves in the region, with a distribution differing completely from the slave trade destinations. In the British Caribbean there were about 720,000 blacks and their descendants, in the French Caribbean 760,000, and in the Dutch and Danish Caribbean 91,000 and in the Spanish Caribbean 600,000.[4]

There has been much debate as to why the demographic lifeline between the Caribbean and Africa was virtually cut off through the abolition of the Atlantic slave trade. The figures mentioned above clearly indicate that the British, French, Spanish, Dutch, and Danish colonies in the Caribbean all required constant importation of new slaves in order to prevent a decline in the number of blacks. In the economically expanding areas such as Guiana and Trinidad, even extra slaves were needed. After the first decades of the nineteenth century, the Spanish Caribbean was also in need of more African slaves in order to satisfy the labor needs of the expanding Cuban and Puerto Rican sugar plantations. After 1840, the slave population in Cuba started to decline more rapidly than before, which made the continuing importation of slaves even more press-

---

scale, however, is not known. For this reason a comparison between these figures and similar statistics concerning the African population in the Caribbean is flawed, since Africans hardly left the region.

4. Figures on slave immigration between 1500 and 1870 from James A. Rawley, *The Trans-Atlantic Slave Trade; A History* (New York 1981), 54 and 428. Figures on the black presence in the Caribbean around 1820 in Knight, *Caribbean*, 238–239 (table 4). Added to the number of blacks are half the number of mulattoes.

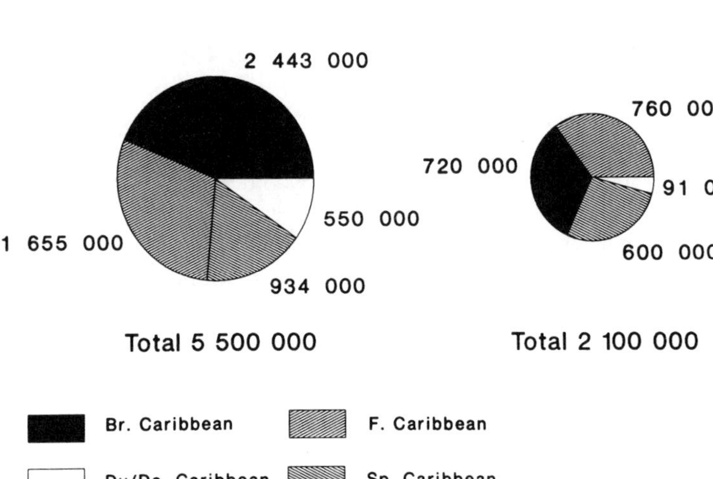

FIGURE 11.2 Africans

ing. In view of these figures, there is little doubt that the abolition of the African slave trade, first by Denmark and then by the other countries owning Caribbean colonies, constituted a case of economic suicide. The abolitionists nor anyone else could provide a viable economic alternative to the labor supply of African slaves.[5]

After abolition, however, the Caribbean sugar industry battled on. It lost some of its competitiveness on the international sugar market, but the sugar plantations in several regions of the Caribbean were able to cope with rising labor costs. The production of coffee and cotton was abandoned in favor of sugar. In view of the centuries-old tradition to obtain plantation labor from Africa, it seemed natural for the Caribbean planters to again turn to Africa in order to recruit both illegally imported slaves as well as "free" Africans, once the legal slave trade had been ended. The large majority of the "free" Africans, however, were not free at all, but made up of slaves freed at the capture of their illegal slave ships and more or less unable to do anything else but to sign a contract of indenture for the West Indies. The source for the recruitment of the only group of really "free" Africans, the Kru from Sierra Leone, dried up very quickly once the first batch of laborers had returned

5. This point is convincingly argued by Seymour Drescher, *Econocide; British Slavery in the Era of Abolition* (Pittsburgh 1977).

home and had been able to give an impression of West Indian labor conditions. Slaves, illegally imported slaves and "free" Africans, constituted the largest group of migrants coming into the nineteenth century Caribbean.[6]

In addition to these continued imports from Africa, Europe increased its migration to the Caribbean in order to again provide laborers to staff the plantations, as had been the case before the 1650s. The great majority of these European immigrants came from the economically depressed Canary Islands and Madeira, as well as from mainland Spain. Their numbers should not be underestimated; Europeans constituted the third largest group of migrants moving to the nineteenth-century Caribbean. Their distribution over time and region was very unequal: 70 percent came from Spain and migrated to Cuba during the period between 1880 and World War I. In comparison to the migration from Africa, a disproportionate number of the European immigrants in the Caribbean were not part of an attempt at filling vacancies on the sugar plantations. Some of the European immigration during the nineteenth century was aimed at changing the economic and social status of the Caribbean, making it into a region of settlement colonies as existed in North and South America. This type of colonization, however, failed, and the Caribbean remained a plantation area with an almost unsatisfiable appetite for plantation labor.[7]

The plantations in the British, French, and Dutch Caribbean found the "answer" to their demand for labor in British India and the Cuban plantations in China. In addition, the Dutch planters imported plantation laborers from Java. The various nationalities migrating into the nineteenth-century Caribbean are surveyed in the table below. In the remainder of this paper, only the indentured labor immigration from India and China will be discussed. The reason for this selection is a simple one: there are only sufficient data concerning the different stages of the migratory process of these two groups. The importation of Asian indentured laborers was carefully

6. David Eltis, "Free and Coerced Transatlantic Migrations: Some Comparisons," *American Historical Review* 88 (1983), 251–280, and David Eltis, *Economic Growth and the Ending of the Transatlantic Slave Trade* (New York and Oxford 1987), 249. On the "free" Africans: Schuler, *"Alas, Alas, Kongo."* On the free migration: Monica Schuler, "Free Emigration to British and French Guiana, 1841–1857" in *Africans in Bondage; Studies in Slavery and the Slave Trade*, Paul E. Lovejoy, ed. (Madison 1986), 155–203.

7. On experiments with European colonization in Surinam: Emmer, "Veranderingen op de Surinaamse arbeidsmarkt," 205–222. On European migration into the nineteenth-century Caribbean: Laurence, *Immigration into the West Indies*, 9, 11, 12, 23, 40. For Cuba: Mörner, *Adventurers and Proletarians*, 62 (figure 11).

administered, mainly due to pressure from the abolitionist lobbies in the various metropoles. The immigration of the 33,000 Javanese into Surinam does not constitute a separate case. Their recruitment, shipment, employment, and return migration were organized under similar regulations as applied to the labor immigration from British India.[8]

It should be noted that thus far only the intercontinental migration into the Caribbean has been mentioned here. As was to be expected, part of the labor needs of the various Caribbean regions were filled by internal migration. First, this happened when slaves from declining plantations were sold to areas with an expanding sugar industry. After emancipation, the internal migration within the Caribbean increased because ex-slaves from densely populated islands looked for jobs in less densely populated areas (notably from Barbados). In addition, some ex-slaves constituted "jobbing-gangs" and migrated elsewhere in the region for a season of cane cutting as the incoming Asian laborers had made such "jobbing-gangs" superfluous at home.[9]

Last, but not least, if we were to bring the Caribbean migration saga up to date, we should also mention the voluminous migration to Europe and North America from all regions and among all echelons of Caribbean society after World War II. It seems that the Caribbean and migration are synonymous.[10]

8. Ismaël, *Immigratie van Indonesiërs*. For a discussion of the differences between the British Indians and the Javanese during the period of their simultaneous introduction into Surinam between 1890 and 1916: P.C. Emmer, "Asians compared. Some Observations regarding Indian and Indonesian Indentured Labourers in Surinam, 1873–1939," *Itinerario* 9, 1 (1987), 149–155.

9. On the inter-Caribbean slave trade: David Eltis, "The Traffic in Slaves between the British West Indian Colonies, *1807–1833*," *Economic History Review* 25 (1972), 55–64. On the migration within the Caribbean of Barbadians: Laurence, *Immigration into the West Indies*, 16, 44; of Jamaicans, Watts, *West Indies*, 482 and Franklin W. Knight, "Jamaican Migrants and the Cuban Sugar Industry, 1900–1934" *Between Slavery and Free Labour; the Spanish-Speaking Caribbean in the Nineteenth Century*, Manuel Moreno Fraginals, Frank Maya Pons, and Stanley L. Engerman, eds., (Baltimore and London 1985), 94–117.

10. Orlando Patterson, "Migration in Caribbean Societies: Socio-economic and Symbolic Resource" in *Human Migration; Patterns and Policies*, William H. McNeill and Ruth S. Adams, eds., (Bloomington and London 1976), 106–146.

TABLE 11.1 Migration into the Caribbean, 1811–1916

	Total	British	French	Spanish	Dutch	Danish
Afr. slaves	799,100	10,600 (1811–1860)	95,700 (1811–1870)	687,800 (1811–1870)	5,000 (1811–1830)	
Br. Indians	543,620	429,286 (1839–1917)	79,700 (1853–1885)		34,304 (1873–1916)	321 (1862)
Europeans	180,729	44,000 (1835–1882)	200–300 (1845–1848)	140,000 (1830–1916)	479 (1845–1873)	
Chinese	145,452	17,185 (1852–1879)	965 (1859)	124,800 (1847–1873)	2,502 (1858–1860)	
Free Africans	58,132	39,632 (1834–1867)	18,500 (1854–1862)			
Javanese	32,956				32,956 (1890–1939)	

Source: see appendix.

The Migration into the Caribbean: Push or Pull?

The emigration of Chinese and Indian contract laborers to overseas destinations was part of a long term push-movement, which seems to have increased dramatically during the course of the nineteenth century. An important caveat, however, should be mentioned: there exists no clear-cut explanation for the increase in long-distance out-migration from China and British India. In both cases demographic, as well as political stimuli, are mentioned.

In the case of China, a rapid increase in population seems to have been a dominant factor: between the years 1650 and 1850 the Chinese trebled in numbers. During most of these two hundred years, an increased efficiency in agriculture helped to absorb the rise in population.[11]

At the same time, there existed a continuous emigration to the overseas Chinese communities all around the Indian Ocean littoral. From the early stages onward, the Chinese were important minorities in the Asian empires of the British, the Dutch, and the Portuguese. During the nineteenth century the Chinese emigration to destinations within Asia itself increased rapidly. The Chinese colony in Singapore grew from 6,600 to more than 50,000 between 1830 and 1860. Between 1830 and 1860 the Chinese more than doubled their numbers in Malacca from 16,500 to 38,000. Perhaps as a result of the rapid demographic growth in China, there was much political unrest following the war with Britain of 1842. A period of "warlordism" started, and the Taiping Rebellion upset matters further between the years 1851 and 1864. Later on during the nineteenth century, areas with endemic rural poverty, disastrous famines and floods, as well as the aftermath of the Boxer rising, provided a continued push for long-distance migration out of China.[12]

It has been estimated that between 1847 and 1874 approximately 1.5 million Chinese, out of a population of 430 million, left for foreign shores. This amounted to 0.3 percent of the Chinese population. Of these 1.5 million Chinese emigrants, only 158,948 went to the Caribbean, amounting to about 10 percent.[13]

The idea of attracting Chinese laborers to work in the West Indies

11. Meagher, "Introduction of Chinese Laborers," 50–56.

12. Ibid., 143–145 and Peter Richardson, "Coolies, Peasants and Proletarians; the Origins of Chinese Indentured Labour in South Africa, 1904–1907" in Marks and Richardson, *International Labour Migration* 167–185.

13. Meagher, "Introduction of Chinese Laborers," 55.

came about during the campaign for the abolition of the slave trade. In 1792 a pamphlet on this matter was published in London, and in 1802 an official proposal was tabled to bring some Chinese to Trinidad. The importations of Chinese into the Caribbean, however, did not start until 1847 for Cuba and 1852 for Trinidad.[14]

The push to emigrate out of India had not been caused by such a drastic increase in population as had been the case in China. The stimuli for migrating out of India are usually described as economic, not as demographic. The push to migrate was linked to the penetration of the expanding world market in the wake of British expansion. The British penetration favored the large landholders, and the subsequent "enclosure movement" pushed considerable numbers of small farmers off their lands and into a state of permanent migration, because their income as derived from their landholdings had dwindled. India in the nineteenth century is described as a country where urban growth was rapid, caused by large numbers of "depeasantized" peasants, who provided the workforce for the developing textile industries. In addition, many of these new city dwellers were recruited to work a long way from home: either overseas or in the tea gardens of Assam. In India the aftermath of the Mutiny seems to have been the only political push-factor stimulating overseas migration.[15]

The idea to import Indian contract labor into the Caribbean was conceived on the small island of Mauritius in the Indian Ocean. The British colonial government of India used Mauritius as a recipient of Indian convict labor (including prisoners who had participated in the Mutiny). In turn, the abolition of slavery caused the Mauritian planters to actively recruit contract labor in India. An influential Caribbean planter visited Mauritius and, subsequently, Indian indentured labor was introduced into British Guiana in 1839, almost immediately after the ending of the period of apprenticeship.[16]

As in the case of the Chinese overseas migration, however, the importation of Indian indentured labor into the Caribbean was small compared to the Indian overseas migration as a whole between 1834 and 1917. It has been estimated that about 20 million Indians, or 6.7 percent of the Indian population (estimated at 300 million), participated in long-distance migration during that period.

14. Ibid., 37–42.

15. Tinker, *New System of Slavery*, 39–61 (chapter 3) and Basdeo Mangru, *Benevolent Neutrality; Indian Government Policy and Labour Migration to British Guiana, 1854–1884* (London 1987), 60–63.

16 Tinker, *New System of Slavery*, 63.

Of these 20 million, only 1.25 million went overseas under government supervised schemes, half of whom (or 3 percent of the total number of Indian overseas emigrants) went to the Caribbean.[17]

In the case of Java, the 33,000 indentured laborers brought to Surinam only constituted 0.001 percent of the total population of the island.[18]

In reviewing the evidence on long-distance emigration out of Asia, it should be noted that: (1) the migration of contract laborers to the Caribbean constituted only a minor percentage of the population of China, India, and Java; (2) the migration of indentured laborers from India and China to the Caribbean, never amounted to more than 10 percent of the Indian and Chinese overseas emigration in general. This figure alone is sufficient evidence to assume that the opening of Asian migration to the Caribbean did not constitute a pull-factor. The Caribbean simply became another destination for the overseas migration out of China and India. This migration itself had been in existence long before Asian indentured laborers arrived in the Caribbean and it continued (and continues) after the Caribbean ceased to be its recipient; (3) the migration of indentured laborers from India, China and Java to the Caribbean was not halted because of a diminishing demand for or supply of migrants. In all three cases migration came to an end because of political decisions.[19]

In accepting the fact that there were obviously strong stimuli to migrate out of certain regions in Asia, it should be pointed out that the Caribbean was not a self-evident destination for the Asian migrants. Outside of the regulated, government supervised migration of indentured laborers between 1839 and 1917, hardly any other Asian migrants went to the Caribbean. Without special contract-cum-transport facilities, Asian migrants would have remained within reach of the Indian Ocean littoral. In view of that, the specific pull factors in the Caribbean should also be mentioned. The main factor was the need for bonded plantation labor. In order to

17. Figures from: Gail Omvedt, "Migration in Colonial India. The Articulation of Feudalism and Capitalism by the Colonial State," *Journal of Peasant Studies* 7 (1980), 188; Engerman, "Servants to Slaves," 272 and Mangru, *Benevolent Neutrality*, 63–65 and K. Davis, *The Population of India and Pakistan* (Princeton 1951), 98–99, esp. table 35.

18. Peter Boomgaard, "Multiplying Masses: Nineteenth Century Population Growth in India and Indonesia," *Itinerario* 9,1 (1987), 135–149.

19. The ending of Chinese emigration: Meagher, "Introduction of Chinese Laborers," 307–346 (chapter VIII) and on the ending of emigration from British India: Tinker, *New System of Slavery*, 334–367 (chapter 9). For the ending of Javanese emigration to Surinam: Ismaël, *Immigratie van Indonesiërs*, 66–76.

satisfy the demand for such labor, the Caribbean planters used local labor and enslaved immigrant labor from Africa. The continuing rise in labor productivity enabled the planters to increase the catchment area for plantation labor by offering higher prices and by recruiting in other continents than had been usual. Toward the middle of the nineteenth century, the planters could afford the labor of illegally imported slaves, as well as the labor of paid migrant labor from Asia and Europe, which were both more expensive than the labor of legally imported slaves.[20]

The Demography of the Sending Regions: The Interconnection Between Internal Migration and the Recruitment for Indentured Service Overseas

In comparing the nineteenth century out-migration from China and India, there seem to have been more differences than parallels between these two movements. In the case of China, the migration to the Caribbean fitted into a pattern of Chinese overseas migration dating back to the seventh century. Most of the emigrants came from China's most southern maritime regions.[21]

The migration within and out of India was of a much more recent date than that of China; it was clearly linked to the incorporation of India into the British empire. It was the colonial government that sent Indian convicts to Mauritius, where they were first used to replace the emancipated slaves on the sugar plantations. The British occupation of India resulted, among other things, in the construction of railroads, which made it possible to recruit in regions completely separate from the catchment areas of the big ports.

The overseas emigration from India was closely connected with the long-distance migration within India, which in turn was also caused by the effects of colonialism. The most important destinations for the migration overland were the recruiting offices of the colonial army, the tea-gardens of Assam, and the textile industries of Bengal. The volume of the internal long-distance migration within India was much larger than that of the government-regulated migration overseas.[22]

20. The drastic increase in labor productivity on West Indian plantations is demonstrated by J.R. Ward, *British West Indian Slavery, 1750–1834; The Process of Amelioration* (Oxford 1988). I am grateful for the advice of David Eltis on this matter.

21. Meagher, "Introduction of Chinese Laborers," 62–68.

22. Tinker, *New System of Slavery*, 50, 57.

The discrepancies between the migratory movements from China and India were reflected in the different ways in which Asian indentured laborers were recruited for service in the West Indies. In China, the recruitment was usually executed by private Chinese individuals or by firms. The increasing demand for Chinese workers had created a professional class of recruiters, which made extensive use of fraud and deception. The majority of the emigrants were found among destitute farmers, who had become refugees from famine-stricken areas and who had crammed into coastal cities. A medical examination was supposed to weed out those who would not survive the sea passage and would not be able to perform the labor in the cane fields.[23]

In spite of the seemingly ample supply, the recruitment of Chinese laborers was marred by frequent cases of kidnapping. In addition to starving farmers, prisoners of the various clan wars were recruited, as well as people with gambling debts. In short, economic hardship alone did not seem to have sufficed in providing enough Chinese laborers for service overseas. The recruiting depots in the various ports of embarkation had armed guards and barbed wire. In the port of Macao alone, 30,000 people earned a living in the recruiting business. Except in the recruitment for British Guiana, Europeans did not participate in the process of obtaining indentured laborers. In fact, it was not until 1866 that the Chinese government finally agreed to put down regulations governing the emigration of Chinese laborers overseas. Before those regulations were applied, the captain of a ship simply sailed into one of the emigration ports of China and contracted with a local merchant for the delivery of a certain number of Chinese laborers, within a certain period. The merchant, in turn, used a whole network of recruiters in order to "produce" these laborers.[24]

The only exception was the recruitment of Chinese laborers for British Guiana during the years 1859 to 1866. In those years, an official British emigration agent supervised the recruitment in China, and recruitment offices were opened in Canton, Amoy, and Swatou. The intending migrants had to report in person to these offices, and subsequently, the migration to Guiana – in contrast to the migration to Cuba – also included some families and women.[25]

23. Richardson, "Coolies, Peasants and Proletarians," 175–178, vividly describes the rural poverty in China at the end of the nineteenth century, which concurs with Meagher's remarks about China's poverty fifty years earlier.

24. Meagher, "Introduction of Chinese Laborers," 68–83.

25. Ibid., 83.

The recruitment in British India of laborers destined for the Caribbean was supervised by the colonial administration. The colonial governments of the British, French, and Dutch possessions in the West Indies, which had obtained the right to recruit Indian labor, all appointed their own "Emigration Agent" in Calcutta or Madras. In turn these "Emigration Agents" used Indian "head-" and "subrecruiters" to do the actual recruiting. Recruitment for the Caribbean was governed by a "season," instituted in order to avoid both travel through wintery conditions around the Cape and to prevent the arrival during the height of the West Indian summer.[26]

There exists no clear-cut opinion in the literature about the advantages and drawbacks of the recruiting system used in India. No doubt, fraud and deception were used, but at the same time, recruiters had to be licensed, and licenses were withdrawn in case of justified complaints. Also, emigrants had to be medically examined and were asked to express their intention to emigrate before an Indian magistrate, while still at the subdepot in the country. This procedure was repeated during their stay in one of the main depots in Calcutta or Madras in front of the Protector of Emigrants, an official appointed by the British Indian government to supervise the migration of indentured laborers.[27]

There are several reasons to assume that over time the recruitment system did succeed in selecting those Indians who were indeed willing to indenture themselves for service overseas. First of all, the percentage of intending emigrants who absconded after having been registered in the Calcutta depot declined drastically over time: from 4.2 percent in the period 1880 to 1890 to 0.9 percent between 1906 and 1916. The majority of the migrants who did not embark were refused on medical grounds. Second, all Emigration Agents were constantly trying to improve the information regarding employment overseas by indenturing "return coolies," who could tell their fellow emigrants about their previous experience. Third, more and more emigrants came from agricultural backgrounds and thus seemed to realize which kind of labor was required overseas.[28]

In assessing the two recruiting systems for labor overseas within

26. Tinker, *New System of Slavery*, 137, 138, and P.C. Emmer, "The Coolie Ships; The Transportation of Indentured Labourers between Calcutta and Paramaribo, 1873–1921" in, *Maritime Aspects of Migration*, Klaus Friedland, ed. (Cologne 1989), 406, 407.

27. Tinker, *New System of Slavery*, 101.

28. P.C. Emmer, "The Meek Hindu; the recruitment of Indian indentured labourers for service overseas, 1870–1916" in Emmer, *Colonialism and Migration*, 187–205.

China and India, it should always be kept in mind that for many intending emigrants, sheer starvation was just around the corner. The decision to enter a recruiting depot, with its regular distribution of food, could literally mean survival instead of death.[29]

Female Migration

There existed a great difference between the participation of Indian and Chinese women in overseas emigration. From China there hardly emigrated any women at all. There were attempts at attracting between 15 percent to 20 percent females among the Chinese migrants to Cuba, but in reality the percentage is estimated to have been even below 1 percent. This percentage concurs with the traditionally low percentage of Chinese women migrating within Asia, such as to Singapore and Java, estimated to have only been 3 percent. Also, the Cuban planters preferred men and declined to pay for the importation of female Chinese. In contrast, the much smaller migration of Chinese laborers to the British Caribbean, notably Guiana, constituted somewhat of an exception. Because of a different method of recruitment, the number of female migrants reached a unique 16 percent.[30]

The proportion of female migrants was set at a compulsory 28 percent for all migration out of India as supervised by the government. During the earlier stages of Indian emigration it had become clear that the percentage of women would not go beyond twenty when left to the law of demand and supply. In spite of protests, both from the Emigration Agents as well as from the planters, the British government set the percentage at 28.5 in order to make it easier for emigrating Indians to build up permanent communities overseas.[31]

The recruitment of comparatively large numbers of women, as required by law, caused some concern to the various recruiting agencies in India. They were forced to recruit more families than would have been the case without such a set percentage. Perfectly healthy male recruits had to be turned away because their wife and children had no chance of passing the medical examinations. Single

29. P.C. Emmer, "The Great Escape: The Migration of Female Indentured Servants from British India to Surinam, 1873–1916" in *Abolition and its Aftermath; the Historical Context*, David Richardson, ed. (London 1985), 251–252.

30. Meagher, "Introduction of Chinese Laborers," 83–97.

31. Tinker, *New System of Slavery*, 88–89, and Mangru, *Benevolent Neutrality*, 96–101.

women were also more difficult to recruit than men, and many times the recruiting agents complained that they were only sending prostitutes to the West Indies. Over time, however, the social background of the female contingent among the Indian migrants changed. The report covering one of the last official tours of inspection among the Indian migrant communities overseas, took great care in pointing out that the majority of the female migrants among the Indian communities overseas had honorable occupations, both during and after the period of their indenture.[32]

The inclusion of a relatively high percentage of women made the Indian migration to the Caribbean certainly more akin to the contemporary long-distance migration from Europe. First, married women saw fewer of their children die overseas than at home. Second, migration gave single Indian women a chance to escape an unhappy marriage or the unfortunate state of widowhood; both were difficult to achieve in India. Also, single women who had not found a male partner in India had more chance to do so overseas. Third, it seems that the position of women in overseas Indian communities gave them more personal freedom than they would have enjoyed in India. Fourth, the mortality among overseas Indians was much lower than the mortality in India, while the fertility was similar, thus allowing the Indian overseas communities to grow rapidly.[33]

These positive developments, however, hardly traveled back to India. During the last years of Indian emigration to the Caribbean in 1914, the chief interpreter of the Surinam Immigration Department returned to his native village. He reported that there were two main questions regarding migration: whether it was really true that the salaries in the West Indies were enormous and whether all female immigrants were forced into prostitution.[34]

Transportation

The number of discrepancies between Chinese and Indian indentured labor migration again increased due to the differences in the way in which the two groups of migrants were transported to the Caribbean. The transportation of indentured laborers from India was much more carefully supervised than that from China. Only if

32. James McNeill and Chimman Lal, *Report to the Government of India on the Conditions of Indian Immigrants in Four British Colonies and Surinam* (London 1915).

33. Emmer, "Great Escape," 255.

34. Emmer, "Meek Hindu," 196.

we compare the transportation of the Chinese to the "pre-European" ways of transporting people, some improvements occurred. At the beginning of the nineteenth century, the flow of Chinese migrants across the Indian Ocean is estimated to have amounted to about 10,000 to 12,000 a year. The migrants were transported in Chinese junks, some of which are known to have carried more than 1,600 persons at a time. There are indications that the shipboard mortality was as high as 50 percent.[35]

Transportation by means of European vessels certainly showed lower mortality rates, in spite of the fact that it was very difficult to apply protective legislation. The Chinese Passenger Act of 1855, setting minimum standards for the transportation of Chinese migrants on British ships, simply made for the replacement of British vessels by American ones.[36] In total, ships of nineteen nationalities took part in the shipping of Chinese coolies. There was no specific type of ship employed in this trade: brigs, schooners, and barks, indeed, "anything that could stay afloat," tried to reap some of the windfall profits to be had in the "coolie trade." Most ships also carried cargo (coal, guano) on their trips to China. Most of these ships were sailing vessels; only a few steamers were employed. The great majority of the ships sailed around the Cape; the Suez Canal was only used sporadically once it became part of an alternative route.[37]

The mortality differed according to the nationality of the vessel. The average rate was 11.83 percent; the lowest mortality occurred on the Spanish ships (10.43 percent) and the highest on the British ships (16.31 percent). It seems that the difference in mortality also coincided with the way in which the Chinese laborers had been recruited. Indentured servants recruited by Chinese contractors for emigration to Cuba were much more prone to die than Chinese laborers recruited by Europeans for service in the British Caribbean.[38]

In contrast to the Chinese case, the transportation from India to the Caribbean had been regulated to the most trivial detail, after a legislative reform in 1870. Before that year, the mortality among migrants from British India had sometimes even been higher than among the Chinese, in spite of the fact that the duration of the

35. Meagher, "Introduction of Chinese Laborers," 142–144.
36. Ibid., 157–158.
37. Ibid., 164–166. Helly, *Idéologie et ethnicité* (Montreal 1979), 133, mentions the frequent use of steamers since 1865.
38. Meagher, "Introduction of Chinese Laborers," 182.

voyage from India to the West Indies on average was shorter than from China.[39] After 1870, the standards of government supervised transportation from India improved drastically. After that year, the rules aboard the coolie ships were more comprehensive and more effectively enforced than on other passenger ships. The most important officer aboard became the doctor, the "surgeon-superintendent."[40] Over time, a small group of physicians became specialized in these voyages, and shipboard mortality dropped to an average of 2 to 3 percent. The use of steamers after the 1890s, cut the average sailing time of ninety days by half and also halved the mortality rate. Two shipping firms monopolized the transportation of indentured laborers from India: James Nourse and Sandback, Tinne and Company, all using clippers.[41]

The transition from sail to steam was a matter of cost: until 1900 sailing vessels charged on average £10 for a passage and steamers £13. Also, the planters felt that they received their indentured laborers in a better physical state than would have been the case without a three months' stay aboard ship, with its regular distribution of food.[42]

The long sea voyage was certainly less beneficial to the Chinese indentured laborers than it was to the East Indians. There usually was no hospital room aboard their ships and no European doctor. There were many mutinies, while only one attempt at such an insurrection was reported aboard a vessel carrying Indian emigrants. Among the Chinese emigrants there was one mutiny on every eleven trips, and 4,000 Chinese passengers, 200 crew, and 12 captains lost their lives due to these violent clashes.[43]

The reason for the difference between the Chinese and Indian emigration is again the way in which the two groups had been recruited. Perhaps as much as two-thirds of all Chinese emigrants were not really willing to move to the Americas. First of all, there always were some kidnapped passengers who had never intended to leave China. The same applied to those emigrants who had signed up in order to pay for gambling debts. Also, it sometimes looked as if some of the emigrants had only come aboard ship in order to start an

39. Tinker, *New System of Slavery*, 163; Meagher, "Introduction of Chinese Laborers," 181–182. I am grateful to Ralph Schlomowitz (The Flinders University of South Australia) for his comments on this issue.

40. Tinker, *New System of Slavery*, 145, 147, 148.

41. Ibid., 116–176; Basil Lubbock, *Coolie Ships and Oil Sailers* (Glasgow 1935), 70–112.

42. Emmer, "Coolie Ships," 411.

43. Meagher, "Introduction of Chinese Laborers," 189.

insurrection, either in cooperation with the pirates of the Chinese sea or with the mysterious secret societies, who seemed intent to put an end to the emigration of Chinese indentured laborers. There were widely differing percentages in the occurrence of mutinies between the voyages originating in Macao (7 percent), Hongkong (9 percent), Amoy (19 percent), Canton (15 percent), and Cumsingmoon (33 percent).[44]

Shipping constituted a subordinate factor in ending both the Chinese, as well as the Indian, "coolie trade." In the case of the Chinese, public opinion in the United Kingdom and the United States was aroused by the frequent and violent mutinies, and this brought the respective governments of these countries to bring pressure to bear on the imperial Chinese government in order to put stricter controls into operation, governing the whole process of emigration. The implementation of these controls priced the Chinese laborers right off the Caribbean labor market in 1874. In the case of Indian emigration, the volume was greatly reduced after 1914 due to the lack of available transportation. The coolie clippers were needed to transport troops in order to help the British in winning the First World War.[45]

Reception and Settlement: Chinese and Indian Indentured Laborers on the West Indian Plantations

Many have remarked that there is little else in the world that changes so little as does the sugar plantation. Because slavery had not yet been abolished, the Chinese indentured laborers faced almost the same conditions on the Cuban sugar plantations as the slaves did. The same situation existed in Surinam. Only in British Guiana did the Chinese arrive after slavery had ended, but it seems doubtful whether this made any great difference in their treatment.

Upon their arrival, the Chinese laborers should have been allotted

44. Ibid., 199; Lubbock, *Coolie Ships and Oil Sailers*, 38–51.

45. The emigration from China to Cuba was halted by the Chinese, British (Hong Kong) and Portuguese (Macao) governments. Laurence, *Immigration into the West Indies*, 33, indicates that Spanish-Chinese negotiations on further imports of Chinese immigrants "achieved nothing" obviously because the Chinese demands would raise the price of Chinese immigrant labor. Meagher, "Introduction of Chinese Laborers," 277, also mentions the relative high costs of introducing Chinese immigrant labor in British Guiana in comparison to indentured labor from India. "It would seem that the Chinese were a kind of luxury that the colonies indulged in whenever they had some extra capital at hand." The end of Indian emigration in Tinker, *New System of Slavery*, 348.

to the plantations according to the numbers as ordered by the planters. In Cuba, however, the Chinese were auctioned for about half the price of a slave. The housing on the plantations was similar to that of the slaves, albeit that the two categories of bonded laborers were not mixed together. The leaders of the Chinese labor gangs were given better housing than the average worker, similar to that of the black drivers. The Chinese obtained a half way position between slavery and indentured labor in that they received both food rations as well as a salary. Like the slaves, the Chinese also cultivated their small subsistence plots, using seeds brought from China. They supplemented their food rations by fishing and hunting. The distribution of clothing soon made the Chinese laborers even look like their enslaved counterparts.[46]

Medical care for the Chinese was more difficult to obtain than it had been for the slaves. Some reports indicate that the mortality rate among the Chinese was as high as 80 to 90 per thousand per year. The mortality in Cuba, however, where the great majority of the Chinese indentured laborers had gone, came to an average of 40 per thousand per year for the period 1847 to 1874. Suicide constituted the cause of fifty deaths per year, which means that more than 0.2 percent of the Chinese mortality was caused by it. There are no comparable data for the population of China at the time.[47]

As far as the allotment of plantation jobs is concerned: both in Cuba and Surinam, the Chinese indentured laborers were kept separate from the field slaves. The Chinese mostly worked in the boiling houses, and specific mention is made of Chinese laborers assisting the European engineers in handling the new and complicated steam engines on the plantations. Also, 30 percent of the Chinese arriving in Cuba were not sent to the plantations; instead, they worked in the retail trade and as domestics. The labor conditions in Cuba, Surinam, and in British Guiana did not cause the Chinese to start insurrections and mass rebellions. Strikes did occur from time to time and opium was widely used, but there are indications that opium was also widely

46. Meagher, "Introduction of Chinese Laborers," 232. Helly, *Idéologie et ethnicité*, 146–178. Humphrey E. Lamur and Jean A. Vriezen, "Chinese kontraktanten in Suriname," *OSO, tijdschrift voor Surinaamse taalkunde, letterkunde en geschiedenis* 4,2 (1985), 169–179.

47. Meagher, "Introduction of Chinese Laborers," 236, and Helly, *Idéologie et ethnicité*, 212. In 1874, on average 50 percent of the imported Chinese laborers had stayed in Cuba for more than 11 years and 50 percent for less than 11 years. The total number of Chinese immigrants imported into Cuba was 125,634. In 1874, 68,825 Chinese were living on the island, that is, a mortality of 450 percent over approximately 22 years or on average 40.9 per mille per annum.

used among the population in China itself.[48]

The experience of the Indian indentured laborers on the Caribbean plantations was somewhat different from that of the Chinese. Because of the exclusive protective legislation and the institution of a special Immigration Department in all the receiving areas set up to safeguard their interests, the indentured Indians were much more "new laborers" in the Caribbean than the Chinese or the ex-slaves. It is true that the strong persistence of traditional labor conditions on the Caribbean plantations hardly allowed for drastic changes in the living and labor conditions. Over time, however, living conditions improved, as shown by the vital demographic data. The prevention of contagious diseases, as based on medical experience, improved considerably in spite of the fact that medical science hardly progressed in treating tropical diseases until the 1930s and 1940s with the introduction of sulpha drugs and penicillin. The very first group of Indians arriving in Surinam in 1873 experienced an extremely high death rate of 185 per thousand. Later on, these rates declined to 28.45 per thousand (1878 to 1882) and even to 18.45 per thousand (1892 to 1902). In Trinidad the decline of the death rate was also noticeable among the indentured laborers on the plantations: from 37.3 per thousand in 1875 to 13.5 per thousand in 1915. The death rate among the Indian population in general, however, remained consistently higher than that among the indentured laborers, and it did not decline, remaining on average 25 per thousand during the period 1906 to 1911. In Guiana the death rate for the Indian population in general remained relatively high: between 37.5 per thousand and 21.3 per thousand for the period 1890 to 1913. In India the death rate at the time averaged around 44 per thousand, and the death rate among the Creole population of Surinam was 43 per thousand, in Trinidad 22 per thousand (1906 to 1911), and in Guiana 32 per thousand. It should be stressed that the Indian indentured population in the Caribbean was mainly made up by people under 35 years of age. Men and women over 30 years of age were usually not recruited in India for service overseas.[49]

48. Scott, *Slave Emancipation in Cuba,* 32, 98. J. Ankum-Houwink, "Chinese Contract Migrants in Surinam between 1853 and 1870," *Boletin de Estudios Latinoamericanos y del Caribe* 17 (1974), 47.

49. P.C. Emmer, "The Importation of British Indians into Surinam (Dutch Guiana), 1873–1916" in Marks and Richardson, *International Labour Migration*, 91 and Emmer, "Great Escape," 255; Trinidad: McNeill and Chimman Lal, *Report* I, 7 and 9; Judith Ann Weller, *The East Indian Indenture in Trinidad* (Rio Piedras 1968), 90. Guiana: McNeill and Chimman Lal, *Report*, 63–64 and Lesley Marianne Potter, "Internal Migration and Re-Settlement of East Indians in Guyana, 1870–1920"

Unlike the Chinese, the Indian laborers were not employed in a restricted number of plantation jobs; they very quickly replaced the workers of other ethnicities. As far as labor discipline was concerned, the plantation regime usually adhered to the old tradition of punishing its laborers for slackness in performing the labor tasks and for being away from the plantation without permission. In addition to the usual sanctions administered by the plantation management, the Indian indentured laborers were also faced with "penal sanctions" imposed by the judicial system outside the plantation. The penal sanctions allowed the colonial judiciary to apply the criminal law in case of a dispute over task work between an employer and an indentured laborer. On average 10.5 percent of the Indian indentured laborers in Surinam were charged with such labor offenses, while 71 percent were actually convicted. In contrast, only 10 percent of the accused employers were convicted for offenses against the regulations of the contracts of indenture. The major complaint in these cases concerned the nonpayment of wages. In British Guiana a similar situation occurred. Gradually, however, the "penal sanctions" lost most of their threat. In 1880 forty-three plantations in British Guiana managed their labor force without recourse to these sanctions. The number of legal complaints in British Guiana declined over time: in 1874 they were applied to 35.56 percent of the total number of indentured laborers and in 1889 only to 24 percent. Convictions even declined by 80 percent. A similar trend could be observed in the number of workers' complaints against their employers. In Trinidad the number of indentured laborers who were brought to trial for labor law offenses came to 30 percent of the total indentured work force, two-thirds of whom were convicted. There also seems to have been decline in the number of these cases over time.[50]

The Chinese laborers, nor the Indian indentureds, ever resorted to large uprisings or to massive violence. There were many strikes, however, especially during the 1880s, when management tried to

(Unpublished Ph.D. thesis, Department of Geography, McGill University, Montreal 1975). I am grateful to Ralph Schlomowitz (The Flinders University of South Australia) for his comments on this issue.

50. Emmer, "Importation of British Indians," 107; Rodney, *History of the Guyanese Working People* 47–48; Moore, *Race, Power and Social Segmentation*, 167–171; Brereton, *Race Relations*, 178. Labor Law offenses in Trinidad: David Vincent Trotman, "Crime and the Plantation Society: Trinidad 1838–1900" (Unpublished Ph.D. thesis, Department of History, The Johns Hopkins University 1981), 267. The decline in numbers of offenses (Ibid., 260–261) is unfortunately not given as percentage of the indentured population.

increase the daily tasks or to lower wages. Some indentured laborers ran away, thus continuing the most common type of slave protest. In Surinam 1.65 percent of all indentured men and women absconded, while in British Guiana this percentage was 3.32 percent. In Trinidad the desertion rate was about 5 percent for the years 1909, 1910, and 1911. The widespread use of "ganga," the relatively high number of suicides (Surinam: 0.06 percent), and the occurrence of violent murders of Indian women are also mentioned as signs of social discontent. When violence occurred, the colonial government usually came to the aid of the planters. During the 43 years of Indian immigration into Surinam, 32 indentured laborers and 5 Europeans were killed in clashes with government troops. In British Guiana the police force was increased by only 150 men in order to cope with possible violence among the 60,000 Indian immigrants residing on plantations. There existed little solidarity between the different ethnic groups on the plantation. Creole and Indian laborers organized separate strikes.[51]

Integration or Isolation? The Indians and the Chinese in the Caribbean after the Expiration of their Contracts of Indenture

The differences between the Chinese and the Indian immigrants in the Caribbean came even more to the fore after their involvement in plantation agriculture had declined. The Chinese only make up a small percentage of the population of the host countries, while the Indians now constitute the most numerous ethnic section of the populations of Guiana, Trinidad, and Surinam. Why?

The answer with regard to the Chinese is simple: no women. There only existed a few stable unions between Chinese and black women, and consequently, the Chinese died out. In 1898 only 15,000 Chinese had remained in Cuba. The majority of this group were classified as simple day laborers. The fact that there still exists a "Chinatown" in Havana today, has little to do with the 120,000 indentured Chinese arriving in Cuba between 1847 and 1874. Instead, the present Chinese community on the island is linked to the

51. Emmer, "Importation of British Indians," 109. Adamson, *Sugar without Slaves*, 154; Emmer, "Great Escape," 256; Moore, *Race, Power and Social Segmentation*, 172–173; Brereton, *Race Relations*, 179. The desertion rate on Trinidad is calculated from McNeill and Chimman Lal, *Report* I, 8 (indentured population figures) and 24 (desertion).

immigration during the first three decades of this century, when more than 22,000 free Chinese laborers arrived in order to work in the sugar industry. In British Guiana there were only 2,600 Chinese present in 1911. Most of the Chinese immigrants had stayed in agriculture after the expiration of their contracts because it was difficult to work in the service sector in British Guiana as this was almost fully monopolized by the Portuguese. Most Chinese in British Guiana have been converted to Christianity.[52]

The demographic experience of the Indians was very different from that of the Chinese. In Surinam their numbers grew rapidly, in spite of the fact that a quarter of the indentured laborers went back to India. The explanation for the explosive growth of the Indian population is the relatively high fertility rate and the relatively low death rate. Compared to India, the general birth rate among indentured populations in Surinam was 34.5 against 47.3 per thousand in India. The fertility rate among Indian women in Surinam, however, was the same as in India: 155 per thousand as compared to 119 per thousand for city women and 154 per thousand for women living in the countryside in India around 1930. The relatively low death rate of 23.5 per thousand as compared to 44 per thousand in India, has already been mentioned. In Trinidad the birth rate averaged 36.6 per thousand (1906 to 1911). Unfortunately, there are no fertility rates available. The birth rates among indentured women, however, were substantially lower than those of the Indian population in general: 13.9 per thousand on average for the years 1907 to 1911. In Guiana the birth rates averaged between 22.6 per thousand and 32.6 per thousand (1890 to 1913). The fertility rate was around 113 per thousand.[53]

Unfortunately, a comparative study of the demography of the Indian communities in the Caribbean is not available. In general, however, it seems possible to remark that the fertility among Indian women was relatively high as compared to the fertility among Creole women in the Caribbean because: (1) Indian women entered relatively early into a stable sexual union; (2) few Indian women remained unmarried; (3) the intervals between sexual unions during the fertile period of Indian women were shorter than those among Creole women; and (4) there were less abortions among Indian women than among Creole women. If we accept the relatively high

52. Corbitt, *Study of the Chinese*, 92. David Lowenthal, *West Indian Societies* (Oxford 1972), 203.

53. Surinam: Emmer, "Great Escape," 253–256; Trinidad: McNeill and Chimman Lal, *Report*, 7, 9; Guiana: Potter, "Internal Migration," 322–332.

fertility level of Indian women in all ex-Indian communities in the Caribbean, then the explanation for the different growth rates of these communities must be found in the differing mortality levels. In Surinam these levels seemed to have declined consistently over time, which was not the case in Guiana and Trinidad. In these two colonies the relatively high percentages of stillbirths, as well as the spread of malaria due to wet rice cultivation, were mentioned as causes of the stagnating growth of the Indian population.[54]

The majority of the "time-expired" Indians did not remain in plantation agriculture. In Surinam only 34 percent of the men reindentured themselves. The percentage of women reindenturing was even lower. It seems that the colonial authorities between 1873 and 1890 considered the Indian indentureds as temporary plantation workers. After 1890, the governments of both Guiana and Surinam actively supported a policy by which ex-indentured Indians could obtain a piece of land. This change led in turn to a third phase in the social and economic ascendancy of the Indians in the Caribbean: small-scale agriculture for the market, be it of foodstuffs, of exportable rice or dairy farming. After World War II, more and more Indians moved to the cities and started to remedy their disproportional representation in civil service jobs. In Guiana the ex-Indians made up 50 percent of the population and held only one-third of the civil service jobs in 1964 and in Trinidad, 40 percent of the population and only 11 percent of the civil service positions in 1962 and 1963.[55]

The key word for the Indians in the Caribbean used to be isolation. No doubt, the tradition to separate themselves from other ethnic groups had its roots on the plantation, where the Indians had completely replaced other ethnic groups except for the management. Indian villages started to grow up, based on wet rice cultivation. Intermarriage was rare, and the strong family ties, as well as the economic drive to save and to invest in the family business, have led sociologists to speak of a "protestant ethic" among the East Indians in the Caribbean. Until recently, the Indian languages were still widely used. There was no massive conversion to Chris-

54. Milton Jacon Brawer, "Fertility Differences, Family Structure and Modernization in two Populations in Trinidad" (Unpublished Ph.D. thesis, Dept. of Sociology, Columbia University 1965); Potter, "Internal Migration," 333–348. On the persistent high mortality rate: G.W. Roberts and M.A. Johnson, "Factors involved in Immigration and Movements in the Working Force of British Guiana in the 19th Century," *Social and Economic Studies* 23,1 (1974), 71.

55. Lowenthal, *West Indian Societies*, 167.

tianity among the Indians, who were 80 percent Hindu and 20 percent Muslim when leaving Indian.[56]

Return Migration

There was hardly any return migration among the Chinese. It has been estimated that only 0.1 percent of all Chinese emigrating to the Caribbean paid for a passage back to China. Until 1866, a free passage was not included in the contracts of indenture and then only for the Chinese emigrating to the British West Indies.

For the Indian indentured laborers, a free return passage was included in the contract of indenture and became available after a period of ten years in the British West Indies and after a period of five years in the Dutch and French Caribbean. In total 31.6 percent of the Indian indentureds returned from Guiana, 19.5 percent from Trinidad, 22.35 percent from Guadeloupe, and 34 percent from Surinam. It has been estimated that the returning Indians brought on average per person £16 (Surinam) to £13 (Guiana) back in cash, in addition to unspecified amounts of jewelry.[57] The differing percentages of returnees seems to have been closely linked to the availability of land. In Trinidad, the distribution of small pieces of land, in addition to a fee for renouncing the return passage, became an early option in the system, while these innovations did not occur in Guiana and Surinam until 1890, immediately reducing the percentage of returnees.[58]

Many returning migrants had great difficulty in readjusting to life in India. A few even tried to get another indenture overseas as quickly as possible after their return, to the delight of the various Emigration Agents, who considered these reindentures as proof of

56. Ibid., 153. For Surinam: C.R. Biswamitre, "Hindostaans leven" in *Cultureel Mozaïek van Suriname: Bijdrage tot onderling begrip*, A. Helman ed. (Zutphen 1977), 205–226. For Guadaloupe: Singaravélou, *Les Indiens de la Guadaloupe* (Bordeaux 1975), 143–152. For Trinidad: Brereton, *Race Relations*, 165.

57. On the Chinese: Meagher, "Introduction of Chinese Laborers," 224. Corbitt, *Study of the Chinese*, 88. Percentages of returnees: Surinam: Emmer, "Coolie Ships," 10–11; Trinidad: Marianne D. Ramesar, "Indentured Labour in Trinidad 1880–1917" in *Indentured Labour in the British Empire, 1834–1920*, Kay Saunders, ed. (London and Canberra 1984), 62; Guiana: Nath, *History of Indians*, 219, 222; Guadaloupe: Singaravélou, *Les Indiens de la Guadaloupe*, 51, 57. Brinsley Samaroo, "'In Sick Longing for the Further Shore': Return Migration by Caribbean East Indians During the Nineteenth and Twentieth Centuries," in *Return Migration and Remittances: Developing A Caribbean Perspective*, William F. Stinner, Klaus de Albuquerque, and Roy S. Bryce-Laporte eds. (Washington D.C. 1982) 45–73.

58. Tinker, *New System of Slavery*, 106; Emmer, "Coolie Ships," 412–414.

popular support for the colonial emigration schemes. Among the sample of 33,000 indentureds going to Surinam, 4.6 percent had been indentured before, half of them in the Caribbean.[59]

The colonial government of India was adamant that return ships were chartered in time, and failure to do so constituted a principal reason for suspending emigration to the French colonies. The return trips from Surinam to Calcutta lasted longer than the other way around: for sailing vessels, on average 155.4 days and for steamers, 50 days.[60] Mortality on the return voyages was lower than aboard ships coming from India, in spite of the fact the two groups were physically quite different. In coming to the Caribbean, the emigrants had passed several medical tests in order to guarantee their physical soundness. Among the return migrants, on the other hand, there was a relatively high percentage of disabled, chronically sick, and insane passengers. The lower mortality among these structurally weak return migrants seems to indicate that the presence of deadly contagious diseases among the sending population was of decisive importance to shipboard mortality. Obviously, such diseases were less frequent and less widespread in the Caribbean than they were in India.[61]

Migration and Capital Movements

There is virtually no information on the relationship between the immigration of indentured laborers into the Caribbean and changes in the structure of plantation investments in the region. In this respect, it should be noted that the indentured immigrants came exclusively to continue the already existing production of sugar. The Caribbean sugar plantations were able to produce sugar at competitive prices only because of the use of bonded labor. There is little doubt that wage costs would have risen steeply without the introduction of indentured labor. After the ending of slavery and apprenticeship, both British Guiana, as well as Trinidad, briefly experienced a period with a free labor market and high wages.[62]

In view of this, there is actually little reason to expect that the

59. Emmer, "Meek Hindu," 197.
60. Emmer, "Coolie Ships," 413; Tinker, *New System of Slavery*, 278–279.
61. Emmer, "Coolie Ships," 413.
62. Adamson, *Sugar without Slaves*, 165 (Guiana) and William A. Green, *British Slave Emancipation; the Sugar Colonies and the Great Experiment, 1830–1865* (Oxford 1976), 197–198 and Wood, *Trinidad in Transition*, 53.

arrival of indentured laborers created a new perspective for plantation agriculture and called for drastic changes in investments. If anything, it seems that the ending of slavery reduced the amount of capital needed to buy a plantation. Certainly, there still was a need for considerable capital outlay in order to finance the increasingly expensive and sophisticated machinery for the boiling houses. In several Caribbean sugar colonies, notably Cuba, railroad tracks were laid in order to facilitate the transportation of freshly cut sugar cane to the sugar refineries. The increase in long-term investments in capital goods on the plantations, however, was more than made good by the fact that such investments in the labor force were no longer necessary after the abolition of slavery.

It seems that the introduction of indentured laborers did not affect the development in plantation financing, which had already started around the time of slave emancipation, if not earlier. On the one hand, there was an increase in the number of local, resident planters owning plantations financed with local capital. On the other hand, large companies in the metropole or in the United States became the financiers of Caribbean plantations. The eighteenth-century combination of planter-owner and merchant-financier had disappeared.[63]

The transition from slavery to indentured labor in the Caribbean has been attributed to the changeover from "mercantile" to "industrial" capital in the financial centers of Europe. During the period of the ancien régime, the financiers of Caribbean plantations were supposed to have been looking for profits by trading tropical cash crops, not by producing them. Therefore, the intensive use of slave labor constituted a relatively expensive form of labor supply. The abolition of slavery had been brought about by the changes in the financial centers of Europe, where the new industrial capitalists had taken over from the old mercantile financiers. This new breed of investors was intent on making a profit in producing cash crops and therefore not opposed to replacing expensive slave labor with indentured labor, which was cheaper.[64]

There is no evidence to support this hypothesis. Capital invested in the Caribbean has always aspired to make profits as high as possible, be it in production or in trade. For that reason, slavery was

63. Green, *British Slave Emancipation*, 255–257. R.W. Beachy, *The British West Indies Sugar Industry in the late 19th Century* (reprint Westport 1978), 118–137. For Surinam: Glenn Willemsen, *Koloniale politiek en transformatieprocessen in een plantage-economie, Suriname, 1873–1940* (Amsterdam 1980), 57–62.

64. Bill Albert and Adrian Graves, "Introduction" in, *Crisis and Change in the International Sugar Economy 1860–1914*, Bill Albert and Adrian Graves, eds. (Norwich and Edinburgh 1984), 3.

introduced into the West Indies and for that reason, indentured labor was imported. Both categories of bonded labor were cheaper than free labor, albeit that slavery was less expensive than Asian indentured labor. Both unfree labor systems ended because of political decisions to cut off supplies. If there existed a difference between the investment policies of "mercantile" and "industrial" capitalists in Europe, it did not surface in the Caribbean.[65]

Migration and Political Movements

It seems difficult to indicate which political changes occurred in the Caribbean due to the arrival of so many Asians in the region. That such changes did occur, however, is obvious. The violent clashes between the "Afro-Guianese" and "Indo-Guianese" during the early 1960s, unfortunately speak for themselves.

In many ways the Caribbean societies seemed ideally suited to accommodate large groups of aliens. They were labeled as "segmented" or – more optimistically – as "plural" societies. Each ethnic group (white, mulatto, black) had created its own social institutions, occupying different economic niches in West Indian society. In the same tradition, the Chinese and Indians were able to constitute another such segment.[66]

As has been mentioned previously, there were many protests by Chinese and Indian immigrants during their period of indenture. These protests, however, were not directed against the Caribbean society as a whole, but limited to the specific living and working conditions on the plantations. Only the slaves had in the past attempted to overthrow the existing order in the Caribbean. Over time, the indentured laborers did settle in, and the number of sick days, suicides, and strikes declined. Around 1900, the Indian community in Trinidad and Surinam founded associations in order to further their socio-economic interests. There was very little contact with the other groups in the society at large. In general, East Indians pursued agricultural activities, and the Caribbean Creoles usually filled the civil service positions and the jobs in the towns. As

65. A nice summary of the problems on the Caribbean labor market over a long time span: Jay. R. Mandle, *Patterns of Caribbean Development; An Interpretive Essay on Economic Change* (New York 1982), 37–52.

66. Anthony Lemon, "The Indian Communities of East Africa and the Caribbean" in *Studies in Overseas Settlement and Population*, A. Lemon and N.C. Pollock, eds. (London and New York 1980), 225–243.

a consequence, there was little competition between these two groups.[67]

After the Second World War, this situation changed when both Afro- and Indo-Caribbeans became increasingly interested in the same type of employment in the cities, which was scarce. Consequently, tensions between ex-Indians and ex-Africans increased. The political systems of the countries involved (Guiana, Surinam, and Trinidad) could not defuse these tensions as most political parties had been founded on an ethnic basis. It is doubtful, however, whether the absence of a considerable Indian segment in the population would have prevented the outbursts of violent social unrest. Caribbean countries without an ex-Asian community have also known considerable social and political violence.[68]

APPENDIX

Sources for Table 11.1: "Immigration into the Caribbean, 1811–1916."
African Slaves: David Eltis, *Economic Growth and the Ending of the Transatlantic Slave Trade* (New York and Oxford 1987), 249. The author underestimated the illegal slave imports into the Dutch Caribbean: J.P. Siwpersad, *De Nederlandse regering en de afschaffing van de Surinaamse slavernij 1833–1863* (Groningen and Castricum 1979), 47–50.

British Indians: K.O. Laurence, *Immigration into the West Indies in the 19th century* (Kingston 1971), 57.

Europeans: To the British West Indies: namely Portuguese indentured laborers (40,000) from Madeira: Laurence, *Immigration into the West Indies*, 18. In addition there were 3,000 European migrants to Jamaica (p. 10). To the French Caribbean: Laurence, *Immigration into the West Indies*, 40. To the Spanish Caribbean: Rebecca J. Scott, *Slave Emancipation in Cuba; the Transition to Free Labor, 1860–1899* (Princeton 1985), 217 mentions the immigration of 24,000 Spaniards to Cuba between 1861 and 1887. Between 1889 and 1894 there immigrated another 58,700. Magnus Mörner, *Adventurers and*

67. Lowenthal, *West Indian Societies*, 156–177.

68. Curaçao (1969) Jamaica (elections of 1980) and Grenada (1983). See also large-scale violence in Cuba after the Second World War, where Asian immigrants had virtually no lasting impact, as well as in Haiti, which received no Asians at all. All these examples indicate that there exists no simple relationship between the ethnic diversity of immigration into the Caribbean and political violence.

Proletarians; the Story of Migrants in Latin America (Pittsburgh 1985), 33, mentions the immigration of 35,000 Europeans to Cuba by 1843. His Figure 9 (p. 59) allows us to estimate the Spanish immigration into Cuba between 1895 and 1916 at about 1,500 per year totaling about 33,000. Figure 2 seems to suggest that there was virtually no European immigration into Latin America (let alone into the Spanish Caribbean) between the years 1844 to 1861. To the Dutch West Indies: P.C. Emmer, "Veranderingen op de Surinaamse arbeidsmarkt gedurende de negentiende eeuw, Smith and Marx in West-Indië," *Economisch- en Sociaal-Historisch Jaarboek* 47 (1984), 213.

Chinese: Joseph Arnold Meagher, "The Introduction of Chinese Laborers to Latin America: the 'coolie trade,' 1847–1874" Unpublished Ph.D. thesis (Univ. of Calif., Davis 1975), 182A, 220, 227A, 289, 290.

Free Africans: Laurence, *Immigration into the West Indies*, 14 (British West Indies), 41 (French West Indies).

Javanese: Joseph Ismael, *De immigratie van Indonesiërs in Suriname* (Leiden 1949), 95.

BIBLIOGRAPHICAL NOTE

There are two bibliographies on this topic: Juan Baily and Freya Meadlam, *Intercontinental Migration to Latin America; A Select Bibliography* (London: Institute of Latin American Studies, University of London 1980) and Rosemary Brana-Shute and Rosemarijn Hoefte, eds., *A Bibliography of Caribbean Migration and Caribbean Immigrant Communities* (Gainesville: University of Florida 1983). The problem is that the first one is very select indeed and that the second one is more extensive, but still seriously flawed; for example, the most important historical surveys on nineteenth-century immigration to Surinam are missing.

The best introduction to the topic of nineteenth-century immigration into the Caribbean is K.O. Laurence, *Immigration into the West Indies*.

The immigration of Europeans to the nineteenth-century Caribbean remains largely unexplored. Unfortunately, the same applies to the European migration during the previous centuries. At this moment there is no comprehensive survey of the two main streams of European immigration: one from Portugal (mainly from Madeira) and Spain (mainly from the Canary Islands) to the British Caribbean and one from Spain to Cuba.

The Chinese immigrants into the Caribbean (and to Latin America) have found a historian, but no publisher. The excellent study of Joseph Arnold

Meagher, "Introduction of Chinese Laborers," should have been made into a book long ago.

The immigration of British Indians is nicely summarized by Hugh Tinker, *A New System of Slavery; the Export of Indian Labour Overseas, 1830–1920* (Oxford 1974). It should be noted that Tinker discusses all Indian indentured emigration and not only the migration into the Caribbean.

Among the monographs on the separate Caribbean colonies, there are only a few books that deal with nineteenth-century immigration: Dwarka Nath, *A History of Indians in Guyana* (London 1970): Singaravélou, *Les Indiens de la Guadaloupe* (Bordeaux 1975); C.J.M. de Klerk, *De immigratie der Hindostanen in Suriname* (Amsterdam 1953); and Ismael, *Immigratie van Indonesiërs.* Duvon Clough Corbett, *A Study of the Chinese in Cuba, 1847–1947* (Wilmore 1971) and Denise Helly, *Idéologie et ethnicité; les Chinois de Macao à Cuba* (Montreal 1979). The "Free Africans" are described in Monica Schuler's, *"Alas, Alas Kongo"; A Social History of Indentured African Immigration into Jamaica, 1841–1865* (Baltimore and London 1980).

There are many more studies of the various Caribbean colonies, which incorporate data and analyses on nineteenth-century immigration. For British Guiana: Alan H. Adamson, *Sugar without Slaves; the Political Economy of British Guiana, 1838–1904* (New Haven and London 1972); Walter Rodney, *A History of the Guyanese Working People, 1881–1895* (Baltimore and London 1981); Jay R. Mandle, *The Plantation Economy; Population and Economic Change in Guyana, 1838–1960* (Philadelphia 1973); and Brian L. Moore, *Race, Power and Social Segmentation in Colonial Society; Guyana after Slavery, 1838–1891* (New York 1987). For Trinidad: Donald Wood, *Trinidad in Transition; the Years after Slavery* (Oxford 1968) and Bridget Brereton, *Race Relations in Colonial Trinidad, 1870–1900* (Cambridge 1979).

Fortunately, more and more detailed studies on immigrants on the Caribbean are being published in order to fill the gap between the volume of studies regarding slave trade and slavery and that of studies on immigrants. John la Guerre, ed., *Calcutta to Caroni; the East Indians of Trinidad*, 2d ed. (St. Augustine 1985). Bridget Brereton and Winston Dookeran, eds., *East Indians in the Caribbean: Colonialism and the Struggle for Identity* (Millwood and London 1982) and David Dabydeen and Brinsley Samaroo, eds., *India in the Caribbean* (London 1987). These two volumes are only the first of many more to come, incorporating papers written for the frequent international conferences on the Indian diaspora in the Caribbean.

The most recent and very fruitful approach to studying immigration and the production of cash crops are monographs and collections of essays dealing with a variety of migration movements executed under similar conditions, both to the Caribbean as well as to other regions importing migrant labor: Kay Saunders, ed., *Indentured Labour in the British Empire, 1834–1920* (London and Canberra 1984) with four contributions on the Caribbean and others on Mauritius, Fiji, Malaya, Queensland, and the Transvaal. In the same category: Bill Albert and Adrian Graves, eds., *Crisis and Change in the International Sugar Economy, 1860–1914* (Norwich and Edinburgh 1984) with six contributions on the Caribbean; Shula Marks and Peter Richardson, eds., *International Labour Migration; Historical Perspectives* (London 1984); P.C. Emmer ed., *Colonialism and Migration; Indentured Labour before and after Slavery* (Dordrecht 1986).

There is little doubt, however, that migration studies concerning the Caribbean have still a long way to go. It should be stressed that there is no dearth of sources: the nineteenth-century colonial administrators usually produced an abundance of materials both on the sending as well as on the receiving areas.

12

Divergent Perspectives

MAGNUS MÖRNER

Push/Pull-Factors

A traditional analytical approach to identifying the dynamics behind migration has been that of evaluating the balance between factors of "push" and "pull."*

In his critique of the approach, as applied to European migration to the Americas, Prof. Nicholas Canny (Ireland) expressed his strong doubts about the usefulness of the push-pull model to understand "why particular migrations occur at particular times." Obviously, most if not all large-scale voluntary migrations were precipitated by dislocations of some kind in the country of origin. Yet, many dislocations occurred without resulting in any out-migration. People might very well starve in one country, at a time when their labor could be usefully employed in another. Moreover, due to the stock effect (or chain migration), a migration flow might continue long after the initial push-factor had ceased to exist. Against those who in such a case would contend that the pull-factor had then become the dominant force, merely reinforced by the stock effect, Canny argued that neither would labor demand, as such, suffice to trigger in-migration. Until it becomes profitable for the carriers of human cargo to make the connection between supply and demand, no major migration would take place. Canny found H. Kjartanson's report on Icelandic migration to provide clear evidence for proving this point. In Canny's view, "carriers," whether from the sending, receiving, or a third country, "must always be considered as an independent force . . . ," merely

* This chapter is an attempt to summarize two days of intense discussions. Even though texts of most special comments have been kindly put at our disposal by the speakers, for reasons of space it has been necessary to summarize them instead. The discussions were tape recorded; however, there are gaps, which have at times hampered my editorial work considerably. M. Mörner.

"marginally influenced" by push-pull.[1] With respect to, for instance, eighteenth-century North America, on both sides of the Atlantic there were "merchants and their agents who created . . . the image of America that lured their migrants to leave their country of origin . . . because transporting a human cargo had become profitable. . . ."

Canny had another reservation about excessive reliance on the push-pull model, namely, that it tended to suggest that the migrants were free agents who could simply choose their destination. This was not so, and not just in the case of non-European labor migrations, such as those treated by G. Clarence-Smith and P. Emmer. Canny also recalled the early migration of indentured servants to North America and masses of "voluntary" migrants as well. "In reality, choice was a luxury . . . open to but a small proportion of migrants . . . usually only to those who possessed a skill . . . in keen demand in several possible destinations." Otherwise, the destination was, in fact, decided upon by the recruitment agent or the relative abroad ready to pay the passage money or to procure employment. The Irish historian, therefore, recommended that the push-pull model be employed "less mechanically" than it had so far and with due attention paid to independent variables. Also, the student must be aware that the push- pull-factors themselves tend to change rather quickly over time and that different categories of people may be influenced by different factors.

During the following discussion, Emmer disagreed with Canny on two issues. First, he noted that in the course of the nineteenth century, governments intervened increasingly, in "coolie" migration at the least, so that carriers lost whatever influence they used to have in the matter. Second, as far as seventeenth-century unskilled indentured servants were concerned, they at least had the choice of joining the army or navy, or going to either North America or the Caribbean. In Canny's view, this was not so much of a choice. He made an important general distinction, however, between Western migration on the one side, and "Third World" migrations on the other. In the first case, information on conditions at the place of destiny was sooner or later likely to reach people at home, constituting either a stimulus (stock effect) or a warning. In the case of the "coolies," it

1. Canny referred especially to Bernard Bailyn, *Voyagers to the West: Emigration from Britain to America on the Eve of the Revolution* (London 1986); Marianne Wokeck, "Promoters and Passengers: the German Immigrant Trade, 1683–1775" in *The World of William Penn*, Richard S. Dunn and Mary M. Dunn, eds. (Philadelphia 1986), 259–81.

did not. On his part, Sune Åkerman agreed with Canny's stress on the stock effect, which "can never, never, be overestimated." In this connection, he pleaded for more attention to the "human beings" involved, that is, individuals and local units. This implied that he rejected Canny's assertion about the lack of choices, something, in fact, inherent in the concept of migration. The latter replied that "when you are in a crisis situation," you have no choice, but admitted that the role of choice increased in a more established situation. Lars Ljungmark, too, stressed the importance of the stock effect, which he had studied in connection with the Swedes in Minnesota. This time, Canny suggested that the choice of destination may decline precisely as a result of the stock effect.

Demography

Geographer P.E. Ogden (Britain) underlined the striking advances taking place in historical demography during the last twenty years. On an explanatory level a basic question had emerged, that is, "whether population change is relegated to the role of dependent variable or whether population trends themselves may be said to influence wider economic and social trends."[2] He believed, however, that "least progress has been made in the study of migration in the past." This was so because demographers themselves had taken relatively little interest in mobility and because sources, methods, and techniques were "of a rather different order from other demographic variables." In very recent years, however, the significance of mobility had become recognized; therefore, relevant studies could soon be expected. Ogden also emphasized the question of different geographical scales of analysis. The "greatest challenge before historical demography today," in his view, was that of breaching the divide between highly localized and national studies by providing regional frameworks as well. As to migrations, this would apply to both sending and receiving territories.

The discussant thought that as far as demography was concerned, the reports presented tended to analyze migration "in something of a vacuum." In particular, he referred to the high degree of mobility in "traditional societies," in rural as well as in urban areas, uncovered by recent research. Therefore, according to Bernard Bailyn,

2. E.A. Wrigley, "Population History in the 1980's," *Interdisciplinary History* 12, 2 (1981), 221.

international movements of the pre-industrial era might be seen "as a reflection and to some extent an extension of domestic migrations. . . ."[3] Against the background of ongoing historical demographic research, Ogden found that most reports "underplayed" demographic issues. He recommended Wilbur Zelinsky's notion of "mobility transition" to associate international movements with economic modernization and rapid population growth.[4] Migration research should also consider recent Malthusian population theory, but it should be aware, of course, of "too facile a correlation between population pressure and emigration." Also, the impact of migration on the demography of sending countries deserved attention in the way Prof. William Smyth did in his report on Irish migration (certainly a striking case). The receiving countries had to be analyzed similarly. "Thus migration streams highly skewed by age or sex had an immediate impact upon destinations where migration was highly localized geographically. In addition, migrants may have brought demographic behaviour sharply different from receiving countries . . . For mortality, effects varied from deleterious – the spread of disease through migration – to the clearly beneficial, where the process of migration may have selected the younger, fitter, more able elements." Finally, the impact of migration upon those who moved should not be forgotten. Out of 90,000 Irish who embarked to Canada in 1847, no less than one out of six died on board or in quarantine or hospitals after landing. As Ogden concluded, the theme of "European Expansion and Migration" is in many ways related to wider questions prevalent in the field of historical demography, something students of migration should keep in mind.

The discussion first dealt with "mobility" as such. As Smyth put it, North American studies sometimes give the impression that mobility only set in when immigrants came ashore. As Ogden saw it, forty years ago, research suggested that sending countries had enjoyed demographic stability. Nowadays you get an impression of mobility that may be equally exaggerated. Prof. Klaus Bade put Ogden's "collectivist" approach in contrast to the individual-oriented approach, for which Åkerman had pleaded during the first

3. Bernard Bailyn, *Voyagers. The Peopling of North America: an Introduction* (London 1986); J. Lucassen, *Migrant Labour in Europe. The Drift to the North Sea* (London 1987).

4. W. Zelinsky, "The Hypothesis of the Mobility Transition," *Geographic Review* 61 (1971), 219–49, and *idem.* "The Demographic transition: Changing Patterns of Migration" in *Population Science in the Service of Mankind*, IUSSP (Vienna 1979), 165–90.

discussion. "Both levels have their own truth" and are complementary, not alternatives, Bade exclaimed. Åkerman also expressed his concern about the linkage between migration and demographic research. He did not find the ignorance of demographers (such as the Cambridge group) about research on migration less grave than the other way around (as underlined by Ogden). Also, even in Scandinavia there is so much that we still ignore about the history of "reproductive systems," such as the linkages to social and urban/rural differentiation. Moreover, students were not aware that in nineteenth-century Sweden, for example, no less than 22 percent of the population never married, or that in Finland, emigration really affected only one county. This was an exaggeration, Harald Runblom stated, referring to data on Finnish emigration in the *Nordic Emigration Atlas* (1980). The chairman pointed out that this work might serve as a goal and model for the ESF Network to extend to the rest of Europe.

Women in Migration

In her brief presentation of the subject, Dr. Béatrice Ziegler-Witschi made clear that the factor of gender (the social aspects of sex) is of the same dimension as race or class for a migrant's identity. The reports showed that the sex ratio tended to be balanced in family migration, but much more skewed with fewer women when migration was unorganized. At the same time, when migrating as family members, women do not appear as actors. Economic and social circumstances at both ends help to explain the degree of participation of women in a migratory movement, but in an insufficient way. Historians have to take into account the specific behavior of gender in the sending, as well as the receiving, country. The push-pull factors may be very different for each gender, Ziegler-Witschi underlined. A country may be most attractive for men, but not for women. Also, other factors may intervene. In some countries, such as Switzerland, women were simply not legally empowered to make on their own the decision of emigrating. Also, single female migrants put their reputation at risk. The discussant also touched upon the very important question of how an excess of males in a migration movement would affect social structure in the sending, as well as the receiving, countries. On the job market, also, demand often differed widely according to gender. In the nineteenth-century Swiss textile industry (and in general, probably), some 80 percent of the workers were female. Ziegler-Witschi's conclusion was that gender simply has to be considered as one of the basic variables of migration research. It is by no means enough to only study certain categories of female migrants.

Prof. Magalhães Godinho started the discussion by pointing to the deviations within Portuguese emigration with respect to female participation. From the Azores, there were always streams of family migration to Brazil, Mozambique, and Angola; otherwise, migration was usually overwhelmingly male. On the whole, over time women did not exceed 15 percent. Mörner referred to the findings of the American scholar Peter Boyd-Bowman, who has shown that no less than a third of Spanish migrants to the New World by 1600 were women, something that radically changes our perception of the colonization process in Spanish America.[5] Prof. J.L. Miège noted that importance of the lack of women in the European possessions in the Indian Ocean. He also stressed the importance of different national patterns in migration. The French normally left without women and logically engaged in exogenous marriages. The Maltese, and the Italians in general, preferred family migration and endogamous marriages. Ziegler-Witschi agreed but stated that the demographic approach was not enough. The situation of women in society had to be taken into account.

Åkerman emphasized the importance of migration for women's emancipation in Scandinavia. Interviews with relatives in the United States had given him many proofs of that. Ziegler-Witschi found it puzzling that Swedish women in the United States would really become emancipated through marriage. Yes, to some extent they did, Åkerman replied, pointing at a wider question: what does marriage mean to women in different societies? At the time, it was more favorable for them in the United States than in, for instance, Sweden. Smith observed that in northern Portugal the question of who would emigrate or stay was part of a very firm family strategy.

Canny gave a fascinating example of female migration to the unhealthy plantation area of the Chesapeake in the seventeenth century. Increasingly, women were sent there as indentured servants. If they did not die or become pregnant by fellow servants after their time of service, they had, he claimed, almost a certainty of becoming "a planter's wife." Yet, that social ascent did not last for

5. See, for example, P. Boyd-Bowman, "Patterns of Spanish Emigration to the Indies, 1579–1600," *The Americas* 33, 1 (1976), 78–95.

long because they were likely to contract malaria and die upon becoming pregnant, with merely one or two children. Evidence suggests, however, that in the early eighteenth century their daughters had acquired a certain degree of immunity. The story made Ziegler-Witschi ask if marriage was really the only goal of such women, did they have no professional ambitions? Kristian Hyidt introduced another country, Denmark, into the discussion. Here the female out-migration rate was strikingly low, while female participation in the rural-urban migration was high. Women were much in demand during the early stage of industrialization. Also, did they remain in the country because they were more attached to the parents? Or, as Ziegler-Witschi added, were they forced to that effect, by social codes or legal institutions?

Transportation

Hvidt (Denmark), in his presentation of the subject, linked it up with the viewpoints on the great role of transportation for the migration phenomena as already made by Canny in his comments on the push-pull factors. His main message was that the transportation system of mass migration has been so far quite neglected as a field of study. Hvidt especially referred to a conference in the 1860s of nine shipowners in Liverpool, a main center of migration traffic, when they more or less seemed to share the European migrant passenger flow among themselves. These shipping lines had great numbers of subagents everywhere, no less than 1,500 in a small country like Denmark. Hvidt suggested that there must exist archives in Liverpool on the traffic through that port, which should highlight the migration traffic and which have not been utilized until now. He also mentioned a second, more international shipping conference in 1885 and, after 1900, the attempts of the Morgan Trust to regulate the worldwide migration traffic. This discussant declared that, generally speaking, "sea transportation has always been cheaper, quicker and easier than land transportation," a fact of basic importance for European history ever since the early Middle Ages. Also, he found imperialism and migration to be a pair of keywords for nineteenth-century Europe as they were closely interrelated phenomena, even though executed by different people. Basically, the imperialists and the shippers shared the same goals. Finally, Hvidt made some reflections on the latest stage of mass migration, that is, during the 1960s, when airlines were to play the same role as had shipping during the early modern era and in the nineteenth century.

Dr. Colin Newbury started the discussion by asserting that the object of the shipping conferences, which had actually been researched rather much, was primarily the formation of a freight cartel. He was therefore "very intrigued" by Hvidt's words about the division of the passenger traffic. He rather thought of the situation in terms of various migration agencies competing with each other, using the brokers of the shipping companies. There should be data on these matters in the Chamber of Commerce Records of Liverpool and of other important harbors. He also mentioned the High Commissioner records for the activities of the agents of the various British colonies and dominions. Newbury finally raised the question about the importance of the expansion of railroads. Here, Hvidt replied that he certainly should have made it clear that from the 1880s onward, railroads challenged the traditional sea transportation dominance, changing the picture radically. With respect to the shipping conference of 1868, Hvidt said that even the Encyclopedia Britannica stated that its aim was a freight cartel. The meeting on passenger traffic must have taken place a year or so earlier.

Smyth pointed out that Hvidt had really only taken up the 1850 to 1900 period. He gave some details about the ways in which, prior to that, large land companies in Canada, with their own cargo ships and agents, helped to direct the flow of migration. Also, most migrants were literate and were able to read information materials. Luigi de Rosa took up the activities of shipping agencies in Italy and also referred to the system of subsidized passages to São Paulo, Brazil, after slave emancipation in 1888, as well as to the Italian settlement enclaves established by railroad companies in Argentina.

Åkerman raised the source problem as alluded to by Hvidt. Oral history was neglected until too late. Occasional migration agency archives have been found, such as the one found in Göteborg by Olof Thörn years ago and used by Berit Brattne in a dissertation.[6] But others had been destroyed when the attics at Sillgatan, where most of these agencies had been housed, were emptied during the Second World War. In Britain, Charlotte Ericson had been looking for such

6. See Berit Brattne, *Bröderna Larson. En studie i svensk emigrantverksamhet under 1880-talet* (Uppsala 1973). See also her article with Sune Åkerman, "The Importance of the Transport Sector for Mass Emigration" in *From Sweden to America: A History of the Migration*, H. Runblom and H. Norman, eds. (Uppsala 1976), 176–200.

archives in vain. In Hamburg, Bremen, and, for instance, Hull, they have been destroyed. When collaborating with Brattne in the 1960s, according to Åkerman the two of them had posed a question that may not be strictly scholarly but is still essential: was the stock effect more important than the propaganda of the agents in triggering migration? Their conclusion was that this was not the case but that the combination between the two was often crucially important. Agents could make use of family relations, for instance. Finally, he agreed with Hvidt that political aspects have often been of vital importance. The migration framework was entirely different in the case of colonial powers and in that of other countries. Hvidt, in his final comment, raised the question about the social implications of lowering passenger ticket rates. Here he found a parallel with the introduction of charter flights in recent times.

The Integration/Isolation of Immigrants

The discussant was sociologist J.J. Mangalam (Canada), himself an immigrant from India. He thought that some of the reports (by P. Emmer, G. Clarence-Smith and P. Marshall) really failed to meet the definition of "migration" as a voluntary movement. Mangalam also criticized Mörner's report for using the concepts of "integration" and "assimilation" more or less synonymously. The former should refer to the extent to which immigrants have internalized the values and norms of the host society so that they, too, can live as members of this society. Political factors should also be taken into account. Assimilation, on the other hand, as he explained at the chairman's request, should be defined as the "final product" of the process of integration. Mangalam also emphasized that historians should duly consider the various social groups that are involved in any process of integration.

Naturally enough, the sociologist's rather provocative – though gracious – remarks triggered considerable discussion. Emmer asked what "integration" of, let us say, East Indian immigrants really meant when applied to the "Caribbean society." Was it the society of the whites, of the "black elite," or that of "ex-slaves?" Mangalam said he was not sure but insisted on the need for definitions. Research must find a "common language." Emmer suggested that it would be useful to make a distinction between divided and more uniform societies. Emigration into these two different types of societies also made the migrant face two completely different ways of assimilating. Mangalam thought it particularly important to "spell out" whether it was the question of a society where integration was still taking place or not. He also criticized the scholarly habit of pointing at the gaps in our empirical knowledge when so many thousands of studies, relevant for the process of integration of migrants, have already been carried out. Therefore, it is really time to attain a common methodology and common definitions of terms that are so commonly used that they should become part of our common heritage.

Mörner made a "confession of sin" for not having distinguished between "integration" and "assimilation" in his own text. He criticized Mangalam, however, for not having done so either, at least not in the handout all participants had received. Moreover, Mörner was not persuaded by the definition of "assimilation" given by the speaker at the chairman's request. Newbury also reminded the audience of the lengthy discussions in the past about the North American "melting pot" and the "sociological despair" that these discussions had revealed. Bade thought it necessary to make clear a basic difference between sociologists and historians. The former put questions to people who are alive and can follow up their inquiries. The latter have to deal with people who are already dead and consequently, are unable to get additional answers. He also recalled the meetings of U.S. social scientists that he had attended, where the "true meaning" of concepts like "integration" and "assimilation" had been interminably discussed. This did not make him overly optimistic about a future agreement on definition. Prof. H.B. Hansen, who himself combined experience as a historian and as a social scientist, agreed to this. Calling Mangalam's request for common definitions "utopian," Hansen recommended as an alternative that historians should attempt the use of sociological concepts, without necessarily subscribing to them, as tools to build hypotheses, to ask questions, and to organize their materials.

In his final comment, Mangalam underlined that his insistence on the necessity of arriving at common definitions, and so forth, was a plea. Granted that social science aims at explanation and prediction, this was simply a basic requirement. Chairman Åkerman concluded that historians, including himself, would so far have considered "Futurology" impossible, a "scientific fake." Yet, recent students of long-lasting basic value systems do believe that these are predictable for some thirty to fifty years ahead. Our knowledge about the basic structures of migration are about as thorough as can be. So perhaps, for all the shyness characteristic of historians, we have to admit that a degree of predictive capacity may be possible in this field.

Return Migration

Return migration was occasionally alluded to in Mangalam's presentation and the ensuing discussion. It was, however, the subject of a special presentation by one of the very few specialists in this field, Dr. Keijo Virtanen (Finland).

To begin, he underlined the lack of sources and of research. Consequently, most research had dealt with groups for which sources are better, such as the Scandinavians and Italians and, to a lesser degree, the Greeks and Irish returning from the United States. During the 1980s international interest increased in the topic. The first European conference on return migration was held in Rome in 1981.[7] As official statistics do not even suggest the scale of return, regional studies could serve as a starting point, as Virtanen had tried himself with a sample of six "communes." Thus, he was able, for example, to separate temporary from permanent returnees. Some kind of quantitative approach had to be attempted, Virtanen believed.

His second point was that, migration being a most complex phenomenon, the study of return migration must comprise four phases: (1) life in the country of origin, (2) emigration, (3) life in the host country, and (4) experience after return. Thus, there is a continuous circuit in which the migrant takes part until it stops one day, either in the host country or in that of departure. With regard

7. K.J. Virtanen, *Settlement or Return. Finnish Emigrants (1860–1930) in the International Overseas Return Migration Movement* (Helsinki 1979). See also Lars-Göran Tedebrand "Remigration from America to Sweden" in *From Sweden to America* Runblom and Norman, eds.; John S. Lindberg, *The Background of Swedish Emigration to the United States. An Economic and Sociological Study in the Dynamics of Migration* (Minneapolis 1930). On the Danes, see Kristian Hvidt, *Flugten til Amerika eller drivkraefter i masseudvandringen fra Danmark 1868–1914* (Odense 1971). On the Norwegians, see Ingrid Semmingsen, *Veien mot vest. Annen del. Utvandringen fra Norge 1865–1915* (Oslo 1950). Betty Boyd Caroli, *Italian Repatriation from the United States 1900–1914* (New York 1973); Francesco Cerase, "The Return to Italy. Nostalgia or Disenchantment: Considerations on Return Migration" in *The Italian Experience in the United States*, Silvano M. Tomasi and Madeline H. Engel, eds. (Staten Island 1970); Robert F. Foerster, *The Italian Emigration of Our Times* (Cambridge, Mass. 1924); Theodore Saloutos, *They Remember America: The Story of the Repatriated Greek-Americans* (Berkeley 1956); Arnold Schrier, *Ireland and the American Emigration 1850–1900* (Minneapolis 1958). The proceedings of the 1981 Conference in: Daniel Kubat, ed., *The Politics of Return. International Return Migration in Europe* (Rome 1984).

to assimilation or adaption, several questions can be asked: Why has the ethnic identity of various groups survived so long? Had the immigrant any reason to try to adapt or to assimilate into the new society if he planned to stay there for only a few years? On the other hand, the immigrant had to find features that eased his stay in the new society. The idea of returning began to fade away gradually, and it was finally the immigrant himself who decided whether he would stay on. In most cases, immigrants did in fact belong to three different worlds: (1) to that of the immigrants themselves, consciously isolated from outside, (2) to that of the receiving country with which they nevertheless, over the years, had become increasingly familiar, thanks to their children and friends, and (3) to that of the old country, which the first generation would never forget. Of the many relevant factors, Virtanen emphasized the length of stay in the receiving area.

Virtanen finally referred to his own effort of establishing a typology of the factors on various levels favoring or mobilizing return migration (Figure 12.1). His model was based on migration from Finland to the United States, but he thought that some of the contributions to this conference regarding other migratory movements showed that his model had a wider applicability. Clarence-Smith, for example, had indicated that African returns from the United States were few because economic opportunities were better in the latter country. Mörner had illustrated that a great contradiction between expectation and reality is likely to produce a high rate of return migration. The influence of distance was reflected in Smyth's conclusions about Irish returnees: those from Australia were few in number, whereas seasonal workers in England and Scotland normally returned home. Virtanen hoped that his model, together with other relevant examples, would show the great difficulties of arriving at generalized conclusions about the return rate, let alone about a "general theory," but he hoped for a step-by-step increased knowledge about this important phenomenon.[8]

Capital Movements Related to Migration

On this subject two discussants had been chosen, Newbury (Britain) and Runblom (Sweden). While the former would take up the macro

8. Virtanen had briefly commented on the pioneers in "migration theory," viz. E.G. Ravenstein, "The Laws of Migration," *Journal of the Royal Statistical Society* 48, 2 (1885) and Everett S. Lee, "A Theory of Migration," *Demography* 3, 1 (1966).

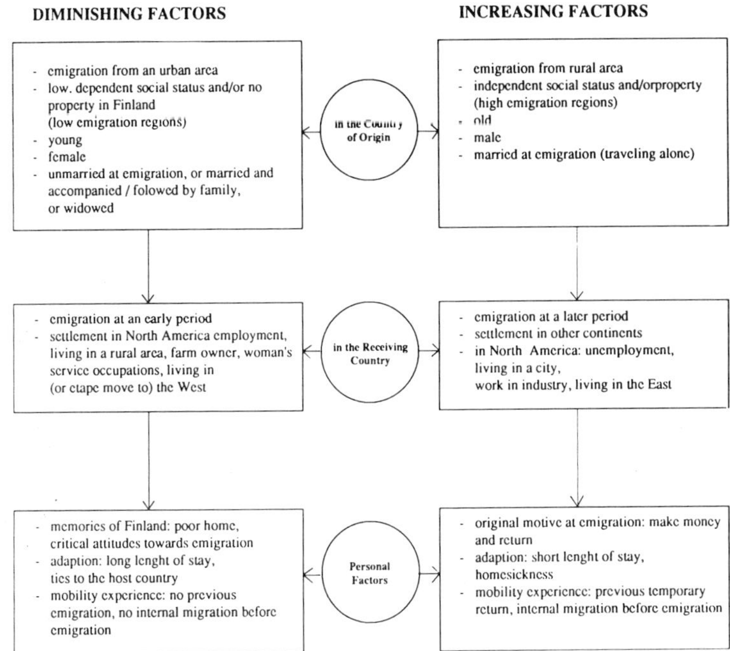

FIGURE 12.1 Factors Influencing the Likelihood of Return Migration Finns Remaining in or Returning from the United States

level, the latter would deal with a micro level, the remittances, and so forth, regarding the financial situation of the migrants themselves. As Newbury observed, most authors of the various reports had merely commented upon the last type of financial movements and not on the "correlation between investment and the movement of labour factors overseas."

In his presentation, he referred to the vast difference in scale between investment (portfolio and direct) in Europe, North and South America, and, to a lesser extent, in Australia, New Zealand, and South Africa, during the era of mass migration from the 1820s to the early 1930s, compared to the marginal investment in enclave development in tropical Africa, plantation territories in the Pacific and the Indian Ocean, and in much of the Middle and Far East.[9] Thus, Europe's exports of capital and manpower, respectively, went

9. For the comparative scale of British overseas investments, see Matthew Simon, "The Pattern of New British Portfolio Investment, 1865–1914" in *The Export of Capital from Britain 1870–1914*, A.R. Hall, ed. (London 1968), 15–144; Lance E.

to regions that developed synchronously but that were typologically quite distinct. Consequently, in the late-nineteenth century, plantations and mines where money was invested had more in common with their eighteenth-century counterparts than with railways and land settlement on the Canadian prairies or with the growth of public utilities in Latin American cities. Newbury declared that no historian of European migration could afford to ignore the "well-established body of research" on the correlation between investment cycles and migration flows, whatever its strengths and weaknesses.[10]

His second major point concerned the "marginal areas of investment and labour recruitment," that is, the role of shipping companies and passenger brokerage, the use of subsidized fares, and other state interventions aiming to remedy labor shortages on plantations. He found a growing differentiation in the nineteenth century between migrants with capital or skills, or with both, who all could pay for their own passages, and "economic refugees." This required careful research because so much depended on the proportions each territory received. The former group also engaged particularly in circular and return migration as they sold their services elsewhere or invested savings in areas from which they themselves had come.

In his comments on the reports, Newbury found that little use had been made of existing data on portfolio and direct investments.[11] These would help to explain the rapid expansion of the Atlantic markets for immigrant labor and provide an insight into the timing of business cycles directly relevant for migration. Interestingly, the investment peaks of 1844 to 1854, 1863 to 1873, 1878 to 1888, and

---

Davis and Robert A. Huttenback, *Mammon and the Pursuit of Empire: The Political Economy of British Imperialism, 1860–1912* (Cambridge 1986).

10. Brinley Thomas, *International Migration and Economic Growth: A Trend Report and Bibliography* (Paris 1961); Richard E. Easterlin, "Influences in European Emigration before World War I," *Economic Development and Cultural Change* 9 (1961), 331–51; Allen C. Kelley, "International Migration and Economic Growth: Australia, 1865–1935," *The Journal of Economic History* 25 (1965), 333–54; Rodney Maddock and Ian W. McLean, ed., *The Australian Economy in the Long Run* (Cambridge 1987), ch. 2; and more generally, Colin Newbury, "Labour Migration in the Imperial Phase: An Essay in Interpretation," *The Journal of Imperial and Commonwealth History* 3, 2 (1975), 234–56.

11. Brinley Thomas, *Migration and Economic Growth: a Study of Great Britain and the Atlantic Economy* (2d ed.; Cambridge 1973); H. Jerome, *Migration and Business Cycles* (New York 1926); Dorothy Swaine Thomas, *Social and Economic Aspects of Swedish Population Movements, 1750–1933* (New York 1941); A.K. Cairncross, *Home and Foreign Investment 1870–1913. Studies in Capital Accumulations* (Cambridge 1953); Irving Stone, "British Direct and Portfolio Investment in Latin America before 1914," *The Journal of Economic History* 37, 3 (1977); Peter Svedberg, "The Portfolio-Direct Composition of Private Foreign Investment in 1914 Revisited," *The Economic Journal* 88 (1978).

1905 to 1913 were reflected in the data on increased migrations, as given in the reports by Bade and Mörner.[12]

In his presentation, Runblom noted that several reports had paid attention to the more limited capital movements, such as the sending of prepaid tickets to relatives or friends back home. He emphasized that it was the question of transfer of capital in two opposite directions: First, money sent from Europe or brought by the migrants themselves to the receiving areas; in this case, the source material is particularly scarce. Second, there were the remittances sent to the home country by the migrants or taken back with them on their return. In these cases, he made a distinction in the ways that money was put to use. Was it the question of active or passive investments? Did money go to the purchase of farms or into investments that would contribute to capital formation? For instance, referring to a recent study of the Swedish island province of Öland, Runblom showed that the remittances received from people who had migrated to the United States could be clearly related to the business cycles in the latter country. He also mentioned a study on Hungarian emigration to the United States that showed the extraordinary socioeconomic importance to Hungary of remittances from Hungarians in America. According to a report in 1911, for example, it was a good guess that 99 percent of the houses constructed in the countryside had been financed with the help of American money.

During the discussion, Clarence-Smith raised the question of the relationship over time between labor and capital flows, as presented by Newbury. The latter explained that, as far as the Atlantic area was concerned, capital, especially in the form of portfolio investment, generally preceded migration of labor until 1865; later, a reverse relationship came about. Labor also became more skilled, and investment in construction became, relatively speaking, more important.

Addressing himself to Runblom, Clarence-Smith then took up the tricky question as to how "productive" investment of remittances or money brought by return migrants in the home country should be

12. Newbury also wanted to draw attention to the growing number of reports from the International Labour Office (ILO) in Geneva (World Employment Programme) on migration both to and from Europe in the context of economic development and the international division of labor. Notwithstanding their focus on contemporary conditions, historians would find them useful. On a theoretical level, he found the network theories of sociologists and social anthropologist working with the analysis of migration in South Africa to be of special interest. He referred to the article by G.K. Garbett and B. Kapferer, "Theoretical Orientations in the Study of Labour Migration," *New Atlantis* 2, 1 (1970), and the introduction in: Shula Marks and Peter Richardson eds., *International Labour Migrations: Historical Perspectives* (London 1984), 1–18.

distinguished from "unproductive" ones. Runblom answered by giving a contemporary example. Yugoslavia, in recent times, is receiving on a large scale both remittances from migrants and returnees with money from Scandinavia and West Germany. But how should that money be invested in a "socialist economy?" The owners of this capital have to buy farm land or to build houses. Also, returnees go back to their home parishes, characterized by very old-fashioned agriculture, which they cannot change. Consequently, money put into the purchase of farms and into the construction of residential houses has to be considered as basically unproductive investments.

Emmer returned to the issue of labor migration and investments. He suggested that a distinction should be made between such territories where investment preceded and made possible the importation of labor and those where labor immigration served to prevent the dissolution of investments made prior to the abolition of slavery. The former group could be exemplified by Uganda, South Africa, and Queensland; the latter by the Caribbean, Réunion, and Mauritius.

External/Internal Migration

In his lecture on this vast and complex subject, Bade (West Germany) started by observing that such a distinction between external and internal migration stems from Anglo-Saxon scholars. Obviously, it is easier to distinguish between these two varieties from the perspective of Europe's largest island than it is from that of the European continent. There, the question of whether a migration movement should be considered external or internal depends on the mere fact of whether it crossed or stayed within the political borders of a given country. Thus, the same movement may at first appear as external and later turn out to be internal, as was the case when the political borders of Germany and Italy changed considerably by the foundation of the nation-state in mid-nineteenth century. In European history, there were "not only people migrating across borders, but also borders moving across people." Moreover, the distinction between external and internal migration leads to isolation of different branches within migration research. In West Germany, for instance, research on transatlantic migration and remigration is quite isolated from that on the history of internal German migration. Furthermore, a third research group, also rather isolated, carries out research on the history of temporary or seasonal migration between Germany and other European countries.

Instead, Bade recommended students to follow Frank Thistlet-waite's famous dictum that the process of migration should be thought of "as a complete sequence of experiences, whereby the individual moves from one social identity to another."[13] The intrinsic coherence and even interdependency between external and internal migration is also decisive, Bade asserted, for a comprehensive analysis of migration processes in the context of population, economy, and society at a given time.[14]

In Germany, the various movements of external and internal migration clearly interacted. The German transatlantic emigration of the nineteenth century reached its peak and also its end during the third wave from 1880 to 1893. Migrants mostly came from the agrarian regions of the northeast. At the same time, though, internal out-migration from these same regions turned into a mass movement. It would surpass transatlantic migration in numbers many times over. In this way, the east-to-west long-distance migration into the industrial areas of central and particularly of West Germany became, in the 1880s, a counterpart to transatlantic migration. Finally, in the 1890s, it would even practically replace transatlantic emigration, due to the economic crisis taking place in the United States at the same time as the industrial labor market expanded in Germany. On the eve of World War I, the increasing demand for industrial labor could, in fact, no longer be supplied within Germany, despite the massive influx of workers from the eastern agrarian regions. In turn, the lack of farmhands became acute in those regions. Consequently, by 1914 some 1.3 million foreign migrant workers had entered Germany, especially Prussia.

Bade then took a closer look at the migration taking place within Prussia, from east to west, especially to the region of Westphalia. This migration meant a transformation of an agrarian proletariat into an industrial one. The sociocultural differences between easterners and westerners were profound. Of the former, many had, in fact, a Polish identity. Also, particular migrant groups from East Prussia populated particular municipalities and even particular coal

13. F. Thistlethwaite, *Migration from Europe Overseas in the Nineteenth and Twentieth Centuries*. Rapport 5. XIe Congrès International des Sciences Historiques (Uppsala 1960).

14. Lucassen, *Migrant Labour in Europe*, and Dudley Baines, *Migration in a Mature Economy: Emigration and Internal Migration in England and Wales, 1861–1900* (Cambridge 1985), were two works he approvingly referred to in this connection.

pits in the Ruhr region. Thus, the "newcomers" literally moved to the very bottom, namely, into these coal seams, or they started out as unskilled industrial workers. In studying the immigrants in Germany, the many parallels with German immigrants in the United States are striking. As Bade puts it, the east-west Prussian movement was "significantly closer to transatlantic emigration than to other simultaneous movements of internal migration in Germany," as far as integration and segregation were concerned.

Bade concluded that it may be more important in migration research to ponder about interactions, interrelations, mutual characteristics, and common grounds of the external and internal migratory movements than to "philosophize" about their respective differences. Moreover, transatlantic emigration from the various European countries also has to be viewed in the common context of European migration, something he thought the conference helped to promote.

When thanking Bade, chairman Ljungmark underlined the great importance for the historian of "external movements" to consider how much smaller in size these have been in comparison to internal migration, the "Big Brother."[15]

The Regional Impact of Migration

In his lecture, geographer Smyth (Eire) started to discuss the concept of regionalism. Historians used it on two levels, he said; first, on a macro level comprising, for example, the whole of Europe, and second, on a more specific, lower level. For a geographer, generally, the region gives "a composite picture of specific areas, spatially expressed, of distinctive economic and social structures." Smyth emphasized how the regional origin of migrants highlights the character of a migratory movement at both ends. Also, regionalism does not merely refer to "spatially defined regions" but might as well refer to individual cities or sections of an urban system. "Basically, migration is viewed as an expression of behavioural choice, but it is susceptible to alterations of the economic, demographic and cultural variables which all operate within the decision-making

15. Bade was also asked by Runblom about the linkage between Jewish east-to-west and transatlantic migration. Here, Bade explained that in the late-nineteenth century, Jews from the east under Bismark were simply not allowed to settle in Prussia. Thus, there was a transit migration, in closed wagons, from the Russian empire to the German seaports carrying Jewish or Polish migrants to their ships.

system." Patterns of regional interaction may persist over decades or even generations; however, "even if the specifics of interactive regional systems may attain a state of prolonged equilibrium, they are as such unstable in the long run." Economy, transportation, and other factors see to that. At the present stage of research, it would be impossible to present any conceptual model that would "articulate the complexities of migration" on a regional level.

Therefore Smyth instead turned to providing an empirical illustration of regionalism on the basis of Irish migration. The nineteenth and early twentieth centuries brought no less than 6 million Irishmen overseas, that is some 10 to 11 percent of the total European transatlantic migration of that period. At an earlier stage, in the eighteenth century, most of the Irish out-migrants came from the northeast part of present Ulster. They were Presbyterians who would above all settle down in the Chesapeake region. Until the early nineteenth century, Irish emigration was originating predominantly from Ulster. Smyth, however, also noted the flow of some 30,000 people who went to Newfoundland from the late eighteenth to the early nineteenth century. They came from the town of Waterford with its hinterland in the southeastern corner of the island. Like Brittany in France and Dorset in Britain, Waterford was heavily involved in the fishing together with provisions trade with Newfoundland. In the nineteenth century, Irish out-migration became diffused and only the western parts of Ireland were underrepresented. At the other end, in the period 1825 to 40, Canada received more Irish immigrants than the United States (even though many went south eventually, like the ancestors of former U.S. president Reagan). The pattern would change radically, however, during the "famine years" (1845 to 1852). Not just every region, but every parish or even family would send migrants to the United States. The frequency was particularly high on the less urbanized western fringe at that time. "No rural society in Europe became so urban as did the rural Irish in the New World," Smyth declared. In the nineteenth century no less than 78 percent of all Irish emigration was directed to the United States. Yet, even within this new, general pattern, the "trickle" of Presbyterians from Ulster to Canada showed a striking persistence. Smyth concluded his contribution by pointing at the distinctive regional trends of Irish transatlantic migration at both ends. It is, indeed, "necessary to get beneath the aggregate picture to get the shifting nuances" in the political, ethnoreligious, and economic spheres.

The discussion was started by Runblom, who thought that Smyth's presentation had been an excellent illustration of the "stock-effect." He was also struck by the strong urbanizing trend of Irish migrants in America. One of the explanations might be, he suggested, that the Irish went to America before North American grain exports had started to flow, whereas Germans and Scandinavians went later, at the time of agricultural expansion in the Midwest, where they usually settled down. Smyth said that this question was not so easy to answer. One main explanation to be found, however, points at the balanced sex ratio of Irish migration. Irish women were absorbed as workers in the urban garment industries in the North American east or they became domestic servants, also in eastern cities.

Both Runblom and Åkerman discussed a phenomenon that is well documented in research on Scandinavian migration, that is, the urban influence fields, or the low frequencies of external out-migration in zones surrounding the cities. The larger this field, the larger the city. Åkerman added that in the Swedish case, emigration to the United States probably did not exceed 8 percent of the total, that is, mainly internal migration. De Rosa underlined the importance of chain migration in the Italian case. As in the case of Ireland, out-migration implied the transformation of impoverished villagers into New World urban dwellers. Thousands of Italian villages became, in fact, deserted.

Canny made an important intervention. Certainly, Irish migrants to North America were overwhelmingly rural in origin, but they were not skilled farmers. They had just eked out their meager existence growing some potatoes and keeping a pig. They did not have the skills, nor the means to settle down in American farming areas, but preferred the urban slums. The other point he made concerned the internal migration of the Irish immigrants within the United States. As shown by Stephen Thernstrom and others, the Irish became quite mobile. At first, they stayed in big harbor cities like Boston and New York, but soon many moved to smaller manufacturing cities in the northeast, where Irish men, as Thernstrom pointed out, worked for lower wages than normally received by American women. Canny also emphasized the importance of railroads in spreading the Irish railroad workers over the country and moving them to large cities like Chicago and San Francisco. Eventually, many Irish immigrants would go directly to one of these western cities after their arrival in Boston or New York from Ireland. Smyth agreed, but he also suggested another important factor: religion. Until the 1840s almost all the Irish disembarked in Quebec. There they had three choices: (1) to go on to the United

States, (2) to stay in Catholic but French-speaking Quebec, or (3) to move on to Ontario, English-speaking but Protestant. It is, indeed, thought-provoking to notice that 65 percent of the Irish in Quebec were Catholic, compared to only 33 percent of those in Ontario.

Migration and Religion

This topic was taken from the previous discussion, as summarized above, and subsequently presented as a subject in its own right by Hansen (Denmark). To begin with, he noted that religion figures in many studies on migration but usually in conjunction with ethnic, social, and political factors, not as the object of an analysis of its specific significance compared to other factors. Thus, Hansen found it hard to arrive at a systematic assessment of the role of religion in migratory processes. He then chose to present a number of scenarios, to identify some aspects of his vast and heterogeneous topic, from novels describing societies of migrants. *The Mosquito Coast*, by Paul Theroux, helped him to identify religion as an individualistic motive behind migration, as well as a reaction against the migrant's own civilization. In Vilhelm Moberg's trilogy on a nineteenth-century group of Swedish settlers in the United States' Midwest, on the other hand, religion's role as a motive was small. Instead, religion was important in that case in helping to maintain the identity of the migrants, along with their language, naturally. Also, the Lutheran Christian ethos sustained their existence and provided guidelines and discipline.[16] The third novel, *Out of Africa*, by Danish author Karen Blixen (Isak Dinesen), describes a prosperous European settler community in Kenya where religion played a minor role, if at all. What is interesting then in this context was the tension between the European settlers and the Christian missionaries who reacted against the settlers' bad treatment of the Africans. The three novels, Hansen claimed, all showed religion as a factor in its own right and as subject to pressure by the surrounding society.

With respect to the seventeenth-century Pilgrim Fathers and Puritans, religious oppression as a push-factor was matched by their wish to build the "Kingdom of God" overseas, making for a pull-factor. For the eighteenth-century Presbyterians from Ireland and

16. He also referred to a comparative study of two Danish communities in the United States with different religious characteristics over time. See Jette Mackingtosh, "'Little Denmark' on the Prairie: a Study of the Towns Elk Horn and Kimballton in Iowa," *Journal of American Ethnic History* 7, 2 (1988).

Scotland, economic factors were clearly stronger than Anglican harassment. Hansen also took up the sequence of events, originating in the revocation of the Edict of Nantes in 1685, and leading to Huguenot migration to Holland and from there to South Africa. As a consequence of this migration, the fundamental role of the Reformed Church in South Africa was reinforced, with the Africans cast in the biblical role of God's enemies. Looking at European emigration over a longer period, however, Hansen found that religion as an explanatory factor became less and less important. He referred to the examples given by his compatriot Hvidt. In the 1840s persecution in Denmark made many Baptists emigrate to America. In the 1850s, many Mormons did the same, but not for the same reason as the new Danish Constitution of 1849 had guaranteed freedom of religion. No, the Danish Mormons migrated because Mormon missionaries encouraged their converts to make the pilgrimage to the "Holy Land."[17]

Turning to Africa, his special field of research, Hansen noted that this continent, except for South Africa and to some extent Kenya, Rhodesia/Zimbabwe, and Angola, was bypassed by European immigrants for being found inaccessible, with few opportunities. There was, however, one interesting kind of European expansion, the missionary movement, whether it can rightly be termed one of migrants or not. Especially important, however, was the attitude of the missionaries, with their considerable influence both on the colonial authorities as well as the Africans toward the various types of migration. When, for example, a campaign started in Uganda in 1903 to recruit Ugandans for the mines of South Africa, the head of the Anglican missionaries effectively put a stop to this kind of labor migration. A few years later, the suggestion was made that people from India should be encouraged to migrate to Uganda, but again the bishop argued strongly against the plan.[18] The missionary attitude was not only prompted by the risk that migrants would spread Islam, but also by the risk that the East Indian presence

17. Hvidt, *Flugten til Amerika*.

18. Hansen's own impressive work, *Mission, Church and State in a Colonial Setting: Uganda, 1890–1925* (London 1984), naturally forms the basis for his observations on Uganda. But a paper prepared for our conference by Dr. Michael Twaddle (London) on "East African Asians through a hundred years" is also very useful for the understanding of the problem. Though not included in the present anthology for technical reasons, it will hopefully appear elsewhere. There were 50,000 Asians who were brutally expelled by the dictator Idi Amin in 1972. *Uganda Now. Between Decay & Development* (London 1988), 242 ff. This anthology was edited jointly by Hansen and Twaddle.

would reduce the chances of the Africans to develop their own land. As educators, the missionaries, in fact, hoped that their African pupils would be able to replace the East Indians and Goans as middlemen in trade and crafts. Also, the Africans would keep their profits in their country instead of sending them abroad. The missionaries also favored African peasant production rather than subsidizing the development of a European settlers' economy. So did the government at last, but for economic, not humanitarian and religious reasons.[19] Interestingly, Hansen also noticed that colonialism in Uganda resulted in a division of offices and land between Protestants, Catholics, and Muslims in the wake of the missionary activities. Like in sixteenth-century Germany, it was a realization of the principle of *cujus regio, ejus religio*. Once religion had become the main structuring principle in society, it also caused internal migrations, a combination of push and pull. As in the case of some early-modern European emigration streams, the Ugandan example showed that the more restricted the freedom of religion, the more significant religion would be as a factor in explaining migrations.

Ziegler-Witschi then gave some examples of the role played by religion in the history of Swiss migration to Brazil. In the 1810s the Brazilian government made an attempt at attracting settlers from Switzerland, provided they were Catholics. This led to a strictly regional movement, from the Catholic Canton of Fribourg.[20] By the mid-century, another wave went, but now half of the Swiss were Protestants. Their letters show that they did not suffer from it. Later on, they joined the German churches existing in Brazil. Interestingly enough, she also showed that yet another category of Swiss migrants, the Catholics, found the mores and traits of Brazilian Catholicism so different, that the same religion, nevertheless, became a feature of differentiation between immigrants and natives. The chairman, Ljungmark, referring to Hansen's observation as to the relative insignificance of religion as a push-factor in nineteenth-century Sweden, suggested that it must have played a rather significant role as a pull-factor instead. That was so in the case of Swedish members of Free Churches, which had their origins and main centers in America.

19. See Hansen's essay, "Christian Missions and Agricultural Change: a Case Study from Uganda," in *The Transformation of Rural Society in the Third World*, M. Mörner and Thommy Svensson, eds. (London and New York, 1991), 241–61.

20. See Martin Nicoulin's excellent work, *La genèse de Nova Friburgo. Emigration et colonisation suisse au Brésil 1817–27* (Fribourg 1973).

Toward a Theory of Migration

This final session had been organized in the form of a panel. It was presided by Emmer with Mangalam, Åkerman, and Miège as participants. As the chairman pointed out, there are some historians who feel no need at all to apply social science theory to the history of migration. Yet, some members of the organizing committee had insisted on a session of this type. Emmer said that the session might also have been called, for example, "some general remarks on the history of migration in the context of European expansion."

The first speaker, Mangalam, declared that the formulation of a migration theory is, indeed, possible and that generalizations are a "must" for research on migration.[21] The theory could be spelled out by means of a series of propositions, namely:

1. Migrants moved from one geographical location to another.
2. Migrants faced deprivations of values in their countries of origins.
3. They perceived that resources existed in the societies of destination to satisfy their needs.
4. Once there, their hierarchy of values would either undergo changes or not, to their satisfaction or not.
5. Social integration and adjustment are the functions of such satisfaction.
6. If the change in their hierarchy of values does not make them dissatisfied, they will become better adjusted and integrated and they will settle down in the country in question. On the contrary, their dissatisfaction will impede integration and they will tend to return to their native land.

To maintain identity and integrity, migrants in the country of destination had to avoid marginality and keep up a sociopsychologically balanced personality, according to Mangalam, even though they were living in two different worlds (in the one of their origin and in the one of their destination); if not, they would suffer from mental problems. Those Irish who, as mentioned by Smyth, were caught in Canada between English-speaking Protestants and French-speaking Catholics ought to have suffered such problems, he suggested. Integration refers to the extent to which immigrants have internal-

21. Mangalam has presented his ideas on migration theory in detail in his important book *Human Migration* (Lexington 1968).

ized the values and norms (folkways and mores) of the host society. Such "internalization (adult socialization) ought to make them participate in the day-to-day life of the host society." It would apply to all the institutional aspects of life and would be time-consuming and arduous. During this period, migration implies considerable change. Migrants may have moved from a "society where extended family relations are dominant to one in which the nuclear family type predominates; from an agricultural economy to an industrial; from a political democracy to a dictatorship; from Roman Catholicism to Protestantism," and so forth. All these changes demand changes in the role performance of the migrants, as well. As far as the concept of "social role" was concerned, Mangalam defined it as a set of norms associated with status position within the social structure. A norm, by turn, is a range of mutual expectations in a group situation. Concluding, Mangalam said that he simply had to make these elementary explanations as he was talking to an audience mostly composed of nonsociologists.

The next intervention was made by Åkerman, who stated that for fifteen years he had not been active in migration research; thus, he had now gained a new perspective on the subject that he wanted to present. Some of the concepts used so far during the conference, such as "stock-effect" and "urban influence field," gave him a sense of déjà vu. He thought that the basic structure of migration comprised three different dimensions, that is, "landscape," "manscape" (creations by man, like environment and farms), and "mentalscape" (ideas, influence, know-how). How could these three dimensions be developed further and at times be merged? Previous research above all neglected the "mentalscape." Åkerman then listed a number of problem areas that he now found especially relevant to future historical research on migration. What did mass migration really mean for the receiving countries? He also thought that Thistlethwaite's demand from 1960, that emigration-immigration-remigration always be studied as a single process and not in isolation, continued to be valid and should be kept in mind. Åkerman then, somewhat provocatively, maintained that one should not just study the migrations of one's own compatriots. Moreover, comparison really imposed itself in this field. In this regard, the present conference had been successful, precisely due to the wide spread of migration movements all over the world (apart from Siberia). What counts, above all, is migration as a common human experience. There is nothing special and, as such, especially interesting about, for instance, Scandinavian migration, possibly apart from the abundance of sources available in that case. Åkerman went on to stress the chronology as well as the spatial aspects that, he thought, at times did not receive due consideration in historical research on migration. Finally, he emphasized that team research in migration history was needed, but in a different way compared to fifteen to twenty years ago. Then, such teams, in Sweden at the least, were made up by historians. Now they should be composed along interdisciplinary lines.

In his talk, Miège stressed the relationship between migration and the various manifestations of European expansion, after all explicitly given by the title of the meeting. He focused on that period of nineteenth-century migrations that coincided with the second phase of European expansion and on the necessity of populating those vast territories that colonial powers now shared among themselves. Strikingly, in Black Africa, by 1913 there were no more than a total of some 20,000 Spaniards, Portuguese, French, and English, that is a mere fraction compared to the volume of even a year of Italian emigration. Miége then discussed primarily the changes taking place in the forces of production during this stage of European expansion. Slaves were partly replaced by beasts, such as mules and horses. As an example, horse breeders from Poitou, France, were called to Argentina in order to display their skills in improving the local stock of horses. Also, steam was introduced into mills previously based on animal energy. Finally, the French specialist on European expansion and migrations in the areas surrounding the Indian Ocean discussed the importance of contract labor in his region of research. These semi-free, semi-slave workers would form the basis of plantation societies of the new type in places such as Mauritius and La Réunion. In this regard, Miège touched upon two aspects in particular: the large-size capital movements and the *mentalités* of such heterogeneous societies.

While Mangalam and Åkerman had attempted a more theoretical approach, Miège's speech fit under the more general alternative heading the chairman had proposed. The ensuing brief discussion was quite diverse. Prof. H. Wesseling found it less than satisfactory that Mangalam's theory excluded categories such as slaves and indentured servants from his concept of "migrants." Thus, his approach would barely serve for migration in the history of European expansion. He was also critical of Mangalam's statement about migrants always facing value deprivation in their country of origin, which he did not find empirically confirmed. Mangalam replied that his theory was not static but dynamic and that it might be improved. He admitted that his definition of migration did exclude the referred-to movements. This was no weakness, however, rather a merit, because we have to keep "our phenomena as pure as possible."

In a few words, Clarence-Smith made clear that, as he saw it, generalization is not theory. "The point about theory is to understand better, not to generalise." Migration was linked to the rise of capitalism as a system, which put demands on all the forces of production. Migration had a content of struggle on the part of those who were used, even though some of the migrants also benefited from that process.

Notes on Contributors

Klaus J. Bade, Professor of Modern History, University of Osnabrück. He has published numerous studies on overseas history such as: *Friederich Fabri und der Imperialismus in der Bismarckzeit. Revolution – Depression-Expansion* (Beiträge zur Kolonial- und Überseegeschichte, Bd. 13, Freiburg, 1975), *Imperialismus und Kolonialmission. Kaiserliches Deutschland und koloniales Imperium* (Wiesbaden, 1982), *Population, Labour and Migration* (Leamington Spa, 1987), *Ausländer-Aussiedler-Asyl in der Bundesrepublik Deutschland* (Hannover, 1990), and *Neue Heimat im Westen: Vertriebene-Flüchtlinge-Aussiedler* (Münster, 1990).

W.G. Clarence-Smith, Reader in the Economic History of Asia and Africa in the University of London. He has published *Slaves, Peasants and Capitalists in Southern Angola, 1840–1926* (1979) and *The Third Portuguese Empire, 1825–1975* (1985). He has edited *The Economics of the Indian Ocean Slave Trade in the Nineteenth Century* (1989).

Pieter C. Emmer, Professor in the History of European Expansion, University of Leiden. He has published (in English), *Reappraisals in Overseas History* (with H.L. Wesseling, eds.) and *Colonialism and Migration* (ed.). Present research: nineteenth century colonial labor migration.

Helgi Skúli Kjartansson, Senior Lecturer in History at the Iceland Institute of Education, Reykjavík. Most of his scholarly publications – mainly in Icelandic – concern the social history of Iceland, 1850 to 1950, including emigration, urbanization, cooperatives, and organized labor.

Lars Ljungmark, Senior Lecturer, University of Gothenborg, Department of History. He has published *For Sale – Minnesota. Organised Promotion of Scandinavian Immigration, 1866–1873* (1971) and *Swedish Exodus* (1979). Present research is in Swedish emigration to Canada.

Vitorino Magelhães Godinho, Emeritus Professor, Universidade Nova in Lisbon and Université de Clermont-Ferrand. He has published extensively on Portuguese social and economic history and on the Portuguese participation in the expansion of Europe. *Documentos sobre a Expansao Portuguesa* (3 vols., 1943–1956); *A Economia dos Descobrimentos Henriquinos* (1962); *L'économie* *de l'empire portugais XVe et XVI siècles* (1969); *Os Descobrimentos e a Economia Mundial* (2 vols., 1982); *Mito e Mercadoria, Utopia e Prática de Navegar (1990)*.

P.J. Marshall, Rhodes Professor of Imperial History, King's College, London University. Author of *The Impeachment of Warren Hastings* (1964), *Problems of Empire: Britain and India 1757–1813* (1968), *The British Discovery of Hinduism* (1970), *East India Fortunes: The British in Bengal in the Eighteenth Century* (1976), (with Glyndwr Williams) *The Great Map of Mankind* (1980), and *Bengal: The British Bridgehead: Eastern India 1740–1828* (1987). Editor (with J.A. Woods) *The Correspondence of Edmund Burke*, (vols. vii and x); Editor, *The Speeches and Writings of Edmund Burke*, (vols. v and vi).

Magnus Mörner, was Professor at the University of Gothenborg, Sweden, from 1982 to 1990. Before that, among other things, he taught at several universities in the United States. He published dozens of books and about three hundred articles on Latin American social history in Spanish, English, and other languages.

Luigi de Rosa, Professor of Economic History in the Faculty of Transport Economics and International Trade, Naples. Editor of *The Journal of European Economic History*; President of the Italian Historical Association; author of many books on Italian Economic History, some of which were awarded with National Historical Prizes. His most recent books are *The Industrial Revolution in Italy*; *Emigrants, Capitals and Banks*; *History of the Banco de Roma*; and *The Adventure of Economic History in Italy*.

William J. Smyth, B.A., Ph.D., Professor of Geography and Academic Vice-President, St. Patrick's College, Maynooth. A graduate of the National University of Ireland, he taught for several years at the University of Toronto before returning to Ireland. His principal research interest is in the field of Irish emigration to Canada. He is co-author of *The Sash Canada Wore: A Historical Geography of the Orange Order in Canada* (Toronto 1980) and *Irish Emigration and Canadian Settlement* (Toronto 1990).

Index